Bar and Beverage Management

Bar and Beverage Management

Noah Carlisle

RANDOM

RANDOM PUBLICATIONS

NEW DELHI - 110 002 (INDIA)

Bar and Beverage Management

ISBN 978-93-51113-02-7

Published in 2014 in India by

Reprint 2020

RANDOM PUBLICATIONS

4376-A/4B, Gali Murari Lal, Ansari Road

New Delhi-110 002

Phone: +9111-43580356, 23289044

E-mail: randomexports@gmail.com; sales@randompublications.com;

info@randompublications.com

Type Setting by: Friends Media, Delhi-110089

Printed at : Mehra Printers, Delhi-110092

Preface

There have been many names throughout history for establishments where people gather to drink alcoholic beverages. Even when an establishment uses a different name, such as "tavern," the area of the establishment where the bartender pours or mixes alcoholic beverages is normally called "the bar." A bar's owners and managers choose the bar's name, décor, drink menu, lighting, and other elements which they think will attract a certain kind of patron. However, they have only limited influence over who patronizes their establishment. Thus, a bar originally intended for one demographic profile can become popular with another. For example, a gay bar with a dance floor might, over time, attract an increasingly straight clientele. Or a blues bar may become a biker bar if most its patrons are bikers. A cocktail lounge is an upscale bar that is typically located within a hotel, restaurant, or airport. A full bar serves liquor, cocktails, wine, and beer. A wine bar is an elegant bar that focuses on wine rather than on beer or liquor. Patrons of these bars may taste wines before deciding to buy them. Some wine bars also serve small plates of food or other snacks. A beer bar focuses on beer, particularly craft beer, rather than on wine or liquor. A brew pub has an on-site brewery and serves craft beers." Fern bar" is an American slang term for an upscale or preppy (or yuppie) bar. A music bar is a bar that presents live music as an attraction. A dive bar is a very informal bar, sometimes referred to simply as a "dive." The counter at which drinks are served by a bartender is called "the bar." This term is applied, as a synecdoche, to drinking establishments called "bars." This counter typically stores a variety of beers, wines, liquors, and non-alcoholic ingredients, and is organized to facilitate the bartender's work. The word "bar" in this context was already in use in 1591 when Robert Greene, a dramatist, referred to one in his A Notable Discovery of Coosnage. Counters for serving other types of food and drink may also be called bars. Examples of this usage of the word include snack bars, sushi bars, juice bars, salad bars, and sundae bars.

Many bars have a happy hour to encourage off-peak patronage. Bars that fill to capacity sometimes implement a cover charge or a minimum purchase requirement during their peak hours. Such bars often feature entertainment, which may be a live band or a disc jockey playing recorded music. The term "bar" is derived from the specialized counter on which drinks are served. Patrons may sit or stand at the bar and be served by the bartender, or they may sit at tables and be served by cocktail servers. The "back bar" is a set of shelves of glasses and bottles behind that counter. In some establishments, the back bar is elaborately decorated with woodwork, etched glass, mirrors, and lights.

It is expected that the book will provide a fund of rich experiences to the students and teachers.

I thank all members of my team who have helped in the preparation of the book. My special thanks go to "Random Publications" who have published the book.

—Noah Carlisle

Contents

1

Bar Management

Tourism

Tourism is travel for recreational, leisure, or business purposes. The World Tourism Organisation defines tourists as people "travelling to and staying in places outside their usual environment for not more than one consecutive year for leisure, business and other purposes".

Tourism has become a popular global leisure activity. In 2011, there were over 983 million international tourist arrivals worldwide, representing a growth of 4.6% when compared to US$ 940 billion in 2010. International tourism receipts (the travel item of the balance of payments) grew to US$1.03 trillion (€740 billion) in 2011, corresponding to an increase in real terms of 3.8% from 2010. In 2011, international travel demand continued to recover from the losses resulting from the late-2000s recession, where tourism suffered a strong slowdown from the second half of 2008 through the end of 2009. After a 5% increase in the first half of 2008, growth in international tourist arrivals moved into negative territory in the second half of 2008, and ended up only 2% for the year, compared to a 7% increase in 2007. The negative trend intensified during 2009, exacerbated in some countries due to the outbreak of the H1N1 influenza virus, resulting in a worldwide decline of 4.2% in 2009 to 880 million international tourists arrivals, and a 5.7% decline in international tourism receipts.

Tourism is important, and in some cases, vital for many countries. It was recognised in the *Manila Declaration on World Tourism of 1980* as "an activity essential to the life of nations because of its direct effects on the social, cultural, educational, and economic sectors of national societies and on their international relations." Tourism brings in large amounts of income in payment for goods and services available, accounting for 30% of the world's exports of services, and 6% of overall exports of goods and services.

It also creates opportunities for employment in the service sector of the economy, associated with tourism. These service industries include transportation services, such as airlines, cruise ships, and taxicabs; hospitality services, such as accommodations, including hotels and resorts; and entertainment venues, such as amusement parks, casinos, shopping malls, music venues, and theatres.

Etymology

Theobald (1994) suggested that "etymologically, the word *tour* is derived from the Latin, 'tornare' and the Greek, 'tornos', meaning 'a lathe or circle; the movement around a central point or axis'. This meaning changed in modern English to represent 'one's turn'.

The suffix *–ism* is defined as 'an action or process; typical behaviour or quality', while the suffix, *–ist* denotes 'one that performs a given action'. When the word *tour* and the suffixes *–ism* and *–ist* are combined, they suggest the action of movement around a circle.

One can argue that a circle represents a starting point, which ultimately returns back to its beginning. Therefore, like a circle, a tour represents a journey in that it is a round-trip, i.e., the act of leaving and then returning to the original starting point, and therefore, one who takes such a journey can be called a tourist."

In 1941, Hunziker and Krapf defined tourism as people who travel "the sum of the phenomena and relationships arising from the travel and stay of non-residents, insofar as they do not lead to permanent residence and are not connected with any earning activity." In 1976, the Tourism Society of England's definition was: "Tourism is the temporary, short-term movement of people to destination outside the places where they normally live and work and their activities during the stay at each destination.

It includes movements for all purposes." In 1981, the International Association of Scientific Experts in Tourism defined tourism in terms of particular activities selected by choice and undertaken outside the home.

In 1994, the United Nations classified three forms of tourism in its *Recommendations on Tourism Statistics*:

- Domestic tourism, involving residents of the given country travelling only within this country.
- Inbound tourism, involving non-residents travelling in the given country.
- Outbound tourism, involving residents travelling in another country.

World Tourism Statistics and Rankings

Total Volume of Cross-Border Tourist Travel: In 2011, there were 983 million international tourist arrivals, with a growth of 4.6% as compared to 2010. In 2012 this rose to more than 1 billion international arrivals.

Rank	*Country*	*UNWTO*	*International tourist arrivals (2011*	*International tourist arrivals (2010)*	*Change 2010 to 2011*
1	France	Europe	79.5 million	77.1 million	+3.0%
2	United States	North America	62.3 million	59.8 million	+4.2%
3	China	Asia	57.6 million	55.7 million	+3.4%
4	Spain	Europe	56.7 million	52.7 million	+7.6%
5	Italy	Europe	46.1 million	43.6 million	+5.7%
6	Turkey	Europe	29.3 million	27.0 million	+8.7%
7	United Kingdom	Europe	29.2 million	28.3 million	+3.2%
8	Germany	Europe	28.4 million	26.9 million	+5.5%
9	Malaysia	Asia	24.7 million	24.6 million	+0.6%
10	Mexico	North America	23.4 million	23.3 million	+0.5%

International Tourism Receipts

International tourism receipts grew to US$1.03 trillion (€740 billion) in 2011, corresponding to an increase in real terms of 3.8% from 2010. The World Tourism Organisation reports the following countries as the top ten tourism earners for the year 2011, with the United States by far the top earner.

International Tourism Expenditure

The World Tourism Organisation reports the following countries as the top ten biggest spenders on international tourism for the year 2011.

Rank	*Country*	*UNWTO Region*	*International tourism expenditure (2011)*
1	Germany	Europe	$101.71 billion
2	United States	North America	$79.1 billion
3	China	Asia	$72.6 billion
4	United Kingdom	Europe	$50.6 billion
5	France	Europe	$41.7 billion
6	Canada	North America	$33.0 billion
7	Russia	Europe	$32.5 billion
8	Italy	Europe	$28.7 billion
9	Japan	Asia	$27.2 billion
10	Australia	Oceania	$26.9 billion

History

Wealthy people have always travelled to distant parts of the world, to see great buildings, works of art, learn new languages, experience new cultures, and to taste different cuisines. Long ago, at the time of the Roman Republic, places such as Baiae were popular coastal resorts for the rich. The word *tourist* was used by 1772 and *tourism* by 1811. In 1936, the League of Nations defined *foreign tourist* as "someone travelling abroad for at least twenty-four hours". Its successor, the United Nations, amended this definition in 1945, by including a maximum stay of six months.

Leisure Travel

Leisure travel was associated with the Industrial Revolution in the United Kingdom – the first European country to promote leisure time to the increasing industrial population. Initially, this applied to the owners of the machinery of production, the economic oligarchy, the factory owners and the traders. These comprised the new middle class. Cox & Kings was the first official travel company to be formed in 1758.

The British origin of this new industry is reflected in many place names. In Nice, France, one of the first and best-established holiday resorts on the French Riviera, the long esplanade along the seafront is known to this day as the *Promenade des Anglais*; in many other historic resorts in continental Europe, old, well-established palace hotels have names like the *Hotel Bristol*, *Hotel Carlton*, or *Hotel Majestic* – reflecting the dominance of English customers.

Many leisure-oriented tourists travel to the tropics, both in the summer and winter. Places of such nature often visited are: Bali in Indonesia, Colombia, Brazil, Cuba, the Dominican Republic, Malaysia, Mexico the various Polynesian tropical islands, Queensland in Australia, Thailand, Saint-Tropez and Cannes in France, Florida, Hawaii and Puerto Rico, in the United States, Saint Vincent and the Grenadines, Barbados, Trinidad and Tobago, Jamaica, St.Lucia Saint Maarten, St. Martin's Island in Bangladesh, Saint Kitts and Nevis, The Bahamas, Anguilla, Antigua and Barbuda, Aruba, Turks and Caicos Islands, and Bermuda.

Winter Tourism

Although it is acknowledged that the Swiss were not the inventors of skiing, it is well documented that St. Moritz, Graubünden became the cradle of the developing winter tourism; since that year of 1865 in St. Moritz, when many daring hotel managers choose to risk opening their hotels in winter. It was, however, only in the 1970s when winter tourism took over the lead from summer tourism in many of the Swiss ski resorts. Even in winter, portions of up to one third of all guests (depending on the location) consist of non-skiers.

Major ski resorts are located mostly in the various European countries (e.g. Andorra, Austria, Bulgaria, Bosnia-Herzegovina, Czech Republic, Cyprus, Finland, France, Germany, Iceland, Italy, Norway, Latvia, Lithuania, Poland, Serbia, Sweden, Slovakia, Slovenia, Spain, Switzerland, Turkey), Canada, the United States (e.g. Colorado, California, Utah, Montana, Wyoming, New York, New Jersey, Michigan, Vermont, New Hampshire) New Zealand, Japan, South Korea, Chile, and Argentina.

Mass Tourism

ass tourism could only have developed with the improvements in technology, allowing the transport of large numbers of people in a short space of time to places of leisure interest, so that greater numbers of people could begin to enjoy the benefits of leisure time.

In the United States, the first seaside resorts in the European style were at Atlantic City, New Jersey and Long Island, New York.

In Continental Europe, early resorts included: Ostend, popularised by the people of Brussels; Boulogne-sur-Mer (Pas-de-Calais) and Deauville (Calvados) for the Parisians; and Heiligendamm, founded in 1793, as the first seaside resort on the Baltic Sea.

Adjectival Tourism

Adjectival tourism refers to the numerous niche or speciality travel forms of tourism that have emerged over the years, each with its own adjective. Many of these have come into common use by the tourism industry and academics. Others are emerging concepts that may or may not gain popular usage. Examples of the more common niche tourism markets include:

Recent Developments

There has been an up-trend in tourism over the last few decades, especially in Europe, where international travel for short breaks is common. Tourists have a wide range of budgets and tastes, and a wide variety of resorts and hotels have developed to cater for them. For example, some people prefer simple beach vacations, while others want more specialised holidays, quieter resorts, family-oriented holidays or niche market-targeted destination hotels. The developments in technology and transport infrastructure, such as jumbo jets, low-cost airlines and more accessible airports have made many types of tourism more affordable. On 28 April 2009 *The Guardian* noted that "the WHO estimates that up to 500,000 people are on planes at any time." There have also been changes in lifestyle, for example some retirement-age people sustain year round tourism.

This is facilitated by internet sales of tourist services. Some sites have now started to offer dynamic packaging, in which an inclusive price is quoted for a tailor-made package requested by the customer upon impulse. There have been a few setbacks in tourism, such as the September 11 attacks and terrorist threats to tourist destinations, such as in Bali and several European cities. Also, on 26 December 2004, a tsunami, caused by the 2004 Indian Ocean earthquake, hit the Asian countries on the Indian Ocean, including the Maldives. Thousands of lives were lost including many tourists. This, together with the vast clean-up operations, stopped or severely hampered tourism in the area for a time.

The terms *tourism* and *travel* are sometimes used interchangeably. In this context, travel has a similar definition to tourism, but implies a more purposeful journey. The terms *tourism* and *tourist* are sometimes used pejoratively, to imply a shallow interest in the cultures or locations visited by tourists.

Sustainable Tourism

"Sustainable tourism is envisaged as leading to management of all resources in such a way that economic, social and aesthetic needs can be fulfilled while maintaining cultural integrity, essential ecological processes, biological diversity and life support systems." (World Tourism Organisation)

Sustainable development implies "meeting the needs of the present without compromising the ability of future generations to meet their own needs." (World Commission on Environment and Development, 1987)

Sustainable tourism can be seen as having regard to ecological and socio-cultural carrying capacities and includes involving the community of the destination in tourism development planning. It also involves integrating tourism to match current economic and growth policies so as to mitigate some of the negative economic and social impacts of 'mass tourism'. Murphy (1985) advocates the use of an 'ecological approach', to consider both 'plants' and 'people' when implementing the sustainable tourism development process. This is in contrast to the 'boosterism' and 'economic' approaches to tourism planning, neither of which consider the detrimental ecological or sociological impacts of tourism development to a destination.

However, Butler questions the exposition of the term 'sustainable' in the context of tourism, citing its ambiguity and stating that "the emerging sustainable development philosophy of the 1990s can be viewed as an extension of the broader realisation that a preoccupation with economic growth without regard to its social and environmental consequences is self-defeating in the long term." Thus 'sustainable tourism development' is seldom considered as an autonomous function of economic regeneration as separate from general economic growth.

Ecotourism

Ecotourism, also known as ecological tourism, is responsible travel to fragile, pristine, and usually protected areas that strives to be low impact and (often) small scale. It helps educate the traveler; provides funds for conservation; directly benefits the economic development and political empowerment of local communities; and fosters respect for different cultures and for human rights.

Pro-Poor Tourism

Pro-poor tourism, which seeks to help the poorest people in developing countries, has been receiving increasing attention by those involved in development; the issue has been addressed through small-scale projects in local communities and through attempts by Ministries of Tourism to attract large numbers of tourists. Research by the Overseas Development Institute suggests that neither is the best way to encourage tourists' money to reach the poorest as only 25% or less (far less in some cases) ever reaches the poor; successful examples of money reaching the poor include mountain-climbing in Tanzania and cultural tourism in Luang Prabang, Laos.

Recession Tourism

Recession tourism is a travel trend, which evolved by way of the world economic crisis. Identified by American entrepreneur Matt Landau (2007), recession tourism is defined by low-cost, high-value experiences taking place of once-popular generic retreats. Various recession tourism hotspots have seen business boom during the recession thanks to comparatively low costs of living and a slow world job market suggesting travelers are elongating trips where their money travels further.

Medical Tourism

When there is a significant price difference between countries for a given medical procedure, particularly in Southeast Asia, India, Eastern Europe and where there are different regulatory regimes, in relation to particular medical procedures (e.g. dentistry), travelling to take advantage of the price or regulatory differences is often referred to as "medical tourism".

Educational Tourism

Educational tourism developed, because of the growing popularity of teaching and learning of knowledge and the enhancing of technical competency outside of the classroom environment. In educational tourism, the main focus of the tour or leisure activity includes visiting another country to learn about the culture, such as in Student Exchange Programs and Study Tours, or to work and apply skills learned inside the classroom in a different environment, such as in the International Practicum Training Program.

Creative Tourism

Creative tourism has existed as a form of cultural tourism, since the early beginnings of tourism itself. Its European roots date back to the time of the Grand Tour, which saw the sons of aristocratic families travelling for the purpose of mostly interactive, educational experiences. More recently, creative tourism has been given its own name by Crispin Raymond and Greg Richards, who as members of the Association for Tourism and Leisure Education (ATLAS), have directed a number of projects for the European Commission, including cultural and crafts tourism, known as sustainable tourism.

They have defined "creative tourism" as tourism related to the active participation of travellers in the culture of the host community, through interactive workshops and informal learning experiences.

Meanwhile, the concept of creative tourism has been picked up by high-profile organisations such as UNESCO, who through the Creative Cities Network, have endorsed creative tourism as an engaged, authentic experience that promotes an active understanding of the specific cultural features of a place.

More recently, creative tourism has gained popularity as a form of cultural tourism, drawing on active participation by travelers in the culture of the host communities they visit. Several countries offer examples of this type of tourism development, including the United Kingdom, the Bahamas, Jamaica, Spain, Italy and New Zealand.

Dark Tourism

One emerging area of special interest has been identified by Lennon and Foley (2000) as "dark" tourism. This type of tourism involves visits to "dark" sites, such as battlegrounds, scenes of horrific crimes or acts of genocide, for example: concentration camps. Dark tourism remains a small niche market, driven by varied motivations, such as mourning, remembrance, education, macabre curiosity or even entertainment. Its early origins are rooted in fairgrounds and medieval fairs.

Doom Tourism

Also known as "Tourism of Doom," or "Last Chance Tourism" this emerging trend involves travelling to places that are environmentally or otherwise threatened (the ice caps of Mount Kilimanjaro, the melting glaciers of Patagonia, The coral of the Great Barrier Reef) before it is too late. Identified by travel trade magazine Travel Age West editor-in-chief Kenneth Shapiro in 2007 and later explored in The New York Times, this type of tourism is believed to be on the rise. Some see the trend as related to sustainable tourism or ecotourism due to the fact that a number of these tourist destinations are considered threatened by environmental factors such as global warming, over population or climate change. Others worry that travel to many of these threatened locations increases an individual's carbon footprint and only hastens problems threatened locations are already facing.

Growth

The World Tourism Organisation (UNWTO) forecasts that international tourism will continue growing at the average annual rate of 4%. With the advent of e-commerce, tourism products have become one of the most traded items on the internet. Tourism products and services have been made available through intermediaries, although tourism providers (hotels, airlines, etc.) can sell their services directly. This has put pressure on intermediaries from both on-line and traditional shops.

It has been suggested there is a strong correlation between tourism expenditure per capita and the degree to which countries play in the global context. Not only as a result of the important economic contribution of the tourism industry, but also as an indicator of the degree of confidence with which global citizens leverage the resources of the globe for the benefit of their local economies. This is why any projections of growth in tourism may serve as an indication of the relative influence that each country will exercise in the future.

Space tourism is expected to "take off" in the first quarter of the 21st century, although compared with traditional destinations the number of tourists in orbit will remain low until technologies such as a space elevator make space travel cheap.

Technological improvement is likely to make possible air-ship hotels, based either on solar-powered airplanes or large dirigibles. Underwater hotels, such as Hydropolis, expected to open in Dubai in 2009, will be built. On the ocean, tourists will be welcomed by ever larger cruise ships and perhaps floating cities.

Sports Tourism

Since the late 1980s, sports tourism has become increasingly popular. Events such as rugby, Olympics, Commonwealth games, Asian Games and football World Cups have enabled specialist travel companies to gain official ticket allocation and then sell them in packages that include flights, hotels and excursions.

The focus on sport and spreading knowledge on the subject, especially more so recently, lead to the increase in the sport tourism. Most notably, the international event such as the Olympics caused a shift in focus in the audience who now realise the variety of sports that exist in the world. In the United States, one of the most popular sports that usually are focused on was Football. This popularity was increased through major events like the World Cups. In Asian countries, the numerous football events also increased the popularity of football. But, it was the Olympics that brought together the different sports that lead to the increase in sport tourism. The drastic interest increase in sports in general and not just one sport caught the attention of travel companies, who then began to sell flights in packages. Due to the low number of people who actually purchase these packages than predicted, the cost of these packages plummeted initially. As the number start to rise slightly the packages increased to regain the lost profits. With the certain economic state, the number of purchases decreased once again. The fluctuation in the number of packages sold was solely dependent on the economic situation, therefore, most travel companies were forced to set aside the plan to execute the marketing of any new package features.

Latest Trends

As a result of the late-2000s recession, international arrivals suffered a strong slowdown beginning in June 2008. Growth from 2007 to 2008 was only 3.7% during the first eight months of 2008. This slowdown on international tourism demand was also reflected in the air transport industry, with a negative growth in September 2008 and a 3.3% growth in passenger traffic through September.

The hotel industry also reported a slowdown, with room occupancy declining. In 2009 worldwide tourism arrivals decreased by 3.8%. By the first quarter of 2009, real travel demand in the United States had fallen 6% over six quarters. While this is considerably milder than what occurred after the 9/11 attacks, the decline was at twice the rate as real GDP has fallen.

However, evidence suggests that tourism as a global phenomena shows no signs of substantially abating in the long term. Much literature, especially that following the Mobilities paradigm, suggests that travel is necessary in order to maintain relationships, as social life is increasingly networked and conducted at a distance. For many vacations and travel are increasingly being viewed as a necessity rather than a luxury, and this is reflected in tourist numbers recovering some 6.6% globally over 2009, with growth up to 8% in emerging economies.

21st Century Trends in International Tourism

Travel and tourism will grow to new heights in the 21st century as it becomes more accessible to a larger cross section of the global population. This will result in commensurate economic opportunities for developed and emerging destinations around the world. It will also create major challenges, not only in attracting and serving increased tourism demand, but also in mitigating the numerous potential negative externalities that will emerge as a result of tourism's rapid growth.

Successful destinations will strike a balance in developing their tourism industries by monitoring international trends, engaging tourism stakeholders, ensuring that the benefits of tourism outweigh any potential negative impacts and pledging a more equitable distribution of tourism revenue. There is good reason for countries to focus on honing their abilities in tourism: it is a big business.

According to the UNWTO, 846 million international visitor arrivals generated US$735 billion (US$2 billion/day) in tourism revenue in 2006. Tourism represents 35 percent the world's export of services and over 70 percent in the Least Development Countries.

The UNWTO predicts that international tourism demand will double by 2020 to an astronomical 1.6 billion visitors generating nearly US$2 trillion in economic activity. Currently, the tourism industry is characterized by a variety of issues and trends, which present a range of inherent threats and opportunities. These include, but are not necessarily limited to:

- There has been an increase in the perception of terrorist threats in many countries most graphically embodied in the Bali bombings in 2002 and 2005. There have also been subsequent terrorism scares and attacks in London, Glasgow, Madrid, Bangkok and other destinations. Well intended safety and security procedures and regulations are creating traveller inconvenience in the form of longer lines at airports and stricter visa policies and standards.
- The notable growth of China into one of the largest source markets in the Asia Pacific region has become a primary focus of the world's tourism industry. Chinese nationals have been increasingly visiting international destinations; a trend the industry widely agrees will continue to increase in the foreseeable future. Equally phenomenal growth is also evident from the Indian outbound market.
- New destination branding campaigns from relative newcomers such as India, South Korea, New Zealand, Egypt, South Africa, Vietnam, Eastern Europe and the Philippines have been recently launched, adding increased competition to mainstay destinations such as Australia, Singapore, Thailand and Malaysia.
- Technology such as the internet has made booking travel-related products easy and convenient, empowering the consumer to be less reliant upon the traditional tourism supply chain. This *disintermediation* opens many possibilities for consumer-direct marketing and distribution.

- In what many refer to as the emergence of a *Leisure Society*, tourism is seen as a basic right – as opposed to an activity for a privileged few – and has become widely accessible for a more diverse global demographic. The rise of low-cost airlines and cut-rate travel deals is fuelling a new wave of demand for tourism in the new millennium. A similar boom last occurred in the early 1970's with the launch of the Boeing 747 and other technological advancements in transport creating a wave of mass international tourism demand by increasing affordability and access.
- The emergence of sub-regional cooperative agreements in which neighbouring countries jointly market multi-nation itineraries in an attempt to increase the value and synergy for the tourist and the participating economies is on the rise.
- Demand is rapidly increasing for niche tourism products that are customised to satisfy the tastes of an increasingly discerning traveller, particularly among business and affluent leisure travellers. Many of these new niches are narrowly defined, but should not be overlooked.
- An increased awareness and consciousness among travellers of the social and environmental impacts of tourism which is fuelling a rapidly increasing interest in responsible, sustainable and green tourism.

Culinary Tourism

Culinary tourism or food tourism is experiencing the food of the country, region or area, and is now considered a vital component of the tourism experience. Dining out is common among tourists and "food is believed to rank alongside climate, accommodation, and scenery" in importance to tourists.

Definition

Culinary/food tourism is defined as the pursuit of unique and memorable eating and drinking experiences. Culinary tourism differs from agritourism in that culinary tourism is considered a subset of cultural tourism (cuisine is a manifestation of culture) whereas agritourism is considered a subset of rural tourism, but culinary tourism and agritourism are inextricably linked, as the seeds of cuisine can be found in agriculture.

Culinary/food tourism is not limited to gourmet food and in fact, "gourmet" is a very small subset, comprising only 8.1% of culinary travelers. This is perhaps best illustrated by the notion that culinary/food tourism is about what is "unique and memorable, not what is necessarily pretentious and exclusive". Similarly, wine tourism and beer tourism are also regarded as subsets of culinary tourism.

In 2012, the International Culinary Tourism Association rebranded as the World Food Travel Association. The rebranding took place because "culinary" in the English language has a more sophisticated sound. The Association is inclusive and rebranded to appear less exclusive and more inclusive of unique and memorable food experiences of all kinds.

Organisations

The World Food Travel Association (WFTA) is considered the world's leading authority on the food travel industry. It provides community, education and development consulting to the food, drink, travel and hospitality industries around the world. The WFTA is a non-profit trade association and was founded in 2003. Food tourism development is usually handled by destination marketing organisations (i.e. tourism offices), although some food/drink trade groups and associations may also have a hand in destination marketing.

Mystery Meet, a social dining group based in the USA, produces the Find Dining Podcast, which is specifically designed for culinary tourists and discusses cities from a culinary perspective.

Delicious Destinations: The Boom in Culinary Travel

In recent years, a culinary vacation usually meant travelling to a famous overseas restaurant or to meet with a famous chef and then watching him or her prepare special dishes.

Not anymore. Welcome to the brave new world of up close, participatory culinary travel. It's become one of the fastest-growing trends in the travel industry today.

According to a 2006 study from the Travel Industry Association, about one in 10 American leisure travelers reported that food or wine was a major factor in choosing their destinations. Translation: These are Deliberate Culinary Travelers. Other travelers took at least one trip where they sought out culinary activities (opportunistic culinary travelers), and then there are the accidental culinary travelers — who stumbled upon the culinary experience while travelling. The culinary travel experience includes everything from visiting a farmers market, sampling artisan products, attending a food or wine festival, going wine, beer or cheese tasting, or driving along a food or wine trail. But almost always, you can choose to have a hands-on experience cooking alongside top chefs.

Cruising

Veteran cruise ship travelers will warn you there are about eight meals a day. Now, on a number of ships, there are nine — the ninth being the hands-on cooking classes taught on board. And that seems almost counterintuitive, since "cruise food" hasn't always been synonymous with "gourmet." But these days, high-end gourmet restaurants are available on many lines: Crystal is partnering with master chef Nobuyuki "Nobu" Matsuhisa to launch the Silk Road and The Sushi Bar on Crystal Symphony. Chef Nobu himself will be on the inaugural trans-Pacific cruise from L.A. to Hong Kong on March 3, 2008.

On the Princess, onboard culinary adventures include a shore excursion to a chef's table on its Alaskan itineraries, where you get a five-course tasting menu of regional dishes.

Holland America has one of the most comprehensive culinary programs out there. The Culinary Arts Centre program, presented by Food & Wine magazine, includes hands-on cooking lessons with top chefs, kids and teen culinary classes, a state-of-the-art demonstration kitchen and wine and cheese tastings.

North America

In Walland, Tennessee (about two hours northeast of Chattanooga), Blackberry Farm is a longtime follower of the local and seasonal food philosophy. It's a combination of luxury resort and working farm — you can spend a day in the life of a gardener, a cheese maker or a chef. Room rates start at $745 a night (two-night minimum), including meals. Cheese making in Texas? In Elm Mott, Texas, the Homestead Heritage School of Homesteading can teach you the fine art of making dairy products such as butter, mozzarella, sour cream and cottage cheese. Prices range from $75 to $245 for a three-day course.

Would you rather sit back and enjoy a meal prepared with the freshest ingredients? Try dining on a farm. That's right, you'll be eating a meal made out of the very ingredients that surround you. Every summer, an organisation called Outstanding in the Field hosts dinners on farms, vineyards and ranches throughout California and parts of Colorado, New Hampshire and New York. 831-247-1041;

Even Canada has its own tradition in culinary excellence. Bet you didn't know that Canadian cuisine has a heritage of British, German and even Mennonite influences. You can learn all about this firsthand at the Wine Country Cooking School, part of Strewn Winery at Niagara-on-the-Lake in Ontario. Owner Jane Langdon and her winemaker husband, Joe, will set you up with their capable staff to create a multicourse lunch. Single-day classes are available for $195 per person, and couples' classes start $340. Just south of the border, Rancho La Puerta's new cooking school is located in the heart of a six-acre organic farm. You can participate in both hands-on and demonstrative cooking lessons, all using fresh produce straight from the farm. Individual cooking classes run $125 each, a four-class package is offered for $425, and the demonstration classes are $60 each.

Asia

You may be familiar with the famous Thai cooking programs at the Oriental Hotel in Bangkok and at the Four Seasons in Chiang Mai. Both options are excellent, but there are plenty of less-expensive, authentic experiences throughout Thailand and other parts of Asia. In Bangkok, a woman named Angsana Andersson operates a cooking class out of her home (she's Thai and married to a Swedish man). She offers private lessons that include three dishes, which you choose from her own family's cookbook. This course is about $60.

If you're looking for a really intensive Asian culinary experience, luxury outfitter Kipling & Clark can cater to your specific tastes. For example, a 14-day Tastes of Southeast Asia Tour includes culinary experiences in Vietnam, Cambodia and Thailand. In Hanoi, you can join a local chef on a tour of Hang Be Market, to learn the story behind Vietnamese herbs, spices and produce before going into the kitchen to prepare a multicourse meal. While in Saigon, you may visit the colourful Cai Be floating market followed by a private cooking class at the Hotel De La Paix. These tours are customized, so prices vary.

Europe

What's a trip to France without an experience in cheese? Check out C'est Cheese Tours, which brings small groups to France to some of the finest cheese and wine regions in the country. You'll get up-close-and-personal with fromagers and affineurs (cheese makers and cheese agers), and learn how to pair the best wines with cheeses. The price includes your full-time guide, who speaks English and French, visits with local residents and experts, tastings, entrance fees, accommodations and meals. Or how about some chocolate? At My Chocolate in London, you can work with owner Hannah Saxton to learn all about the fine art of chocolate making. Of course, the most popular class of the bunch is, surprise, more about tasting and less about making — it traces the history of chocolate followed by a lesson in tasting techniques.

Not only do you go home with recipes for every delicious treat from vanilla truffles to chocolate fudge, but you'll have 20 home-made chocolates in hand (though it's doubtful that they'll make it all the way back home!). The workshop costs about $100 per person.

What's the first thing that comes to mind when you hear "Irish food"? If it's "potatoes," you're not alone. But you may be surprised to learn that Ireland is undergoing its own renaissance in culinary tradition — and the centre of it all is not in Dublin, but in East Cork at the Ballymaloe Cookery School.

Culinary Travel and Tourism

Are you a *foodie* who loves to travel? An ardent fan of Anthony Bourdain? Or do you simply enjoy sampling the cuisine of destinations you visit? If yes, then you are very familiar with culinary travel.

In this section I plan to share information about different aspects of culinary travel, including trips, tours, and cruises that you may want to consider. I'd also like to hear your perspective. Check back as I add more over the coming weeks.

Culinary Trips and Cruises

Culinary Travel vs. Culinary Tourism: In my own, unofficial view, culinary travel takes you anywhere in the world in pursuit or enjoyment of authentic, local culinary traditions. Officially, culinary tourism is a broader concept that can include travel away from home or down the street. According to the International Culinary Tourism Association (ICTA), culinary tourism is "the pursuit of *unique and memorable* culinary experiences of all kinds, often while travelling, but one can also be a culinary tourist at home." The ICTA considers wine and beer tourism and spa cuisine to be subsets of culinary tourism. Unique, memorable, and authentic culinary experiences encompass a broad range of sites and activities, including "cooking schools, cookbook and kitchen gadget stores, culinary tours and tour leaders, culinary media and guidebooks, caterers, wineries, breweries, distilleries, food growers and manufacturers, culinary attractions and more. "

Whether you travel to Munich or Brussels to celebrate their world-renowned beers or follow your local taco truck around town from day to day, you are participating in culinary tourism.

Culinary Destinations

These can be anywhere in the world where food is consumed! For the industry's perspective, consult the latest ICTA map to see the current, emerging, and cooling culinary tourism hot spots. As of this writing, Ontario and Scotland are on top. Emerging areas include India, China, Thailand, Vietnam, South Australia, New Zealand, Peru, Alberta, and Texas. California, British Columbia, Mexico, UK, and Sweden are losing their lead. Where are Italy and France? Who knows... no survey results, perhaps?

Slow Food and Slow Travel

No discussion of culinary travel would be complete without a recognising the role played by these movements in promoting authentic, local, ecological food and travel experiences around the world. Slow Food is a grassroots organisation of over 100,000 members worldwide "who are linking the pleasure of good food with a commitment to their community and the environment." It was founded in 1989 "to counter the rise of fast food and fast life, the disappearance of local food traditions and people's dwindling interest in the food they eat, where it comes from, how it tastes and how our food choices affect the rest of the world." You are most likely familiar with growers, markets, restaurants, wineries, and others in your area who are collaborating on local, sustainable food and beverage production, distribution, preparation, education, and celebration. You can find these when you travel as well. Slow Travel promotes a slower, more meaningful form of travel in which travelers spend more time in a single place and get to know it on a deeper level. Typically you stay in a vacation rental or private home, shop and dine where the locals do, and learn about the local way of life. Culinary experiences are an important part of this type of travel. You are encouraged to share your travel stories and trip reports with others on the web forums.

Enotourism

Enotourism or Wine tourism or Vinitourism refers to tourism whose purpose is or includes the tasting, consumption or purchase of wine, often at or near the source. Where other types of tourism are often passive in nature, enotourism can consist of visits to wineries, tasting wines, or even taking an active part in the harvest.

History

Enotourism is a relatively new form of tourism. Its history varies greatly from region to region, but in places such as the Napa Valley

AVA, it saw heavy growth once a concerted marketing effort was implemented in 1975 that was given a further boost by the 1976 Judgment of Paris. Other regions, such as Catalonia, Spain have only started marketing enotourism starting in the mid-2000s, primarily focusing on how it is an alternative form of tourism to the beach for which Spain is overall known. There was also a rise in the profile of enotourism among English speakers with the 2004 release of the film, Sideways whose two central characters visit wineries and wine in the Santa Barbara region of Southern California.

Currently

The industry around enotourism has grown significantly throughout the first decade of the 21st century. In the United States 27 million travelers, or 17% of American leisure travelers, engaged in culinary or wine-related activities. In Italy the figure stands at approximately five million travelers, generating 2.5 billion euros in revenue.

Activities

Most visits to the wineries take place at or near the site where the wine is produced. Visitors typically learn the history of the winery, see how the wine is made, and then taste the wines. In some regions, staying in a small guest house at the winery is also offered. But, most importantly, visitors buy the wines made by the winery at the premises, accounting for up to 33% of their annual sales. More elaborate tastings can include horizontal and vertical tastings as well as full meals focused upon showcasing the wines. As the enotourism industry matures, additional activities have been added to visits such as riding electrically assisted bicycles, called, "burricleta"

Future

Most tourism agencies see it as a segment of the industry with tremendous growth potential, stating that in some regions, it's only functioning at 20% of its full potential. The success of enotourism has been problematic as it becomes a major form of income for wineries whose tasting fees continue to escalate in regions such as Napa Valley. This can, in turn have the opposite effect desired wherein potential visitors are driven away and turned off enotourism.

A private initiative by Recevin holds an annual "Enotourism Day" on the second Sunday of November each year to promote cellar visits in Germany, Austria, Slovenia, Spain, France, Greece, Hungary, Italy, and Portugal.

Italian Food Culture

Wondering what culture surrounds the unique Italian cuisine? Find out how the eating etiquettes of the Italians and the traditions that surround the activity. Just as there is a special art to preparing top class Italian food, there is also the art of eating Italian food. Over the years the Italians have developed their own culture surrounding the eating of their food. It is a well known fact that Italians are very serious about their food and why shouldn't they be?

After all, it is the food that brings together friends and families after a hard day at work in the office. This is why we find Italian people to be very fond of spending long hours at the table and meal times occuring at a leisurely pace over the span of a couple of hours.

Eating is the favourite past time cum recreational activity for families. Unlike faster paced societies in the world meal time in Italy is a time to kick back and relax. When the Italians sit down to eat they literally forget about the world and are in no hurry whatsoever to gobble down their food and get back to work. This is why the culture of Italian food is relaxed and slow paced with families getting the chance to bond with each other.

Family Meals

In cases where the extended family is being invited over for dinner the preparations get underway well in advance. The tradition in Italy is such that the hosts generally prepare a lot more food than could actually be consumed during the event. One of the strikingly different things about the food culture in Italy is that the event does not get underway unless and until all the members on the guest list have arrived and all the food has been prepared. You would often see children pinching little bites off the table in anticipation of the food.

The actual sitting down and eating process on an Italian dinner table is long, relaxed and spread over a couple of hours. To be precise the average Italian meal is three hours long during which the participants consume their food in a many as ten courses. Another prevalent tradition in Italian homes is that each guest brings with himself an interesting homemade dish as well which adds to the already overwhelming menu. Since the courses are so numerous they are usually small in quantity so as to be able to get a taste of everything. The food is served in large platters which makes it easy to reach but as a guest you ought to be careful not to stuff yourself on the first few servings because there is always more to come on an Italian dinner table.

It is fascinating to witness the culture that has developed around Italian food over the years. Even the people that are sitting down to eat on the table have their unsaid places as the elders sit at the head of the table with the younger generation sitting at the centre of the table and the women rushing back and forth from the kitchen. Most people like to stay on and keep talking even after the meal has ended and the dinner party goes on for as long as there is an after taste in your mouth.

Wine Festival

Annual wine festivals celebrate viticulture and usually occur after the harvest of the grapes which mainly is at the end of September until well into October. They are common in most wine regions around the world and are to be considered in the tradition of other harvest festivals. The oldest known cultivation of wine took place in the ancient Egypt. The knowledge was passed on from there along the mediterreanen sea where over the nowaday territories of Israel, Turkey, Greece it reached Etruria and Rome. Although already the Egyptians god Osiris was dedicated to wine the oldest historically documented wine festivals can be traced back to the Greek celebrations for their wine god Dionysos. Until the very day drinking wine in company is the centre of all wine festivals. It usually goes along with regional foods and music.

In Culture

The grape, and the extraction of the juice to produce wine, have become meaningful parts of mankind's history that is more than a food or drink. It is both rich in flavour, nutrients, and an icon symbolizing virtues used in religion and culture. Although the alcohol content could lead to intoxication, the festivals embody the enlightened spirit of mankind.

Wine Competition

A wine competition is an organised event in which trained judges or consumers competitively rate different vintages or bands of wine. There are two types of wine competitions, both of which use blind tasting of wine to prevent bias by the judges.

Types of Wine Competition

The most common form of wine competition is intended to obtain valid comparisons of wines by trained experts. The awards are given to groups of wines in various categories on the basis of the blind tasting. The awards are frequently bronze, silver, gold, and double gold medals. However, ribbons of various colours are also sometimes used.

These competitions often include a "Best of Class" award, producing a clear category winner among those vintages awarded a gold medal, for example the Los Angeles International Wine & Spirits Competition.

The other form of competition is most often organised by wine lovers and is consumer-oriented. The judges also evaluate the wines blind. However, instead of giving numerous awards, the wines are ranked by number from high to low in each wine category, a process known as ordinal ranking. Thus, there is only one first place winner, one second place, one third place, and so on down to the lowest place.

There are critics who argue that the results of such competitions may be misleading and should not be relied upon as a measure of quality. Other commentators argue that, because of wine competitions, wine quality has improved in many countries around the world.

Wine Competitions

- *World Wine Competition:* Annual global competition which by entries considered the largest in the world, founded in 1991.
- *International Wine Challenge:* Annual British based wine competition led by Charles Metcalfe and a team of eminent wine judges such as Oz Clarke and Tim Atkin MW. The results are published at the London Wine Fair and the Awards Dinner is held in the autumn.
- *Decanter World Wine Awards:* Each year the competition receives entries from over 47 countries worldwide and in 2012 received 14,119 entries, making it the largest wine competition in the world. The results of the competition are published online and in Decanter's October Edition, which, is released in September.
- *International Wine and Spirit Competition:* 300 experts, considered to be the oldest and most prestigious wine and spirit competition in the world
- *International Wine Contest:* A competition organised since 1961 in Brussels by Monde Selection, an international quality institute.
- *New York Wine Tasting of 1973:* Fourteen experts, including France's Alexis Lichine, ranked 23 Chardonnays from France, California, and New York State.

- *Paris Wine Tasting of 1976:* This notable wine competition known as the "Judgment of Paris". The tasting was repeated at the San Francisco Wine Tasting of 1978 and at the tenth anniversary Wine Spectator Wine Tasting of 1986 and French Culinary Institute Wine Tasting of 1986
- Concours Mondial de Bruxelles "wine world-championship" with more than 6000 participating products from the four continents. As a whole, these samples represent more than 500 million marketed bottles.
- *Wine Olympics (1979):* A French food and wine magazine organised a competition of 330 wines from 33 countries evaluated by 62 experts.
- *Great Chardonnay Showdown (1980):* A total of 221 Chardonnays from around the world were evaluated by 25 judges.
- *Grand European Jury Wine Tasting of 1997:* European jury tasted three vintages (1989, 1992 and 1994) of 27 Chardonnays from seven countries.
- The Tasting that Changed the Wine World: 'The Judgment of Paris' 30th Anniversary. A 30-year anniversary replication of the 1976 Paris competition.

2

Wine Production and Tourism

Wine tourism is now acknowledged as a growing area of special-interest tourism throughout the world, and it is an increasingly important tourism component of for many wine-producing regions. With its wide range of benefits, including foreign-exchange earnings, the creation of both full- and part-time jobs, and the generation of secondary economic activity, wine tourism is emerging as a lucrative industry sector with the ability to generate substantial long-term wealth and sustain steady tourism growth for these regions. Consequently, support for and investment in the wine-tourism sector is now regarded as an essential regional economic-development strategy by government and by the wine and tourism industries.

Despite optimistic expectations of growth, wine tourism is confronted by a range of critical development issues that have the potential to interfere with its sustainability and long-term profitability. One such issue is that of visitors' perceptions of the service received at the cellar door—that is, at the winery—and the effect of that service on consumer satisfaction, brand loyalty, and long-term behavioural intention. Attention to this issue has, in turn, led to a heightened concern by producers and consumers for the quality of service being offered. Whereas a winery's success was once determined solely by the quality of its wine, the development and important of the cellar-door concept now means that the quality of service received during a visit is just as likely, if not more likely, to drive future wine sales.

This article seeks to add to our understanding of customer service in the emerging wine-tourism sector. It first seeks to define the concept of wine tourism and the linkages between wine quality and brand values, as well as the role of a visit to the cellar door in reinforcing these linkages. {Note to the authors: As you see, I struggled with the preceding sentence. Did I get it correct on the rewrite, or did I misstep and are the linkages among all three? If the latter, what is the "these" being reinforced in the final phrase?-gw} That said, the main aim of this paper is to identify the attributes of service quality as they apply to visits to wineries. This article reports on a survey of visitors to wineries in Western Australia. From this, a framework will be developed within which areas for service-quality investment or disinvestment can be identified.

An Overview of Wine Tourism

As we stated at the outset, wine tourism has emerged as a strong and growing area of special-interest tourism throughout the world, and is now seen as an increasingly important component of the tourism product of most wine-producing countries. Some commentators suggest that wine tourism is fast replacing eco-tourism as the hot new buzz word of global tourism development and is becoming an important new niche market with considerable growth. Indeed, both the wine and tourism industries have achieved high levels of growth over recent years, and seem to be in the midst of what might best be described as a wine-tourism boom. Below we explain who is a wine tourist and what this booming new industry sector is all about.

Among the several definitions for wine tourism, the most widely used is that presented by Johnson, who describes the phenomenon as "visitation to vineyards, wineries, wine festivals, and wine shows for which grape wine tasting or experiencing the attributes of a grape wine region are the prime motivating factors for visitors." Getz suggests that wine tourism has three major characteristics, comprising the regional destination, the wineries themselves, and the tourists. As such, a typical wine tourist may be viewed as any person, whether day-tripper or overnight visitor, who engages in the act of wine appreciation while visiting a wine producing region. Of course, there is no such thing as a stereotypical wine tourist, with Hall citing evidence to suggest a typology of wine tourists that includes wine lovers, wine-interested people, and the curious tourist. This list might even be extended to include a fourth classification as suggested by Spawton, the mobile drunk.

As an emerging activity, wine tourism has been identified as one of a few tourism sectors that is genuinely concentrated outside traditional metropolitan areas and, hence, is viewed as playing a vital role in regional development, employment generation, business growth, tourism, and corporate investment. This view is supported by Kennedy who suggests it is helping revitalize and create jobs in traditionally rural and economically deprived regions. It has the potential to give a strong competitive advantage to regions with a grape and wine industry, and to generate profitable business for wineries, other wine-related products, and for visitor services. Therefore, the benefits of wine tourism can be felt throughout the whole region and not by just the wineries themselves.

It is not surprising therefore, that the wine-tourism phenomenon has taken on truly global proportions, with individuals from both sides of the supply chain coming together to offer a broad range of wine-tourism experiences in most of the world's wine-producing regions. Europe, of course, and France in particular leads the way with many well established wine-tourism experiences including the popular Beaujolais, Bordeaux, Burgundy, Champagne, Côtes-du-Rhône, and Provence wine trails. Over recent years this list has been extended to include Corsica, Jura, the Pyrennées, and Savoie regions. Other European destinations offering a similar style of experience include Italy, Spain, and certain of the emerging European wine nations including Bulgaria, Romania, and Hungary. Next on the ladder in terms of truly outstanding wine tourism experiences is the United States, which currently sits at number four in terms of global wine production. Renowned as a wine-producing country, the U.S., principally through its Napa Valley region, is fast becoming known as a leader in global wine-tourism destinations. Given that Napa Valley has over 270 vineyards, each offering its own distinct wine-tourism experience, it is not surprising that some five million wine tourists make their way to and through the Napa Valley annually. The Napa Valley, of course, is just one of a number of wine-producing regions in California. Indeed wine tourism is big business throughout the state, with estimates of some 10.5 million visitors a year being put forward for the entire state. Lesser known, yet nonetheless growing in significance as a wine-tourism destination, is Washington state. According to Tice, wine tourism there is "taking off, fuelled by the growing cachet of the state's wineries." This assertion is backed by a recent study by the Washington Wine Commission which showed that industry efforts to lure tourists to the region were paying off. With some 135 wineries statewide, it is estimated that almost two million visitors walk through winery doors annually and that these visits are worth an estimated $18.9 million a year.

Hot on the heels of the U.S. is Australia, where wine tourism has long since been recognised as a vital and necessary plank for the economic survival of many rural areas. According to one analyst Australia's wine-growing centres shine out as success stories generating an estimated AU$500 million (approximately US$100 million) for rural Australia each year. The Winemakers Federation of Australia estimates total Australian wine tourism figures to be on the order of 5.3 million visits per annum—worth $428 million in 1995 and expected to grow substantially to around $1100 million by 2025.

Given this global growth, many smaller and lesser known wine-producing regions are now emerging as serious wine-tourism destinations. Countries like New Zealand, South Africa, Bulgaria, and various republics from within the former USSR are now tapping into this market potential. Even India, it seems, is trying to cash in. *Express Travel and Tourism*, India's premier travel business magazine, reported on a recent attempt to put India on the world wine map and position India, through its Chateau Indage winery in the Sahyadri Valley, Maharashtra, as a new world wine destination.

Understanding Visitor Perceptions

Despite optimistic growth forecasts and expectations, wine tourism in Australia is still a relatively infant tourism activity. As we said at the outset, this activity is confronted by a range of critical development issues that have the potential to cripple its sustainability and long-term profitability. One such issue is that of visitors' perceptions of the service quality experienced at the cellar door and its effect on consumer satisfaction, future purchase intentions, and brand loyalty. Not surprisingly, there has been a heightened concern by both producers and consumers regarding the quality of services being offered. Indeed, the structure of the industry requires such attention. To take Australia for example, in 1997 the top three companies crushed over 50 percent of all grapes processed and the largest 20 producers were responsible for 98 percent of all wine produced. There were 914 wineries in Australia at that time, and there are over 1,150 as we write—reputedly with an additional winery coming into production every 84 hours. This makes the market highly fragmented and increasingly competitive.

Differentiation is central to achieving the competitive edge required for survival and growth. Put simply, there is a need to understand the attributes influencing wine tourists' decision in selecting wineries to visit and wines to purchase, as well as whether customers will repeat their retail and cellar-door purchasing. It has been suggested that many wine producers have been concerned in the past that the economic benefits of tourism have often been captured by tourism operators and other non-wine businesses, while wineries themselves have been left to bear the costs of providing the experience.For example, Hubscher comments that while the payback to the tourism industry is obvious, the payback to the wineries is less clear.

This may in part be explained by the fact that many wine producers do not perceive themselves as offering a tourist product and are unaware of how to best attract visitors to their vineyard. In some cases, production-focused wineries (particularly small wineries) have seen tourism negatively, because tourists taste wines and demand vineyard tours, but are rarely interested in buying the wines themselves. Where such attitudes underlie a winery operator's thinking, profitably improving the quality of customer service at the cellar door will be a challenge.

In wine tourism, as with all aspects of tourism activity, the consumer's perception of service quality is critical, with many commentators now suggesting clear and direct links with customer satisfaction, future behavioural intention, and long-term brand loyalty. {I propose that we not go in that direction, since this is not really the topic of your article, and instead build your core thesis.-gw} A number of conceptual differences distinguish wine tourism from other forms of service activity. Wine tourism involves customers' visiting a vineyard where the experience of tangible and service-production processes are an essential part of the service benefit—in particular, the tangible product (the wine). It is on this benefit that many vineyard operators focus and use as a means of introducing and promoting their product. Many visitors to wineries may be on vacation with little likelihood of repeat visits in the near future. However, benefit to the winery may derive from visitors' seeking out the winery's wine when they get back home and through word-of-mouth referral. Indeed, high levels of service can encourage the development of relationship-marketing strategies (e.g., through the use of mailing lists and targeted incentives), as well as a relationship to the brand in a more traditional sense.

For the winery owner, customers' visits to the cellar door offer three benefits: distribution at a low marginal cost, the development of brand equity, and a chance to add value to their enterprise. With much of the world's wine industry based on small and medium-size enterprises, cellar-door sales can be a critical outlet for sales dollars and customer contact. This view is shared by the Winemakers' Federation of Australia, which in its National Wine Tourism Strategy suggests that "for small, especially newly established wineries, their ability to tap wine tourism will determine their viability." For example, in Western Australia's Margaret River region, cellar-door sales account for approximately 34 percent of annual sales revenue for wineries, with 15 percent of outlets reporting this enterprise to be in excess of 80 percent of sales revenue. These figures indicate the significance of cellar sales to these wineries. The minimal distribution costs (bypassing wholesalers) and consequent high margins make sales at the cellar door are particularly attractive to wine producers.

Creating brand loyalty takes on considerable significance in a competitive marketplace. Dodd and Bigotte state that "in addition to sales revenue, wine tourism offers benefits such as opportunities for market intelligence, increased margins above other retail outlets, and the chance to encourage brand loyalty toward a winery." Similarly, Nixon suggests that "the changing face of the winery tourist is a smart consumer. But they will be a loyal customer if we give them a reason and a means to be loyal." The challenge is to find a means of providing "added value" elements to attract customers. Zekulich, for example, suggests that "new producers struggling to crack the retail market could seek greater reliance on cellar-door sales and direct marketing.... It could also mean associated facilities like food services and arts and crafts helping people sell their wines." This is already evident, with many wineries' having restaurants, merchandise on sale, and some even having overnight accommodations to attract visitors. Regardless of the approach, the cellar door is a vital link in the service chain. It is often the first contact that consumers have with a winery and its wines. Therefore, every aspect of the cellar door (including layout, appearance, and staff) can be of importance. Staff members, for example, can play a vital part in the quality of the wine tourist's experience at the winery. The staff's friendliness, courteousness, and knowledge, along with the quality of service received from winery personnel are important attributes in a customer's decision to purchase wine at the winery. In that regard, appropriate employee selection and training can be critical to the success of any tasting room.

Given the production orientation of many wine producers, not all of them have a highly developed understanding of tourists' expectations. It is to advance understanding in this area that this article is directed. However, the fact should not be overlooked that there are many wineries that have developed their tourism activities to the point where these have become a dominant part of the business. By adding catering, conference, and exhibition services, among others, a relatively stable form of income can be generated. In such a visitor-based winery, the focus for quality management shifts from a sole preoccupation with the wine to a much broader management of the intangible visitor experience. We now discuss methodological issues raised in the identification of service-quality criteria in wineries offering visits to tourists.

Research Methodology

Although it has been argued that service quality at the cellar door has considerable implications for wine producers, the issue has not been widely researched. Our study seeks to fill that gap by adopting a largely quantitative approach to identify significant trends among current visitors to wineries. It is recognised that a quantitative approach is not well suited to exploring the underlying symbolism or meaning of a visit to a winery, or gaining a deep understanding of the needs and motivations that lead individuals to visit a winery. Such an approach would form a future avenue of inquiry, and our quantitative survey may indicate questions that could usefully be explored with deeper qualitative research.

This study of customers' perceptions of service quality at the cellar door was carried out over a three-day period in the high season at four cellar-door operations in the Margaret River region of Western Australia. The survey took the form of a 23-item self-completion questionnaire which visitors were asked to complete immediately prior to departing each winery. For each item respondents were asked to rate their perceptions of the dimensions listed on a five-point Likert scale anchored at strongly disagree (1) and strongly agree (5). In addition respondents were also asked to rate the level of importance attributed to each dimension on a similar scale anchored at low importance (1) and high importance (5).

Scale items were based on the 22 items of the original SERVQUAL instrument. In the absence of a previously validated scale that has been applied to wine tourism, this appeared to be the best basis for a measurement scale. This scale has been widely replicated in both inferred and performance-only-based disconfirmation measures and the factor structure has been found to be appropriate to a wide range of consumer services.{Except earlier you said wineries are different, not typical. So, in keeping with that thought I've modified this section. Plus which, you next say that you made considerable changes to the survey instrument, further suggesting a lack of typicality. If I'm wrong, I'll restore the original phraseology, but it didn't scan to me.-gw} Because of the differences between cellar-door sales and other service activities, we modified the scale extensively to take account of the particular service setting to improve its content and face validity.

This was achieved through an initial review of the published literature on wine tourism, which extracted common points related to consumer evaluation criteria. This was supplemented with five focus-group discussions involving winery staff and customers. All discussions were recorded and subsequently analyzed. The resulting analysis was then cross-checked against independently transcribed notes for accuracy and, where appropriate, item wording was changed to better fit the context of the cellar-door experience. These discussions led to the exclusion of two of the original SERVQUAL items due to cumbersome language. Two items, which related to the range and quality of wines tasted and on offer, deemed by participants to be highly relevant to the evaluation of service quality in the cellar-door domain were added (scale items five and ten). An additional item was included as an overall measure of service quality for the purposes of assessing convergent validity. A final refined list of scale items was shown to two participating winery owners and agreement reached that the items were valid indicators of service quality in the context of cellar-door operations.

Our research design applied the adapted SERVQUAL scale items to an Importance–Performance Analysis (IPA) framework. IPA has gained popularity over recent years for its simplicity, ease of application, and diagnostic value. This analysis is best described as an absolute measure of performance that also seeks to identify the underlying importance ascribed by consumers to the various quality criteria under assessment. Importance is viewed as a reflection by consumers of the relative value of the various quality attributes. It is this additional information that makes the technique more suited to the task of directing improvement based on what is deemed most important by consumers. Low-importance ratings are likely to play a lesser role in affecting overall perceptions, while high-importance ratings are likely to play a more critical role in determining customer satisfaction. Lovelock, Patterson, and Walker have noted that Importance–Performance Analysis is an especially useful management tool helping to "direct scarce resources to areas where performance improvement is likely to have the most effect on overall customer satisfaction."It also has the benefit of pinpointing which service attributes should be maintained at present levels and "those on which significant improvement will have little impact."

Research Sample and Setting

The sample was drawn from visitors to four participating wineries in the Margaret River wine region over the three-day period spanning the Annual Margaret River Wine Festival, in December 2002. The selected wineries were chosen based on their willingness to participate in the research and on the fact that they offered an extensive cellar-door service. Margaret River is a tourism destination about 3.5 hours' drive south of Perth—with a number of natural and eco-tourism features, good surfing, and vineyards and wineries to attract visitors. Its reputation as a premium wine-producing region has been forged over the last 15 years, and it now has an international reputation for its wines—particularly based on the Cabernet Sauvignon and Chardonnay grape varieties. The region has some 130 wineries, of which just over 60 maintain a cellar-door operation. Six hundred questionnaires were administered, of which 353 were returned, representing a response rate of approximately 59 percent. Surveys were administered to all patrons as they exited each winery over the three-day period, and a small incentive in the form of a prize drawing for a mixed case of premium Margaret River wines was offered to help bolster the response rate.

Research Results

The results of the study are presented in three sections, followed by a section containing analysis. Section one provides a brief description on the demographic characteristics of the sample. Section two addresses the performance of the research instrument and includes reliability data and the results of the factor analysis. Section three presents an analysis of mean scores. Section four brings together mean scores for each service attribute within an Importance–Performance matrix, and, finally, comparison is made between two underlying dimensions of service quality that emerged during the analysis.

Demographic Characteristics

The principal demographic characteristics of the sample are shown in Exhibit 1. Of the 353 subjects included in the study, respondents were distributed almost equally by gender—160 (45.3 percent) men and 189 (53.5 percent) women (with four missing entries accounting for the remaining 1.2 percent). Respondents were categorized into one of five age groups, as shown in table. The 40 subjects aged between 18–24 years accounted for 11.3 percent of the sample, 25–34 years for 33.4 percent (118 respondents), 35–44 years for 20.1 percent (71), 45–54 years for 16.4 percent (58), and 55 years and over for 17.6 percent (62) of the total.

Of those surveyed approximately 54 percent (189) were first-time visitors to the winery. Moreover, 85 percent (297) of respondents visited a winery less than once a month. Previous research suggests that 65 percent of visitors to the region have visited it at least twice, suggesting a fairly high level of repeat visitation.

Table: *Demographic profile of visitors (N=353)*

Frequency of ages			***Frequency of gender***		
18-24	40	11.3%	Male	160	45.3%
25-34	118	33.4%	Female	189	53.5%
35-44	71	20.1%	Not given	4	1.2%
45-54	58	16.4%			
55+	62	17.6 %			
Not given	4	1.2%			

Further examination of the demographic statistics reveals that the cellar-door customer was generally a managerial or professional person (67 percent) between 25 and 44 years old, indicating a well-educated customer base. While the majority of visitors were from Australia (just over 88.7 percent) only 11.6 percent (41) of the total were from the South West region, indicating a strong out-of-area interest in the region's wine-tourism offerings. The remaining 11 percent (53) came from overseas. Almost 96 percent (338) of visitors stated that they would return to the wineries where they were surveyed. This is consistent with the relatively high mean performance values recorded for all attributes of the cellar-door experience. In addition, almost 96 percent (338) of respondents stated that they would be happy to recommend the wineries they visited to others, and some 50 percent of customers surveyed reported that they had purchased wine during their visit. Almost 71 percent (249) of those surveyed stated that they had come across, tasted, or purchased the wines sampled on a previous occasion, and almost 38 percent (186) of respondents stated that they had heard of the respective wineries based on personal recommendation and other word-of-mouth sources. In addition, almost 36 percent of respondents indicated that they had previously visited the wineries under investigation. This supports the view from the literature that the majority of cellar-door customers are genuine buyers.{But earlier we said that wineries were frustrated because people came, demanded tastings, and then didn't buy. Should we not delete that earlier assertion, given this finding?-gw}

Performance of the Research Instrument

While the overriding goal of the study was to address the issue of visitors' perceptions of service quality, it also proved useful to test the use of the measurement instrument (that is, the adapted SERVQUAL) for measuring service quality within this service setting, that is, the cellar-door operation. Zeithaml, Parasuraman, and Berry defined service in terms of five "RATER" dimensions (reliability, assurance, tangibles, empathy and responsiveness). To this end a factor analysis using the principal component extraction technique was performed on respondents' perception scores. The analysis made use of the OBLIMIN oblique factor rotation procedure in SPSS-X and is in keeping with the original SERVQUAL study. While visitors were asked to complete the perception and importance sections of the questionnaire, only the perception (performance) scores from the 22-item scale were initially used to operationalize the service quality construct.

Table: *Dimensions of the Cellar-Door Experience*

Variable	*Comp I "Relate"*	*Comp II "Logistics"*
1. Facilities for visitors		.824
2. Decor of the winery		.722
3. Winery staff appeared neat		.745
4. Brochures and signs		.852
5. Range of wines		.496
6. Problem solving	.638	
7. Ethos of right first time	.851	
8. Right first-time delivery	.822	
9. Convenience of tasting times		.634
10. Quality of wine tasted		.564
11. Knowledgeable staff		.597
12. Non-excessive wait time	401	.452
13. Staff willingness to help	.514	.435
14. Staff responsiveness	.522	
15. Staff behaviour instilling confidence	.621	
16. Feeling of security in dealing with the winery	.600	
17. Staff being consistently courteous	.519	
18. Staff having product knowledge	.617	
19. Being made to feel like a special person	.946	
20. Staff having visitors' best interests at heart	.891	
21. Staff understanding the specific needs of visitors	.915	
22. Staff giving individualized attention to visitors	.844	
Eigenvalue	13.382	1.278
% of variation	60.829	5.811
Coefficient alpha	.96	.90

Note: Factor analysis of respondents' performance scores only.

Above table strong factor loadings (item to total correlations) along two dimensions with coefficient alpha scores of 0.90 and 0.96. {There isn't actually a range, is there? Just two scores.-gw} This is clearly at variance with the original SERVQUAL factor structure. From the analysis, extracted component one is reflective of a combination of the reliability, assurance, and empathy dimensions from the original SERVQUAL instrument.

Viewed in the context of the cellar-door experience, component one (labelled here as "Relate") seems to focus on issues of contact and the personal and relational aspects of the cellar-door encounter. Component two is largely reflective of the relatively tangible and logistical dimension of the original SERVQUAL and is labelled here as "Logistics." These items appear to focus on the physical and process aspects of the service encounter, for example, the setting, décor, appearance of staff, and timeliness of the service received.

The instrument performed well in terms of both reliability and validity. Overall reliabilities were alpha = 0.94 for the importance scale and 0.96 for the performance scale. Overall reliability for the importance-performance (IP) difference scores was also high, at alpha = 0.93. These reliability scores clearly exceed the usual recommendation of alpha = 0.70 for establishing internal consistency of the scale.

Construct validity was also addressed in terms of both convergence and the research instrument's ability to discriminate between the underlying dimensionality of the service-quality construct. Convergence was investigated by calculating the mean difference scores for each of the 22 scale items and (using Pearson's product moment correlation) correlating these with the mean score from an overall single-item measure of quality, which was also included in the instrument. A correlation of 0.376 was found which, while low, was nonetheless significant at the 1-percent level.

Analysis of Item Mean Scores

The next stage of the analysis was to examine the sample responses across the 22 item attributes to assess visitor perceptions of service quality and the relative importance assigned by visitors to each. For each respondent, an Importance–Performance score was calculated to analyze the gap between the two. This information is presented in Exhibits 3 and 4, where mean scores for all respondents are shown for each of the service-quality attributes as per the underlying factor structure.

Table: *Importance–Performance analysis for the component "Relate"*

Quality Attribute	*Mean Importance*	*Meanper Formance*	*Performance Minus Importance*	*t value*	*Sig(2 Tailed)*
Problem solving	4.05	3.93	-0.12	-1.58	
Ethos of right first time	4.01	3.91	-0.10	-1.54	
Actual service right first time	3.99	4.02	0.03	0.231	
Knowledgeable staff	4.38	4.26	-0.12	-1.40	
No excessive waiting time	4.40	4.35	-0.05	-0.617	
Staff always willing to help guests	4.50	4.47	-0.03	-0.882	
Never to busy to respond to guests	4.48	4.32	-0.16	-2.86	.004
Staff behaviour giving confidence	4.34	4.31	-0.03	-0.62	
Staff making customers feel secure	4.12	4.27	0.15	2.50	.013
Staff consistently courteous	4.47	4.45	-0.02	-0.48	
Knowledge to answer guest questions	4.43	4.33	-0.10	-2.02	.044
Made to feel like a special individual	3.99	3.90	-0.09	-198	.049
Visitors' best interests at heart	4.04	4.04	-0.00	-0.263	
Understood the specific needs of guests	4.07	3.98	-0.09	-2.08	.039
Individualized attention to guests	4.28	4.14	-0.14	-2.18	.030
Overall mean values	4.21	4.16	-0.05	1.57	0.118

To complete the Importance–Performance analysis, a series of paired-samples t-tests were run to evaluate where mean performance scores differed significantly from mean importance scores. The analysis highlights a high degree of collinearity within the results for both the perception and importance measures, which at first glance may be looked on as a weakness of such measurement scales. We believe, however, that given the time required to complete the questionnaire and the discriminant evidence provided that these results are a true and accurate reflection of visitor perceptions when recorded.

Importance–Performance Matrix

The next stage in the analysis examined the relative positioning of the individual service quality attributes in relation to overall mean performance and importance for operators. One of the advantages of using a weighted performance measure is that attributes can be plotted graphically on a matrix, and this can assist in quick and efficient interpretation of the results. Exhibit 5 highlights the relative positioning of attributes in matrix format, with the importance values on the vertical axis and performance values on the horizontal axis. This matrix shows three individual items where there was a significant difference between importance and performance scores. On two of those items, the appearance of the staff and winery décor, the wineries were actually overshooting with regard to the importance ascribed by visitors. The only important item on which the wineries fell short was the availability of the wines.

When presented in matrix format (Exhibit 5) the results present operators with the following strategic alternatives.

(1) Quadrant A (high performance, low importance) indicates a misuse of the operator's resources. While judged to be performing well above average in relation to the provision of the particular service attributes, customers in their assessment of the overall cellar-door experience have deemed these attributes relatively unimportant. It is unlikely therefore that any further investment or improvement in this area will lead to a greater perception of quality on the part of the consumer.

(2) Quadrant B (high performance, high importance) reflects a situation where operators are perceived to be performing above average in relation to the delivery of those service attributes deemed most important by customers.

(3) Quadrant C (low performance, low importance) reflects the fact that certain aspects of the cellar-door experience are not being performed to their full potential. When viewed in the context of the corresponding importance weighting, however, any pertaining improvement effort would have to be questioned.

(4) Quadrant D (low performance, high importance) is where the greatest improvement effort is indicated. Attributes that fall into this category are deemed to be of great importance to customers in their overall evaluation of the service experience, yet the wineries are underperforming in the customers' eyes. It should be a priority to focus improvement efforts in this area.

Analysis of Service-Quality Dimensions

The final stage of analysis examined the service quality dimensions extracted during the initial factor analysis.

Table: *Importance–performance scores for service-quality dimensions*

SERVQUAL dimension	*Mean importance*	*Mean performance*	*Performance minus importance*	*t value*	*Sig. (2 tailed)*
Relate	4.21	4.16	-0.05	1.57	0.118
Logistics	4.21	4.26	0.05	1.49	0.154

As with the preceding individual-variable analysis, Exhibit 6 illustrates that operators are performing well above the midpoint of the measurement scale in relation to each of the two quality dimensions that we identified. Operators do seem to be experiencing some difficulty, though, with respect to the relational aspects of the cellar-door experience, although this aspect was not found to be significant. Analysis reveals that both dimensions are rated as equally important to visitors. This is an interesting finding, and reinforces the importance of both the technical and relational aspects of the service-quality construct at the cellar door. The corresponding performance scores illustrate that operators have performed better in relation to the "Logistics" dimension ($m = 4.26$) of the cellar door experience. Using a paired samples t-test, the "Relate" and "Logistics" means were found to be significantly different at the level of 1 percent ($t = -5.098$; $p < 0.0001$).

This is no doubt reflective of the importance that most operators attribute to the physical aspects of their operation—that is, the wines. This relates not solely to the actual cellar door counter, but to each tangible element on show at the winery, including signs, entrance roads, staff presentation and grooming, production and bottling plant, viticulture machinery, display of testimonials and awards, surrounding gardens and vineyards, parking facilities, and even children's play areas. While the quality of the wine on offer for tasting is undoubtedly at the forefront of most visitors' minds, operators understand that there is great potential for the physical surroundings and other tangible cues to have a profound effect on the perceptions patrons form and take away about the service they receive.

The chapter has sought to highlight the emergence and significance of wine tourism as a new growth sector of truly global proportions. Additionally, the paper has also sought to stress the importance of the cellar-door concept and corresponding service levels to the future success of wine tourism operations. It has shown that success depends not only on the quality of the wine being offered but also on the way it is offered for sale within the cellar-door environment. {I'm sorry, Professor O'Neill, but your study just does not support that assertion.

The customers are overall quite satisfied with their cellar door experience. There is exactly one problem, and that is the premium wines being unavailable for free.-gw} While this study reported that the non-availability of wines was seen as a significant failing of wineries, the study in itself cannot explain the complexity of factors that led visitors' to stress such high importance to this attribute. This study has not been able to build a picture of the consequences of failure to deliver on that attribute.

The approach adopted in this study cannot segment visitors into categories of knowledge and liking for wine, as distant from casual visitors who may be novice wine tasters. To answer these questions, further qualitative research would be useful. Finally, this study was undertaken in the context of Western Australian's wine tourism sector. Given that the industry is still young, and Australians have been relatively late adopters of quality wine, compared with many "old world" countries, limitations when extrapolating to other countries should be noted. It is likely, for example, that attributes of importance may differ in France and Germany, where there is a much longer tradition of buying wines from the cellar door.

Wine, Product Differentiation and Tourism: Exploring the Case of Chile and the Maule Region

As world wine output grows at 1.35%, wine consumption just grows at 0.26 % per year anticipating a surplus of output with negative results in the long-run for both winegrowers and for consumers. Thus, an alternative for emerging exporters, like Chile, is to identify and to target productive efforts towards reaching refined segments and niches of the market, instead of selling generic produce to the market at large. Naturally, their wines should be differentiated in a memorable way. Paradoxically, those countries which are large wine exporters seem to be also larger importers of wine.

The content of this paper explores the case of Chile as an emerging country, particularly from the New World in the world wine trade, assessing the effect of globalization in the Chilean exporting process. Output and consumption as well as wine trade are analyzed, with special reference to the European and French markets. This is complemented with identification of the source of investments, Chilean trade policies, production and processing technology in this industry. Conclusions state the need for a wider vision in the strategic development of the sector, stating research and collaboration needs between winegrowers, consumers and local communities; locals should be involved in wine tourism exalting terroir. Research needs are identified. This paper explores initially the wine world trade and Chilean contribution with special reference to vineyard size and variety composition wine-growing trends, origin and nature of new investment, actual market shifts for Chilean wine trade. Next it is discussed new challenges facing this industry, such as the actual price policy applied, falls in the rate of exchange. A special mention is made to wine routes development and their contribution to the creation of wine culture as an alternative to improve Chilean wine chances of success. Finally, conclusions are drawn and research needs are identified.

The world wine market is changing both from supply and from the demand sides. Recent trade changes have been led by new trends in consumption, as well as shifts in technology and source of supply. Thus, from the consumer side there is a significant drop in the low quality or table wine drinking which is being replaced by wines of improved quality and of higher prices, a special role has played the "appellation d'origin contrôlée". Additionally, low quality vineyard has been replaced by classic grapes varieties, by a higher wine quality as well as a significant improvement in the infrastructure and in the actual wine processing.

New World countries are more likely to get into crisis in the short run, due to a forthcoming supply surplus. Thus, Chilean wine producers should closer monitor competitors market performance of close competitors such as Australia, South Africa, USA, New Zealand, Argentina, Hungary and Bulgaria. Major producers and consumer countries such as France, Spain, Italy and Germany are already taking steps towards these new challenges.

World Wine Market

Currently wine market has followed general trends of the agri-food systems moving towards internationalization. Although the exchanges are growing in value, the economic relevance of the sector appears static due to a stable consumption. One of the main problems is the weak balance between wine production and wine consumption.

Vineyards Size: In 2001 there were 7.9 million hec. in production. This surface size has not been reached smoothly. Until 1980 there was a sustained growth, and since then there was a drastic drop of 2.3 million hec. in a period of ten years, recovering quickly during 2000-2001. Projections for the year 2005, suggest the world-wide surface will be reduced, whereas certain vineyards of the New World will keep growing constantly. Western Europe countries will have an important reduction, whereas in the rest of the world some important increases in the surface appeared, as it is the case of South Africa, New Zealand, Canada, the United States, among others.

World Output: The main world producing countries are Italy, France and Spain until period 1981-1985. It began to decrease sharply until lapsed in 1991-1995, remaining with a decreasing tendency in the following years, with an average of 250 million hec. Yet, in 1999 a new cycle seemed to have began increasing production again, which was soon halted again. The world-wide wine production increased.

World Consumption

The main wine consuming countries are France, Italy and Gemany. Also, when comparing the consumption per capita between the different countries, can be seen that those that have a greater wine consumption are Luxembourg (63.5 lt), France (57.0 lt) and Italy (54.7 lt). Frothy wines represent just 20% of wine consumption and constitute the category with lower growth and smaller value. Still wines (80%) would have to show an increase of 10% in next the 5 years, whereas the frothy wines could show one slight recovery, of around 3% by the year 2006. When comparing the consumption across continents, the growth of the in America and Northern Europe, as well as, in a smaller degree, in Australia, is off set by a new reduction of the drinking in the traditionally producing countries of Western Europe and South America.

The consumption of wine more expensive than 10 euros the bottle would have to increase by 42% between 2001 and 2006; however, this category just represents now only 3.7% of the total bottled trade. The category of more than 5 euros is equivalent at the moment to a 12.9% of the world-wide consumption and increases a 7% annually. Towards year 2006 it is anticipated that 88% of the growth of the wine consumption will be made up of to wine in bottles costing more than 5 euros.

International Trade

The world-wide wine market has been estimated by the O.I.V. in 68 million hectolitres, allowing for re-exporting and the exports from wine producing countries. The five main producers from the U.E are also main wine traders, representing in period 1996-2000 around 71% of the world-wide interchanges, against 15% of the countries from the Southern Hemisphere and the U.S.A. France, Italy and Spain are the main world exporting wine countries. Nevertheless, is worth to emphasize that Australia and South Africa, are set to increase their exports considerably.

With regard to imports, a paradox occurs when identifying main importers countries. They are Germany, England and France. Germans seem to have reached the maximum level some six years ago and now are gradually drinking less wine. The British, on the other hand are still increasing wine drinking at a rate of 6.1% per year. The whole set of main importers countries are drinking somewhat more wine at a rate of 2.2%, although in the last year observed there was a reduction of 1.3%, which should began to worry to the world wine industry. France, the largest wine exporting country, also imports large amount of wine.

Chilean Wine Market Background

Chile has vineyard of 108 thousand hectares just 1.4% of world. They are located between regions IV and VIII in the Central Valley. This is industry involves a US$ 650 million business to December of 2003. The wine exports have been one of the most dynamic sub-sectors within the Chilean agricultural exports and remains a main item.

In the last 12 years Chile has reached notoriety in world-wide the wine industry and has been recognised, along with Australia, South Africa, New Zealand and Argentina, as one of the emerging country in the market of fine wine export. In this activity had a key role to play in Free Trade Agreement signed with Union European and the United States in 2003. As a result, wine is one of the Chilean exports that are expected to increase its presence in the European and North American markets. Apart from a dry Mediterranean weather with dry summers cold and rainy winters and cold nights, another natural conditions for Chilean wine industry is the sanitation and quality of cepage. Incidentally, due to protection policies, good weather conditions and natural isolation, Chile, has become a filoxera free country. The original vine were "país" variety a low quality one, brought in by the Spanish conquerors in the XVI century. That was improved with noble French vine varieties were planted by newly rich silver miners between 1860 to 1880. Since then this cepage have survived from extinction, as they have been kept well and alive, while elsewhere these varieties have been almost suppressed by widespread of this disease.

Chilean vineyards is growing at 3.5% for the last two decades. Additionally, there are some 52,00 hec. of table grapes vineyards and 10,000 hec of vine for making "pisco", a local aromatic spirit made out of destilled wine. More than three quarters (78%) of Chilean vineyards for wine-making are made up of fine French varieties, with a potential for wine production of exportable quality. Foreign investments are directly managed or they are in join venture. This is an exemplary case of what foreign capital and technology, as well as market networking can do for today's globalization process. Tat link is still much stronger. In many cases, investor groups are also well-established brand names in importing countries, while Chilean wine investment began to spread to neighbouring countries.

Chilean main varieties are for red wine. They are Cabernet Sauvignon (35.7%) which trebled in six year; and país (14%). The second one has remained static over decades. A significant rise occurred for Merlot, growing at 50% per year reaching 12,887 hec. in the year 2001. Pinot Noir grew even faster at 67.5% per year. Others have seen an explosive growth, like Carmenère growing 16 time in five years, to reach 5,407 hec. in 2001, the same occurred with Syrac and Cabernet Franc. An opposing trend occurred with cepage for white wine, which did not grow or actually have decreased. Thus, farmers' aim is clear: to elaborate red wines of high quality for exports. The performance is that Chilean vineyard size almost double in six years. As far as the storage system, at national level there is storage capacity of approximately 1,426 million litre (SAG, 2003), which is made up of different quality: cement storage (47%), stainless steel (33%), wood (15%), barrels (1%) and others (4%). These wine storage containers are of large capacity as 47% are larger than 10 million lt, 44% between 10 to 1 million lt. Chilean wine is produced in very different conditions from one region to another, the degree of specialization for agricultural activities, the actual cepage and size of vineyards, as well as wine making techniques applied. In Chile there is a wide range of wine qualities. A significant effort to inform consumers about quality has been the application of "appellation du origin" system. However, there still much to be done on linking wine production to the "terroir", the local environment and to local communities.

Paradoxically, in spite of this significant growth in both quantity and quality, Chilean wine consumption in Chile, has been drastically reduced from 59,0 lt. per capita in 1972 to 13.1 lt. in 1997, while slightly recovering to 14.6 lt. per capita in 2001. Thus Chilean although they are producing a high quality wine, they are drinking just one quarter than thirty years ago, and just 20% less than a decade ago.

Chilean Wine Exports. In the last decade, Chilean exports have experienced a remarkable growth from 0.4% to 4.5% of wine world trade in 14 years. At the beginning of the nineties exports grew to rates that exceeding 30% per year, to maintain a growth from 10%

to 20%. However, in the last months there has been increasing difficulties to market production. There has been a reduction in prices paid to the producer, together with a structural fall in the dollar exchange rate to the Chilean peso. This last effect began to be relevant soon after the signature of the two trade agreements, with the European Union and with the U.S.A.

By the year 2002, the destination of the Chilean wine exports has shifted. During the 80's years, more of 80% of the exported wine was directed to the market Latin American, just a very small percentage was sold in Europe (2%). This has changed, as just over one half of Chilean wine exports goes to European market (53%), an important part (28%) also gets to North American countries (mainly USA and Canada), and 11% gets to the Far East (China and Japan), but only a small amounts now reaches Latin American countries. This major changes can only be explained by the Chilean trade policies and trade agreements reached with both the European Union and the U.S.A., as well as some other thirty bilateral trade agreements, strong investment policies in this industry, and significant improvements in technology and infrastructure.

Nevertheless, some 43% of Chilean wine exports are sold in-bulk while the rest is sold bottled. Average export prices depends mainly on the type of wine and the degree of elaboration and value added; thus bottled wine gets six than the wine sold in-bulk. In 2003, average export value in US$ per lt was 1.7, but for bottled wine 5.6, champagne 2.8, and in-bulk 0.44. However, the trend is to increase wine exports as bottled, at the expense of in-bulk exports. Three main buyers of bottled Chilean wine by 57% and they are the United Kingdom (25,8%) and the U.S.A (25%) and Denmark (5.9%). Exports of wine in bulk, on the other hand are not that concentrated in few countries; important buyers are Germany (22.4%), China (19.1), Denmark (13.6%), United Kingdom (9.8%) and France (9.6%).

Nowadays, the main Chilean wine exporters are the vines Concha and Toro, San Pedro, Santa Rita, Santa Carolina and Caliterra, exporting wines of high quality and low costs. All of them collect grapes and mostos from various regions, disregarding regional denomination system. Viña San Pedro, for example, has a 3,000 hec. in Lontué, vineyard Concha y Toro, the largest one has important vineyards in various regions of Chile, has introduced intensive automatization, robotics in the process, as well as mechanical harvesting operations. Nevertheless, its own vineyards are not enough for its processing capacity; thus every year the company buys a huge amount of both grapes and mosto from farmers in various locations in the country, but processing and selling them in the domestic and overseas markets only under Concha y Toro brand names. Naturally, these large exporters usually are at odds with quality control systems, like "Appelation d'origin controlée". The quality of their produce varies substantially form year to the next due to enormous span of weathers, soil composition, cepage mixtures and farming practices at their vineyards. Thus usually their exporting prices of their bottled wine are not high, and also they sell important amount of their wine in-bulk. This industrial agribusiness has certain features of coffee tree old "plantations" of cotton or sugar cane

Competing with the largest exporter is another group self-called "boutique wine-growers" grouped in the association self-called Wine of Chile, which integrates the whole process from farming and grape production to wine-making in one single location. This system, they claim, ensures a better control over the whole process, starting with soil quality, uniform weather conditions, homogeneous and high quality product, farming practices, selected cepage, standarized processing, storage, bottling and transport, conditions, all of which contributes towards and improved quality of the final output. They are strong supporters of the "Appellation d'origin" system and they aim to sell most of their wine under viñas own names. Leaders in Wine of Chile in the Maule Region are: Viña Miguel Torres, Viña Balduzzi, and Viña Casa Donoso. Naturally, they are getting higher prices, but they still lack of enough output and bargaining power for consolidating their trading position. Chilean wine exports enter into world trade as a cheap wine during the eighties and beginning of the nineties. However, that policy now has turned into its major problem. How to increase prices and they have already positioned Chilean wine in the lower end of the price scale.

Chilean Wines Competitiveness

Comparative advantages for quality wine production in Chile seems to have remain for a long time. They are special climate and soil, sanitary and genetic patrimony, availability of manual labour and the like. Most of these factors have been in existent since long time ago in Chilean wine-growing activity. Yet, the growth in Chilean wine exports did not happen until mid 1990's. Country competitive advantages, however are the dynamic factors explaining this take off: quality management of resources of production, sizeable domestic demand, dynamic sectorial organisations and quality and inexpensive supplies industries, plus supportive and public authorities.

Liberalization policies, new technology in production and management, suitable infrastructure and investments linked to consume market, are also a part of the Chilean model. That seems to be the main source of competitive advantages supporting this Chilean new trade drive for wine exports. Unlike other exporting countries, the specially United States and France, the domestic market in Chile has not represent a significant source of competitiveness, as this has been substantially and consistently reduced. Additionally, there were a few negative factors also influencing performance of the Chilean wine industry. For example, the lack of a strongly organised industry and the lack of systematic support from public institutions. That is represents a weakness for the national wine-growing industry in relation to its main competitors. In addition, input supply industries do not represent any relevant source of competitive advantage for the sector, as most of them had to be imported (cork, labels).

As anticipated, the Chilean price policy applied to enter foreign markets has been based until now on a non-sustainable good relation price-quality, selling high quality wine at very low price. Also, this drive was supported by an exceptional growth in Chilean gross domestic product from the early nineties. Summarising, Chilean export drive in wine is a peculiar case of success as in ten years its share of the world market has grown ten times in a decade, up to reaching a 4.5%. Official bodies suggest that there still a good scope for keeping up that positive drive, although Chilean should have face up to new challenges. Low production cost are not longer sustainable. Wages, rate of foreign exchange to the Chilean peso, cost of inputs are all increasing. Therefore, low prices and high quality simultaneously cannot be kept in the long run. The average value for the wine exported should be increased, both for cost and market reasons. The image of Chilean wine has been damaged by earlier policies and need urgent re-shaping, if ever the Chilean wine is going to get a premium price.

Securing Overseas Markets: In order to secure export markets, the Chilean government has developed an aggressive trade agreements policy. Most well known are the one signed with the European Union and with the U.S.A. and quite recently with South Korea, all of them in 2003. Other 30 agreements have been signed. Under negotiations are with Japan, India and China.

Chile has improved its image and negotiating positioning abroad. Also these agreements are providing a greater security and a reduced risk for Chilean export business, because of the setting up of official fair conflict resolution procedures. As objective arbitration of conflict does not allow to impose unilateral directives. A small country tries to get equal terms in trade competition.

Organisation for Wine Trading: One of the policies for supporting the entry of Chilean wine into international markets was the setting up of Wines of Chile organisation. This is an attempt to get a more coherent commercial strategy. Wines of Chile was officially launched in April of year 2002. Its objective is to put in practice a strategy of international development and to develop an unified vision towards overseas trade, to construct brand labels that generates loyalty in the international consumers and to become the organisation representing the interests of all the Chilean wine growers at international level. Thus producers expect that commercial cooperation between wine-growers will establish a suitable wine image, while supporting an improved positioning in the mind of the consumer, increasing prices, and providing a product of superior quality with a set of unique differentiating attributes.

Investments for Wine Exports: Disregarding their size, Chilean wine-making companies have carried out great investments in technology and in new plantations, taking advantage of the natural conditions of the country that allow to grow vines with their "terroir". A strong investment commitment, near US$1000 million will change the shape of this industry, in the next few years. These resources will be invested in more and better wine-processing infrastructure for both processing and storing wine. Already are being built a number of new cellars, vineyards, and warehouses using latest generation technology involving mechanization, informatics, automation, robotics, etc. Also a part of overseas investment are being made in improving the access to retail chains. That is the case of Concha y Toro buying shares of a USA large supermarket concern.

Foreign Investments: The great potential of the Chilean wine-growing industry has not pass unnoticed for foreign investors who, individually, or associated at Chilean capitals, are aiming towards excellence wines. Miguel Torres from Spain was one of pioneers, in 1979. This continued until Odfjell Vineyards S.A. from Norway buying an existing vineyard and building processing facilities. France also has provided capital for the Chilean wine industry. Most notable are the Societé Domaines Barons de Rothschild (Lafite), in Viña the Basoues, Les Vignobles, Domain Orientale in Viña Casa Donoso, Villard Fine Wines, G.E. Massenez in Chateau the Boldos, Viña Aquitania, Viña William Fevre, Casa Lapostolle, Viña de Larose. Famous is Pernod-Ricard, consolidating investment of Baron Phillippe de Rothschild and Viña Concha and Toro to produce Almaviva, a premium wine in new installations built with an investment of around US$ 4 million.

North American investments from the USA and Canada has also arrived in Chile. American interests came from Kendall Jackson of California (Vine of the Haze), Seagram of Chile with Cuvée Mumm, Caliterra in Viña Errázuriz and R. Mondavi, Mildara Blass in Viña Santa Carolina, among others. From Canada arrived Canandaigua Brands buying Franciscan State to control Viña Veramonte, and Magnotta Winery. Chilean Wineries Investing Abroad. An important feature of globalization is the flow of capital to and from a dynamic industry. Successful Chilean wine corporations are now investing abroad, expanding their wine varieties and using opportunities to expand output at even lower costs. Argentina, a neighbouring country is receiving Chilean investors in wine. That is the case of Viña Concha and Toro, who is controlling Viña Patagonia in Mendoza, gaining a storage capacity of 2.4 million litres, that already has been extended in 2 million litres and 150 hectares of vineyard. Viña Santa Rita, acquired in Luján of with 730 hec. Viña San Pedro purchased an estate of 200 hectares, in the South of the province of Mendoza.

Wine Tourism

The concept of "terroir" is a complement of the "Appellation d'origin" system, supporting a wine culture. Both are essential component of the wine quality, as much actual wine chemical attributes, as has been probed in the French's practice, with wine tourism. Thus, wine produced in places where consumers have gained memorable experiences at vineyards and wineries, it is expected that commitment to brand names and images be consolidated, creating such a levels of loyalty that purchasing would remain although price may have been substantially risen. This is an attempt to link producers with consumers in the context of globalization.

This view is particularly relevant for Chilean, as this wine has began to be noticed in foreign market as a cheaper one. Therefore, the setting up of significant rural tourism services based upon wine-making is the current paradigm for this emerging wine exporter.

In Chile, in the last five years has began to appear a few wine routes as an attempt to diversify production and to support wine sales. They have been set up by "boutique wineries", plus one of the large corporation (San Pedro), whose vineyards are mainly concentrated on one side of the main motorway to Santiago. The Chilean government has initially supported these initiatives. Now are operating, for example, Ruta Casablanca, Ruta Cachapoal, Ruta Colchagua, Ruta Curico and Ruta Maule. They are run by small group of local wine producers. The emphasis is on routing their various winery members, wine tasting and in hard selling the various vintage wine. Local tourism attractions have been gradually added to the route.

However, managers have obtained disappointed outcomes, which have worried members. There has been great controversy about the component of these wine routes, the degree of involvement of non-wine tourist attractions and of the local community. Also there are disagreements as to how to manage and how to assess the outcome of these projects. Members of participating groups feel that they have not take off, due to the poor wine sale levels and or low number of visitor achieved during their first years of operation. However, this winegrowers are quite happy in investing huge amounts in infrastructure, equipment, vineyards or in processing technology, disregarding any major investment in consumer loyalty. Here, there is a case for both researching and for transferring successful experiences across the world.

Proposing Hypothesis

From these background information a few hypothesis may be stated:

Hypothesis A: Long term effect of agricultural subsidies policies in the investment globalisation context. A long term effect of the EU Agricultural Policy subsidies for uprooting European vineyards ended invested in developing countries like Chile, which in due course has contributed towards an increase flow of quality wine imports into the EU. This, in turn, contributes to deepen profitability problems for local EU wine producers. If this hypothesis is proved, then agricultural policies should be re-shaped in order to cater for self-inflicted unwanted long term effects.

Hypothesis B: Country Of Origin Or Supplies From Competitors. The fact that France, the largest wine producing and consuming country in the world and that holds a significant wine surplus, also has to resort to import wine. This fact calls for a deeper understanding of the re-shaping in the post-modern wine trade and of domestic markets. Hypothesis C: Special Nature Of Wine Route Performance Indicators. Successful wine routes should place more emphasis on current local tourism and on developing brand loyalty, rather than in short term win selling to visitors. Wine routes cannot be outlined as self-contained and self-supporting initiatives. Wine tourism project should be designed as another tourism offer, and thus should cater for all services and activities required by tourists, from the decision to travel to that destination up to arranging all supporting services for the return back home. Wine and wine selling although they always should place an important component of wine routes, per se are not enough to develop the "terroir". Both local culture and local community always should place an essential part of the brand image which should reinforce the building of brand loyalty.

Hypothesis D: Assessment Span For Wine Routes. The outcome of Wine Tourism should be regarded as investments in consumer loyalty and therefore they have to be assessed only in the long run, as the most valuable effect, liking "terroir" to brand product image, building trust and commitment towards building brand loyalty. That can occur only in the long run, after a relationship is established with the brand, the location, the organisation, the contact staff at the counter and visit service. Thus the wine route is just an input which should be memorable to contribute towards the strategy for building consumer loyalty.

All a Question of Taste – Wine Tourism and Destination Development

In regions where wine is produced, vineyards are often the dominant factor in the shaping of the landscape and wine growers contribute great parts to the agricultural production of the area. The beauty of the landscape and the possibility to see first-hand where and how wine is produced appeal to wine consumers who then go on vacation in the wine-growing area, where they will then be known as wine tourists. Mueller/Dreyer distinguish between wine tourism in a narrow and broad sense. In their opinion, when wine is the key motivational factor for the visit and the wine experience itself plays an important role during the visit, it is to be called wine tourism in a narrow sense. In a broader sense, the visitor does not come to the region only for the wine, but also for the wine. (Mueller/Dreyer 2010; pg.11)

Due to its size, the second group, wine tourism in a broader sense, seems (economically) more important. Other definitions, lacking the distinction into narrow and broad sense of wine tourism, include for example the definition by the South Australian Tourism Comission (1997): It focused on activities suggesting that wine tourism is "any experience related to wineries or wine production in which visitors participate when on a day trip or longer visit." It added that "wine tourism can range from a visit to a single cellar door outlet while en route to a main holiday destination, to intensive, week-long experiences focused on the wine process." (Dowling/Getz 2001: pg. 50)

Mueller/Dreyer do not name any research talking about the motivation for a wine vacation, though: experts in the field criticize that lots of research has been conducted directly at the cellar door or in the wine region itself (for convenience), but has only recently started to explore the motivations behind wine tourism (Getz/Brown 2007; pg. 149). In their article "Critical success factors for wine tourism regions: a demand analysis", Getz and Brown describe market research explaining what the long-distance wine tourist expects from the wine tourism destination. It is worth questioning the importance of the long-distance wine tourist due to their relatively minimal numbers.

They found out that distance does not play an important role in the decision-making process and that wine destinations compete with any other possible destination because other destinations might appeal more to respondents and their friends. Wine tourism destinations therefore are not considered a special group among all possible destinations. Even though not consciously making Dreyer's distinction between wine tourism in a narrow and broad sense, their survey showed that wine in combination with cultural activities is more popular than an all-wine vacation. This leads to the conclusion that the above mentioned hypothesis – that wine tourism in a broader sense in more important than wine tourism in a narrow sense – is proven.

The top five wine region features for wine consumers for the decision to visit a long-distance wine region are as follows:

1. The wineries are visitor friendly
2. There is a lot to see and do in the region
3. Attractive scenery
4. Winery staff are knowledgeable about wine
5. Group tours of the wineries are offered

Altogether, Getz/Brown ranked twenty-seven wine region features, all more or less important and categorized into three fields: The core wine product, core destination appeal and the cultural product.

As final food for thought, I would like to cite two statements by Dowling/Getz and Getz/Brown: Ultimately, "it is the consumer who defines the wine tourism 'product', but it should be remembered that there are at least three major perspectives on the subject – that of wine producers, tourism agencies (representing the destinations) and consumer." (Dowling/Getz 2001; pg. 51). "Those charged with developing wine destinations might be prone to over-emphasizing the attractiveness of their wine or wineries, rather than the bundle of cultural and recreational experiences that consumers desire". (Getz/Brown 2006; pg. 156)

Important Wine Travel Destination

Rioja, Spain

Among Spanish wine regions, Rioja ranks as the granddaddy of them all. Located in northeast Spain along the Ebro River, protected to the north by the Cantabrian Mountains and anchored by the city of Logroño, Rioja boasts centuries of winemaking history. It entered the modern commercial era in the 19th century, when French winemakers, looking to escape the spreading phylloxera plague, crossed the Pyrénées and settled in Rioja. Today, Rioja offers an elite mix of Iberian history, stunning scenery, proprietary cuisine, brilliant wines and a unique meshing of old and new. Welcome to Spain's greatest wine region.

Where to Dine

The quintessential food experience in Rioja centres around strolling the bustling streets of Laurel, San Agustín and San Juan in central Logroño and feasting on regional tapas accompanied by glasses of local wine. Top spots include Las Cubanas for roast suckling pig and Tastavin for elevated tapas like tempura bacalao (a dried salted cod). For fine dining in the so-called Spanish vanguardia style, Francis Paniego's Restaurante El Portal del Echaurren in Ezcaray can provide moments of brilliance, while the chef's more casual restaurant in Logroño, Tondeluna, captures the essence of contemporary cooking.

Where to Stay

Lodging options in Rioja range from the five-star Frank Gehry-designed Hotel Marqués de Riscal in Elciego to boutique hotels in small villages, as well as basic European-style three-stars that won't break the bank. The aforementioned Marqués de Riscal, which houses a Caudalie Vinothérapie spa, is Rioja's signature luxury hotel, with an affluent clientele. The Hotel Viura in tiny Villabuena de Álava is a personal favourite, with luxe touches and a cool design. Heredad Ugarte, near Laguardia, features a newly constructed hotel with outstanding views of the Ebro Valley.

Where to Taste

Over the past decade, Rioja wineries with public tasting rooms and tours by appointment have increased exponentially. Bodegas

Franco-Españolas is the only major Rioja winery located within Logroño's city limits. Situated on the north bank of the Ebro River, the restored winery dates from 1890 and offers photos spanning more than a century and tastings. Viña Real, part of the CVNE family of wines, was designed by Bordeaux architect Philippe Mazières and incorporates plenty of pine and Canadian redwood. It's a stunning bodega, operational since 2004, with caves extending 150 metres into the hillside. At Bodegas Muga in Haro, a visit (appointment required) revolves around seeing the winery's own cooperage in action, lessons in racking and tastings of several of Muga's world-class wines.

When to Go: Spring and fall are the prime visiting seasons. Late September into October is harvest time.

Prominent Wines

With more than 600 wineries spread across the subzones of Rioja Alta, Alavesa and Baja, variety is a regional theme. Quality and prices start at simple and cheap and expand to outstanding and expensive. The main grape in the region is Tempranillo, but Rioja's vineyards also grow Garnacha, Graciano and Mazuelo (Carignan), among red grapes. The principal white grapes of Rioja are Viura (Macabeo) and Malvasia.

Budget Tip

At Centro Hípico Navarrete, owner Katharina Gachnang offers informative one-hour horseback rides through the vineyards overlooking the town of Navarrete (approximately $24).

Local in-the-know

Taquio Uzqueda, local artist and historian says, "I've spent more than a quarter-century visiting the monasteries of Yuso and Suso in San Millán de la Cogolla, where history says the modern Spanish language began during the 10th century. When you are there, you think about the era of monks, Moors and Christians, and the battles that these monks listened to in silence. Every corner of each monastery is filled with magic."

Other Activities

What is arguably the best wine museum in the world resides at the Dinastía Vivanco winery in Briones. Unveiled in 2004, the Museo de la Cultura del Vino features almost 3,000 corkscrews and more than 8,000 wine-related pieces and exhibits spread throughout five salons. A top-level restaurant and a wine-and-tapas bar provide postvisit refreshment and nourishment.

Danube, Austria

Stretching from the imposing Monastery of Melk to the city limits of Vienna, the prime winegrowing areas of Wachau, Kremstal, Traisental, Kamptal and Wagram are strung like pearls along the blue Danube River. The river winds through a stunning landscape that varies from steep, terraced vineyards to rolling hills and forests that are marked by historic cloisters and majestic castles. The region's rich art, wine and culinary traditions are not a thing of the past, but continue to evolve and be lived today. These treasures can be explored by car, train, boat, bicycle or foot.

Where to Dine

For haute cuisine and an eclectic wine list in an elegant country manor atmosphere, Landhaus Bacher in Wachau is one of the region's best eateries, and is acclaimed internationally. Delicious organic regional specialities can be enjoyed in a scenic garden setting at the biodynamic wine-farm estate Gut Oberstockstall in the Wagram. Weingut Nigl, nestled in the vineyards of Senftenberg near Krems, offers its delicious wines paired with classy Austrian dishes and an enchanting view of the Ehrenfels Castle ruins.

Where to Stay

The Hotel Schloss Dürnstein is located in the heart of the Wachau Valley UNESCO World Heritage Site. The rooms in this historic castle are furnished with precious antiques and fragrant fresh flowers, and the spa and restaurant offer luxurious indulgence. The stylish, new boutique hotel Malat is located in Furth and enjoys an impressive view of the Göttweig Abbey. This family operation is famous for generous breakfasts served with its own sparkling wine.

Where to Taste

The modern, friendly tasting room and wine shop at Domäne Wachau is open seven days a week from April through October and offers superb tours and tutored tastings twice a day. Sandgrube 13 Wein.Sinn in Krems and Loisium Wine & Spa Resort in Langenlois are both ultramodern wine centres that offer visitors the chance to experience the creation of wine from the vineyard to the glass. The new regional wine event centre, Weritas, a shimmering glass structure perched on the edge of a loess precipice, boasts 35 wine specialities from the Wagram available for tasting. The Stift Klosterneuburg is one of Austria's architectural jewels and has been the centre of spiritual, economic, social and cultural life in the region for nearly 900 years.

See how state-of-the-art winemaking is seamlessly integrated in the expansive Baroque cellar on the winery tour that descends 118 feet underground.

When to Go

There is a choice of 800 delicious events during the Lower Austria Autumn Wine Festival.

Prominent Wines

The Danube wine regions produce some of the world's tastiest and sought-after white wines. Austria's most famous grape, the peppery Grüner Veltliner, is the most prolific variety. Generally, crisp, delineated and mineral-driven Grüner Veltliner are grown in soils made from primary rock, while the exotic, full-bodied versions come from the warm and sandier loess soils. The Danube is also renowned for classy, muscular Rieslings that exude fragrances of apricot and peach. And you will be remiss if you don't seek out a bottle of the delicate, floral Roter Veltliner. It won't be easy to find, but well worth the hunt. Several juicy, must-try cool-climate reds, including Zweigelt and Blaufränkisch, are produced in small quantities and are so popular among the locals that they are often hard to find outside the country.

Budget Tip

Family wine farms often have heurigen (wine taverns) that offer homegrown regional dishes and wines by the glass. A bush branch hung near the door signals that the new wine is being served.

Local in-the-Know

Roman Horvath, MW, of Domäne Wachau: "Stroll along the Art Mile of Krems from the historic old town to the medieval quarter. An absolute must is the Manfred Deix exhibition in the Karikatur Museum [in Krems]. Deix is one of Austria's most important satirical artists, and his works offer an authentic view into the depths of the Austrian soul. Several restaurants and wine bars provide plenty of nourishment for body and mind!"

Other Activities

Wachau Schiff offers a gourmet cruise from Krems to Emmersdorf and a view of the Wachau vineyards from the Danube River. Delight in a return trip on the nostalgic Wachaubahn railway. Book a cooking class with the award-winning chef Toni Mörwald at his Toni M. Cookery School set in the Wagram vineyards of Feuersbrunn.

North and South Forks of Long Island, New York

Fringed by sandy beaches and bustling fishing villages, rolling farmland and forest sanctuaries, Long Island wine country is unlike any region in America. The North and South Forks of the island, collectively known as the East End, extend into the Atlantic Ocean like a two-tined fork, with picturesque Shelter Island wedged between the spears. Just a two-hour drive from Manhattan, it's a unique amalgam of metropolitan influences against a core of hearty, agricultural tradition. Family-owned farms, artisanal food producers and small-production winemakers mingle amongst tony Hamptonites, sharing the wealth of the region's land, sea and vines.

Where to Dine

Conceived by four veterans from some of Manhattan's most lauded restaurants (Aureole and Gramercy Tavern, among others), The North Fork Table & Inn in Southold combines a farm-to-table philosophy with a menu that's innovative and impeccably executed. Noah's in Greenport is casual yet elegant, offering a variety of small plates and squeaky-fresh clams, oysters and scallops delivered daily from local waters. While in Greenport, stop at Aldo's for freshly baked biscotti and espresso from artisan roaster Aldo Maiorana.

Where to Stay

Shinn Estate Farmhouse in Mattituck offers an unparalleled winery experience, complete with vineyard views, captivating wines and gourmet breakfasts prepared by multitalented owner/chef/ winemaker David Page. The Jedediah Hawkins Inn in Jamesport offers the ultimate in Victorian luxury and on-site access to the renowned Luce & Hawkins restaurant. For a downtown vibe and harbor views, the Harborfront Inn at Greenport will place you within steps of restaurants, nightlife and the North Ferry, which connects to Shelter Island.

Where to Taste

With the bulk of the region's 50-plus wineries situated in the North Fork along Route 25 (Main Street) and Route 48, winery hopping is a breeze. Top producers like Paumanok Vineyards, Macari Vineyards, Shinn Estate Vineyards and Farmhouse, Lenz, Bedell and Sparkling Pointe are all located on the North Fork, each with unique tasting rooms open to the public. In Peconic, The Winemaker Studio by Anthony Nappa Wines is a cooperative tasting room offering an unusual collection of private-label selections from local winemakers like its owner, Anthony Nappa. It also features limited-production and library choices from area wineries. The South Fork is home to only three wineries, but with outstanding producers like Wölffer Estate Vineyard and Channing Daughters, it's well worth a day trip.

When to Go

Summer is glorious, but autumn is also prime; farm stands and fish markets are brimming with local offerings.

Prominent Wines

Encouraged by similarities in maritime climate and northerly latitude with Bordeaux, Long Island used to be predominantly Merlot country. Indeed, there is an abundance of well-crafted Merlot here. In recent years, Cabernet Franc has shown great promise, delivering aromatic wines with brambly red-cherry and violet notes. A number of standout Chardonnays shows balance and complexity, as does a handful of high-quality Sauvignon Blancs and traditional method sparkling wines. There's even a Chenin Blanc of note.

Budget Tip

Dine alfresco on the beach, or at one of the many wineries offering picnic areas to enjoy wines, with local cheeses and charcuterie from The Village Cheese Shop in Mattituck.

Local in-the-Know

Kareem Massoud, winemaker at Paumanok Vineyards in Aquebogue: "[Enjoy] sailing out of Greenport, Sag Harbor [or] Montauk and fishing in and around Peconic Bay...Shelter Island and Gardiners Island. It is a seafood lover's delight out here for sport fishermen—for clams, oysters and crabs... Peconic Bay scallop season starts the first Monday in November—a true delicacy of the region."

Other Activities

To travel between the North and South Forks by ferry, it's necessary to drive through Shelter Island, a sleepy islet occupied by the Mashomack Preserve, hiking trails and beaches. During the summer, Crescent Beach transforms dramatically into a bass-thumping, miniature St. Tropez, thanks to hotelier André Balazs's beachside bar and boutique hotel, Sunset Beach.

Stellenbosch, South Africa

The town of Stellenbosch, situated on the banks of the Eerste (First) River, was founded in 1679 by the Governor of the Cape, Simon van der Stel, and named after him. This university town, its historic streets lined with European oak trees and heritage buildings, is surrounded by majestic mountains, giving the impression of a giant amphitheater. Vines—part of the scenery since the 17th century—are planted across the undulating valley, on mountainsides and close to the sea. Although Stellenbosch boasts the largest number of wineries of any of the Cape's regions, all are accessible within a day's drive. The region offers something for everyone, whether your interest is in the arts, culture, food, wine, hiking or surfing.

Where to Dine

Spectacular views across the Stellenbosch Valley accompanied by chef George Jardine's fine food make Jordan Restaurant hard to beat. A favourite with locals is 96 Winery Road Restaurant, which features one of the region's best wine lists and chef Natasha Harris's country cooking. For a true South African experience, AmaZink is a show highlighting authentic musical traditions in the townships and takes place in the suburb of Kayamandi. When exploring the town, Wild Peacock Food Emporium is conveniently situated for a quick, tasty lunch.

Where to Stay

For quiet and relaxation among the vines, L'Avenir Country Lodge offers comfortable elegance. Perched at the top of the Helshoogte Pass (also known as R310), The Lodge at Delaire Graff Estate provides luxury and privacy, with sweeping views of the Stellenbosch Valley and Table Mountain in the distance. Oak trees and the Eerste River bring a bucolic feel to Beauclair Guest Cottage, a stately manor on the outskirts of town. Coopmanhuijs Boutique Hotel & Spa, a beautifully restored 18th-century private residence, is situated in the heart of historic Stellenbosch, surrounded by shops, galleries and museums.

Where to Taste

Vergelegen Estate's impressive modern hilltop winery and classic wines are contrasted by the old manor house and 300-year-old camphor trees in its lush gardens. Learn about going biodynamic at South Africa's only certified producer, Reyneke Wines. Kanonkop Wine Estate, which produces red wines only, is considered a South African "First Growth" (an unofficial honour that indicates a consistent record of excellence). Local art is displayed in the gallery attached to the cellar. Rustenberg Wines and Muratie Wine Estate offer thoroughly modern wines served in Old World settings with beautiful surroundings. The

Stellenbosch Wine Festival, to be held this year from Jan. 25–Feb. 3, 2013, will offer tastings of the best wines from the area.

When to Go

October and November offer cool, fine days in early summer. Harvest time is January to March.

Prominent Wines

Among red wines, Cabernet Sauvignon is king. From the warm inland slopes of the Simonsberg, the wines are muscular and rich; grapes grown closer to the sea make for fresh, tight wines. Cabernet also features in top Bordeaux-style blends. But the area's varied soils, aspects and altitudes allow for much more: vibrant Sauvig-non Blanc, rich Chardonnay, elegant white blends and full-bodied Shiraz, plus a stylistic rainbow of Chenin Blanc and the country's signature Pinot Noir-Cinsault cross, Pinotage. All are book-ended by Cap Classique (South Africa's rendition of sparkling wine) and botrytized dessert styles.

Budget Tip

Expand your knowledge of wine and food at the many farms offering wine with specific food pairings, everything from biltong (cured spiced meat) to chocolate.

Local in-the-Know

Ken Forrester, owner of Ken Forrester Vineyards and chairman of Stellenbosch Wine Routes, says, "Visitors shouldn't miss going to the fantastic open-air Amphitheatre at Oude Libertas, where both local and international artists perform. A picnic on the lawns before the show perfectly sets the scene. At the same venue, the Saturday morning Slowmarket, where everything has been made by the producers themselves, is also a must."

Other Activities

This is an area for the great outdoors. Golf, horse riding and mountain bike trails, the Villiera Wildlife Sanctuary—where you might spot red hartebeest, bontebok and grysbok—a moonlight hike in the Klapmutskop Renosterveld Conservancy and guided walking tours of the town are some of the activities available.

Monterey County, California

Monterey County is one of California's premier wine-producing regions, but it also has long been a destination for travelers. It has beautiful scenery, including Big Sur, the 17-Mile Drive and the Pebble Beach golf courses. It has the tourist venues of Cannery Row and

Fisherman's Wharf. It has the upscale galleries and bistros of Carmel-by-the-Sea. In short, Monterey has diverse draws for wine-oriented visitors. Glamorous resorts dot the county, featuring world-class cuisine, stellar local wines and full spas that pamper with style. The city of Monterey is only about 100 or so miles from downtown San Francisco, making it an easy detour for a multiday trek.

Where to Dine

When Restaurant 1833 opened in downtown Monterey, it instantly raised the city's culinary reputation. Located in one of California's oldest adobe buildings (hence the name, which honours the year in which the structure was built), it offers fresh, skillfully crafted cuisine and a wine list so extensive, it has been described as an auction catalog. The cocktail selection is easily the best on the Monterey Peninsula. The atmosphere is lively, crowded and happy, with most entrées coming in around or above $25.

Where to Stay

The chic Monterey Plaza Hotel & Spa is conveniently located on Cannery Row in the city of Monterey. Many rooms have expansive views of Monterey Bay (and sounds, too—the crashing of surf, the barking of harbor seals and sea lions).

Where to Taste

A Taste of Monterey on crowded Cannery Row features the offerings of over 85 local wineries in a tasting bar-type setting. It's the perfect place to sample the best of Monterey, especially if you're staying nearby and don't want to drive. For individual winery visits, start with Morgan. The tasting room is in Carmel, and you can sample a wide range of reserve and regular Chardonnays, Pinot Noirs, Syrahs and other wines from this well-regarded producer. Talbott Vineyards offers some of the region's most complex Chardonnays and Pinot Noirs at its location on the River Road Wine Trail, which winds scenically along the base of the Santa Lucia Mountains. Chalone Vineyards is a true pioneer in California Pinot Noir. Its tasting room is way up in the Gavilan Mountain Range, above Soledad, east of the 101 Freeway.

When to Go

September and October offer the driest, sunniest weather, with rain more likely as November nears.

Prominent Wines

Monterey has a relatively cool climate, so its signature varieties are Pinot Noir and Chardonnay. Dependable producers include the

Testarossa Winery, Pessagno Winery, Roar, Morgan, Pisoni and Talbott Vineyards. Cool-climate Syrah abounds, too, from the likes of Novy Family Wines and Wrath. While most of the county is too cool for Cabernet, the warm Carmel Valley, sheltered by the Santa Lucia Mountains, features elegant, earthy Cabernets from Bernardus Winery and Galante Vineyards. A particularly successful small region is Arroyo Seco, nestled on the west side of the sprawling Salinas Valley. It's known for crisp, inexpensive red and white varieties. Insider tip: Wines with a Monterey or Monterey County appellation can be extremely good values, so if you're in the market, be sure to scoop up a few cases.

Budget Tip

Dig into the famous Ambrosia Burger with a sauce that includes chili salsa, for $14.50, at Nepenthe in Big Sur. Wash it down with local wine on the outdoor deck while enjoying fabulous views.

Local in-the-Know

Rhonda Motil, executive director of the Monterey County Vintners and Growers Association, says: "Dennis the Menace Park is one of my family's beloved places for adventure. From making sure you have steady feet on the swaying bridge, to squealing with delight as you ride the coaster slide, to testing your skill on the rock climbing wall, and finally capping the experience by pretending you are the conductor on the model train—it's fun for kids and grown-ups alike."

Other Activities

Take a drive, with the top down, on Highway 1, which boasts one of the most gorgeous drives on the planet. The winding two-lane highway hugs the coastline and offers unsurpassed vistas of the majestic Santa Lucia Mountains and the deep-blue Pacific. Head south out of Big Sur and in minutes the relatively pricier convertible rental will pay for itself.

Vale dos Vinhedos, Brazil

Forget about the sandy beaches and bikini-clad beauties of Rio de Janeiro, and instead picture the rolling hills of Italy's Piedmont region. In the late 1800s, southern Brazil experienced a mass influx of Italian immigrants, primarily from northern Italy. The largest and most important wine region in the country, Serra Gaúcha and its Denominación de Origen, Vale dos Vinhedos, now account for almost 90% of Brazil's fine wine production. These green hills, dotted with wineries, hotels and restaurants, attract approximately 150,000 visitors per year. Italian cuisine is prominent, and many aged residents speak an almost-lost Venetian dialect interspersed with Portuguese.

Where to Dine

At Valle Rustico, don't miss Chef Rodrigo Bellora's filet mignon with house-made chimichurri sauce or polenta with wild boar ragu. With a wine list boasting 21 sparkling, six white and 35 red selections, it's hard to choose just one. At Cabanha's Churrascaria, this traditional pampa-style restaurant features prime cuts of beef that are grilled to perfection over a wood-burning fire. The attached wine shop makes picking your wine fun, educational and easy.

Where to Stay

With 128 luxurious rooms, lavish public areas and a world-class spa, Hotel & Spa do Vinho Caudalie is the place to base yourself while touring Brazilian wine country. Don Giovanni Vinhos Vinhedos Pousada is a quaint, family-run bed-and-breakfast, and is a bastion of Old World charm. Eight guest rooms, a winery and an award-winning restaurant are set in a historic house built in 1930.

Where to Taste

Roughly 130,000 visitors per year pass through Miolo winery's gates. Under the guidance of consultant Michel Rolland, it makes highly regarded red, white and sparkling wines. At Pizzato Vinhas e Vinhos, father and son Plinio and Flavio Pizzato make excellent wines from Cabernet Sauvignon, Merlot, Chardonnay, Pinot Noir (for sparkling) and some lesser-known varieties. Visitors are often surprised by the impressive European-style buildings at Casa Valduga. Make sure to tour its extensive sparkling wine cellars.

Vinícola Aurora is a co-op with 1,100 member families and a variety of bottlings. The red-wine-spouting, gold-toned Bacchus fountain is a fun photo op. Also, visit Vinícola Salton. Started in 1910, the winery now produces more than 30 wines.

When to Go

Most of Brazil is south of the equator, so the seasons are opposite ours. Go in March to catch the harvest.

Prominent Wines

Red wines are made using Merlot, Cabernet Sauvignon, Cabernet Franc, Tannat, Ancellotta, Pinot Noir, Touriga Nacional and Teroldego. White grapes include Riesling, Chardonnay, Muscat, Malvasia and

Glera (formerly known as Prosecco). Sparkling wines are produced in dry and sweet styles, and are among Brazil's more sought-after sips. The only red grape that can be labelled as a single varietal in Vale dos Vinhedos is Merlot. Notable examples are made by producers like Miolo, Casa Valduga and Pizzato. The Indicação de Procedência Pinto Bandeira allows production of both sweet and dry sparkling wines, and dry reds and whites.

Budget Tip

Buy a bottle of Brazilian sparkling wine and some pão de queijo (cheese bread) and head out to Floresta de Tijuca Municipal Park for a relaxing afternoon amid the local flora and fauna.

Local in-the-know

Flavio Pizzato of Pizzato Vinhas e Vinhos likes to spend his days away from the winery actively engaged with nature. "The region is very steep, green and full of barely explored areas. [Mountain range] Paredão da Eulália is close to our winery, and you can just see the sights there or do a deep forest exploration. Also, Serra Gaúcha's main river, Rio das Antas, is very good for rafting." One of his favourite outfitters is CIA Aventura.

Other Activities

Take the family for a relaxing day in Serra Gaúcha's hot springs. Caldas de Prata offers a variety of packages to suit your needs and budget, from a simple pool soak (approximately $9.50) to a luxurious spa day (prices vary by treatment). Make sure to visit the beautiful local waterfall, Cascata da Usina.

Willamette Valley, Oregon

The Willamette Valley is a big place, and it's stuffed with friendly wineries, gorgeous scenery, toy towns and a dazzling array of outdoor activities. Visitors should plan to explore the countryside, not just the main towns. That means lots of driving on twisty, two-lane roads, so try to focus each day's excursions on a confined area. Headquarter in Newberg or Dundee for quick access to the American Viticultural Areas (AVAs) of Dundee Hills and Ribbon Ridge, where many of the region's finest boutique wineries reside. Carlton is a sweet little town with good restaurants and tasting rooms. It's best to call ahead for an appointment at small tasting rooms.

Where to Dine

In Newberg, The Painted Lady is tops. Jory, at The Allison Inn & Spa, has a deep Oregon wine list. Also in Newberg are Recipe, a winemakers' favourite for rustic, delicious specials; and Panadería y Taquería González, which offers authentic Mexican fare. Thistle is the best in McMinnville, while the Joel Palmer House in Dayton is famed for its locally sourced mushrooms. In Dundee, try Paulée or Tina's for fine dining, while The Dundee Bistro and Red Hills Market offer simple country and takeout foods.

Where to Stay

The Allison Inn & Spa is far and away the most deluxe lodging option in the valley, offering full resort services. In Newberg, The DreamGiver's Inn, Le Puy and Lions Gate Inn all get high marks for both comfort and romance. The Chehalem Ridge Bed & Breakfast has spectacular views. In storybook Carlton, try the Lobenhaus Bed & Breakfast & Vineyard or Abbey Road Farm Bed & Breakfast for tranquility amidst splendid scenery.

Where to Taste

The Carlton Winemakers Studio, conceived and built by winemaker Eric Hamacher, has as many as a dozen garagiste wineries on site. It's a great one-stop opportunity to taste through some of the newest and rarest of the region's offerings, including wines from Andrew Rich, Hamacher, Merriman, Retour and Utopia Vineyard. In downtown Carlton, the Scott Paul tasting room also pours rare Burgundies, imported by proprietor Scott Wright. Angel Vine, Lemelson Vineyards and Soter Vineyards are must-sees nearby. The Ribbon Ridge AVA is home to a number of outstanding boutiques, notably Ayres Vineyard, Beaux Frères, Brick House Vineyards, Patricia Green Cellars and Trisaetum. Close by are Adelsheim, Bergström and Penner-Ash Wine Cellars. Most require reservations, but Adelsheim is always open, and pours an array of single-vineyard Pinots.

When to Go

The best weather months are May–June and September–October.

Prominent Wines

Consider Willamette Valley your Burgundy of the states, producing world-class Pinot Noir and Chardonnay. The weather is relatively mild throughout the year, with cool, wet winters, dry, warm summers and coastal marine influences. The resulting Pinot Noirs are elegant and structured, with a striking balance between ripe fruit and earth. For wine lovers looking beyond the classics, the valley also cultivates outstanding Pinot Blanc, Pinot Gris, Riesling and Viognier for still wines, as well as sparkling wines made from traditional Champagne varieties.

Other Activities

The Evergreen Aviation & Space Museum, just outside of McMinnville, is home to the famous Spruce Goose, a World War II-era wooden aircraft and the largest plane ever built, along with other vintage aircraft. Also on-site are an IMAX theater and the Wings & Waves Waterpark. Other nonwine options include golfing (Chehalem Glenn Golf Course in Newberg and nearby Pumpkin Ridge Golf Club in Aloha), biking, hiking and ballooning.

Budget Tip

Press Wine Bar and Bottle Shop, at The Inn at Red Hills in Dundee, offers many hard-to-find, small-lot Oregon wines at very competitive prices. A wine club is due to launch soon.

Local in-the-Know

Kelley Fox is the winemaker for Scott Paul and the owner and winemaker of Kelley Fox Wines. "A classic," she says, "is Nick's Italian Café in McMinnville. It has been and always will be a watering hole for winemakers. I have the fondest memories of washing David Lett [founder and winemaker of The Eyrie Vineyards]'s tasting room glasses in Nick's kitchen, often while Nick himself was rolling out the day's ravioli. Great jazz, too."

Hunter Valley, New South Wales, Australia

Australia's Hunter Valley is perfectly situated for wine tourism, just a couple of hours by road from Sydney, the country's largest city. Various companies run tour buses to the region direct from downtown, and chauffeured limo services are readily available. As a result, many visitors come to the Hunter just for the day. But to really explore the Hunter, it's best to get up into it and stay overnight, or longer. As one of Australia's traditional grape-growing regions, there's plenty of history to discover, alongside vast open spaces and some terrific wines made in styles found nowhere else on the planet.

Where to Dine

Many of the Hunter's best restaurants are located at resorts or wineries. Il Cacciatore ("The Hunter") at the Hermitage Lodge offers Italian cuisine using local ingredients and a range of Hunter wines. The most extensive wine list in the region is found at Tower Estate and its two affiliated restaurants—Roberts and Nine—a legacy of the era when legendary bon vivant Len Evans was a partner in the business. Also notable is Muse Restaurant & Café, run by chef Troy

Rhoades-Brown, an alum of Roberts, with a wine list that includes some aged treasures at reasonable prices.

Where to Stay

For the ultimate in luxury, Tower Lodge is a Relais & Châteaux property. Guests at this boutique hotel feel completely at home, despite the setting being anything but ordinary. At Peppers Convent, guests stay in an actual convent that has been relocated nearly 375 miles and magnificently restored. The nuns never had it so good. Pokolbin Village offers several different types of accommodations, with chocolate, cheese and wine shops on the property.

Where to Taste

The region's proximity to Sydney and its legions of tourists have led most of the wineries to develop sophisticated cellar-door operations. Many include restaurants, or at least the prospect of ordering cheese or charcuterie to accompany your tastings. Hope Estate regularly hosts expansive outdoor concerts, and in March 2013, will host a multiday country and folk music festival. McWilliam's Mount Pleasant Estate was where Maurice O'Shea, perhaps Australia's greatest winemaker, plied his work. Lake's Folly is unusual for its pursuit of Cabernet and Chardonnay, sold almost exclusively through a mailing list or at the cellar door, when wine is available (call first). Also notable: Brokenwood, Hungerford Hill, Keith Tulloch Wine, Lindeman's, McGuigan Wines, Tulloch (try the Verdelho), Tyrrell's Wines (ask if any aged Semillons are on offer) and Wyndham Estate.

When to Go

Spring and fall are the best times to experience the Hunter. Summer can be too warm for comfort.

Prominent Wines

The Hunter Valley is home to two distinctive wine styles, unduplicated elsewhere. As the region is warm and prone to late-season rains, growers historically harvested their grapes early. Semillon (ditch the French accent and pronounce it SEM-a-lon), is typically under 12% abv. With its high acidity and greenish tinge, it's fine young when served with raw shellfish, but aged examples develop golden hues and honeyed, toasty richness. Hunter Valley Shiraz is also traditionally moderate in alcohol, emphasizing aromas and flavours of leather and spice rather than jammy fruit. Chardonnay does well in the Upper Hunter Valley, where it develops warm, tropical flavours.

Budget Tip

Many folks visiting from Sydney come just for the day, but upscale meals and accommodations are less expensive in the Hunter. Stay over and enjoy not having to drive back after a long day of tasting.

Local in-the-Know

Keith Tulloch, a fourth-generation Hunter winemaker who produces an eponymous label, says, "Take a short drive up to the top of the mountain range to a spot that overlooks the whole Hunter vineyard area, with views that extend down to the ocean about 30 miles away. There's nothing to beat such a great view, especially with a plate of fresh seafood, or barbecue, and a glass or two of our best wines."

Other Activities

Award-winning Hunter Valley Gardens features 10 different themed gardens and approximately five miles of walking paths. The rose garden alone contains more than 8,000 specimens of flora. Hot-air balloon is a popular way to see the region, or stay closer to ground and rent a bicycle to traverse the scenic byways.

Douro Valley, Portugal

You will fall in love with the Douro. Northern Portugal's claim as the most beautiful wine region in the world is supported by the grandeur of its landscape and wines. Hewn from schist mountainsides like unpolished granite, the steep-terraced vineyards rise above the majestic Douro River's ribbon of water far below. For centuries, its remoteness—the journey on twisting, cobbled roads—made it hard to reach. Today, it's easy. Even so, this is a place where neighbourhood dogs sleep in the village streets and the annual cycle of the vines seems timeless. Sit on a terrace in the evening, a glass of white Port and tonic in hand, and listen to the distant, mournful hoot of the evening river train. The land is calm, and calming.

Where to Dine

Eat at DOC, between Pinhão and Peso da Régua, the winemakers' hot spot for celebrated modern cooking. The Douro wine list is impressive. Arrive by river if you want—there's a boat dock. On the riverfront in Peso da Régua, Douro In is popular with wine locals for its modern interpretations of classic Portuguese dishes. For a friendly welcome and traditional family food—especially fresh fish and chicken—head for Ponte Romana near Pinhão's old bridge.

Where to Stay

Quinta do Vallado Wine Hotel is run by the descendants of the 18th-century grande dame of the Douro, Dona Antónia Adelaide Ferreira. Stay in the renovated historic manor house or in the 21st-century wing. For classic home cooking, stupendous Douro views and a great art collection, try Casa do Visconde de Chanceleiros on the hills above Pinhão. Romaneira Quinta dos Sonhos, a Relais & Châteaux property, is the ultimate in luxury. The aim is total relaxation: no phones, cell phone reception or TV, but there is public Wi-Fi.

Where to Taste

Sandeman's winery and award-winning visitors' centre at the Quinta do Seixo wine centre offers an atmospheric venture into Port wine production, including tours of the open lagars (fermenting vats). Keep an eye out for the Sandeman Don. Afterward, enjoy tastings in the modern bar with views over the river. There's a family-style welcome at Quinta do Crasto after a twisting, sometimes scary, cliff-hugging drive. Climb up to the chapel for a dramatic view. Fonseca's Quinta do Panascal sends you into the terraced vineyards with an audio guide (stout footwear recommended). Visit Panascal's restaurant or taste on the terrace overlooking the torrent of the Távora River after the walk. A short drive up from the Douro Valley is Quinta do Portal, a beautiful, modern, family-owned winery where you can visit, taste and dine. But don't limit yourself to these suggestions: Stop along the way at any quinta, and make sure to taste the Douro table wines as well as the Ports.

When to Go

March–June for almond blossoms, wild flowers and budding vines; September for harvest.

Prominent Wines

Famed for its Port wines, the Douro also offers redoubtable red table wines. Rich and powerful, they vie with the wine world's top selections. Still, no one goes to the Douro without tasting Port. Naturally, every option is here, straight from the quinta—a Port lover's heaven. Try the late-bottled vintages (LBVs), vintages, the tawny variations (golden-brown from aging in wood for 10–40 years) and the rare vintage-dated colheitas—there's no experience that can compare to tasting a Port older than you are. All the Port and table wines are products of some of Portugal's finest native grape varieties: Touriga Nacional, Touriga Franca and Tinta Barroca are among the best.

Budget Tip

Take a picnic to the chapel of São Salvador do Mundo near São João da Pesqueira. Enjoy the best Douro River views down almost vertical slopes.

Local in-the-Know

Quinta de la Rosa's co-owner, Sophia Bergqvist, takes the train along the Douro through vineyards, villages and the moon-like granite landscape from Pinhão to Ferradosa. "At Ferradosa, you can walk to a small restaurant with beautiful views over the river and feast on some great traditional food," says Bergqvist.

Other Activities

The Foz Côa prehistoric rock-art site in Douro Superior features 20,000-year-old rock carvings interpreted by clever guides. The Côa Valley Archaeological Park is remote and arid. Carvings, long a part of shepherd gossip, were recognised in the beginning of the 1990s when it was to be flooded for a dam. Make reservations for four-wheel-drive tours.

Puglia, Italy

Flanked by two seas, magical Puglia is a thin peninsula packed tight with the same attributes that attracted us to Italy decades ago: It's an undiscovered land with an enviable quality of life. The octagonal Castel del Monte, a 13th-century castle, inspires architects today, and the historic city of Lecce offers the purest expression of Moorish-Italian Baroque. Weathered stone and whitewashed buildings pop against green olive groves. Trulli are the mysterious cone houses in the Itria Valley, and all of Puglia's stunning beauty is surrounded by some of the bluest waters in Europe.

Where to Dine

To say that Puglia has Italy's best food is no exaggeration. It offers fresh ingredients, whether pulled from the sea or picked from the nearest tree. Masseria Il Frantoio is a foodie's paradise, with a never-ending appetizer spread and grandmothers kneading orecchiette pasta in the kitchen. Ristorante Masseria Spina is slightly more sophisticated, but equally rooted in tradition. Antica Cucina 1983 Ristorante, Le Lampare al Fortino and Osteria Gia Sotto L'Arco offer excellent seafood dishes at various price points. Ristorante Penny boasts an excellent wine list.

Where to Stay

County manors, or masserie, from the 16th and 17th centuries are routinely being refurbished as luxury hotels. One of the most beautiful is Masseria Torre Coccaro, with a cooking school and romantic, wild botanical garden. The Justin Timberlake-Jessica Biel wedding was staged at the sea-facing Borgo Egnazia resort. Equally luxurious, if slightly formal, is Masseria Torre Maizza. If you are looking for homey, rustic charm, try the gorgeous Borgo San Marco. And, if you are visiting the town of Alberobello and want to sleep in one of the iconic trulli, book a cone-shaped room at Le Alcove.

Where to Taste

Puglia's rapidly expanding wine scene has something for all tasting types. Don't miss the grand cellar room at Tormaresca. Owned by Antinori, the property represents one of the biggest local investments in quality wine. Equally impressive are Masseria Altemura, inaugurated by the Zonin family with a wine shop and visitors' centre, and Castello Monaci. You can tour the postcard-perfect 16th century castle just beyond the winery. If your passion is organic farming, Agrinatura is a unique model. It presents a sustainable organic platform that spans wine, olive oil, pasta sauce and seasonable crops (all on sale). For boutique tasting rooms with great wines, consider these by-appointment visits: Castel di Salve; L'Astore Masseria, with an ancient olive press; and Rivera. The Movimento Turismo del Vino Puglia acts as a wine tourism and information centre.

When to Go

Summer, for epic seafood meals on pristine beaches and all-night pizzica dancing.

Prominent Wines

Puglia excels at warm-climate wines made with indigenous grapes. Castel del Monte delivers red wines from Uva di Troia, Bombino Nero and Aglianico. Interesting work is being done with crisp Bombino Bianco white wines and sweet Moscato di Trani. Further south, the Primitivo grape (Primitivo di Manduria) is famously linked genetically to Zinfandel. Local wines show ripe berry nuances, inky concentration and soft tannins. Salice Salentino is planted to Negroamaro (sometimes blended with Malvasia Nera) for hearty reds. The past five years have a remarkable rise of crisp white wines from Greco, Fiano, Malvasia and Chardonnay.

Budget Tip

Feast on raw sea urchins at one of the many beachfront ricci di mare shacks in the Salento. Scoop out the bright orange roe with whole-grain bread, and wash it down with red table wine.

Local in-the-Know

"Castel del Monte is an astronomical machine more than a castle," says Sebastiano de Corato, export manager for Rivera in Andria. "Go in the late afternoon as the setting sun reflects off the white stone. Built in the 1200s by Emperor Frederick II, the eight-sided castle was constructed according to the Golden Ratio, and symbolic shadows are cast during the equinox and different times of year. It has all sorts of Da Vinci Code-like appeal."

Other Activities

This is a land of superstitions, and old-timers warn that poisonous tarantulas will bite humans (mostly young females), forcing them into a frenzied, trance-like dance called tarantella. This mystical affliction continues today with the contemporary pizzica dance and music festivals all summer long, where you can see the dance performed. Young women in flowing skirts swirl and stomp to rhythmic tambourine beats late into the night.

Aroma of Wine

It is through the aromas of wine that wine is tasted. The human tongue is limited to the primary tastes perceived by taste receptors on the tongue-acidity, bitterness, saltiness, sweetness and savoriness. The wide array of fruit, earthy, floral, herbal, mineral and woodsy flavour perceived in wine are derived from aroma notes interpreted by the olfactory bulb. In wine tasting, wine is often smelled before being drunk in order to identify some components of the wine that may be present. Different terms are used to describe what is being smelled. The most basic term is aroma which generally refers to a "pleasant" smell as opposed to odor which refers to an unpleasant smell or possible wine fault. The term aroma maybe further distinguished from bouquet which generally refers to the smells that arise from the chemical reactions of fermentation and aging of the wine.

Aroma vs. Bouquet

In professional wine tasting, there is generally a distinction made between "aromas" and a wine's "bouquet" while in casual wine tasting these two terms are used interchangeably. An aroma refers to the smells unique to the grape variety and are most readily demonstrated in a varietal wine—such as lychees with Gewürztraminer or black currant with Cabernet Sauvignon. These are smells that are commonly associated with a young wine. As a wine ages chemical reactions among acids, sugars, alcohols and phenolic compounds create new smells that are known as a wine's bouquet. These can include honey in an aged Sauternes or truffles in a Pinot noir. The term bouquet can also be expanded to include the smells derived from fermentation and exposure to oak. In Burgundy, the aromas of wines are subdivided into three categories-primary, secondary and tertiary aromas. Primary aromas are those specific to the grape variety itself. Secondary aromas are those derived from fermentation and oak aging. Tertiary aromas are those that develop through bottled aging.

The technique of microoxygenation has an impact on the aromatic bouquet.

Components of a Wine's Aroma

Within wine there are volatile and non-volatile compounds that contribute to the make up of a wine's aroma. During the fermentation and for the first few months of a wine's existence, chemical reactions among these compounds occur frequently and a wine's aroma will change more rapidly during this period than at any other point. As a wine ages and matures, changes and developments in aroma will continue to take place but at a slower and more gradual pace. Volatile aroma compounds are present in the skin and juice of a grape berry and will vary in composition according to the individual grape variety. It is theorized that the *Vitis* vine developed these compounds as a evolutionary tool to aid in procreation by attracting insects to assist with pollination and birds and other animals to eat the berries and disperse the seeds. The diverse spectrum of aromas associated with individual grape varieties is a reflection of the vine's adaptation to ecological conditions and competition among other plants.

The majority of volatile compounds responsible for aroma combine with sugars in the wine to form odorless glycosides. Through the process of hydrolysis, caused by enzymes or acids in the wine, they revert into an aromatic form. The act of tasting wine is essentially the act of smelling these vaporized aroma compounds. Olfactory receptors cells, each sensitive to a different aromas, pick up these compounds and transfers the information to the brain by way of the olfactory bulb. In the 1980s there was renewed focus in studying the correlation between aroma/flavour compounds in grapes and the resulting quality of wine. Scientists were able to use chromatograph-mass spectrometres to identify volatile aroma compounds in various grape varieties.

Study of the compounds responsible for aroma and flavour, as well as their correlation with a wine's quality, is ongoing. As understanding of these compounds grows, there is concern that wines in the future could be "manipulated" through the use of chemical additives to add complexity and additional aromas to wine (such as creating a manufactured perfume) . In 2004, a winery in South Africa was found to have added illegal flavouring to their Sauvignon blanc to enhance the aroma. Viticultural studies have focused on how aroma compounds develop in the grapes during the annual growth cycle of the vine and how viticultural techniques such as canopy management may contribute to developing desirable aromatics in the wine.

Identified Aroma Compounds

Some of the identified aroma compounds include the following:

- Methoxypyrazine-grassy, herbaceous aroma compound associated with Cabernet Sauvignon and Sauvignon blanc.
- Monoterpenes-responsible for the floral aromatics of varieties like Gewürztraminer, Muscat and Riesling. Includes geraniol, linalool and nerol.
- Norisoprenoids-Carotenoid derived aromatic compounds that includes megastigmatrienone which produces some of the spice notes associated with Chardonnay and zingerone responsible for the different spice notes associated with Syrah. Other norisoprenoids include raspberry ketone which produces some of the raspberry aromas associated with red wine, damascenone which produces some of the rose oil aromas associated with Pinot noir and vanillin.
- Thiols-sulfur contain compounds that can produce an aroma of garlic and onion that is considered a wine fault (mercaptans). They have also been found to contribute to some of the varietal aromas associated with Cabernet Sauvignon, Gewürztraminer, Merlot, Muscat, Petit Manseng, Pinot blanc, Pinot gris, Riesling, Scheurebe, Semillon and Sylvaner.

Esters

Some of the aromas perceived in wine are from esters created by the reaction of acids and alcohol in the wine. Esters can develop during fermentation, with the influence of yeast, or later during aging by chemical reactions. The precise yeast strain used during fermentation and temperature are two of the strongest indicators of what kind of esters will develop and helps explain partially why Chardonnay grown in the same vineyard but made by two different producers could have different aromatics. During bottle aging hydrogen ions, found in higher concentration in low pH (high acid) wines, serves as a catalyst in the formation of esters from acids and alcohols present in the wine. However, at the same time these hydrogen ions encourage esters to also split apart back into acids and alcohols. These two counterbalancing acts gradually inch a wine closer to a state of equilibrium where there is equal parts alcohol, acids, esters and water (a by product of the reactions). During this period the ester influenced bouquet of the wine is constantly changing due to the concentration, formulation and splitting of different esters. This is partly the reason why a wine will have one set of aromas at one time and other aromas later in its life.

In Wine Tasting

The sense of smell and detecting the aromas in wine is the primary means through which wine is tasted and evaluated. Prior to tasting the wine, wine drinkers will often smell the wine in the glass. Large bowl glasses with tapered openings, some of which are specifically designed to enhance aromatics of different wines, can assist in capturing more aromatics within the glass for the drinker to detect. Wines served at warmer temperature will be more aromatic than wine served cooler due to heat's ability to increase the volatility of aromatic compounds in the wine. Swirling, or aerating, the wine will increase available surface area, increasing the rate at which aroma molecules volatilize. Some subtle aromatics can be overwhelmed by more dominant aromatics that arise after swirling, so most professional tasters will sniff the wine briefly first before swirling. The closer the nose is to the wine, even right inside the glass, the greater chances of aromatics being captured. A series of short, quick sniffs versus one long inhale will also maximize the likelihood of aromatics being detected. The human nose starts to "fatigue" after around six seconds and so a pause may be needed between sniffs.

When wine is sipped, it is warmed in the mouth and mixes with saliva to vaporize the volatile aroma compounds. These compounds are then inhaled "retro-nasally" through the back of the mouth to where it is received by nearly five million nerve cells. The average human can be trained to distinguish thousands of smells but can usually only name a handful at a time when presented with many aromas. This phenomenon, known as the "tip of the nose phenomenon", is countered when a person is given a list of possible choices, through which they can often positively identify the aroma. Professional wine tasters will often mentally cycle through a list of potential aromas (and may use visual aids like the aroma wheel, developed by Ann C. Noble of University of California, Davis) until one choice stands out and can be identified in the wine.

Detecting an aroma is only part of wine tasting. The next step is to describe or communicate what that aroma is and it is in this step that the subjective nature of wine tasting appears. Different individuals have their own way of describing familiar scents and aromas based on their unique experiences. Furthermore, there are varying levels of sensitivity and recognition thresholds among humans of some aromatic compounds. This is why one taster may describe different aromas and flavours from another taster sampling the very same wine.

Wine Clubs

Wine clubs are a developing extension of modern wine culture. Wine clubs are designed to provide customers with a series of wine bottles on a monthly or quarterly basis that they would otherwise have to find and purchase on their own. Wine clubs often behave in a themed manner, providing recipients with red wines, white wines, or a mixture of the two. Wine clubs are most frequently offered by vineyards or speciality wine shops, but they can also be found as independent bodies.

Origin

Paul Kalemkiarian, Sr. claims to have invented the idea of wine in the mail in 1972, while managing a small liquor store in Palos Verdes Estates, California. When a customer needed advice on a wine purchase, Paul Kalemkiarian, Sr. would direct him or her toward a bottle of red and a bottle of white that he had designated as the "monthly selections." Soon customers began to request that these selections be delivered to their homes, and newly-licensed Paul Kalemkiarian, Jr., Kalemkiarian's teenage son, would load up the truck and make his rounds. The number of customers requesting this service increased over time, serving as the impetus for the Wine of the Month Club as it exists today. The Club, now owned and operated by Paul Kalemkiarian, Jr., continues its tradition of delivering two bottles of wine—both of which have been pared down from among the hundreds that Kalemkiarian, Jr. tastes each month—to the homes of its members nationwide.

Variations and Costs

Most wine clubs involve all red bottles, all white bottles, or a combination of both, known as "mixed" clubs. However, there have arisen many stylistic variations in what wines are shipped (including grape varietals and wine regions and how many bottles. Various wine clubs can have a set theme or many themes that alternate with each shipment. The cost range for wine clubs is vast since wine itself can range vastly in price. The type of wines being selected for club shipments and the number of bottles, as well as the frequency of shipping, will influence the overall cost of a wine club. Common wine clubs are created by wineries themselves, wine stores, internet retailers or large media companies such as the New York Times and Wall Street Journal, among others.

Tasting Room Etiquette

Many small, boutique wineries are family-run. When visiting a wine tasting room consider yourself a guest. The owners and staff are proud of their facility and want everyone to enjoy their visit. Expectations in wine tasting rooms are different than at wine festivals or in busy bars. After visiting 450 wineries in the last three years and talking with numerous wine hosts and visitors, we have created a selection of ideas to keep in mind when visiting a winery tasting room. Simple rules of etiquette can help to make the experience enjoyable for all. The atmosphere in a winery tasting room is one of a subtle sophistication. While shorts and athletic shoes are acceptable so are semi-dress clothes. Do not wear perfume or cologne the day you are visiting winery tasting rooms. The smell will interfere with a wine's aroma, not only for you, but also for those near you.

In the sophistication of a winery tasting room, loud outside voices are not appropriate. Conversational tones are perfect and fit in well with talking about the wines you taste and meeting other wine enthusiasts who have common interests. Do take the time to talk to other visitors. It is interesting to meet others with a passion for wine. Some visitors are new to wine. Never belittle someone for what they think about a wine. Don't act or sound like a wine snob. There are always those who know less and more about wine than you.

If you appear drunk, the tasting room attendant is not permitted, by law, to serve you even if it is a tasting. Drunken behaviour has no place in the atmosphere of the tasting room. Wineries deal with this behaviour in different ways, most often you will be asked to leave.

Tasting rooms can be crowded on weekends. Weekdays are generally slower and wine hosts have more time to talk about the wines you taste. In either case, if the tasting room is busy, do not elbow your way to the tasting bar. If the tasting room is busy, consider stepping back to discuss your wine and enjoy the tasting with other like-minded people. This gives others room to step up for a tasting. On busy days, some wineries will set up tasting tables or bars outside the tasting room. Give yourself plenty of time at a winery. Relax and enjoy the wine tasting and the ambiance of the tasting room. Many wineries have gift selections to browse while tasting wines. Take your time tasting and browse the shelves.

The wines for a tasting are presented in a particular order based upon the style of wine. If you choose not to drink a particular wine that's fine. Gently cover your wine glass with your fingers to indicate you do not want to taste a wine. It is so much more subtle than declaring, "I don't like that wine." Not all wine drinkers like all wines and wine hosts understand this. Visitors do not need to announce to everyone that they dislike a particular wine. Remember that it is perfectly acceptable for you to dislike a wine. However, keep in mind that the person next to you may very well enjoy it.

What should you do with the wine in your glass you have tasted? If you do not want the rest of the wine in your glass, you can pour it into a dump bucket. It is really okay. In addition, it is a good idea to spit your wine into the bucket. However it might be easier to spit into a cup. Ask if there is a cup that you can use. You can then dump the contents from the cup into the dump bucket. Even though tastings are small, they do add up after a number of tastings.

Do you think wineries are being stingy when they set out tiny crackers or tiny bites of cheese? Remember this is not your lunch. The purpose of the crackers, dips or cheese is to cleanse the palate and to help one decide how the wine pairs with food. Some wineries have restaurants, so if you want lunch check out the restaurant.

Picnic lunch? Many wineries encourage visitors to bring a picnic lunch. Frequently picnic tables or patio tables are available. Ask in advance if it is okay to bring a picnic lunch and where to picnic on the grounds. Do not bring wine from another winery or any other kind of alcohol. Laws restrict wineries and many are only allowed to have their own alcohol on their premises. Besides, if you were going to someone's home for dinner, it would be tasteless to bring your own entrée.

Staff and visitors always appreciate good manners. If you have the opportunity to visit a vineyard, do not pick the grapes. If you would like to taste a wine grape at harvest time, be sure to ask a staff member. One winery we visited mentioned how they don't mind visitors walking through the vineyards and taking pictures, but one day a visitor walked out of the vineyard with several bunches of grapes to ask what they were.

It did not dawn on him until an owner reminded him that the grapes would have made wine. The visitor tried to give them to the owner who replied, "They aren't good now. They aren't ready for making wine." Another major faux pas is to pick up a bottle and pour your own tasting. Let the wine consultant pour the wine. We did visit a winery in Pennsylvania and one in Colorado that permitted people to pour their own tasting. Two wineries out of 450 isn't the norm however.

The best motto to follow in a winery or vineyard would be the National Parks motto, "Take only pictures and leave only footprints."

When you visit a winery, if you like the wine and want to buy it that is great, but you do not need to purchase a bottle of wine. Do not buy a bottle of wine unless you like it. Participating in a winery tasting room can be a delightful experience for everyone.

Advance planning is the key to a successful winery visit. The majority of wineries in the United States have websites. A google search by state makes it easy to locate the websites. Websites may include hours, types of wines, tour availability and directions.

Call in advance if your group will be larger than five. Some wineries do not have room for buses or limousines. Other wineries like to know in advance if large groups will be arriving so they can provide enough staff.

Tasting or drinking wine on an empty stomach is not a good idea. Eat well before you go to the winery. The more food in your stomach the less alcohol will affect you. Take bottled water and be sure to drink it especially if you will be visiting another winery. Plan on drinking as much water as you do wine. This is also vitally important when the weather is hot. If a tour is available, go ahead and participate in it. Each winery tour focuses on what is important to their winery. However, most wineries include a visit to the press pad where the grapes arrive from the vineyard. Also included will be the tank room and barrel room. Most wineries like to include the history behind their winery. Some of these histories include winemakers who have come to the new world to start a winery and others are entrepreneurs who are fascinated with winemaking. Tours add to the experience and can provide great photo opportunities.

The winery staff is usually very knowledgeable about the wine, winery and vineyards. In some cases, the staff will have a notebook behind the counter where they can check for information. Remember not everyone knows everything about wine. The wine culture can be a fun learning experience for everyone.

Keep these tips in mind and more than likely you will have an experience you will remember for years to come.

3

Wine Festivals as Tourist Destinations

San Diego Bay Wine and Food Festival

The San Diego Bay Wine & Food Festival is an international showcase of wine and spirits, chefs and culinary personalities, and gourmet foods, produced by World of Wine Events, LLC. Attendees able to take cooking classes, sample food from celebrity chefs and local restaurants, and participate in wine tastings from 170 wineries, breweries and spirit booths. The festival takes place in November and has been held annually since 2004.

History

The San Diego Bay Wine & Food Festival was created in 2004 by co-producers Ken Loyst and Michelle Metter. Proceeds from the auctions benefit the American Institute of Wine & Food Culinary Arts Scholarship programs for students in San Diego.

Production

The San Diego Bay Wine & Food Festival is produced by World of Wine Events and Fast Forward Event Productions, an event management and festival production company specializing in the creation of wine, culinary trade, and consumer events.

Naples Grape Festival

Naples Grape Festival is an annual festival in Naples, New York, United States, dedicated to grapes. The town of Naples is in the centre of Finger Lakes American Viticultural Area (AVA), a region known for grape-growing and wine making in the Finger Lakes area of Upstate New York.

The festival, which has been held since 1961, includes arts and crafts vendors, a wine-tasting tent, food, live music, and a grape pie contest.

Other Grape Festivals

Grape festivals elsewhere include the Turpan Silk Road Grape Festival in Turpan, Xinjiang Uygur Autonomous Region, China and the Lodi Grape Festival and Harvest Fair in Lodi, California.

Zielona Góra Wine Fest

***The Zielona Góra Wine Fest (Polish:** Winobranie w Zielonej Górze*) is a wine festival held in the Polish town of Zielona Góra. The tradition is related to the period of harvest of grapes from the local vineyards which were then turned into wine. The first festival took place in October 1852. Nowadays it starts in the first or second week of September and lasts for nine days.

The festivities starts on a Saturday with a parade through the city centre. It is preceded by a symbolic ceremony when the Roman wine god Bacchus and his Maenads receive the keys to the town from the local authorities. During the nine days a lot of cultural and sport events take place, among which the International Festival of Folklore is one of the most prominent. There are also theatre meetings (including street theatres) and music concerts. The centre of the town turns into a big marketplace for the time of the fest, with a separate street allotted for the antiques market.

Pittsburgh Wine Festival

Pittsburgh Wine Festival	
Frequency	Annual
Inaugurated	2003
Organised by	Pittsburgh Wine Festival LLC

The Pittsburgh Wine Festival is an annual festival celebrating wine in Pittsburgh, Pennsylvania. The festival is sponsored by the Pennsylvania Liquor Control Board. The Pennsylvania Liquor Control Board maintains an on-site wine shop. The Pittsburgh festival follows a similar one in Philadelphia. Its success inspired the Pittsburgh Whiskey & Fine Spirits Festival.

The festival receives generally positive review from wine critics. It was named to the Top 10 list of wine events in the United States by the *Quarterly Review of Wines* Tickets generally sell out.

The first event was held in 2003. Early in its tenure, some skeptics questions whether a "beer" city like Pittsburgh could sustain a wine festival.

Proceeds benefit charity. By the fourth year, in 2007, the festival had raised over $400,000 for charity. By 2009, that figure had grown to $6 million, with large portions going to Children's Hospital of Pittsburgh and the Pittsburgh Cancer Institute.

Hong Kong International Wine and Spirits Fair

The Hong Kong International Wine & Spirits Fair is a trade fair organised by the Hong Kong Trade Development Council (HKTDC), scheduled to be held annually with its inaugural event held in 2008 at the central location in Hong Kong of the Hong Kong Convention and Exhibition Centre. The next fair is in 2012 HKTDC Hong Kong International Wine & Spirits Fair 2012 8 - 10 November at the Hong Kong Convention and Exhibition Centre.

The 2009 fair attracted over 520 exhibitors from 34 countries and regions, including Argentina, Australia, Chile, the Chinese mainland, Hungary, India, Italy, Japan, Korea, Moldova, New Zealand, Portugal, Slovenia, South Africa, Spain, Thailand, the United States and Uruguay.

Following the removal of wine duty in 2008, Hong Kong became the only major economy in the world to impose no duty and no sales tax on wine. Hong Kong is ideally placed to host this major international wine event and it gives direct access to the expanding markets of the Chinese mainland and the rest of Asia.

The fair offers more than 50 special activities, including wine auctions, wine-tasting sessions, master classes and seminars. It opens to the public on the last day.

Major Exhibit Categories

- Liquor & Beverage Products
- Wine Production & Logistics
- Wine Accessories & Equipment
- Other related services

North Carolina Wine Festival

The North Carolina Wine Festival is one of several annual events showcasing vineyards from all across the state of North Carolina. It is the largest one-day wine festival in the state. It began in 2000 as a way to showcase the over 100 different wineries in the state. It was held at Tanglewood Park, in Clemmons, North Carolina. The 12th annual festival was held on May 26, 2012 and had 30 participating wineries. The general manager for WSJS-AM, Tom Hamilton, is also the festival director.

More than just a wine-tasting, the event features many bands, activities, food and apparel vendors. Attendance in 2012 was estimated to be between 12,000 and 15,000 people. Revenue from wineries produces over $1.2 billion in annual sales, making North Carolina the 10th largest U.S. state in wine production. North Carolina is the world's largest producer of muscadine wines.

2005 Split

In 2005 several wineries of the Yadkin Valley AVA pulled out of the event citing low sales and little exposure compared to other events and activities taking place at the festival. The Yadkin Valley Winegrowers Association formed their own festival held shortly after the NC Wine Festival.

Naples Winter Wine Festival

The Naples Winter Wine Festival is a multi-day charity wine festival featuring celebrity chef-hosted dinners and an auction. The event has been held yearly in Naples, Florida since 2001. The 2012 festival raised $12.2 million for 20 charitable organisations in Collier County.

Past Festivals

- 2001—The festival's first year saw $2.7 million ($3.54 million in 2012 dollars) raised for charity. Jeff Garguilo, of Garguilo Vineyards, was the chairman.
- 2002— $3.4 million ($4.39 million in 2012 dollars) raised for charity, with $2.5 million coming from the auction. Brian Cobb was the chairman.
- 2003—$3.96 million ($5 million in 2012 dollars) was raised. Tom Wajnert was the chairman.
- 2004—The Festival's auction set a world record for a charity wine auction; $6.67 million ($8.21 million in 2012 dollars). Shirleen Elkins was the chairwoman, and Robert Mondavi was the honoured vintner.
- 2005—The auction set another world record, with $11.1 million ($13.2 million in 2012 dollars).

- 2006—The auction raised \$12.19 million (\$14.1 million in 2012 dollars). Grace Evanstad, of Domaine Serene, was the festival's chairwoman.
- 2007—Another record year — \$16.5 million (\$18.5 million in 2012 dollars). A single lot went for a record \$2 million (\$2.24 million in 2012 dollars); a 2008 Rolls Royce drophead coupe.
- 2008—The auction raised \$14 million (\$15.1 million in 2012 dollars).
- 2009—Due to the economy, the auction only raised \$5.06 million (\$5.48 million in 2012 dollars), the lowest auction total since 2003.
- 2010—The festival bounced back with \$8.06 million in auction lots (\$8.59 million in 2012 dollars).
- 2011—The auction brought in \$11.9 million, but the chairs added another \$100,000 to make it an even \$12 million (\$12.8 million in 2012 dollars)
- 2012—The auction raised \$12.2 million; HRH Prince Robert of Luxembourg was the featured vintner. He donated several vintages of his wine, Château Haut-Brion, which had 2 bidders involved in a bidding war. He donated a second lot to the losing bidder; the combined price for both was \$1.1 million.

The Great Led Zeppelin Wine Pairing

The Great Led Zeppelin Wine Pairing is a series of "wine and music pairings," created by noted restaurateur and viticulturist Joe Bastianich and writer-musician Mike Edison, along with writer and wine expert David Lynch. Bastianich and Lynch are both recipients of the James Beard Award. The idea was formed when Bastianich and Edison were pondering how to pair the songs of Led Zeppelin with various wines. "Our passion for wine is only rivaled by our passion for Zeppelin," said Bastianich, and encouraged attendees to "taste with their ears and listen with their mouths."

Edison, in an interview with publishing blog Galley Cat, said, "Either you see this as a hyper-intellectual exercise in promoting the lexicon of oenology as a valid critical system while simultaneously subverting it and subjecting it to ridicule—or you think it is just some dudes who want to drink some really good wine and listen to Led Zeppelin. No matter what, it is still going be the best salon since Dorothy Parker made that crack about horticulture."

Why Led Zeppelin?

Edison has explained that "Zep is the perfect band to pair with wine—maybe the only band. They have all the right qualities: They can be earthy and intense, or dark and mellow, or just insanely huge. They've got some very real, edgy twang, and some rich, complex textures. They embrace both the Old World and the New. I can't think of any other band that shows so much depth and development, both within individual songs and across entire records," adding, that the wine pairings were both "freakishly sophisticated and patently absurd."

Quotes

Joe Bastianich: "I think because of the sheer complexity and the deep roots of the music—where the music comes from, and how profound it is— Led Zeppelin's music can only really be paralleled with the kind of evolution, importance and complexity of wine, as both a cultural thing as well as a beverage."

Mike Edison: "Back when I was in seminary school, attempting to pair Boones Farm apple wine with "Stairway to Heaven" and having disastrous results, I stumbled upon this little theory: "Led Zeppelin IV" is the record that when you're stoned and listening to it really loud you think the phone is ringing when it's really not. 'Black Dog' is like a fully fucking awesome motherfucker—this is when they got really heavy."

David Lynch (referring to the "Black Dog" pairing): We're bringing the thunder. We're bringing the tannin. We're bringing the viscosity. We're coming at you with guns blazing, with a Malbec from Argentina.

Wine Tasting

Wine tasting (often, in wine circles, simply tasting) is the sensory examination and evaluation of wine. While the practice of wine tasting is as ancient as its production, a more formalized methodology has slowly become established from the 14th century onwards. Modern, professional wine tasters (such as sommeliers or buyers for retailers) use a constantly evolving formal terminology which is used to describe the range of perceived flavours, aromas and general characteristics of a wine. More informal, recreational tasting may use similar terminology, usually involving a much less analytical process for a more general, personal appreciation.

Tasting Stages

The results of the four recognised stages to wine tasting:

- appearance
- "in glass" the aroma of the wine
- "in mouth" sensations

- "finish" (aftertaste) – are combined in order to establish the following properties of a wine:
- complexity and character
- potential (suitability for aging or drinking)
- possible faults

A wine's overall quality assessment, based on this examination, follows further careful description and comparison with recognised standards, both with respect to other wines in its price range and according to known factors pertaining to the region or vintage; if it is typical of the region or diverges in style; if it uses certain wine-making techniques, such as barrel fermentation or malolactic fermentation, or any other remarkable or unusual characteristics. Whereas wines are regularly tasted in isolation, a wine's quality assessment is more objective when performed alongside several other wines, in what are known as tasting "flights". Wines may be deliberately selected for their vintage ("horizontal" tasting) or proceed from a single winery ("vertical" tasting), to better compare vineyard and vintages, respectively. Alternatively, in order to promote an unbiased analysis, bottles and even glasses may be disguised in a "blind" tasting, to rule out any prejudicial awareness of either vintage or winery.

Blind Tasting

To ensure impartial judgment of a wine, it should be served *blind* — that is, without the taster(s) having seen the label or bottle shape. Blind tasting may also involve serving the wine from a black wine glass to mask the colour of the wine. A taster's judgment can be prejudiced by knowing details of a wine, such as geographic origin, price, reputation, colour, or other considerations. Scientific research has long demonstrated the power of suggestion in perception as well as the strong effects of expectancies. For example, people expect more expensive wine to have more desirable characteristics than less expensive wine. When given wine that they are falsely told is expensive they virtually always report it as tasting better than the very same wine when they are told that it is inexpensive. French researcher Frédéric Brochet "submitted a mid-range Bordeaux in two different bottles, one labelled as a cheap table wine, the other bearing a grand cru etiquette" and obtained predictable results. Tasters described the supposed grand cru as "woody, complex, and round" and the supposed cheap wine as "short, light, and faulty."

Similarly, people have expectations about wines because of their geographic origin, producer, vintage, colour, and many other factors. For example, when Brochet served a white wine he received all the usual descriptions: "fresh, dry, honeyed, lively." Later he served the same wine dyed red and received the usual red terms: "intense, spicy, supple, deep." One of the most famous instances of blind testing is known as the Judgment of Paris, a wine competition held in 1976 where French judges blind-tested wines from France and California. Against all expectations, California wines bested French wines according to the judges, a result which would have been unlikely in a non-blind contest. This event was depicted in the 2008 movie *Bottle Shock*.

Vertical and Horizontal Tasting

Vertical and horizontal wine tastings are wine tasting events that are arranged to highlight differences between similar wines.

- In a vertical tasting, different vintages of the same wine type from the same winery are tasted. This emphasizes differences between various vintages.
- In a horizontal tasting, the wines are all from the same vintage but are from different wineries. Keeping wine variety or type and wine region the same helps emphasize differences in winery styles.

Tasting Flights

Tasting flight is a term used by wine tasters to describe a selection of wines, usually between three and eight glasses, but sometimes as many as fifty, presented for the purpose of sampling and comparison.

Tasting Notes

A tasting note refers to a taster's written testimony about the aroma, taste identification, acidity, structure, texture, and balance of a wine. Online wine communities like Bottlenotes allow members to maintain their tasting notes online and for the reference of others.

Glassware

The shape of a wineglass can have a subtle impact on the perception of wine, especially its bouquet. Typically, the ideal shape is considered to be wider toward the bottom, with a narrower aperture at the top (tulip or egg shaped). Glasses which are widest at the top are considered the least ideal. Many wine tastings use ISO XL5 glasses, which are 'egg'-shaped. Interestingly, the effect of glass shape does not appear to be related to whether the glass is pleasing to look at.

Wine Colour

Without having tasted the wines, one does not know if, for example, a white is heavy or light. Before taking a sip, the taster tries to determine the order in which the wines should be assessed by appearance and nose alone. Heavy wines will be deeper in colour and generally more intense on the nose. Sweeter wines, being denser, will leave thick, viscous streaks (called *legs* or *tears*) down the inside of the glass when swirled.

Process

Figure: *Judging colour is the first step in tasting wine.*

There are five basic steps in tasting wine: colour, swirl, smell, taste, and savor. These are also known as the "five S" steps: see, swirl, sniff, sip, savor. During this process, a taster must look for clarity, varietal character, integration, expressiveness, complexity, and connectedness.

A wine's colour is better judged by putting it against a white background. The wine glass is put at an angle in order to see the colours. Colours can give the taster clues to the grape variety, and whether the wine was aged in wood.

Characteristics Assessed During Tasting

Varietal character describes how much a wine presents its inherent grape aromas. A wine taster also looks for integration, which is a state in which none of the components of the wine (acid, tannin, alcohol, etc.) is out of balance with the other components. When a wine is well balanced, the wine is said to have achieved a harmonious fusion.

Another important quality of the wine to look for is its expressiveness. Expressiveness is the quality the "wine possesses when its aromas and flavours are well-defined and clearly projected. The complexity of the wine is affected by many factors, one of which may be the multiplicity of its flavours. The connectedness of the wine, a rather abstract and difficult to ascertain quality, describes the bond between the wine and its land of origin (terroir).

Connoisseur Wine Tasting

A wine's quality can be judged by its bouquet and taste. The bouquet is the total aromatic experience of the wine. Assessing a wine's bouquet can also reveal faults such as cork taint, oxidation due to age, overexposure to oxygen, or lack of preservatives and wild yeast contamination due to *Brettanomyces* or acetobacter yeasts. Although low levels of *Brettanomyces* aromatic characteristics can be a positive attribute, giving the wine a distinctive character, generally it is considered a wine spoilage yeast. The bouquet of wine is best revealed by gently swirling the wine in a wine glass to expose it to more oxygen and release more aromatic etheric, ester, and aldehyde molecules that comprise the essential components of a wine's bouquet. Sparkling wine should not be swirled to the point of releasing bubbles.

Pausing to experience a wine's bouquet aids the wine taster in anticipating the wine's flavours. The "nose" of a wine - its bouquet or aroma - is the major determinate of perceived flavour in the mouth. Once inside the mouth, the aromatics are further liberated by exposure to body heat, and transferred retronasally to the olfactory receptor site. It is here that the complex taste experience characteristic of a wine actually commences. Thoroughly tasting a wine involves perception of its array of taste and mouthfeel attributes, which involve the combination of textures, flavours, weight, and overall "structure". Following appreciation of its olfactory characteristics, the wine taster savors a wine by holding it in the mouth for a few seconds to saturate the taste buds. By pursing ones lips and breathing through that small opening oxygen will pass over the wine and release even more esters. When the wine is allowed to pass slowly through the mouth it presents the connoisseur with the fullest gustatory profile available to the human palate. The acts of pausing and focusing through each step distinguishes wine tasting from simple quaffing. Through this process, the full array of aromatic molecules is captured and interpreted by approximately 15 million olfactory receptors, comprising a few hundred olfactory receptor classes.

When tasting several wines in succession, however, key aspects of this fuller experience (length and finish, or aftertaste) must necessarily be sacrificed through expectoration. Although taste qualities are known to be widely distributed throughout the oral cavity, the concept of an anatomical "tongue map" yet persists in the wine tasting arena, in which different tastes are believed to map to different areas of the tongue. A widely accepted example is the misperception that the tip of the tongue uniquely tells how sweet a wine is and the upper edges tell its acidity.

Scoring Wine

As part of the tasting process, and as a way of comparing the merits of the various wines, wines are given scores according to a relatively set system. This may be either by explicitly weighting different aspects, or by global judgment (although the same aspects would be considered). These aspects are 1) the appearance of the wine, 2) the nose or smell, 3) the palate or taste, and 4) overall.

Different systems weight these differently (e.g., appearance 15%, nose 35%, palate 50%). Typically, no modern wine would score less than half on any scale (which would effectively indicate an obvious fault). It is more common for wines to be scored out of 20 (including half marks) in Europe and parts of Australasia, and out of 100 in the US. However, different critics tend to have their own preferred system, and some gradings are also given out of 5 (again with half marks).

Expectoration

Figure: *Spitting into a spittoon at a wine tasting.*

Because wine can affect the consumer's judgment, wine tasters generally spit the wine out after they have assessed its quality at formal tastings, where dozens of wines may be assessed. However, since wine is absorbed through the skin inside the mouth, tasting from twenty to twenty-five samplings can produce an intoxicating effect, depending on the alcoholic content of the wine.

Visiting Wineries

Travelling to wine regions is another way of increasing skill in tasting. Many wine producers in wine regions all over the world offer tastings of their wine. Depending on the country or region, tasting at the winery may incur a small charge to allow the producer to cover costs. It is not considered rude to spit out wine at a winery, even in the presence of the wine maker or owner. Generally, a spittoon will be provided. In some regions of the world, tasters simply spit on the floor or onto gravel surrounding barrels. It is polite to inquire about where to spit before beginning tasting.

Attending Wine Schools

A growing number of wine schools can be found, offering wine tasting classes to the public. These programs often help a wine taster hone and develop their abilities in a controlled setting. Some also offer professional training for sommeliers and winemakers. It is even possible to learn how to assess wine methodically via e-learning.

Sensory Analysis

Tasting plays an important role in the sensory analysis (also referred to as organoleptic analysis) of wine. Employing a trained or consumer panel, oenologists may perform a variety of tests on the taste, aroma, mouthfeel and appeal of wines. Difference tests are important in determining whether different fermentation conditions or new vineyard treatments alter the character of a wine, something particularly important to producers who aim for consistency. Preference testing establishes consumer preference, while descriptive analysis determines the most prominent traits of the wine, some of which grace back labels. Blind tasting and other laboratory controls help mitigate bias and assure statistically significant results. Many large wine companies now boast their own sensory team, optimally consisting of a Ph.D. sensory scientist, a flavour chemist and a trained pancl.

Wine and Food Matching

Wine and food matching is the process of pairing food dishes with wine to enhance the dining experience. In many cultures, wine has had a long history of being a staple at the dinner table and in some ways both the winemaking and culinary traditions of a region will have evolved together over the years. Rather than following a set of rules, local cuisines were paired simply with local wines.

The modern "art" of food pairings is a relatively recent phenomenon, fostering an industry of books and media with guidelines for pairings of particular foods and wine. In the restaurant industry, sommeliers are often present to make food pairing recommendations for the guest.

The main concept behind pairings is that certain elements (such as texture and flavour) in both food and wine react differently to each other and finding the right combination of these elements will make the entire dining experience more enjoyable. However, taste and enjoyment are very subjective and what may be a "textbook perfect" pairing for one taster could be less enjoyable to another. While there are many books, magazines and websites with detailed guidelines on how to pair food and wine, most food and wine experts believe that the most basic element of food and wine pairing is understanding the balance between the "weight" of the food and the weight (or body) of the wine. Heavy, robust wines like Cabernet Sauvignon can overwhelm light delicate dish like a quiche while light bodied wines like Pinot grigio would be similarly overwhelmed by a hearty stew. Beyond weight, flavours and textures can either be contrasted or complemented.

From there a food and wine pairing can also take into consideration the sugar, acid, alcohol and tannins of the wine and how they can be accentuated or minimized when paired with certain types of food.

History

Wine has had a long history of being served as an accompaniment to food. The early history of wine has it origins as another dietary staple and a beverage that was often more sanitary than the local water supply. There is little evidence that much serious thought was given to pairing particular dishes to particular wines with most likely whatever wine was available being used.

However, as culinary traditions in a region developed, so too did local winemaking tradition. Many pairings that are considered "classics" today emerged from the centuries old relationship between a region's cuisine and their wines. In Europe, lamb was a staple meat of the diet for many areas that today are leading wine regions. The red wines of regions such as Bordeaux, Greece, Rioja, Ribera del Duero, Rhone and Provence are considered classic pairings with the lamb dishes found in the local cuisines of those regions. In Italy, the intimate connection between food and wine is deeply embedded in the culture and is exemplified by the country's wine.

Historically, Italians rarely dined without wine and a region's wine was crafted to be "food friendly", often with bright acidity. While some Italian wines may seem tannic, lean or tart by themselves they often will show a very different profile when paired with boldly flavoured Italian foods. There have been some historical anecdotes that have related to food and wine pairing before modern times. One anecdote often attributed to British wine merchants is *"Buy on an apple and sell on cheese"* meaning that if a wine tastes good when paired with a raw, uncooked apple it must be truly good and pairing any wine with cheese will make it more palatable to the average consumer and easier to sell.

The principles behind this anecdote lies in the food pairing properties of both fruit and cheeses. Fruits that are high in sugar and acidity (such as the malic acid in green apples) can make wines taste metallic and thin bodied. In contrast, hard cheeses such as cheddar can soften the tannins in wines and make them taste fuller and fruitier. Another historical anecdote, still repeated today, is *"White wine with fish; Red wine with meat"*. The root of this adage rests on the principle of matching the body (weight) of the wine with the weight of the food. Meat was generally heavier and "red" in colour so it was assumed that a red wine (which was usually heavier than white wine) paired better. Similarly fish was generally light and "white" in colour so it was often paired with white wine.

This adage has become out dated somewhat due to the variety of wine styles prevalent in modern winemaking where there are now many "heavy" white wines such as "New World" oaky Chardonnay that can have more body than lighter reds such as Pinot noir or Italian Merlots. Another older idea was "to pair strong cheeses with strong wines," for example, asiago, a sharply flavoured cheese, with zinfandel, a dark red wine with fruit tones.

Modern History

In recent years, the popularity and interest in food and wine pairings have increased and taken on new connotations. Industries have sprung up with print publications and media dedicated to expounding on the principles and ideals of pairing the perfect wine with the perfect dish. In the restaurant industry, there is often a dedicated individual or staff of sommeliers who are trained to recommend wine pairings with the restaurant's fare.

The origins of this recent phenomenon can be traced to the United States in the 1980s when Neo-Prohibitionists prompted the wine industry to reexamine the context of wine-drinking as a component of dining rather than as just an alcoholic beverage meant for consumption and intoxication. Winemakers started to emphasize the kind of food dishes that their wines would go well with, some even printing pairing suggestions on back wine labels. Food magazines began to suggest particular wines with recipes and restaurants would offer multi-course dinners matched with a specific wine for each course. Today there are multiple sources for detailed guidelines and tips on food and wine pairing. But many wine drinkers select wine pairings based on instinct, the mood of the meal or simply a desire to drink a particular wine at the moment they desire to eat a particular meal. The subjective nature of taste makes it possible to drink any kind of wine with any kind of food and have an enjoyable experience. Wine expert Mark Oldman has noted *"Food and Wine pairing can be like sex and pizza: even when it's bad, it can still be pretty good"* and gives the example of wedding cake with a dry sparkling wine.

A very dry wine with a very sweet food is, according to Oldman, *"the equivalent of nails on a chalkboard"* and is not a "good pairing" according to most guidelines but the atmosphere of the occasion and the subjective nature of taste can trump any rule or guideline. Today, many wine experts and advocates in the realm of food and wine pairing try to focus on the more objective physical aspects of food that have an effect on the palate, altering (or enhancing) the perception of various aspects of the wine.

Matching Weight

In food and wine pairings, the most basic element considered is "weight"-the balance between the weight of the food (a heavy, red sauce pasta versus a more delicate salad) and the weight or "body" of the wine (a heavy Cabernet Sauvignon versus a more delicate Pinot grigio). In wine tasting, body is determined primarily by the alcohol level of the wine and can be influenced by the perceptions of tannins (from the grape skins or oak) and extract (the dissolved solids in the wine derived from winemaking processes like extended maceration and sur lie aging).

An oaked Chardonnay from a warm wine region, such as Australia will be "heavier" in body than a stainless steel fermented Chardonnay from a cooler wine region such as Chablis. Pairing heavy wines with light dishes or vice versa, can result in one partner overwhelming the other. The "weight" of a food can also be described in terms of the intensity of its flavours-such as delicate and more subtle flavours versus dishes that have more robust and hearty flavours. A key to pairing upon this principle is to identify the dominant flavour of the dish. Sauces can be the dominant flavour instead of the meat or main component. While poached fish is usually light bodied and better served with a light white, if the fish is served with a heavy cream sauce it could be better balanced with a fuller bodied white wine or light red.

Weights of Wine

Below is a rough guideline of the various weights of wines. Winemaker and regional style as well as oak treatment can cause a wine to be lighter or heavier in body. For example, Pinot noir can vary from being very light to more medium bodied. Another example is the influence of regional climates. Warmer climate wine regions tend to produce wines with higher alcohol levels and thus more fuller bodied wines so that a Sauvignon blanc from California may have a heavier weight than a Sauvignon blanc from the Loire.

Lighter Whites: Pinot gris, Pinot blanc, Riesling, Sauvignon blanc, Chablis, Champagne and sparkling wines, Gruner Veltliner, Vinho Verde

Medium to Heavy Whites: Oaked Sauvignon blanc, Alsatian wines, Albarino, White Bordeaux (Semillon), White Burgundy, Rhone whites (Viognier, Roussanne, Marsanne), Tamaioasa Romaneasca and New World Chardonnay

Lighter Reds: Beaujolais, Dolcetto, some Pinot noir

Medium Reds: Chianti, Barbera, Burgundy, Chinon, Rioja, Cabernet franc, Merlot, Malbec, Zinfandel, some Pinot noir

Heavier Reds: Syrah, Brunello di Montalcino, Cabernet Sauvignon, Port, Barbaresco and Barolo

Focus of the Pairing

While a perfect balance where both food and wine are equally enhanced is theoretically possible, typically a pairing will have a more enhancing influence on one or the other. Master Sommelier Evan Goldstein notes that food and wine pairing is like two people having a conversation: *"One must listen while the other speaks or the result is a muddle"*. This means either the food or the wine will be the dominant focus of the pairing, with the other serving as a complement to enhance the enjoyment of the first. In regards to weight and intensity, if the focus of the pairing is the wine then a more ideal balance will be a food that is slightly lighter in weight to where it will not compete for attention with the wine but not too light to where it is completely overwhelmed. If the focus of the pairing is to highlight a dish then the same thought would apply in pairing a wine.

Complement and Contrast

After considering weight, pairing the flavours and texture can be dealt with using one of two main strategies — complement or contrast. The first strategy tries to bring wine together with dishes that complement each other such as an earthy, Burgundian Pinot noir with an earthy, mushroom dish. The second strategy operates under the truism that "opposites attract" and brings together food and wine that have contrasting traits such as a crisp, acidic Sauvignon blanc and a fish with a creamy lemon sauce.

The crisp acidity of the wine serves as a contrast that can cut through the creaminess of the sauce and give a different, refreshing sensation for the palate as oppose to what a complementary pairing, such as a creamy, buttery Chardonnay, would bring. For most of history, the "complementary strategy" was the prevailing thought on food and wine pairing. In the 1980s, as more people started to discover and experiment with pairings, the idea of using contrast started to gain more favour. It follows the same idea that the "salty/sweet" pairing does in cooking (such as salty peanut butter with sweet jelly). The same food may be complemented *or* contrasted: a hard, nutty cheese such as Hirtenkase should have "a nutty, slightly sweet wine with it," *or* a full bodied red wine.

Physical Properties of Wine

While it is often said that "taste is subjective", there are quantifiable taste characteristics (like bitter, sweet, salty or sour) that can be perceived and measured as low, moderate or high—such as measuring the sweetness of honey or the saltiness of oysters. Flavours, such as butterscotch, char and strawberry, are more personal and can't be quantifiable. Flavours are either perceived to be present or not. The perception of flavours is linked to our sense of smell, while tastes come from the sensory glands of the taste buds. Though individual sensitivity to the different taste "senses" can vary, wine experts will often recommend pairings based on these more objective measurements rather than the more subjective concept of "flavours". In wine there are three basic tastes-bitter, sweet and sour. These three tastes can each be identified with a primary component of the wine-tannins (bitter), residual sugar (sweet) and acidity (sour). A fourth component, alcohol, is identified in wine tasting with a perception of "heat" or hotness in the back of the mouth and is the primary factor influencing the body of the wine. The residual heat of the alcohol can be considered in food pairing with some ingredients minimizing the heat of the wine while some will accentuate it.

Acidity

Acidity is a dominant player in any food and wine pairing due to the pronounced and complex ways that it can heighten the perception of flavours. In wine tasting, acidity is perceived by a mouth watering response by the salivary glands. This mouth watering can also serve to stimulate the appetite. In wine there are three main acids that have their own associated flavours-malic (green apples), lactic (milky) and tartaric (bitter). In dishes that are fatty, oily, rich or salty, acidity in wine can "cut" (or standout and contrast) through the heaviness and be a refreshing change of pace on the palate.

In cooking, acidity is often used in similar fashions such as a lemon wedges with a briny seafood dish such as oysters. The acidity of the lemon juices can make the oysters seem less briny. A wine that is less tart than the dish it is served with will taste thin and weak. A wine that comes across as "too tart" on its own maybe soften when paired when an acidic and tart dish. The complementing "tartness" of the food and wine cancels each other out and allows the other components (fruit of the wine, other flavours of the food) to be more noticeable.

Sweetness

The sweetness of wines is determined by the amount of residual sugar left in the wine after the fermentation process. Wines can be bone dry (with the sugars fully fermented into alcohol), off-dry (with a hint of sweetness), semi-dry (medium-sweet) and dessert level sweetness (such as the high sugar content in Sauternes and Tokays). Sweet wines often need to be sweeter than the dish they are served with. Vintage brut champagne paired with sweet, wedding cake can make the wine taste tart and weak while the cake will have off flavours. In food pairings, sweetness balances spice and heat. It can serve as a contrast to the heat and alleviate some of the burning sensation caused by peppers and spicy Asian cuisine. It can accentuate the mild sweetness in some foods and can also contrast with salt such as the European custom of pairing salty Stilton cheese with a sweet Port. Sweetness in a wine can balance tartness in food, especially if the food has some sweetness (such as dishes with sweet & sour sauces).

Bitterness

The astringency associated with wine is usually derived from a wine's tannins. Tannins add a gritty texture and chalky, astringent taste. It can enhance the perception of "body" or weight in the wine. Tannins are normally derived from the skins, seeds, and stems of the grapes themselves (leeched out during the maceration process) or from contact with oak during barrel aging. Tannins react with proteins. When paired with dishes that are high in proteins and fats (such as red meat and hard cheeses), the tannins will bind to the proteins and come across as softer. In the absence of protein from the food, such as some vegetarian dishes, the tannins will react with the proteins on the tongue and sides of the mouth—accentuating the astringency and having a drying effect on the palate. Various cooking methods, such as grilling and blackening can add a bitter "char" component to the dish that will allow it to play well with a tannic wine. While fish oils can make tannic wines taste metallic or off. Astringent tannic wines like Barolo and Cabernet Sauvignon can overwhelm a lot of foods but can be soften by fatty foods with a lot of proteins such as hard cheeses or meats. The dry tannins also serve as a cleansing agent on the palate by binding to the grease and oils left over in the mouth. Spicy and sweet foods can accentuate the dry, bitterness of tannins and make the wine seem to have off flavours.

Alcohol

Alcohol is the primary factor in dictating a wine's weight and body. Typically the higher the alcohol level, the more weight the wine has. An increase in alcohol content will increase the perception of density and texture. In food and wine pairing, salt and spicy heat will accentuate the alcohol and the perception of "heat" or hotness in the mouth. Conversely, the alcohol can also magnify the heat of spicy food making a highly alcoholic wine paired with a very spicy dish one that will generate a lot of heat for the taster.

Other Pairing Principles

Beyond the basic guidelines listed above, food pairings can dive even further into matching several layers of texture and flavours. The term "bridge ingredients" refers to ingredients and flavours that have certain affinities to wine pairing (such as slow cooked onions to creamy wines, etc.). It can also refer to using particular herbs and spices perceived in the wine (such as rosemary in some Cabernet Sauvignon) and adding them to the dish as an ingredient. Their presence in a dish may increase the likelihood that the certain wines will pair well. The above principles can be used for pairing wines with Asian cuisine. Pair for the flavour of the dish - whatever the 'main ingredient' may be - it is not the meat, seafood, or vegetables that stand out as the predominant flavour. Rather the true flavour of the dish is determined by the cooking method (for example, the toasty flavours of a stir fry), the sauce (from curries to sweet-and-sour), the use of seasonings (such as ginger and coriander leaves to mask fishy tastes), or the blending of ingredients to for new flavours (as in sukiyaki or satay). Indeed it may result from a combination of any of these elements. Also, note that in the case of an Asian meal, several dishes are served at the same time and are shared by everyone present. The wine chosen for such a meal has to be versatile.

Local Food – An Opportunity for Tourism

In an age where the population is being encouraged to think about eating more healthily, and celebrity chefs are highlighting the often unsavoury side of mass farming, local food is a valuable resource which makes a significant contribution to local economies and encourages diversification amongst rural communities. Where once a particular farm produced lamb for the supermarkets, the same business now produces and sells its meat directly to customers, the old farm buildings house craft shops and activity rooms and the farmer offers B&B and self-catering.

Alongside this shift in emphasis the research company FARMA has proven through research a growing interest and enthusiasm in local foods. At the beginning of the decade calculations from the New Economics Foundation (NEF) estimated that for every £1 spent on local food £2.50 is generated for the local economy. This was significantly more than the £1.40 generated when that same £1 was spent in a supermarket. NEF believes this value increases further when that purchase is part of a local food project. This article considers the role of local food initiatives and the inspiring projects which have secured the future of farms at risk, opened up new business opportunities and ultimately made a significant contribution to local economic growth.

It aims to review some of the underpinning concepts and provide a set of considerations for managers to maximise the opportunity local food can offer to businesses and the wider community.

Multiplier and Leakage

A key issue in the promotion of local food is the multiplier and leakage effect, which describes the contribution a product makes to the local economy. In very simple terms, money spent on a product either stays in the local economy, and multiplies its value, or leaks out of the economy. In the case of food, this effect is apparent among major retailers, such as supermarkets, where leakage is rife, and small independent businesses selling local products from local businesses, where the multiplier effect is clear.

This effect relates most to the tourism industry in the rural areas of the UK where high numbers of day trippers spend little money and therefore have little impact on the local economy (a particular challenge in National Parks). The average day visitor buys petrol before they leave home, often takes a picnic and is likely to buy only snacks and postcards at their destination. However, the leakage problem is not just a problem of the visitor's making – many retailers lack the local produce to sell. Many 'touristy' shops and gift shops at attractions err towards mass production and homogenisation, and are often, therefore, selling items produced outside the economic boundary.

Most of the shelves in souvenir shops are lined with pens, pencils and souvenirs which are purchased, ready branded, from incentive suppliers. The cookies and fudge more often than not acquire a postcard glued to the front of the box to give some sort of locational significance to the purchase, while other products, such as Kendal Mint Cake, are ubiquitous and have nothing to do with destinations outside the Lake District. As a result such shops are missing the opportunity to sell produce sourced locally.

Authenticity

Given a choice consumers like to purchase 'authenticity'. More often than not that authenticity is signified by packaging and image. The greater the authenticity the higher the ascribed value to the buyer. However there is a threat to this in the form of postcards glued on boxes and the constant reappearance of certain categories of food regardless of geographic origin. There are a number of things tourism businesses can do to enhance authenticity, for example:

- adding signs to tell customers that a jam was produced locally
- citing a magazine article about the local fudge maker next to his fudge
- telling each customer who produced the local cheese.

As a consequence visitors leave with a closer connection to the destination, and potentially purchase more of the product to take home with them.

There is also an opportunity for shops and restaurants to build a relationship with their suppliers. For example, telling the customer at the counter that the honey they're purchasing was only produced yesterday at the farm two miles away and is their best yet may encourage the visitor back to the shelves to buy more of the high quality product.

The same principle applies in accommodation businesses selling local produce. Owners might consider selling the produce that the guest has eaten at breakfast, so that the guest can take away the local bread, local jam, sausages, eggs, etc as a memento of their visit. Using and selling the local produce creates a new income stream.

Barriers to Selling Local Food

Price: The biggest issue for local food, indeed any local product, is price. Local produce is bought within a smaller economy of scale – for example, to produce oatcakes in a household kitchen by hand, using smaller batches of ingredients and packaging, takes longer and costs more than mass producing thousands of biscuits for each and every UK supermarket. This adds real costs, that not only the consumer has to bear, but that the retailer also has to consider. Whilst it may be a small increment on a pack of fudge, it could be a substantial increase when selling fish, meats, cheese and other products. Communicating the origin of the food should assuage customer concerns and add value to the product and can overcome price objections.

These added costs and new production technologies also make the producers themselves reluctant to change production and supply chain routes when the market is uncertain. In many cases it also requires investment in new equipment, (eg machinery for sweet production) or in other new businesses (local meat has to be slaughtered locally so a local abattoir is required or the farmer needs to also become a butcher).

Lack of Confidence about the Market

Whilst the supermarket trade may not pay much for the meat that is produced on a sheep farm, and the wool may not fetch huge sums of money, there is a guaranteed market. What farmers need, then, to feel confident enough to change their production methods, is the security that there is a market for their produce. Clear demonstration of demand for the product from local retailers, opportunities to test the market through farmers' markets, and support from funded projects can all help assuage these concerns.

Confusion with Other Categories of Food

There is a danger with local food that some of the main messages can be lost along the way, or confused with other projects. Local food does not, for example mean organic, although some local organic food may not be accredited as organic but produced with the ethos of organic farming.

Of course packaging plays a large role in managing and influencing customer expectations, but media coverage of healthy living and environmental protection may also confuse consumers. Ultimately local producers need to identify systems to communicate the quality and value of their produce through clear labelling, relevant quality standards and membership of local or regional food projects.

Commercial Competitors

Whilst local produce has until recently been the preserve of small business, supermarkets are seeing the ethical and financial benefits of local and/or organic food, notably led by Waitrose and Marks and Spencer, with their predominantly AB class shoppers.

Consumer Confusion

Again, consumer confusion here is rife. Does the consumer buy the organic potatoes from Africa, or the non-organic food from the local farm? If choosing the latter then how is this production measured as any better than any other supermarket supply chain, and can the consumer be sure they are contributing effectively to local economies? If choosing the former how do the air miles and carbon footprint equate to the benefits of buying organic? The same issues arise with Fairtrade products which in some cases cannot be sourced locally (tropical fruits, rice) and farm assured or other industry standard schemes. There is no measure of how an overseas standard equates to a UK standard and there is no legislative requirement for food producers to identify the source and type of ingredients in their products.

There are also aspects of the larger grocery sellers' operations which may impact on the local food product. Supermarkets have to consider corporate social responsibility and local and organic food sales are a very visible clue for the consumer. But could this growing market start to impact negatively on the local producer again?

Case Study: The Peak District Foods for Tourism Project

In the aftermath of the outbreak of foot and mouth disease (FMD), a number of projects were set up in the Peak District National Park to support rural businesses and encourage farmers to diversify. These projects were primarily European-funded and offered a range of business advice, training, environmental benchmarking and economic growth initiatives. Of particular interest is the Peak District Foods for Tourism Project, comprised of two sub-projects (as follows), supported by other European funded programmes.

- *Peak District Foods:* This project supports local producers, primarily farmers, to sell their products locally, as 'local products'. Often the businesses also encompass organic farming principles, and sell to the local trade and direct to visitors. Some of the farms are also accommodation providers and are able to use their produce for catering.
- *Peak District Cuisine:* This project works to encourage local businesses to use local produce, sourced form the Peak District Food Project members. Most of these members comprise local accommodation providers, catering outlets at tourist attractions and pubs.

Branding is an important element of the project % branded stickers, banners and blackboards are provided to participants to place around their businesses. Participants are also encouraged to use the branding on their menus and on packaging. A project manager coordinates a working group for each project, manages funding for *Savour the Flavour* (a guide to local food), organises events and coordinates free marketing materials. The project funding runs out in March 2008 and the project will then rely on the groups involved in the project to self-finance and manage the current funded aspects of the project.

Other Routes to Market

The project also supports farmers' markets, local food delivery and catering companies and the Great Peak District Fair. Farmers markets in the National Park were popular and well attended, and those involved were keen to make the most of new routes to market and opportunities to diversify from the core product. One local honey producer also offers visitors a chance to 'meet the bees' with special tours and talks about the apiary. To fit this into the national picture it is worth noting that research by the National Farmers' Retail & Markets Association (FARMA) identified that in 2006 there were over 550 farmers markets nationwide, creating 9,500 market days and 230,000 stallholder opportunities, valued at £220m.

Key Issues to Consider

It is useful to summarise the key issues associated with local food, before considering the essential steps of setting up successful local food projects.

Positives

The positive aspects for of local food production and consumption generally include the following.

For Consumers:

- better tasting, better quality food
- ability to make a contribution to the local economy
- traceability and trust in the food source
- food will have travelled less distance and is therefore a more sustainable product.

For Producers:

- better retail or wholesale prices
- opportunity to develop a good reputation
- opportunities for diversification
- less susceptible to mass-market forces.

For Retailers:

- the concept of freshness and quality is implicit
- use of local produce can be promoted through marketing materials, menus and quality standards
- enhances the multiplier effect in local economies
- creates a unique selling proposition for business involved in local food projects
- local food is susceptible to seasonality, which forces producers to offer varied menus with seasonal produce
- reduced food miles and in some cases reduced overall costs.

Negatives

The negative aspects associated with such projects include the following.

For the Consumer:

- the cost of local produce is higher
- there is confusion over what the product is (local, organic or fair trade)
- seasonality and weather conditions limit choice.

For Producers:

- initial investment costs may be high
- routes to market may need research and participation from businesses
- business requires an understanding of marketing and promotion, food hygiene, etc and qualifications that traditional farming doesn't demand

- research is required into supply chains and logistics
- seasonality may affect what can be supplied and therefore year-round consistency is not possible
- potential threat of changing marketplaces (another outbreak of food and mouth disease that 'closes' the countryside would ruin local suppliers in a given destination).

For Retailers:

- higher costs for purchase (although offset by higher sale price)
- perishability of some products may be reduced
- confusion may exist about what is local, what is organic and which is best to stock
- retailer needs a greater product knowledge.

Recommendations for Developing Local Food Projects

Synergies are essential for successful retailing of local produce. The relationship between the producer and consumer, or retailer (or secondary producer in the case of catering establishments) and retailer/ producer and consumer is crucial. Key aspects to be considered in the development of food projects include the following.

Funding

Funding streams constantly change, and less UK funding is available through the EU, but there is still money available through the UK Government, European Social Fund, European Development Fund and Interreg. There is also the new Making Local Food Work project, supported by the Big Lottery, which will invest £10 million into local food initiatives across rural and urban England over the next five years. It is up to potential projects to choose a source of funding which allows the most relevant outputs to be achieved. Many funding schemes will require proof that there is a 'need for the project', so research with local farmers, retailers, visitors and the community (year-round customers, rather than seasonal ones) is required.

Branding

Branding needs to be linked to the destination identity and there needs to be a quality standard or benchmark scheme. Peak District Foods & Peak District Cuisine both borrow styles and colours from the Peak District and Derbyshire destination brand. This reinforces the quality and values of the product in consumers' minds and ensures the products are associated with the destination. In the case of these projects retailers were supplied with software to produce food labels, signs and menus which included the project logos.

Quality Standards

Any use of quality standards need to be clearly communicated to customers so they are understood. National standards such as the Soil Association accreditation for organic foods are valuable. It may also be that membership of a local food group requires the producer to sign up to standards regarding traceability, production standards and a guarantee that all ingredients are locally sourced, not just the primary components.

Other Research

A review of existing supply chain mechanisms and formalisation of local food suppliers and users is required. These existing businesses will form the foundations of a project. An audit of potential participants is required to establish if the project can be self-funding and to check that sufficient businesses will engage with the concept. It is worth considering what other infrastructure already exists: consider local markets, key industry players, and examples of best practice.

Publicity: Interpretation and story telling, publicity and events are essential aspects of building awareness.

Benefits to Tourism

With the growing interest in selling local foods and increasing consumer demand it could be very easy to expect to see the benefits of local food to the economy. However this will not necessarily associate the food product with the tourism industry. Local food initiatives are crucial to a vibrant tourist economy, especially in rural areas, but as yet few destinations really value existing projects.

What is Wine Tourism?

Wine is not a very complex drink, considering the basic idea of wine. It is made from grapes that have been turned into juice. The juice is allowed to ferment and the result is wine. That's it! But, it is this fermentation process that is critical in wine-making, this itself decides most palate properties of the wine. Not that the quality of grapes is irrelevant, though. There are a number of different varieties and types of wine, beginning with the basic white and red. People around the world are beginning to love wine. They are enjoying it, in fact, so much that many are touring the world just to taste brands specific to some parts of the world.

Wine Tour

A wine tour is when a traveler goes to specific destinations in order to view wine being made or taste a variety of different wines.

Some are lucky enough to have vineyards a short distance away, but others need to travel thousands of miles in order to taste that elusive glass of wine that they have been searching for. Not that they would mind! The difference in wines comes in the fermenting process and in the grapes. There are dozens of types of grapes, and each grape ferments a little differently than any other. When more than two grapes are added together, another type of wine is formed. This means that there are dozens of different subtle nuances in the smell, look, and flavour of the wine.

Wine Culture

It used to be that people only drank wine when they were out at a fancy restaurant. Now, however, wine is widely available, even at places you may not normally expect - try your neighbourhood grocery store for some inexpensive flavour! There are inexpensive wines, including some that come in boxes, and there are expensive wines, which are more elaborately decorated and packaged. Most agree that it is not necessarily the cost that matters when it comes to the taste, but that more expensive wines often taste a bit more refined. Some people even try to collect wines that they enjoy, especially wines that considered to be vintage.

France

France has long been a tourist destination, and not without compelling reasons. A great traditional background, great food, and great wines! Tourists in France can visit the many vineyards in France and watch how wines are made. Trust us, next time, the same wine will taste better! They can also sample a number of different types and years of wines that were made at the vineyard. They can often even travel around the vineyard and pick grapes right off the stem. Anybody that enjoys wine would enjoy a trip that is revolves around wine tourism. This is not to say that the tourist can not enjoy the other sites as well, but when wine is the centre of the trip, the tourist is sure to have a good time. Enjoy your drinking, but remember, don't drive after that!

Food in Okinawa, Japan

Okinawa is a prefecture, or island, that is located in Japan. It is considered to be the largest island in population as well as in size. There are a number of islands that make up the Okinawa Prefecture. Some are famous for their beaches while others are known for their beautiful jungle atmosphere. The climate of Okinawa is hot, making it the perfect place to visit for those looking towards a tropical vacation.

Traditional Cuisine

Okinawan cuisine is extremely different from the cuisine normally served in Japan. Okinawa has a different climate and vegetation, which means that it is nothing like the food available on the mainland. Most people in Okinawa exist on whole grains and vegetables. Meat is served, but not extremely often. Of the meat that is served, Spam, Soki (a type of pork spare rib) and other pork meat are the favourites. Both white rice and brown rice are served, as well as noodles, but that is truly the only similarity between Japanese and Okinawan dishes.

Traditional Dishes

One traditional dish is chanpurû. Chanpurû is a stir fry dish that is made in a number of different ways. Each way is slightly different, but each way has vegetables, tofu and a type of meat or fish in it. Sometimes pork belly is used as the meat, other times tuna is. One favourite is Gôyâ chanpurû. This is made with a bitter melon (known as the gôyâ melon), as well as other vegetables, tofu, Spam and bacon. Other chanpurû is made with pasta and eggs. Okinawa soba is a dish that is so popular in Okinawa, it was named after the country. It is a noodle soup that is made using thick wheat noodles. The noodles are then topped with either scallion, pork belly, pork ribs, pickled ginger or a fish cake. Often diners add Korean pepper to the dish in order to spice it up. Okinawa soba can be found in almost any restaurant on the island. Another popular dish is taco rice. Taco rice is begun with a base of rice. Lettuce is then laid on top of the rice and taco meat is piled on top of that. Cucumber, cheese and tomato are crumbled over the mixture to complete it. Sometimes the dish is served in a tortilla roll. This meal is served frequently for lunch and is found in many school cafeterias.

Drinks

Awamori is an alcoholic beverage that is made only in Okinawa. It is created by distilling rice. This drink is exported to Japan, although the exported brands are not as strong as those that stay inside the country. It is also sometimes called island sake.

Food in Oceania

Oceana is the section of the world located in the Pacific oceans. It includes a number of different countries, as well as small volcanic islands that have no names. Some of the countries that reside in Oceana are Australia, Indonesia, Samoa, Solomon Islands, Marshall Islands, and New Zealand.

Traditional Cuisine

Because there are so many different islands, each with a different culture inhabiting it, there is no one cuisine that is shared by them all. There are some common ingredients and spices that some of the islands share between them, but the dishes are extremely varied in flavour as well as texture.

Fish

One ingredient that is shared by many of the islands is fish. There is an abundant supply of fish that surrounds these islands, and the natives learned to make use of the surplus by creating delicious meals that centred on the protein without becoming boring. When served plain, fish is often grilled whole and served in the middle of the table for guests to pick at. Sometimes fish is chopped up and a fish base is created for a stew or soup, while other times it is served raw in the form of sashimi or sushi.

Coconuts

Coconuts are found on a number of the tropical islands. They grow wild and are usually found in abundance. Natives on the islands figured out a number of different ways to use the coconut. Coconut meat can be eaten plain or can be used to garnish dishes. Many use coconut meat in desserts such as cookies or cakes. Coconut milk has saved more than one starving lost person in the islands. It is extremely nutritious and is one of the few things that people can drink when in a foreign country without having to worry about getting any parasites. Coconut milk is used in a number of different dishes on the island. It is sometimes used to sweeten a stew or soup, and other times is used to marinate a meat in. Coconut milk has a way of softening up a piece of meat that not many marinades do.

Other Dishes

Many of the islands in Oceana that are close to Asia use rice and noodles, just as the Asian culture does. The starches are a staple in the diet, served with almost every meal. One dish that is popular is called nasi goreng. Nasi goreng is created when fried rice is mixed with other items. Sometimes the leftovers from the night before are thrown into the dish and it is served for breakfast. Chicken is also cooked frequently on the islands. Some islands spice the chicken up and grill it, while others make a type of chicken soup out of it. Many of the island chickens are allowed to run wild and are skinnier and have more muscles because of it.

Food in North America

North America is an extremely diverse culture. Some call it a melding pot, because many people immigrated to the continent from other cultures. Many French immigrants settled in Canada, but while the French influence is still there, it has been diluted over centuries of other cultures finding their home in the beautiful wilderness as well. The Mexican people have a more tightly-knit culture, as their ancestors passed down the "old ways" successfully to the younger generation. The United States is extremely diverse, with older traditions staying in the east and newer traditions popping up in the west.

Canada

Canadian cuisine began with the French but has since morphed to include some of other cultures, including those of Great Britain and the United States. Those living in the province of Quebec still tend to cook French food. Their dishes are hearty fare that has simple flavours, all of which meld together well. In the wilds of the North, game is much more popular and is eaten on a regular basis. One can get caribou, moose or venison without much trouble. Smoked meat is delicious in Canada, especially in the city of Montreal. Salmon is on the menu frequently, especially when visiting either coast of the country.

Mexico

Traditional Mexican food has been handed down through generations of family members. It was created by using the available resources, which means that many of the dishes are very spicy. This is because spices were always plentiful in Mexico. Spanish rice is familiar to most. It is a dish created by blending garlic, tomatoes, onions and a few other spices in with white rice. The result is a spicy rice that goes perfect as an appetizer.

Chicken is popular in the southern area of Mexico, while beef is the main protein in the northern area. Both areas make a version of burritos. This meal is a filing one that uses thin tortilla's as a base. Some put rice in the tortilla, others put meat, and still some use leftover beans as a way to be economical. Burritos had their start as a way to eat food cheaply and easily, but have now become extremely popular in many parts of the world.

The United States

When people immigrated to the United States hundreds of years ago, they settled on the east coast. This may be why most of the food in the east coast is more reminiscent of the past than the food in the west coast is. In the east, the food tends to be very filling and warm. This may be because of the difficult and long winter months. Stews are extremely popular, as are other dishes that can be combined in one pot, such as casseroles. Beef and chicken are the two most popular proteins. In the northeast, citrus has to be shipped in from the south or the west, as there is not a long enough growing season for it to thrive. Those in the west coast live on a much lighter fare. People moving to the west from the east met people from other cultures and integrated their food into the recipes they currently had. This made a new type of food called fusion, which is when foods from two different cultures are meshed together. Fruit is popular in the west because it grows so well in the bright sunshine.

Food in Middle East

The Middle East is located in south-western Asia, between Europe and North Africa. It is an area that has suffered from a number of wars, sometimes devastating the countries that lie in the beautiful area. The cuisine in the Middle East ranges from light, tasty fares to heavier, more filling foods. Some of the ingredients that are used in a majority of the countries include sesame seeds, chickpeas, pitas and honey.

Savory Foods

Some countries in the Middle East, such as Egypt, prefer to eat savory foods that are full of herbs and spices. Lamb is a protein that is often used in the Middle East as it is plentiful. Many of the cultures mix sweet foods with lamb in order to dilute the gamey taste a bit. Vegetables are also used frequently in Middle Eastern cuisine. In Israel and in Egypt, vegetables such as eggplant or peppers are stuffed with mixtures, such as rice and beef or rice and beans. Beans, such as fava beans, are used as a base for many dishes. In Egypt fava beans are mashed and mixed with garlic and olive oil in order to make a dish called ful medames, which is eaten in the morning.

The Pita

Pita bread is eaten quite often in the Middle East. It is a soft bread that is shaped in a circle. The centre is hollow, and when the bread is cut in half, a pocket is opened and ingredients are stuffed into the pocket. This makes the sandwich very easy to make and enjoy. Many Middle Eastern countries use the pita to put falafel in. Falafel is a meat product that is often eaten as a quick meal or snack.

Pitas were first created in the Middle East but have since become used throughout the world. Some cultures stuff deli meats into the pocket while others prefer vegetables or tuna fish.

Couscous

Couscous is another dish that is found in a majority of the Middle Eastern countries. Couscous is a dish that is created when small wheat granules are coated in wheat flour. The granules are then steamed in either water or a flavoured broth. There are a number of ways that this dish can be served. Some countries serve it plain while other countries mix vegetables or meat, such as lamb, into the dish before serving. Couscous has also become popular in the West where it is available to purchase in a box mix.

Fast Food

Fast food is available to purchase in the Middle East. Some countries have fast food stands, such as McDonalds, that are available to eat in, while others rely on outdoor vendors. Most of these vendors are extremely sanitary, but tourists should always insist that the food is created in front of them so that they know that the food they are eating is fresh. Kebobs are often found at roadside vendors, as are falafel sandwiches.

Food in Hawaii

One of the most popular vacation spots, Hawaii is known for its beautiful beaches and its amazing vistas. There are nineteen separate volcanic islands that are attached to the name, and each one has its own perks. The most popular island is called Hawaii, much like the state is, but goes by "The Big Island" in order to avoid confusion. It is home of some of the major resorts and is also home to the most active volcano in the world. Oahu and Maui are the next most popular islands. Waikiki beach is on the island of Oahu and is one of the most popular beaches in the world. Maui is home to a tall crater named Haleakala.

Traditional Cuisine

The cuisine of Hawaii is hard to define. It is a mixture of foods that were brought by the many different types of immigrants that settled on the islands. The dishes created make the best use of the flora and fauna on the island, as well as the animals that were imported there. Local ingredients include things like yams, coconuts, mussels, fish, seaweed, bananas, breadfruit and taro. A number of ingredients are regularly imported onto the islands such as soy sauce, Spam, tofu, wasabi, melons and fish sauce.

Traditional Dishes

A plate lunch is often the first things that tourists find when they begin to eat in the islands. This is a lunch that generally consists of a few scoops of rice, a macaroni salad that is made very simply with just macaroni and mayonnaise, and a choice of toppings. Some of the toppings include gravy, hamburger and a fried egg. The dish is served in the majority of restaurants, especially those on the Big Island.

One dish that has made it to the mainland of the United States is poke. Poke is a fish salad that is created by slicking up one-inch cubes of a number of vegetables, seaweed and fish. It is served as an appetizer. This dish is often purchased, even by the locals, at a supermarket or a fish hut. Most stores have a variety of different types of poke to choose from. Mahi-mahi is a food that most tourists try before they leave the island. The Mahi-mahi is a fish that is also called the "dolphin fish". This fish has a sweet taste and is similar to a swordfish. It is enjoyed by many different cultures because it is both kosher, for Jewish people, as well as halal, for Muslims. This is because it has scales as well as fins through its entire life.

Loco moco is another popular Hawaiian dish. It begins with white rice which is then covered with a hamburger patty. A fried egg goes on top of the hamburger and gravy gets poured over the entire thing. This dish became popular when the American soldiers were stationed on the islands. So popular, in fact, that many of them brought the recipe home with them. It is now served in a number of establishments in the United States.

Food in Europe

The area of Europe is a large area that is located between Asia, Africa, and the Arctic. Europe is often visited by tourists. Some head to see the culture of France or the United Kingdom, while others head to Spain, Greece or Italy in order to enjoy the warm weather and the beautiful beaches.

Traditional Cuisine

Europe is considered to be the cultural centre of fashion, interior design, and cuisine. The only problem with this statement is that what is considered to be high fashion, great interior design and delicious cuisine varies from country to country. The cuisine in Europe, no matter which country is visited, is almost always delicious. Gourmet cooking has become a fine art, and visitors to the area can find almost any type of food, from Italian to Spanish to Chinese, no matter which country they are visiting.

Heavier Foods

The cooler climates tend to serve the heavier foods. England, Belgium, Ireland, Germany and Hungary are just a few of the countries that boast of a heavy fare for the casual traveler. Countries that are mostly landlocked, such as Hungary and the Czech Republic, learned how to create filling meals on very little. In Hungary, goulash is a meal that is found on almost every menu. Some consider it to be the national dish. Goulash is made by first browning meat in a skillet. Water is then added to the skillet along with onions, peppers and garlic. Sometimes potatoes are added as a way to thicken the broth. This hearty dish is served with mashed potatoes. People in these cold climates needed to create foods that kept them warm and kept them full, so that they could work a long day without having to worry about food. This is why heavy sauces and thick stews are so popular. Those used to a lighter fare may have a hard time adjusting to some of these meals. In the United Kingdom, for instance, some consider it sacrilegious to serve a shank of meat without adding a gravy to it.

Lighter Fare

Food in the Mediterranean, which includes countries such as Greece, Monaco, Italy and Spain, generally has a much lighter feel to it. Emphasis is placed more on blending the tastes together rather than in creating a filling meal. In many of these countries, it is considered rude to not be served at least three courses during a full dinner setting. Coffee is also an important part of the Mediterranean culture. Espresso is a favourite coffee drink, as is cappuccino and caffe late. These drinks have migrated over into the Western cultures to become extremely popular. People that eat a Mediterranean diet generally eat a number of fruits and vegetables, as well as fish. Heavier meats are eaten, but are generally served in thin slices, not large chunks.

What is Food Tourism?

It used to be that people travelled to distant lands in order to see historic monuments or to have an adventure. Now, however, some people are heading to distant lands in order to eat historic food or have a culinary adventure. Food tourism is sweeping the world and is becoming something that everyone should know and understand. But what, exactly, is food tourism?

Food Tourism

We've all seen the little tourist centre at the popular vacation destinations. You walk in and the guide will help you to find the best lodging, shopping, and things to do in the area. These tourist centres are a great help to someone who is unfamiliar to the area and just wants to enjoy the sites. But what about people who travelled to the area specifically to try the cuisine? Culinary shows have become the rage in most parts of the world. Shows like "Ramsey's Kitchen Nightmares", and "Top Chef", are helping ordinary people to understand the ins and outs of all types of cuisines. Cookbook sales have gone through the roof, all because people want to attempt to recreate the dishes that they see on these television shows.

Reasons to Visit

Some people believe that instead of trying to recreate a dish, they should go to the country that is famous for it. Take, for instance, John. John enjoyed eating Chinese takeout from the local fast-food Chinese restaurant. One day John decided that he wanted to see what traditional Chinese food was like, so he hopped a flight over and spent a week travelling the country, trying different foods. It might sound a bit incredible, but this type of a situation is occurring more and more regularly.

One survey found that one in six of 150 million United States tourists took a food tour or tried a cooking class in another country while they were on vacation. Some of those people actually travelled to their destination spot just to try the specific cuisine. There have been people that have travelled to New York City in order to eat from one end of the Big Apple to the other, and those who have gone "down under" just to have a steak off the infamous "barbie".

Planning a Trip

Food tourism is something that is becoming more commonly understood. But how would someone decide where to go, and what to see? It's fairly simple, actually. Tourists should first decide which type of cuisine they would like to try. Start by figuring out which food they love the best and by doing a little research. Then, after the tourist arrives in the city, they should seek the advice of others. Ask the local cab driver or the hotel clerk where the best places are to eat. Don't think that you have to stick to gourmet restaurants. Sometimes the smaller restaurants that are on the side streets are the best places to try traditional cuisine.

Food in Egypt

Egypt is a large country in Africa that is connected to Asia by the Sinai Peninsula. It has long been known for being the home of

Egyptian civilization, with mysterious pyramids, spooky mummies and interesting hieroglyphs. Cairo is the destination of most tourists, as it is the home of not only the Egyptian Museum, but the Giza Pyramids as well. Luxor is where the gateway to the Valley of the Kings lies, and Siwa is a hidden oasis town that has much to offer it's visitors. Egypt is truly a country that caters to adventurers and casual travelers alike.

Traditional Cuisine

Like much of the eastern Mediterranean countries, traditional Egyptian cuisine consists of many different herbs and spices. Lamb is the popular protein and vegetables are often stuffed and eaten as a side dish.

Traditional Dishes

One dish that is considered to be the national dish of Egypt is called ful medames. Ful medames is a dish that is usually eaten for the breakfast meal. Fava beans are cooked in a copper pot extremely slowly and for a long period of time. This makes the beans easy to mash. After they have been mashed, olive oil and garlic is added. Onion, garlic and lemon juice are also used to season the mashed fava beans. Baladi bread is sometimes served along side the dish, as well as hard boiled eggs and other vegetables.

Shawerma is another popular Egyptian dish. It is a sandwich that is made up using either lamb, chicken or goat. A large piece of meat is skewed with onion and tomato on top. It is roasted for a number of hours. The meat is then shaved off in thin slices and is put into a pita bread or other flatbread. Sometimes hummus, Amba sauce or pickled vegetables are put into the bread. It is often eaten as fast food and is available on a number of carts around the larger cities. Dukkah is another quick snack. It is a mixture that is created using nuts, seeds and other spices. Often pita bread is dipped into olive oil and then the mixture. This gives the bread a different taste and is extremely nutritious to eat. Kushari is a popular dish and is served in most of the restaurants in the country. Kushari is created using a base of lentils, chickpeas, macaroni and rice. These are topped with garlic and tomato sauce and fried onions are often put on top. It is similar to the Western spaghetti and meatballs meal, but has a much more spicy taste.

Food in Denmark

Denmark is a small country located in Northern Europe. It used to be the home of the Vikings, which meant that it was a major power in Europe. Now, however, Denmark is a modern nation that is helping with the economic integration of Europe. Most tourists head to

Copenhagen, which is one of the major cities of the country. Others head to Legoland, which is perfect for families or Lego-lovers to visit, and Ribe, the oldest town in Denmark.

Traditional Cuisine

Traditional Denmark cuisine is much like the cuisine of Norway and Germany. Most dishes are very heavy and have a lot of meat and carbohydrates in them. People survived on the foods that they could grow until the 1860's, when Denmark finally became a member of trade with other nations. This means that vegetables and fruits played a large part in the majority of early dishes.

Traditional Dishes

The first meal of the day is usually buttered bread that is served with cheese, jam and coffee. Sometimes salami is served as well. Some Danish people eat cereal with a crumbled bread on top, or an porridge. On a special occasion, morgenbord is served. This is a buffet of different foods that are laid out during an anniversary or birthday. It will have a number of different breakfast selections on it.

Smorrebrod is a type of sandwich that is eaten during the lunch hour. It is a buttered rye bread that is topped with cold cuts, meat or cheese. There are a number of different combinations that can be made, but all of these open sandwiches are created using a base of a dark buttered bread and a meat or cheese. Just like the Danish have a special celebratory meal for breakfast, so do they for lunch. Kolde bord, or cold table, is a smorgasbord of lunch items that are served on a large table. Different items, such as pickled herring, Danish sausage, Veal medallion, cold cuts, and different breads, are laid out for people to choose from. Dinner is the main meal of the day, and is when the family gathers together. Regular dinners may include dishes such as frikadeller. Frikadeller are a Danish meatball that is made using ground veal or pork, onions, eggs, and spices. It is made into balls, flattened, and fried in pork fat. They are often served with potatoes and gravy or red cabbage. These are also a popular dish in a smorgasbord.

Christmas Lunch

Christmas time is a special time in a Danish household. A Christmas lunch is often served. This lunch can be for family members or for a business. It includes traditional smorgasbord items, such as liver, cold cuts, salads, cheeses, and fruit. One thing that separates a Julefrokost from a traditional lunch buffet is the selskabssang, or party song. These are songs that are sung during the meal, making the occasion extremely festive.

4

Principles of Food Production

Food Hygiene Includes all Practices, Precautions and Procedures Involved in:

a. Protecting food from the risk of biological, chemical or physical contamination.

b. Preventing any organisms multiplying to an extent that would expose consumers to risk or result in premature decomposition of food.

c. Destroying any harmful bacteria in food by thorough cooking or processing.

Benefits from high standards of food hygiene include:

a. Reduced risk of food poisoning, foreign body contamination and spoilage.

b. Compliance with MOD and legal requirements.

c. Economic advantages, including increased shelf life and reduction of waste.

d. Consumer satisfaction and enhanced reputation.

e. Increased morale of personnel.

Hazard Analysis

The Food Safety (General Food Hygiene) Regulations 1995 (FS(GFH)R) refer to *Hazard Analysis* (HA). HA is based on five principles, detailed at Annex A to this chapter and are summarised below:

a. Analysis of the potential food hazards in a food operation.

b. Identification of the points in those operations where food hazards may occur.

c. Deciding which of the points identified is critical to food safety ("critical points").

d. Identification and implementation of effective control and monitoring procedures at those critical points.

e. Review of the analysis of food hazards, the critical control points and the control and monitoring procedures periodically and whenever the catering operation changes.

In order to meet the requirements of HA across the MOD, a practical guide for the MOD has been produced, based on the principle that there are four main methods of preparing food. The guide, *Hazard Analysis-The Four Line Method*, is at Annex B to this chapter, which is to be used as a template in all Service establishments. Universally recognised Critical Control Points (CCPs) have been identified, however additional Control Points or Critical Points may be applicable in each case. This will be entirely dependant on the type of catering function and the supporting infrastructure. When preparing individual HA profiles, units are advised to consider the following definitions in order to determine the type of risk that applies at each stage of food preparation:

a. *Control point* – specific stages in those operations where food hazards may occur.

b. *Critical point* – control points which are considered critical points where the hazard must be controlled to ensure that it is eliminated or reduced to a safe level.

c. *Critical control point* – is a critical point in the process where a specific hazard must be controlled on the basis that no further process will adequately eradicate that hazard.

Written records are also important in establishing a Due Diligence defence under the Food Safety Act 1990. HA, as defined in the FS(GFH) R, includes the principles of: Critical Points and the Control of those Critical Points. In this document the term Hazard Analysis (HA) will be used, but this is be taken to be synonymous with HACCP.

Regulation 4(3) of FS(GFH)R states that: "a proprietor of a food business shall identify any step in the activities of the food business which is critical to ensuring food safety and ensure that adequate safety procedures are identified, implemented, maintained and reviewed". This Regulation is designed to make caterers focus on the activities critical to food safety and to find ways of controlling them. The systematic analysis of each individual food item would result in a heavy burden for most MOD catering operations and would be impractical to implement. An approach, that considers the catering operation step by step, from supply through to consumption, is achievable, effective and forms the basis of food HA in the MOD. The HA approach to ensuring food safety and hygiene is intended to give a clearer focus on the controls that are important to Service caterers to ensure that safe food is provided.

Where catering is provided by contract, the contractor is to use a Hazard Analysis system that meets legislative requirements or adopt the Four-Line Method. Specialist advice, through the Chain of Command may be obtained from DCG Service Support Contracts

Supply of Food and Water

The FS(GFH)R state that no raw materials or ingredients shall be accepted by a food business if they are known to be contaminated with parasites, pathogenic micro organisms, toxic, decomposed or foreign substances and that, after normal sorting and/or preparatory processing procedures, they would still be unfit for human consumption.

Delivery Monitoring Routine checks must be made on deliveries of food for signs of damage, contamination and the presence of pests. The general condition of the food is to be checked, together with more specific checks such as date marks (Best Before and Use By) and temperature.

Unfit food or food past its "Use By" date must not be accepted and is to be immediately returned. Temperature monitoring should be conducted at the time of delivery and should form part of the quantity & quality check. For chilled and frozen foods, checks are to be made that the food is delivered at the correct temperature (less than 8oC for chilled and less than –12oC for frozen). The Delivery Monitoring form is no longer required to be completed, the vehicle temperature printed record must now be attached to the Price Advice Note (PAN). For bulk stock "between pack" temperatures are to be taken using an air probe and recorded directly onto the PAN. A note stating "Quality & Date Coding Checked" is to be hand written onto the PAN. A commercially produced ink stamp could also be utilised for this task. Potable Water Supply. It is essential that galleys and kitchens be supplied with potable water for the purposes of food preparation and cleaning.

Food Storage

The FS(GFH)R requires food products and ingredients to be stored in food premises in appropriate conditions, designed to prevent harmful deterioration and to protect food from contamination. Dry Provisions Storage. These storerooms are to be kept clean and orderly to minimise the potential hazards from "foreign bodies" and to prevent the harbourage of pests. Where practicable these stores are to be proofed against pest ingress. Part used packs are to be adequately to prevent contamination. High ambient temperatures (above 13oC) and high humidity are to be avoided. Dry goods should be stored on suitable racking raised off the ground.

Chilled Storage (5oC). Cool rooms and refrigerators are to be kept clean and tidy. It is the responsibility of the Catering Manager to raise the appropriate request if refrigerated space is considered inadequate. Best Practice guidance indicates that the ideal operating temperature of a refrigerator is 1-4oC.

Frozen Storage(-18—21oC). Freezers are to be kept clean and tidy at all times. Best Practice guidance indicates that the ideal operating temperature of a freezer is between –18oC to –21oC. Satisfactory storage is essential if a galley/kitchen/mess is to serve clean and safe food. This should include routine turnover of stock and checks of Best Before Dates. There are four main groups of foods that require differing storage conditions. The groups are as follows:

Where reference is made to a Priced Advice Note; this also means any other form of Invoice or Delivery Note

a. *Fresh Fruit and Vegetables.* These may be contaminated by soil bacteria and are to be stored away from other foods in a cool area, with adequate ventilation, preferably refrigerated at a temperature appropriate to the product.

b. *Dry Foods.* (including Canned Foods, Cereals and Flour). These are to be stored in dry, well-ventilated rooms ideally at 13oC. Food is to be put on racks, shelves or pallets off the floor.

c. *Frozen Foods.* These are to be stored in a freezer as soon as they are delivered. Frozen foods are to be used within 1 month. 'Kitchen prepared' chilled foods that are subsequently frozen are also to be used within 1 month.

d. *Perishable Foods.* Perishable food temperatures in a refrigerator must not exceed the legal limit of 8oC. Therefore, perishable foods are to be stored in a refrigerator cabinet, set at a target temperature of 5oC. Such food includes chilled dishes, meat, poultry, eggs, cooked meats and vegetable dishes, prepared salads, soft cheeses, sandwiches, fresh pasta, low acid desserts, smoked or cured meats, fish and dairy produce. Best Practice advice, is that chilled foods are to be used within 48hrs. Food that is spoiled or past its "Use By Date" must be removed from food rooms and appropriate action taken prior to disposal. Broken packaging must be avoided.

Food Displays/Serveries. Food displays and serveries should be set at the correct temperature with adequate time allowed for the equipment to achieve target temperatures. It is good practice to have sneeze screens attached to hot and cold food displays to minimise the risk of contamination of food. The handles of utensils should not contact food; this can be achieved by using utensils with longer handles than the service containers.

Cross Contamination

Cross contamination is the process whereby pathogenic bacteria present in raw food, such as meat, poultry, and vegetables, come into contact with ready to eat food, either directly or indirectly, through contact with surfaces, equipment, splashes, drips, utensils, hands and cloths. To prevent cross contamination, raw and ready to eat foods are to be kept apart. Good management planning of workflow through the kitchen can assist in this. The flow of waste is also be considered, along with raw products and prepared food. Additionally, it is to be ensured that:

a. Where possible, there are separate designated preparation areas for raw and cooked foods. If, due to limitation of space, preparation surfaces are used for both high and low risk foods then these activities must be separated by time (ideally low risk foods prepared first). Preparation surfaces must be thoroughly cleaned and disinfected between the two operations.

b. If raw and cooked food is to be stored in the same refrigerator, raw foods are always to be stored (and adequately covered) below cooked or salad foodstuffs.

c. Food handlers always wash their hands between handling raw and cooked foods and change their protective clothing once heavily soiled.

d. Separate colour coded cutting boards (red for raw meat, blue for raw fish, green for fresh fruit, salad and vegetables, white for cooked foods) and colour-coded knives are used (details of NSNs for these items are contained in JSP 308). Always thoroughly wash and disinfect cutting boards and knives in between and after use.

e. Separate machines for raw and cooked food are used, or slicing and mincing machines are thoroughly cleaned and disinfected between raw and cooked food. If separate machines are not available, cooked food must be prepared before raw food.

f. All food is kept in covered, dated and labelled containers during storage and before service.

g. Storing and Cooking with Eggs. Some eggs can contain salmonella bacteria inside or on their shells so care must be taken with their use. They are to be stored in a cool dry place or refrigerated, with exterior packaging removed and kept away from other foods. All egg dishes are to be served immediately or cooled quickly and chilled. Commercially pasteurised egg products should be used in preparation of any recipe that is served uncooked or partially cooked. This includes mayonnaise; bearnaise and hollandaise sauces, some salad dressings, ice-cream, icings and tiramisu.

h. Washing of Fruits and Vegetables. All fruits and vegetables should be washed in potable water before use. In addition fruits and vegetables purchased locally overseas are to be immersed for 30 minutes in water containing either of the agents listed. The items should then be rinsed to remove taste of disinfecting agent:

   (i) Calcium hypocholrite granules-one level teaspoon per two gallons of water

   (ii) Milton: 5 teaspoons per gallon of water.

Defrosting Food

It is essential that frozen meat and poultry are thoroughly thawed on trivets, or if unavailable in a designated defrosting area, or ideally in a defrosting cabinet. Frozen vegetables must be cooked directly from frozen.

Cooking

It is essential that food is cooked thoroughly to destroy any bacteria on or within it. Food is to be cooked to a core temperature of 75°C, checked with a calibrated digital probe (disinfected with bactericidal wipes). It is important that food such as rolled joints, burgers, and chicken are cooked to 75°C at its thickest part.

Chilling Food

When chilling cooked food for later cold or hot consumption, it is essential that the food be cooled as quickly as possible. In accordance with 'Best Practice' hot food is to be taken through the recognised 'Danger Zone' of 60-10°C within 4hrs, and subsequently stored in a refrigerator at 8°C or cooler.

(These requirements refer to the temperature of the food, not the air temperature of the equipment). If the target temperatures are not achieved food is to be discarded. The chilling of food to a recognised safe temperature may be achieved using the following methods:

a. Break food down into shallow trays and cover.

b. Cool initially to a low ambient temperature, then refrigerate or blast chill to below 'Danger Zone'.

c. Store in a refrigerator.

Reheating Food

It is advised that the reheating cooked foods is avoided, but if this is not possible it must only be reheated once and the following steps are to be taken:

a. Ensure that the food reaches a core temperature of at least 75°C. (In Scotland it is a legal requirement for the centre of the food being reheated to reach 82°C).

b. Use digital probe thermometers to check the temperature at the centre of the food. (Probes are to be disinfected using bactericidal wipes between each use).

c. The food is to be served and eaten as soon as possible.

d. After reheating, any leftover cooked food is to be thrown away.

Temperature Control and Monitoring

The Food Safety (Temperature Control) Regulations 1995 (FS(TC)R) impose two holding temperatures of below 8ºC or above 63ºC. The purpose of the regulations is to inhibit or prevent harmful micro organisms from multiplying by keeping food outside of the recognised 'Danger Zone' of 60ºC to 10ºC.

The FS(TC)R allow limited periods outside temperature control during preparation, display, service, storage or transport, but it is an offence to keep food out of temperature control for so long that it could become unsafe. The requirements do not apply to foods, which by their nature or their packaging (e.g. canned foods) are inherently safe from the growth of such organisms. In such cases the manufacturer's guidelines are to be followed.

Refrigerator and Freezer Temperature Recording. The operating temperature of all appliances should be monitored and recorded thrice daily using either of the templates at Appendices 1 and 4 to Annex B of this Chapter. As a guide, the target operating temperature for a refrigerator is 5°C and for a freezer is-18°to-21°C, but this will depend on the efficiency, age, contents and capacity of the appliance.

Note: The template to be utilised is dependent on establishment size and the number of appliances. Catering Standing Orders are to specify the corrective action (including Out of Hours/Weekend actions required) to be taken in the event of refrigerators/freezers not achieving recommended operating temperatures or failing completely.

Food Holding Temperatures

Two and Four Hour Rule

Hot food must be kept at 63°C or above. It must either be consumed within 2 hrs from the time the food temperature drops below 63°C, or be disposed of. Chilled food may be displayed (away from under temperature control) for a maximum period of 4 hours. Only one such period is allowed, no matter how short. If, for example a refrigerated dish has been on display for 1 hour in a non-refrigerated environment, refrigerating it does not mean it can be displayed for a further 3 hours later. Where food is being cooled prior to refrigeration, cooling is to be achieved as quickly as possible as described in paragraph. When hot or cold food is displayed outside a temperature controlled environment, it is to be consumed or discarded.

Target Temperatures

Food Safety legislation and the Dept of Health require that certain temperatures be maintained throughout the food storage and production process.

- Cook
- Temp
- Service
- Temperature
- (At or above)
- Reheat Reheat
- Scotland
- Chilled
- Storage
- Frozen
- Storage
- Legally Required
- Temperature
- 0°C for 2 mins 63°C 75°C 82°C 8°C-18C.

Temperature Measurement and Temperature Probe Calibration

Measurement. A digital thermometer with attached probe is to be used for measuring food temperatures, including final cooking temperatures. The probe is to be disinfected with food safe wipes between measurements. There are also 'Between Pack Probes' are available that are to be used to measure temperatures of frozen and chilled foodstuffs, primarily at the delivery stage. Details of these items can be found in JSP 308.

Table: Numbers of parts as available as follows;

Description	*NSN*	*Remarks*
Wipe Clean Thermometer	7320 99 0173073	
Robust Penetration Probe	7320 99 2154600	
Thermometer Between Pack Probe	6685 99 9906711	6 x 200 pack
Bacterial Probe wipes	7320 99 995890	
Pocket Stick Thermometer	6685 99 0007159	

Calibration: The digital thermometer is to be re-calibrated annually or in accordance with the manufacturer's instructions and warranty. A monthly calibration check is to be undertaken with an appropriate device in accordance with the manufacturer's instructions, and recorded on the template at Annex C to this chapter. The Test Plug is also to be calibrated in accordance with manufacturer's instructions and warranty.

Records

Records. Records are an important aspect of any due diligence defence and are essential in proving that the temperature requirements were being met in the event of any prosecution or food poisoning outbreak. Records (including Calibration records) are to be retained for 6 months. The mandatory records that are to be kept with unit files are listed below:

a. Delivery monitoring records.

b. All refrigerator and freezer temperature monitoring documents.

c. Food temperature monitoring records.

d. Calibration records for temperature probes.

Personal Hygiene

Good personal hygiene is a legislative requirement, ensuring safe food. Induction training must ensure that new staff joining are aware of the required standard Food handlers are a potential source of bacterial and physical contamination of food, and so personal hygiene is a key element in ensuring that food is prepared safely. Staff training is to include all the basic elements of personal hygiene (including hand washing training) covered in this section and personnel are to understand the relevance of the precautions. The FS(GFH)R lays down criteria for the personal hygiene of food handlers and the actions to be taken if a food handler is infected. These regulations require every person working in a food handling area to maintain a high degree of personal cleanliness.

Any person suffering from a disease that is likely to be transmitted through food must inform the person in charge of the galley/kitchen. A separate regulation states that any such infected person may not be permitted to work in any food handling area, in any capacity, where they might contaminate food.

Specific Requirements

a. *Hand washing.* The hands of food handlers are the principal agents in the transference of bacteria to food. Hand washing facilities (a separate basin that is only to be used for hand washing) in galleys/kitchens and heads/toilets are to include hot and cold running water, soap, nail brush and a suitable means of drying the hands. Regular checks by senior staff are to be made to ensure these facilities are available and are being used effectively. As a minimum, hand washing, is to take place:
   (1) On entering a food room.
   (2) Between handling raw and cooked food.
   (3) After handling waste food or refuse.
   (4) After smoking or eating.
   (5) After visiting the WC.

b. *Cuts.* Open cuts harbour bacteria and must be covered with clean blue waterproof dressing to aid detection. Stocks of these are to be available in food preparation areas and readily accessible to food handlers.

c. *Jewellery.* The wearing of wristwatches, ear rings ('Studs' are acceptable) and other exposed body piercing, bracelets and rings, is not acceptable as they harbour bacteria and there is a risk of physical contamination of food. The wearing of a plain wedding ring is acceptable.

d. *Smoking.* Smoking is not permitted in food areas, as it transfers bacteria from the mouth to hands. Cigarette ends and ash also pose physical contamination risks.

e. *Protective Clothing and Changing Facilities.* Food handlers must wear suitable clean protective clothing (including appropriate footwear and hats) to prevent contamination of food from normal clothing. Such clothing is to be changed at the end of a shift, or sooner if the situation requires, in order to maintain hygienic standards. It is not to be worn outside food areas and associated premises. If necessary, an outer garment is to be worn over protective clothing whilst away from food production environment. Adequate changing facilities must be provided, with locker space for clean and soiled protective clothing. Changing facilities must be kept clean and tidy at all times.

f. *Visitors.* All visitors to a food preparation area are to be viewed as potential sources of contamination. They must therefore be provided with protective clothing and briefed upon good food hygiene practices before entering the food area. Before entering a food preparation area, visitors must confirm that they are not suffering from diarrhoea and/or vomiting, or heavy cold. Individuals who are suffering should not be allowed to proceed.

g. *Eating/drinking.* Food handlers are not to eat or drink in food rooms. It is acceptable for cooks to taste dishes during preparation in a manner that does not contaminate the food i.e. a clean spoon each time.

h. *Toilet Facilities.* Where possible toilets for catering personnel are to be separate from those for non-catering personnel and visitors. Toilets are not to be located directly within a food preparation area. There is to be an intervening ventilated space between toilets and food rooms. Food is not to be stored in that space. Toilets must be ventilated such that associated odours are prevented from permeating into food rooms. They must also be kept clean and tidy, in good repair with adequate supplies of toilet paper, hand washing facilities, nail brushes, soap and hand towels.

Infected Food Handlers

Dispersed Feeding

Dispersed feeding is the production and transportation of food for consumption away from an established unit/galley/kitchen or mess for example to personnel on security duties who are unable to be fed in-mess, non-public section functions, such as barbecues or sports meals.

This method of feeding is recognised as high risk, because the majority of foods used require controlled temperatures during transportation in order to comply with Food Safety Legislation. Dispersed feeding should only take place when there is no suitable alternative. Documentation. Before food leaves the kitchen, the Shift NCO (or equivalent if DEL or contract catering staff) is to ensure the completion (in duplicate) of FCAT 1013.

Dispersed Feeding Record (demanded from DSDC Llangennech)

A copy is to be retained with the food safety records and a copy handed to the person (recipient) taking the food out of the kitchen. The recipient is to be briefed on the following points:

a. Chilled Products. Chilled foods are to be consumed within 4 hours of being removed once cold products leave from a temperature controlled environment i.e. refrigerator or chilled servery and when and the product temperature rises above 8oC, products are to be consumed within 4 hours.

b. Hot Products. Hot foods are to be consumed within 2 hours of being placed into a container. Food is to be served at 63°C. If a hot container meal arrives at its final destination and the product temperature is below 63°C, it is to be consumed as soon as possible (but always within 2 hours from when the product was placed into the container). This time will have been recorded in column (b) of the FCAT 1013.

c. When temperature monitoring is unavailable at a dispersed feeding location, the food is to be consumed within 2 hrs (hot product) or 4 hours (cold product) of being placed in the insulated container or leaving a refrigerated environment. Once again the time of service is to be recorded in column (b) of FCAT 1013.

Transport of Food

Movement of temperature-controlled foods may include:

a. The collection of food from suppliers and transportation to the main ration stores and messes.

b. The transportation of prepared food from messes to satellite or dispersed feeding facilities.

Transport can include items such as trolleys, bags, boxes, trays and crates. These articles must be kept clean. Where transport is also used for materials other than food, it must be thoroughly cleaned between loads to avoid the risk of cross contamination.

Non-catering personnel collecting foodstuffs from the mess are to be briefed on the importance of maintaining the integrity of the food chain, and how this is achieved. During transport, all food is to be covered and is to be transported in appropriate insulated containers. High-risk food must be kept separate from anything that could cause contamination. When transporting prepared meals, dispatch and receipt temperature checks are to be recorded in accordance with paragraph.

Cleaning

The FS(GFH)R requires adequate facilities are provided for the cleaning and disinfecting of work utensils and equipment. These facilities must be constructed of materials resistant to corrosion, must be easy to clean and have an adequate supply of hot and cold water. Equipment items that come into contact with high-risk foods will need to be cleaned and disinfected as necessary. Facilities must be provided to clean and disinfect all tools and equipment, crockery, cutlery, glasses and serving dishes. There are to be sufficient cleaning materials and equipment to match the size of the catering facility. Staff involved in cleaning must wear suitable and adequate protective clothing, which must be changed, at the end of each shift.

Colour coded cleaning equipment, e.g. mops must be cleaned, dried and stored in a designated area once finished with. Drying of equipment must not cause recontamination, e.g. from soiled cloths. A full list of NSNs of colour-coded equipment is shown in JSP 308. Equipment must be of durable construction and resistant to corrosion, especially items that will come into contact with powerful cleaning chemicals.

Sinks. It is a legal requirement that, where appropriate, adequate provision must be made for any necessary washing of food. Every sink or other facility for the washing of food must have an adequate supply of hot and/or cold potable water as required, and be kept clean. Separate facilities must be provided for hand washing, food preparation and equipment washing if the volume of preparation in the kitchen demands it. In small catering operations, one sink may be used for both equipment and food washing, provided that both activities can be done effectively and without prejudice to food safety, i.e. the sink is to be thoroughly cleaned between each process. It is good practice to have signs above sinks indicating what they can be used for. Hot water supply is not essential if a sink is to be used exclusively for food preparation.

Disinfection. Disinfection is a process that reduces microorganisms to a level that will not lead to harmful contamination or spoilage of food. Sterilisation is a process that destroys all living organisms. The word 'sterilise' is sometimes used in food hygiene literature and in some official publications where the word 'disinfect' would be correct. Cleaning products are often described as 'detergent/sterilise' when 'detergent/disinfectant' would be a more accurate description. The following definitions clarify the relationship between disinfection and cleaning:

a. A disinfectant is a chemical agent used for disinfection after cleaning.

b. Sanitisation is a term used mainly in the food and catering industry. It is a process of both cleaning and disinfecting utensils and equipment.

c. A sanitiser is a chemical agent used for sanitisation.

d. Sterilisation is a process intended to destroy or remove all living organisms. It is not to be confused with disinfection.

e. Cleaning, Heat, and Chemical Disinfectants. Disinfection is essential in food hygiene. It is achieved by:

   (1) Cleaning. This is the most useful and practical method of removing food residues, dirt, grease and other undesirable debris. It can be used alone or in combination with the other two methods. A high proportion of microbial contamination is removed from equipment, food preparation surfaces and hands by thorough cleaning.

   (2) Disinfection by Heat. This is considered the most reliable of the three methods of disinfection. Immersion in water at 65°C for 10 minutes, or at higher temperatures for shorter times can be relied upon to destroy most microorganisms harmful to health, with the exception of bacterial spores. Boiling water is an effective and cheap disinfectant although bacterial spores may survive boiling. The temperature of the washing or rinse cycle in a dishwashing machine can be adjusted to include heat disinfection in the cycle, in accordance with the manufacturer's instruction.

   (3) Some chemical disinfectants are active against a wide range of bacteria; others have a narrow range of antibacterial activity. In all circumstances chemical disinfectants must be used in accordance with the manufacturer's instruction. It is military policy to use general-purpose detergent for general cleaning with surface sanitisers. Chemical disinfectants (stored in a designated

Cleaning Procedures

Cleaning of food premises is carried out to remove dirt and grease from all surfaces and equipment, including pathogenic bacteria, that could compromise food safety, as well as food debris.

It is imperative that high standards of cleaning are maintained for the following reasons:

a. To comply with the legal requirements of the FS(GFH)R.
b. To reduce the risk of food poisoning by removing food residues, which could contain harmful bacteria.
c. To deny pests harbourage and food.
d. To reduce the risk of foreign objects physically contaminating food.
e. To promote hygiene awareness amongst catering personnel.
f. To provide a pleasant working environment and a favourable image to personnel.

Cleaning Schedule: A planned cleaning schedule programme is important in ensuring that high standards of cleanliness in all food areas are achieved and maintained. This can be achieved by adhering to a written cleaning schedule. Food preparation surfaces must be regularly cleaned whilst in use. This is particularly important where space is limited and the cross contamination risk is increased.

a. Instructions for cleaning specific areas or pieces of equipment are to include the following information relative to the task:
   (1) Job description.
   (2) Cleaning materials and chemicals to be used (in accordance with manufacturer's instruction).
   (3) Safety precautions.
   (4) Job method.
b. The cleaning schedule is to state how often a specific area or piece of equipment is to be cleaned and who is responsible for checking that all cleaning tasks have been completed to a satisfactory standard.
c. General information concerning the cleaning of food equipment, surfaces and the material structures, including a list of cleaning equipment and agents used in food rooms/kitchen/galley/mess, are at Annex D to this chapter.
d. Catering managers are to implement a cleaning schedule that relates to all food areas within their department. A schedule

detailing the frequency of routine cleaning tasks should be produced for each catering facility. It is to be contained within Catering Standing Orders and communicated to all personnel (e.g. by displaying the schedule on a notice board). A matrix showing the frequency, details of the task, type of cleaning required and a signature block is considered the most useful layout and should be readily available for operatives to follow and sign off. A signature block should also be included for a supervisory check.

Deep Cleaning: All galleys/kitchens and associated areas are to be deep cleaned in accordance with single Service instructions. Catering managers are to ensure that deep cleaning contracts are adequate to meet the tasks required.

Food Preparation Areas

Surfaces. The FS(GFH)R require that those surfaces which come into contact with food must be maintained in a sound condition, be easy to clean and, where necessary, disinfect. This requires the use of smooth, washable and nontoxic materials. To comply with this legal requirement, it is important that surfaces that come into contact with high-risk foods must be capable of being disinfected regularly.

Examples of such surfaces, assuming that they are properly fixed, applied or installed and maintained, include: stainless steel, ceramics, and food grade plastics. Wooden boards are inappropriate for the preparation of high-risk foods. Food preparation surfaces must either be continuous in their construction or have properly sealed joints.

Design and Layout. The design and layout of food areas are to:

a. Permit adequate cleaning and/or disinfection.

b. Protect against dirt, contact with toxic materials, and formation of condensation and mould.

c. Encourage good food hygiene practices and prevent cross contamination by foodstuffs, equipment, materials, water, air supply or personnel and external sources of contamination such as pests.

d. Where practicable, suitable temperature conditions should be provided for the hygienic preparation of food.

Structural Requirements. In areas where food is prepared, consideration is to be given to floor and wall surfaces, ceilings and overhead fixtures, windows, doors and other openings. There are to be adequate washbasins, sanitary conveniences, ventilation, and drainage. Any maintenance requirements and requests to catering premises are to be recorded in either the Maintenance of Catering Premises – Record of Work Services Template at Annex E to this chapter or the unit works service record. Priority awarded to work service request is entirely dependent on the type of establishment and the impact of the equipment failure. The following priorities are to be applied:

MOD Standards. Defence Estates (DE) Design and Maintenance Guide 18 deals with the design of kitchens and serveries for all ranks, and dining rooms for Junior Ranks. Details of dining rooms for Officers and SNCOs are given in JSP 315 Services Accommodation Code, Scales 29 and 34. The guide is also to be read in conjunction with DE Specification 42 on Catering Equipment and JSP 315, Scales 01, 39, 40, 45, 47 and 52. For HM Ships and Submarines, the relevant Naval Engineering Standards (NES) publication provides guidance in the design, layout and equipping of Galleys, Storerooms (refrigerated and dry) and associated areas.

Pest Control

Pests are known to carry a number of pathogenic organisms that can be transmitted to humans through contaminated food. In addition, pests will damage food stocks causing financial loss. It is therefore important that food premises are kept pest free. The Prevention of Damage by Pests Act 1949 and the FS(GFH)R impose legal duties on owners and occupiers of buildings to keep their premises free from infestation.

A wide variety of insect and rodent pests will enter food premises for a number of reasons:

a. Food. Even in small quantities, food will enable pests to survive and multiply. Regular and thorough cleaning of spillages is therefore imperative.

b. Warmth. Pests of all types are attracted to buildings, which offer even limited warmth away from outdoor conditions. A few degrees increase in temperature will provide conditions in which breeding is enhanced and proliferation encouraged.

c. Shelter. Almost every building provides a variety of harbourages for pests.

Contrary to common belief, it is the newer buildings with suspended ceilings, panelled walls, service ducts and enclosed electrical trunking, which are more likely to create a problem, than older buildings without such features. Access must be provided to these spaces for the effective control of pests.

Denial of food, warmth or shelter will prevent the survival of pests. This form of control can be termed 'environmental control' and is the first line of defence against possible infestation. Environmental control may be considered as denial of access (proofing), food and harbourage. Flying Insect Control. Emphasis is to be placed on the environmental and physical control detailed previously to reduce the risk of food contamination. Areas around food premises are to be kept clean and tidy to reduce the number of possible breeding sites.

External refuse containers are to be clean and in good repair, and have tight fitting lids. If skips are used they are to be completely enclosed. Waste food containers must be washed out before being stored outside. Windows and other openings which provide ventilation are to be fitted with close fitting and cleanable fly screens where required. Doors are to be kept closed or fitted with screens or clear plastic heavy-duty strips. Electronic fly killers, where required, are to be installed but must not be sited above food preparation areas. The bulbs within electric fly killers must be changed in accordance with the manufacturer's instructions.

Recording Sightings

All personnel employed in a kitchen/galley have a duty to report to the Head Chef any evidence of pest infestation. Kitchen Managers are to record such sightings in the Pest Management Register at Annex F to this chapter. Under operational conditions or on exercise, trained Service personnel carry out pest and vector or vermin control. In peacetime (except in some overseas Commands and HM Naval Bases where MOD Civilian pest control operators are employed) civilian contractors normally carry out pest control. There are two ways in which a pest control contractor may be used:

a. To deal with and eradicate a single infestation.

b. To act as a long-term contractor who will visit the premises regularly and carry out pest control treatments as necessary. This proactive approach is more suitable and is recommended.

Waste Disposal

The FS(GFH)R require that food waste and other refuse must not be allowed to accumulate in food rooms, except so far as is unavoidable for the proper functioning of the catering department. It is recommended that systems of work are in place to ensure that refuse containers in food rooms are not over filled and are emptied regularly. All waste is to be removed at the end of the working day. Food waste and other refuse must be deposited in sealed containers which must be of an appropriate construction, kept in sound condition, and, where necessary, be easy to clean and disinfect. Lids are not required on refuse containers used for temporary storage of waste in food preparation areas.

They are frequently touched by the hands of food handlers and may be a serious source of contamination. Any refuse containers used for storage of waste awaiting collection and removal are to have a lid and to be constructed of durable material, which makes them easy to clean and disinfect. Refuse containers are to be included in the cleaning schedule. The FS(GFH)R state that adequate provision must be made for the removal and storage of food waste and other refuse. Refuse stores must be designed and managed in such a way as to enable them to be kept clean, prevent access by pests, and protect against contamination of food, drinking water, equipment or premises. Areas for indoor storage of refuse must be remote from food rooms and not sited near the main delivery entrance. In establishments it is good practice to have a separate area designated for the storage of outdoor waste with well-lit hard standing. A hose is to be provided for cleaning purposes.

Environmental Protection (EP) and Marine Pollution Regulations (MARPOL)

Disposal of food waste must meet the requirements of EP (JSP 418), DEFRA instructions and MARPOL legislation. Revised legislation relating to the disposal of raw meat and fish produced as waste product came into effect 01 Jul 03. Such products can no longer be sent to landfill for disposal. A transitional period until Dec05 has been granted before which DCG will publish policy regarding disposal of such products.

The Five Principles of Hazard Analysis

Analysis of the Potential Food Hazards in a Food Business Operation

Food Hazard-A hazard is anything that could cause harm to the consumer. There are three main hazards that may arise with food served in catering premises. These are contamination of food by:

- Bacteria or other microorganisms that cause food poisoning.
- Chemicals, for example by cleaning materials or pest baits.
- Foreign materials such as glass, metal, plastic and so on.

Of these, the most important hazard is likely to be harmful bacteria or other germs that may contaminate and multiply in food. Identification of the Points in those Operations where Food Hazards may occur. Food passes through many steps; delivery, storage, preparation, cooking, cooling and so on. Hazards can occur at many or all of the steps. For each type of food, the hazards that may occur at each step are to be identified. Mostly these will be steps in the operation where:

- Food can become Contaminated with microorganisms, chemicals or foreign material.
- Bacteria can Multiply if the food is held too long at the wrong temperature.
- Micro organisms Survive a process that should kill them, e.g. when cooking or disinfection of equipment is inadequate.

Deciding which of the critical points identified are critical to ensuring food safety.

Critical Points are steps at which the hazards must be controlled to ensure that a hazard is eliminated or reduced to a safe level.

- Any step where food may be become Contaminated is to be controlled. Controls include clean and disinfected equipment, the personal hygiene of staff, and separation of raw and cooked food. All food is to be protected from contamination by foreign bodies, pests or chemicals.
- Steps where bacteria may be able to Multiply in food must be controlled. The time and temperature at which food is held, stored or displayed are likely to be critical.
- Any cooking or reheating step is to be able to Kill harmful microorganisms. It will be critical that heating is thorough. Cooking is normally the most important control step in most food preparation. Chemical disinfection of equipment is another control point designed to Kill microorganisms.

Identification and implementation of effective control and monitoring procedures at those critical points

Controls must be set for the Critical Points, then Checks Introduced

Controls will either reduce the hazard to an acceptable level or get rid of it completely. The controls are to be precise as possible. For example, it is better to state that certain products will be stored under refrigeration at a set temperature, rather than to simply say that it must be kept in the chiller. A control target is to be set for every critical control point that has been identified. When controls have been set, it is then possible to Monitor the critical points whenever that preparation step is used. The targets can be checked. The frequency of checks is to be set for each control. Checking temperatures does not always involve probing food with a thermometer.

Delivery vans or storage chillers may be fitted with temperature monitors and these can be checked. Other critical controls are more difficult to measure, e.g. cleaning & disinfection of equipment or the personal hygiene of staff. They will be often vital to the safety of food, and there are to be regular checks that standards are kept up. Review of the analysis of food hazards, the critical control points and the control and monitoring procedures periodically, and whenever the food business's operations change. It is not satisfactory to go through this process once and forget about it. Occasionally the system may need to be reviewed and amended, for example:

- If controls or methods of checking are found to be ineffective or impracticable.
- The menu changes. New dishes may have new hazards and controls.
- The method of preparation changes.
- New equipment is introduced.

Annex B-Hazard Analysis

The Four-line Method

This annex contains:

a. Flow Diagram-An Overview of the Four-Lines.

b. Flow Diagram – LINE A – Food/dishes served cold.

c. Flow Diagram – LINE B – Food/dishes served hot.

d. Flow Diagram – LINE C – Food/dishes cooked, chilled and served cold.

e. Flow Diagram – LINE D – Food/dishes cooked. Chilled and reheated.

f. Hazard Analysis Flow Chart – LINE A.

g. Hazard Analysis Flow Chart – LINE B.

h. Hazard Analysis Flow Chart – LINE C.

i. Hazard Analysis Flow Chart – LINE D.

j. Galley/Kitchen/Mess Management Records:

(1) Daily Food Safety management Record (Template)
(2) Advance Food Preparation Record (Template)
(3) Food Time/Temperature Record (Template)
(4) Galley/Kitchen/Mess Fridge/Freezer/Blast Chiller Daily Monitoring Record (Template)
(5) Galley/Kitchen/Mess Fridge/Freezer/Blast Chiller Monitoring Record (Template).

Use of the Four-Line Method

All caterers are to use this guide as a reference document. Each catering establishment will have unique hazards, which are to be annotated onto the template as a Control Point, a Critical Point or a Critical Control Point.

The Four-Line Method is to be used as follows:

a. Monitoring and Recording of the HAL's. Record the daily menu on single Service record forms. Determine high-risk menu items and, by referring to the Four-Line method guidance, annotate on the record the relevant Hazard Analysis Line (HAL) to the individual food dish.

b. Whilst the Four-Line method provides a system of HAL within kitchen and provision areas, other factors will need to be considered in ancillary kitchen areas e.g. delivery bays and pot/crock wash.

Food Hygiene in Catering Establishments

Legislation and Model Regulations

Food and Agriculture Organization of the United Nations: The World Health Organization, through its Food Safety Programme, which is aimed at ensuring the safety of foods for the consumer, initiated a survey of legislation related to food hygiene in catering establishments. The results of the survey, which are summarized in this publication, and the model food hygiene regulations for catering establishments, also included here, were reviewed by a joint FAO/WHO expert consultation held in Geneva from 28 April to 2 May 1975.

This meeting was funded by the United Nations Environment Programme (UNEP) as part of its activity to "support, and accelerate or expand the work of the FAO/WHO Codex Alimentarius Commission on international standards for pollutants in food and strengthening of FAO/WHO capabilities to assist developing countries in food control".

In this activity the Food and Agriculture Organization of the United Nations and the World Health Organization are cooperating agencies. Many of the legislative texts on which this survey was based have been published, in full or in summary, in:

(1) International digest of health legislation. Geneva, World Health Organization (published quarterly); and

(2) Food and agricultural legislation. Rome, Food and Agriculture Organization of the United Nations (published quarterly).

The survey covers a reasonably representative cross-section of the legislation of Member.

States in all Parts of the World

Food control has two principal objectives: protecting consumers against health risks, fraud, and adulteration of foods and assuring fair practices in the food trade. The survey described here was concerned with the first of these objectives, namely, the safety and cleanliness of food, i.e., food hygiene. The need for a high standard of food hygiene and for adequate control measures is particularly important in catering^ establishments of all kinds. The fourth report of the WHO Expert Committee on Environmental Sanitation-' points out that:

> *"One careless food handler, or one human carrier of disease, preparing food at home will jeopardize the health of only a small number of persons, mainly members of the family. When one such person works in the kitchen of a restaurant, hospital, factory, canteen, school, or other place where meals are supplied to many people, the number of potential victims is correspondingly greater."*

The present report is therefore concerned essentially with the promotion of food hygiene in catering establishments. Nevertheless, since the basic principles of food hygiene are common to all types of food establishments and food handling activities, the model regulations annexed to this report can be used as the basis for the legal control of all types of food "Food hygiene" has been defined as, "The measures whereby the wholesomeness, soundness and safety for human consumption are secured or increased, covering all facets of food production, harvesting, processing, distribution, preparation and service and of possible causes of toxicity (physical, chemical or microbiological)".

Geneva, World Health Organization

The model code sets out in detail, but in simple terms, the various points which should be legally enforceable in any country and should be embodied in regulations or secondary legislation. It is intended, in particular, for the guidance of developing countries wishing to build up an effective organization for the control of standards of hygiene in catering establishments. In drawing up this code account has been taken of a statement by the Codex Alimentarius Commission on general principles of food hygiene.

Measures for Promoting Food Hygiene

Effective legislation is essential in any adequate system for promoting food hygiene, but this is only part of such a system. However comprehensive the legislation, it will be ineffective unless it can be enforced. This means that there must be an agency, or agencies, charged with that responsibility. These responsible bodies must in turn employ an adequate number of capable and well trained staff for enforcement duties. Indeed, one of the first steps which developing countries wanting to build up a service to improve standards of food hygiene should take is the development of a trained field staff.

Field staff cannot, however, be engaged solely in law enforcement activities. Their principal role must be to exercise constant surveillance over catering establishments so that they are fully aware of the standards of hygiene being observed and are able to take prompt action to correct any faults that they discover. This work will involve frequent inspections of premises and the collection of samples for bacteriological and chemical analysis, and supporting services such as laboratory facilities will be required. The field staff will also have advisory and educational functions, obtaining improvements in the handling of food through persuasion and consent and the education of managements.

To establish and maintain an adequate field staff with the support services required and to meet related expenditure on, for example, transport, equipment and materials, will require adequate financial resources. Part of the finances required may come from licensing or registration fees or other charges on the catering industry, but the major part will usually have to be obtained from central or local governments, or both. Governments have to decide how the funds are to be provided but it may be necessary to present strong arguments to justify the request, particularly where a country has previously not had a comprehensive food control service. Since the primary object of a food hygiene programme is to protect the health of the public, it is not always easy to present a case on a cost-benefit basis.

It must be recognized that promotion of food hygiene is only one of a number of measures for protecting and improving human health that fall within the scope of environmental health. According to a WHO Expert Committee on National Environmental Health Programmes: Their Planning, Organization, and Administration, environmental health "refers to the ecological balance that must exist between man and his environment in order to ensure his well-being".

Within the field of environmental health, environmental sanitation was defined by a WHO Expert Committee in 1950 as "the control of those factors in man's environment which exercise or may exercise a deleterious effect on his physical, mental, or social well-being". The report of Joint FAO/WHO Food Standards Programme, Codex Alimentarius Commission. Recommended international code of practice: general principles of food hygiene. Rome, 1969.

WHO Technical Report Series, No. 439, 1970.

Committee on Environmental Sanitation). the WHO Expert Committee on National Environmental Health Programmes lists 17 item considered to be included in, or related to, environmental health. Among those items are water supplies, wastes disposal, vector control, and food hygiene. Food hygiene, therefore, is an integral part of a health service and it is important to appreciate that it is difficult to develop in isolation a satisfactory programme for raising standards of food hygiene. High priority should be given to achieving proper standards in this particular field, but progress will be made more easily if efforts are also made to improve general environmental health.

In other words, a food hygiene programme should be developed within the context of progressive environmental health and personal health programmes. Good food hygiene is impossible without adequate supplies of safe water, proper means for wastes disposal, effective pest control, and reasonable living conditions. It is also difficult to reduce the incidence of food-borne infections where disease is widespread among the population and adequate steps are not taken to reduce sources of infection.

Basic Principles of Food Hygiene Legislation

General

An essential part of the health services of every country must be to ensure that food is safe, wholesome and not injurious to health, and that proper hygienic standards are observed at all stages from production or manufacture until it reaches the consumer. The requirement that food must not be injurious to the consumer means that food traders must be under a legal obligation not to sell food which they know to be unfit for human consumption or could with reasonable diligence ascertain to be unfit. They must also have a duty to take due care to ensure that adequate standards of food hygiene are observed at all times in the conduct of their business.

It is not sufficient merely to place legal obligations on food traders. There must also be official agencies charged with the duty of exercising close surveillance of all types of food premises, including catering establishments. Many environmental factors can influence the maintenance of satisfactory standards of food hygiene and, as indicated on p. 3, progress will be made more easily if a food hygiene programme is developed within a progressive environmental health and personal health programme. Where food hygiene is the responsibility of the agency responsible for general environmental health there should be no problems in securing coordination of effort. Where separate agencies are responsible it is important that there should be close liaison between them. Agencies with the duty of controlling food hygiene should not be regarded merely as law enforcement bodies, though they should possess adequate legal powers to establish and maintain the required standards. Their officers need to have authority to enter food premises during business hours without warning in order to carry out the necessary inspections and investigations, and it should be an offence to obstruct officers who are carrying out these duties.

Effective legislation is necessary to secure the proper observance of hygienic practices. The basic legal requirements should be embodied in national statutes but the more detailed and technical requirements should be contained in regulations which can be readily and quickly changed to keep pace with scientific and technical developments.

There is a need also for codes of practice which, while not legally enforceable, give guidance to food traders and the officials responsible for inspection and control of food premises on equipment, materials and practices for maintaining the desired standards. Although the basic legal requirements embodied in national statutes and the more detailed and technical requirements contained in regulations will cover very many points it is not advisable that legal provisions should be too rigid or too detailed.

Often, the more satisfactory approach is to prescribe the objective to be achieved and to allow some flexibility in the choice of methods to be used to achieve that objective. In any case, it is impracticable for laws to be drafted in sufficient detail to take account of all possible circumstances.

Basic Legal Requirements

The principal points that should be included in the basic legal requirements are as follows :

(a) the authorities responsible for the enforcement of food hygiene legislation should be specified;

(b) it should be an offence to sell food that is diseased, unsound, or unwholesome;

(c) recognized officers of the responsible authorities should be authorized to inspect food intended for sale, to take samples, and to seize and condemn food that appears to be unfit for human consumption;

(d) recognized officers should have power of entry to all food premises;

(e) all food premises of prescribed types should be required to be registered by the responsible authorities before being opened for business and these authorities should be empowered to revoke registration where continued use of the premises constitutes a potential danger to health; particular types of premises would be registered under regulations made in accordance with point (f) below;

(f) authority should be given to the appropriate minister to make regulations containing specific and detailed legal requirements with respect to food hygiene in particular types of premises and different food handling activities; compliance with the appropriate regulations would be a condition for the registration of premises;

(g) physicians who become aware, or suspect, that patients they are attending are suffering from food poisoning should be required to notify the local public health authority;

(h) authority should be given to recognized officers to prohibit the use or removal from the premises of food which they believe is likely to cause food poisoning until investigations have shown whether it may safely be used for human consumption;

(i) persons engaged in the handling of food should be required to notify their employers if they become aware that they are suffering from any condition that might lead to the infection of foods and employers should be under an obligation to inform the local medical officer.

Model Food Hygiene Regulations for Catering Establishments

The basic legal requirements for the control of food hygiene which should be embodied in a national statute have been set out in the preceding section. As indicated in point (f), detailed legal requirements should be stated in regulations or secondary legislation made under the authority given by the statute. It should be noted that in these model regulations expressions such as "adequate", "suitable", and "sufficient" are frequently used.

This is because a legal document of this kind must have sufficient flexibility to meet the varying circumstances found in different types of establishment and in different parts of the world. The interpretation of these terms is left to the discretion of local control authorities. The following Model Code details those matters which it is suggested should be included in the food hygiene regulations for catering establishments.

Registration

(a) No premises shall be used as catering premises unless they are registered for that purpose by the local authority. Any person who uses unregistered premises shall be guilty of an offence.

(b) Application for registration must be made before the premises are opened and the application must be refused if the premises do not comply in all respects with food hygiene regulations for catering premises.

(c) Registration may be revoked if at any time serious breaches of the food hygiene regulations occur.

Where a licensing system is preferred, points (e) and (f) should be amended accordingly.

Where a system of licensing is preferred this section should be amended accordingly.

Construction and Maintenance of Premises

(a) No catering business shall be carried on in any premises in which food is exposed to the risk of contamination.

(b) The premises shall be of adequate size, sound construction and in good repair. Areas used for the handling of food shall be completely separated from any part of the premises used as living quarters.

(c) The internal walls, floors, windows, ceilings, woodwork and all other parts of every room shall be so constructed and maintained in such good order, repair and condition as to enable them to be cleaned effectively and to prevent, as far as practicable, infestation by rats, mice, insects and birds.

(d) The premises must be kept free from rodent and insect pests, and birds, and dogs, cats and other domestic animals must be excluded from areas where food is processed or stored. All rodenticides, insecticides and other toxic substances must be clearly labelled and, when not in use, be kept in separate, locked cupboards.

(e) The premises must be kept in a clean condition and no water must be deposited or allowed to accumulate in rooms in which food is prepared, stored or served, except in so far as this may be unavoidable for the proper conduct of the business.

(f) All rooms in which food is stored, prepared or served, or in which utensils are washed, and all sanitary conveniences shall be well ventilated and well lighted.

(g) No room in which food is stored, prepared or served may be used as a sleeping place or communicate directly with a sleeping place or sanitary convenience.

Water Supply

(a) An ample supply of water of drinking quality must be provided at all premises; where possible this should be from the public supply main but if from any other source it must be approved by the health authority and checked for bacteriological and chemical quality at intervals.

(b) An adequate supply of hot and cold water or of hot water at a suitable controlled temperature shall be provided in all areas where food is prepared and where equipment and utensils are washed.

(c) Water used for making ice shall be of drinking quality.

Drainage

(a) All premises shall be provided with an adequate drainage system which, where practicable, shall be connected to the public sewerage system.

(b) Where connexion to the public sewerage system is not practicable the method of sewage disposal must be approved by the health authority.

Personal Washing Facilities

(a) An adequate number of suitable wash-hand basins shall be provided for the use of all persons engaged in the handling of food. These basins must be conveniently accessible to these persons and in any case must be located in or immediately adjacent to all sanitary conveniences. In all new premises, and where practicable in existing premises, hand-washing facilities must be provided within or immediately adjacent to food preparation areas. All wash-hand basins shall be properly connected to the drainage system and be provided with an adequate supply of hot and cold water or of hot water at a suitable controlled temperature. At each basin shall be provided an adequate supply of soap or other suitable detergent, nail brushes and clean towels or other suitable drying facilities.

(b) Facilities for personal washing must not be used for any other purpose.

Sanitary Facilities

(a) An adequate number of conveniently located sanitary conveniences shall be provided for all employees. Separate conveniences shall be provided for each sex. An adequate supply of toilet paper must be available at all times.

(b) In or near every sanitary convenience a clearly legible notice must be displayed in a prominent position requiring users to wash their hands after using the convenience.

Storage of Clothing

Adequate facilities shall be provided for the storage of employees' clothing and personal belongings not being worn during working hours and such clothing and belongings shall not be kept on the premises other than in the accommodation provided.

First-aid Materials

(a) A sufficient supply of suitable bandages, dressings (including waterproof dressings) and antiseptics shall be provided for the first-aid treatment of persons engaged in the handling of food.

(b) This material must be kept in suitable locations readily accessible to employees and clearly labelled.

Storage of Refuse

(a) A sufficient number of watertight containers of durable and nonabsorbent material with tight-fitting or self-closing lids shall be provided for the storage of food waste and other refuse.

(b) Adequate space shall be provided for the temporary storage of waste; this space must not be in any room where food is stored, prepared or served.

Food

(a) Food, while being stored, prepared, displayed or served, shall be protected from dust, flies, rodents and other pests, and other contamination and all persons engaged in the handling of food shall take all reasonable steps to protect the food from risk of contamination.

(b) Raw meat, poultry, fish, shellfish, milk or uncooked products containing those foodstuffs shall not be permitted to come into contact with any cooked foods. Any persons handling any of these raw or uncooked foodstuffs must, before handling any cooked food, thoroughly wash their hands and carefully cleanse all surfaces, utensils and equipment with which the foodstuffs may have come into contact.

(c) All perishable food consisting in whole or in part of milk or milk products, eggs, meat, poultry, fish, shellfish or other ingredients capable of supporting the rapid growth of pathogenic organisms shall be kept at a temperature that is not within the range from 4.5°C (40°F) to 65.5CC (150°F), except during necessary periods of preparation and service.

(d) Raw, unprocessed fruits and vegetables shall be thoroughly washed in clean drinking-water before use.

Equipment

(a) All articles of equipment with which food comes into contact, or may come into contact, must be kept clean, be so constructed, placed, of such materials, and kept in such good order, repair and condition as to:

(i) enable them to be thoroughly cleaned;

(ii) prevent, so far as is reasonably practicable, any matter being absorbed by them; and

(iii) prevent, so far as is reasonably practicable, any risk of contamination of the food.

(b) An adequate number of sinks or other suitable facilities for the washing of food and equipment when necessary shall be provided. These sinks or other facilities shall be provided with an adequate supply of hot and cold water or of hot water at a suitable controlled temperature, or with cold water only where the sink is used only for washing fish, fruit or vegetables. These facilities must not be used for any other purpose.

(c) Equipment shall be so installed as to facilitate its cleaning and the cleaning of adjacent areas.

Personnel

(a) Every person handling or coming into contact with food, or with any equipment or utensil used in its preparation, processing or service shall:

  (i) keep as clean as may be reasonably practicable all parts of his body that are liable to come into contact with the food and, in particular, he shall wash his hands thoroughly before commencing work and after using a sanitary convenience;

  (ii) wear clean, washable outer garments and headgear that confines his hair;

  (iii) keep any open cut or abrasion on any exposed part of his body covered with a suitable waterproof dressing; and

  (iv) refrain from spitting and using tobacco in any form while engaged in the handling, preparation or service of food, while handling utensils or equipment, and while he is in any room containing open food.

(b) No person who is affected with any disease in a communicable form may work in any catering premises and the proprietor of any catering establishment shall not permit any such person to work in the establishment. Immediately a person engaged in the handling of food becomes aware, or has reason to suspect, that he is suffering from, or is a carrier of, typhoid, paratyphoid or any other Salmonella infection or amoebic or bacillary dysentery or any staphylococcal infection likely to cause food poisoning he shall immediately inform the person operating the catering premises in which he is employed and that person shall immediately notify the medical officer of the health authority.

Turnover & Retention

As one F&B manager Interviewed Noted: "Employee retention is important for consistency of products and customer service standards, so customers know what to expect". Hinkin and Tracey (2000) list the following productivity-related costs of staff turnover: pre-departure productivity loss; learning curve; errors and waste; supervisory and peer disruption. Turnover can also negatively affect productivity within interdependent worker groupings and teams. However not all staff turnover has negative implications. Moderate turnover can help to replace unproductive employees, enable career progression, enhance job and employee matching and is therefore viewed as enhancing productivity by some (Ilmakunnas et al., 2005).

A recent study of Auckland hospitality workers (Poulston, 2006) indicated short lengths of employment are common (87% have been in their current job fewer than five years), and that the majority work part-time. The latest survey conducted by the Restaurant Association (March 2006) indicates an average annual staff turnover of 29%, up from 26% in 2005. A New Zealand study of productivity found that high-involvement work practices and employee retention were strongly associated with strong enterprise performance (Guthrie, 2001). While turnover increases exposure to disruptions associated with the loss of employees in high involvement work practices this damage is greater than in settings where processes are more automated, for example the preparation areas of fast food establishments.

Several managers stated in the interviews that they have real problems with staff turnover, tending to attribute much of the problem to the tight labour market rather than to factors that are directly within their control. Of the managers who completed the web survey question asking whether staff turnover affects productivity in their business, 54% feel it does, 29% feel it does not, and 17% responded 'not applicable'. The need for training new staff was seen as having the greatest negative effect on productivity. The time and cost involved are also detrimental effects stemming from staff turnover.

> *"Turnover is costly and involves extra training-there's also a trust issue with long term staff".*

Large hotels are the most proactive in developing strategies to cope with turnover and to increase retention. Such strategies include succession planning, valuing internal communication to develop teams, and offering incentives for staff to stay. Training and flexible hours are also seen to be important in improving retention.

Overall, employees agreed that new staff often reduce productivity, because they are inefficient in their job, and because it is a burden on experienced staff to train someone new. Some employees, however, give new staff credit saying they usually are the most willing to learn. Longer term staff not only have more industry experience, which helps to increase overall productivity, but also a stronger relationship with the kitchen staff, seen by many as prerequisite for having a *"good night"*.

Technology

In its discussion of productivity drivers the Department of Labour has identified that:

> *"innovation is a key part of raising workplace productivity. The appropriate introduction of advanced*

> *technology is linked with higher productivity, greater market share and employment growth".*

The introduction of advanced technology has been cited by several authors as an important and positive influence on productivity. Positive impacts however do not simply 'appear', rather they stem from the competent use and exploitation of IT capabilities (Sigala, 2003). Technology has been found to 'support employees, enhance the quality of service, improve efficiencies, gain competitive advantage, maintain relationships with customers and increase profitability', while poor investment in technology (along with poor training) is likely to reduce profitability. Several studies have shown that SMEs in the hospitality sector have special difficulties in maximising the productivity potential of information technologies.

Such enterprises are more likely to recognise the limitations of technology and emphasise the importance of 'the human touch'. At the same time SME owners and managers are more likely to have to out-source aspects of IT maintenance and may feel more removed from its application to the business setting. The web survey found that 89% of managers have introduced new technology in the last two years with the view to improving productivity in their workplace. The interviews revealed a similar trend. A range of technologies have been introduced by managers, primarily in the front of house area with computers being the most common purchase. Smaller businesses have a slower uptake of 'cutting edge' ICT devices such as wireless personal digital assistants and text message ordering.

Both managers and employees are divided on the issue of technology and productivity. Some think it enhances staff efficiency, saves time and improves productivity. Others say it in fact creates inefficiencies when it breaks down or requires updating. While technology was discussed as an important contributor to productivity, most of the technology identified as bringing real efficiency gains is in the front of house environment. In particular, technological innovations are central to streamlining ordering and point of sale processes.

5

Food and Beverage Services

Food and beverage services are among the most visible locations at ski areas, and a ski area's environmental commitment is often judged by the environmental practices within these establishments. Pollution prevention (P2) opportunities for restaurants address a broad range of operations, including solid waste management, grounds and facility maintenance, and restaurant supply purchasing. A restaurant's pre-tax profit is typically only 3 to 9 percent of its total revenue; therefore, money saved through reductions in operating costs (that is, through reduced energy consumption and water use) can significantly increase the profit margin. While some restaurants have already taken advantage of the many P2 opportunities available to them, a survey by the National Restaurant Association shows that for some of the most common P2 techniques and best practices, there is still room for improvement across the industry. Numerous programs exist for the food and beverage service industry that help restaurants and their customers minimize environmental impacts. This chapter uses the Green Restaurant Association's approach as an outline to present the environmental practices a restaurant should consider.

Green Restaurant Association

Involvement in environmental programs is a good way for a restaurant to learn more about environmental best practice opportunities. An environmental resource for the food service industry is the Green Restaurant Association (GRA), which helps member restaurants reduce environmental impacts with twelve "eco-steps". The GRA's primary operational components are research, environmental consulting, education, public relations and marketing, and community organizing and consumer activism. To become a member of the GRA, a restaurant must sign a statement of its commitment to making environmental improvements based on the 12 "eco-steps" listed below. After a member restaurant has made positive environmental changes, the GRA will include the restaurant in the "Green Restaurant Guide," which serves as a directory for environmentally conscious restaurants. The GRA also offers fee-based consulting services to member restaurants and initiates public relations and marketing initiatives, such as having restaurants featured on CNN, to increase restaurant exposure and consumer awareness.

GRA's 12 eco-steps are outlined below and discussed further in Sections 9.2 through 9.13.

1. Elimination of Polystyrene Foam (commonly known as styrofoam). Replace all polystyrene foam products with environmentally friendly alternatives: paper, bamboo or sugarcane paper, recyclable plastic, biodegradable plastic, and so on. *This is the minimum environmental standard for becoming a member of the GRA.*
2. Comprehensive Recycling. Initiate or improve recycling programs for glass, plastic, bimetal, cardboard, and mixed paper.
3. Waste Reduction and Reuse. Increase bulk purchasing and reduce excessive packaging for food, condiments, and so on. Replace disposable products with reusable alternatives: eating ware, aprons, tea strainers, cups, and so on.
4. Biodegradable Plastic. Transition to corn-based "plastic" products that are biodegradable and petroleum-free: cups, utensils, garbage bags, and straws.
5. Recycled Products. Transition to recycled products with the highest postconsumer content available and non-tree-fiber paper products: napkins, paper towels, toilet paper, office paper, take-out containers, coffee jackets, plates, and bowls.
6. Non-Chlorine-Bleached Paper Products. Transition to non-bleached or non-chlorinebleached paper products: cups, wax paper, plates, take-out containers, bags, pastry bags and grabbers, napkins, paper towels, coffee filters, and office paper.
7. Nontoxic Cleaners, Landscaping and Pest Management. Replace hazardous chemical products with biodegradable and nontoxic alternatives; dish detergent, germicides, disinfectants, toilet bowl cleaners, drain cleaner, floor wash, floor polish, glass cleaners, degreasers, and laundry detergent. For landscaping,

switch to nontoxic, nonsynthetic, and organic fertilizers, pesticides, or herbicides. For pest control, use nontoxic products or services.

8. Energy Efficiency. Improve the energy efficiency of lighting, refrigeration, air conditioning, gas appliances, and so on. Obtain assistance with using government and private rebate programs. Make connections with energy consultants to learn about more extensive programs.
9. Water Efficiency. Improve the water efficiency of toilets, faucets, laundry, sprinkler systems, and so on.
10. Composting. Divert food waste from landfills and create nutrient-rich soil for gardening and landscaping.
11. "Green" Electricity. Change to an energy provider that uses solar, wind, small-scale hydroelectric, geothermal, or methane-based power that is renewable and less polluting to ecosystems.
12. Employee Education Program. Train all employees, managers, and owners. Topics covered should include
    - An environmental profile of the restaurant industry
    - A history of environmental issues relevant to food service: landfills, water pollution, air pollution, clear-cutting, and global warming
    - Data describing the restaurant impacts (positive and negative) on the environment.

Elimination of Polystyrene Foam

Polystyrene foam (Styrofoam) is widely used in restaurants in insulated cups for hot beverages and take-out containers. Production of polystyrene involves use of known (benzene) and suspected (styrene and 1,3-butadiene) human carcinogenic substances (styrene and 1,3-butadiene). Styrene is also known to be toxic to the reproductive system. Polystyrene can be recycled; however, its recycling rates are low. Styrofoam is light in weight, but bulky in size, so hauling Styrofoam to the nearest available recycling facility is often not economically feasible. The value of a load of Styrofoam may not even cover the cost of shipping. To reduce environmental impacts, restaurants should consider switching from Styrofoam to non-bleached paper wraps, cardboard containers, or other sustainable food packaging.

According to a report published by the Environmental Defence Waste Reduction Task Force, McDonalds has completed the switch from polystyrene foam "clamshells" to paper-based wraps for packaging its sandwich items. The wraps provide a 70 to 90 percent reduction in packaging volume, resulting in significantly less space being consumed in landfills. Compared to the polystyrene foam boxes they replaced, the new sandwich wraps also offer a substantial savings in energy used and substantial reductions in pollutant releases measured over the full life-cycle of the packaging. McDonalds is also testing Earth Shell packaging products in 300 of its restaurants throughout the U.S.. These sustainable containers are made from potato starch, natural limestone, 100 percent postconsumer recycled fiber, biodegradable polymer and wax coatings, and water.

Comprehensive Recycling

The "Recycling Guidebook for the Hospitality and Restaurant Industry" provides a general overview of developing and implementing a comprehensive recycling program. The first step mentioned in this resource is to conduct a waste audit in order to evaluate the waste stream, enabling a restaurant to better target the commodities that should be included in a recycling program. Materials that are commonly recycled in restaurants include;

- *Paper*, including cardboard, computer paper, register tape, and telephone books
- *Metals*, including aluminum, tin, and steel cans
- *Green, brown, and clear glass*
- *#1 Polyethylene* (PET) and *#2 high-density polyethylene (HDPE)* plastics
- *Printer cartridges.*

Convenience is the key to a successful recycling program. An EPA Waste Wise tip sheet notes that a convenient collection system will encourage both customers and employees to carefully sort recyclables by material type and to eliminate contaminants. Collecting uncontaminated recyclables (commodities that are properly sorted and free of excess food and beverage waste) will save time otherwise spent in sorting out contaminants.

Further, uncontaminated recyclables have higher value if they are sold. Presented below are other restaurant recycling tips listed in the "Recycling Guidebook for the Hospitality and Restaurant Industry."

- Recycling and trash bins should look different from each other and be clearly marked. Both types of bins should be conveniently located in the kitchen and bar areas so that employees will use them.

- Self-serve establishments should post signs to inform customers about the recycling program and provide specific instructions. Either strategically places bins for collection of recyclable commodities, or have customers leave such commodities on a designated counter for collection by staff.
- If lack of space is a problem, specially designed equipment such as can, glass, and plastic crushers are available to reduce the volume of recyclable materials.
- Recyclable collection bins in public areas should be well-marked. Choose bins with specialized openings, such as a hole for cans or a slot for newspapers, for these areas.
- Set up a logbook or a receipt system to record the volume of recyclables leaving the premises in order to facilitate tracking and compensation.

Waste Reduction and Reuse

Waste reduction and material reuse should be the first step in minimizing the waste that a restaurant produces because it is more efficient to reduce waste at the source or reuse material than it is to recycle. As mentioned in audit is an effective way to evaluate a restaurant's waste streams. Doing so enables staff to identify wastes that are nonessential to operations, such as excess packaging material. This process can also identify disposable products that can be replaced with durable, reusable ones. For example, disposable plastic tableware and silverware should be replaced with washable or compostable utensils.

EPA's Waste Wise program is a free, 3-year, goal-oriented program that assists businesses in assessing and reducing their waste streams.11 EPA designed Waste Wise to be a flexible program, in which the participant determines how much time and money to invest. Key aspects of successful Waste Wise programs include;

- Waste assessments
- Employee education
- Measurement and reporting
- Program maintenance.

The above aspects are fundamental in assessing, developing, implementing, and maintaining a viable waste reduction and reuse program. Waste assessments provide a full understanding of waste streams and provide a basis for targeting specific waste reduction goals. However, these goals will only be reached with the full support of the restaurant – from managers and servers to cooks and food preparation staff. Therefore, employee education is critical to the success of the program. It is also important that program efforts be measured regularly.

Tracking and documenting the costs, savings, and effects of a waste reduction and reuse program are the only ways to determine the environmental and economic impacts of implementing the program. Program data can also provide insight into the effectiveness of employee education programs. Lastly, program maintenance is imperative to realize long-term benefits from a waste reduction and reuse program. A successful program is not a result of one-time changes but a cumulative result of permanent procedural and behavioural changes. Several other guidance documents provide specific waste reduction and reuse ideas for the restaurant industry. Presented below are some examples of common waste reduction techniques that are discussed in "Food for Thought: Restaurant Guide to Waste Reduction and Recycling."

- Purchase and serve beverages in bulk rather than in bottles, cans, or individual packets.
- Buy bar mixes, juices, and coffee in bulk.
- Use health department-approved, refillable condiment containers.
- Purchase cleaning supplies in concentrated form.
- Use cloth towels and reusable table linens and tableware.
- Use vendors that take back packaging material and pallets.

Another way that restaurants can minimize their waste and overall environmental impact is purchasing products through local food supply vendors and grocers. Local sourcing is of particular benefit to the tourism sector, where visitors appreciate locally distinctive food, drink, and other products. For example, several Aspen Skiing Company-owned restaurants purchase natural, chemical-free beef and hamburger from local ranchers to support the ranching community and thus preserve open space, as well as to provide guests with healthy food. The pilot program began in winter 1998 and expanded significantly in 2000. The beef costs twice as much per pound, however

Aspen Skiing Company absorbs the additional cost. By purchasing local produce and supplies, restaurants minimize the affects of excessive transportation and shipping. Such efforts should be accounted for when evaluating the environmental impact and overall performance of a restaurant.

Biodegradable Plastic

As long as customers wish to take their food "to go," restaurants will need to stock disposable goods such as food containers and silverware. According to Biocorp, a manufacturer of biodegradable plastic tableware and silverware, nearly 113 billion disposable cups, 39 billion disposable eating utensils, and 29 billion disposable plates are used in the U.S. every year, and half these items are made of plastic. Because restaurants cannot control what happens to these items once they are in customers' hands, the most effective way to minimize their environmental impacts is to purchase biodegradable products. Biodegradable products are typically made of corn, starch, or paper with an easily biodegradable coating. The Earth Shell is one example of a biodegradable food service product. Biocorp also manufactures biodegradable composting bags, silverware, plates, and beverage containers. "Scientists Perfecting Planet-Friendly Plastics," an article published by the Environmental News Network, explains that the starch used to create these biodegradable plastics– typically wheat gluten – costs about 15 cents per pound, whereas the least costly commercial plastics cost about $1 per pound. Thus, when this starch-based plastic becomes widely available to manufacturers, it could be the cheapest plastic available.

Currently, however, most manufactured environment-friendly plastics cost about $2.50 per pound, although recent projects have brought their costs down to approximately $1.50 per pound. Because biodegradable plastics are more expensive than regular plastic, the biodegradable plastic industry has a challenge in breaking into a very competitive market.

Recycled Products

Restaurants use several types of products that can be replaced with items made from recycled materials. Most of the products with recycled content that can easily be purchased are paper products such as napkins, toilet paper, tissues, paper towels, paper tablecloths, take-out containers, register tape, and office paper. Since 1998, EPA has required federal facilities to purchase products with recycledcontent material. The resulting increased demand for recycled content paper has driven down its cost to the point that recycled-content products are the same price or less expensive than virgin material products.

Case Study: Composting At Keystone Ranch

Keystone Ranch, a horse ranch resort in Keystone, Colorado, implemented a composting program that combines horse manure with vegetable and meat scraps from the Ranch Restaurant. The ranch rents a 30-cubic yard container from a local hauler that holds almost 20 tons of material. Biodegradable cornstarch-based bags are placed at four stations to collect food waste during food preparation and uneaten food from customers. Keystone Ranch estimates that between 10 and 15 percent of the contents of the full 30-cubic yard container is food waste.

The rest of the compost mixture is manure collected from the stalls of 15 to 80 horses. The hauler transports the container to the Twin Landfill Corporation in a nearby town, where the compost is further processed, screened, and then sold to landscapers and farmers. As a result of the composting program, which complements an established glass, aluminum, tin, cardboard, and paper recycling program, the Ranch Restaurant is "rapidly approaching a zero-waste status." Because the tipping fee for compostable material is 30 percent less than that for solid waste, the program sustains itself financially and has diverted 450 tons of organic waste from the local landfill.

Green Electricity

In addition to efforts to minimize their energy use, restaurants can minimize the environmental impacts of the energy they do use by purchasing renewable electricity. By using a renewable source of energy, a restaurant decreases its dependency on nonrenewable fossil fuels and eliminates greenhouse gas emissions associated with its electricity use. Renewable energy sources include wind, solar, geothermal, and biomass. The availability of green electricity varies from region to region, so restaurants interested in purchasing energy from a renewable source should contact their city or state government agencies or local electric utility. Non-profit green energy certification programs, such as Green-e and Cleaner and Greener, may also be able to help direct restaurant owners to local green energy providers.

Employee Education Program

The development of an employee education program is critical to maintaining an environmentally responsible restaurant. An environmental education program should teach both the "how" and "why" of each aspect of the program. An understanding of why an employee should ensure that certain environmental procedures are followed adds meaning to the task. Because of high turnover in many restaurants, environmental education should be a regular, multimedia program, and should include both written and verbal instruction in all languages of the employees. Environmental awareness expectations should be outlined during new-hire training and reinforced throughout the period of employment.

Restaurant managers should consider acknowledging employees who demonstrate superior dedication to minimizing environmental impacts. For example, employees may be offered a percentage of the cost savings resulting from environmental projects implemented at their suggestion. Such recognition would not only reward the employees, but would send a message to customers that the restaurant is actively pursuing "greener" practices. Once the expectation of excellent environmental performance is established, maintaining the program will require less effort. Finally, restaurant managers should encourage employees to provide feedback regarding areas for improvement. Many employees will have ideas of how to improve the environment they work in, and with a forum to voice ideas, innovations can be made.

Chefs, Head Cooks, and Food Preparation and Serving Supervisors

Chefs, head cooks, and food preparation and serving supervisors oversee the daily food service operation of a restaurant or other food service establishment. *Chefs and head cooks* are usually responsible for directing cooks in the kitchen, dealing with food-related concerns, and providing leadership. They are also the most skilled cooks in the kitchen and use their creativity and knowledge of food to develop and prepare recipes. *Food preparation and serving supervisors* oversee the kitchen and non-kitchen staff in a restaurant or food service facility. They may also oversee food preparation workers in fast food, cafeteria, or casual dining restaurants, where the menu is fairly standard from day to day, or in more formal restaurants, where a chef provides specific guidelines and exacting standards on how to prepare each item. All of these workers—chefs, head cooks, and food preparation and serving supervisors—hire, train, and supervise staff, prepare cost estimates for food and supplies, set work schedules, order supplies, and ensure that the food service establishment runs efficiently and profitably. Additionally, these workers ensure that sanitation and safety standards are observed and comply with local regulations. Fresh food must be stored and cooked properly, work surfaces and dishes clean and sanitary, and staff and customers safe from illness or injury to avoid being closed by the health department or law enforcement.

While all chefs have a role in preparing the food, developing recipes, determining serving sizes, planning menus, ordering food supplies, and overseeing kitchen operations to ensure uniform quality and presentation of meals, different types of chefs may have unique roles to perform or specialize in certain aspects of the job. *Executive chefs, head cooks, and chefs de cuisine,* are primarily responsible for coordinating the work of the cooks and directing the preparation of meals.

Executive chefs are in charge of all food service operations and also may supervise several kitchens of a hotel, restaurant or corporate dining operation. A *sous chef,* or sub chef, is the second-in-command and runs the kitchen in the absence of the chef. Many chefs earn fame both for themselves and for their kitchens because of the quality and distinctive nature of the food they serve.

As a greater variety of establishments prepare and serve food, chefs and head cooks and first-line supervisors of food preparation and serving workers can be found in a greater variety of places. Grocery and specialty food stores employ these workers to develop recipes and prepare meals for customers to carry out. They increasingly work in residential care facilities, such as nursing homes, and in schools and hospitals. Some chefs and head cooks work for individuals rather than for restaurants, cafeterias, or food manufacturers. *Personal chefs* and *private household cooks* plan and prepare meals in private homes according to the client's tastes or dietary needs. They order groceries and supplies, clean the kitchen, and wash dishes and utensils. They also may serve meals. Personal chefs usually prepare a week's worth of meals in the client's home for the client to heat and serve according to directions. They may be self-employed or work as part of a team of personal chefs and employed by a company that provides this service. Private household cooks typically work full time for one client, such as corporate executives, university presidents, or diplomats, who regularly entertain as a part of their official duties.

While the work of chefs and head cooks is concentrated in the kitchen or in providing overall guidance, food preparation and serving supervisors oversee specific areas of operation in food service establishments or the kitchen and counter areas of quick service restaurants. In fast food and casual dining restaurants, they may share many of the same functions with food service managers. They are responsible for dealing with customer complaints, balancing the books at the end of the day, scheduling workers, and ordering supplies. They also supervise and train kitchen and food preparation staff and ensure that these workers know how to gather food supplies, operate equipment, and assemble orders.

Work environment. Restaurants and other food service facilities where these workers are employed are required to be clean and sanitary. Although the seating areas of eating places are often attractive, kitchens can be crowded and hot and filled with potential dangers, such as hot ovens and slippery floors. Job hazards for those working in kitchens include slips and falls, cuts, and burns, but these injuries are seldom serious. Chefs, head cooks, and supervisors are under constant pressure to get meals prepared quickly, while ensuring quality is maintained and safety and sanitation guidelines are observed. Because the pace can be hectic during peak dining times, workers must be able to communicate clearly so that food orders and service are done correctly.

Work hours in restaurants may include early mornings, late evenings, holidays, and weekends. Schedules for those working in offices, factories and school cafeterias may be more regular. In fine-dining restaurants, work schedules tend to be longer because of the time required to prepare ingredients in advance. Many executive chefs regularly work 12-hour days because they oversee the delivery of foodstuffs early in the day, plan the menu, and prepare those menu items that require the most skill. Depending upon the days of operation, some chefs or other supervisors may take less busy days off to offset the longer hours on other days.

Investment in Property

Funding Real Estate Projects for the Hospitality Industry: Emerging Perspectives

Up until 2007, most hoteliers, investors and developers were buoyant when it came to the growth prospects in the hospitality industry. They had enough reason to be optimistic as every factor which would influence the industry, directly or indirectly, was on a growth trajectory. The GDP was growing like never before and the whole world had its eyes on the Indian growth story. Plans of expansion filled the newspapers and press releases and investors were keener than ever to get a fair share of the pie.

The recession, however, had plans of its own and devoured most of the pie. The global economic slowdown and its effect on the Indian economy has doused the fire of excitement of even the most optimistic developers and investors. It has resulted in an extreme crunch for investment in the hospitality sector, coupled with the decrease in demand for rooms. This double whammy put to rest most of the ambitious plans of expansion across the country.

All players have been reviewing their plans of development, owing to the increasingly challenging macro economic situation at the moment. The total number of rooms estimated to be added is today nearly half of what was announced earlier. One-fourth of the announced plans have fallen completely flat and the rest are hanging on the edge of viability. DLF, Parsvnath and other developers of similar cadre have scaled down or slowed down their plans of expansion.

Parsvnath, which had plans of adding at least 10,000 rooms, has now stopped acquiring land for any further plans other than the twenty hotels for which they have already done the same. There have been reports that DLF has been in talks with various hotel companies to sell eight to nine of their land parcels demarcated for hotel projects to raise funds. Unitech has sold its Gurgaon hotel project to reduce its huge debt burden. Developers are keener to finish the projects on hand rather than plan further. Divesting the investment heavy hotel plans seems to be the best way out for the cash strapped, heavily indebted players to survive the present-day economic scenario.

Financial Projections Going Awry

The seeds were sown, the crops were nurtured through the tough inflationary times but when the time to harvest came, the floods of recession washed away the anticipated bounty. Cost and revenue assumptions made during the good times have thus gone for a toss. When it comes to loan disbursements, real estate is presently the black sheep of the family.

Private banks from which loans were freely available earlier have dried up. Public sector banks which continue to lend, albeit cautiously, now require a higher collateral to lend the same amount. Non-banking finance companies are either not lending at all or looking at returns in the post 20 per cent range. Private equity interest in the hospitality sector has all but dried up. Due to the severe global liquidity crunch and flight of capital to 'places of origin', there is a diminishing interest for private equity players in foreign markets. This has added to the financial woes of the capital thirsty developers.

The risk associated with a hospitality project being relatively larger, the premium at which funding is available has gone up. Due to this, only the most stable projects in the market would be able to take up the risk of delivering higher returns to the lenders.

Many developers had invested heavily in land in the past when the land values were significantly higher. At present, the value of the same land parcels has come down significantly. The dependency on the appreciation of these assets has turned out to be a major dampener to the development plans of the various developers. The lower value of land means that the value of collateral has come down for project loans. The cycle of cost of construction has taken the industry on a roller coaster ride over the past couple of years. The global commodity cycle has drastically changed its course. Steel and cement which form a significant chunk of the civil construction costs have lost up to 40 per cent from their historic highs twelve months ago.

The hotels which have opened recently have faced the brunt of the cost fluctuations in a similar fashion. Greater costs were incurred, owing to the period in which their construction phases passed through. The cost of materials was higher, the market was booming and along with the high material costs, the various architects and consultants demanded a premium as a result of a never-before-seen demand. Despite the increased amount of investment that the developers had to put in, they now face a world with reduced revenue prospects.

The main factor that has directly and indirectly influenced the stability of revenue-side financial projections in the hotel industry is the lack of 'stickiness' relative to other real estate sectors. Stickiness of the hotel industry is low. In order to explain, take lease agreements into consideration. These are long term in nature and hence revenues are more secure in the case of an office or retail space as they have a considerable lock-in period. However in case of the hospitality industry, the revenues are more directly susceptible to market conditions. This being the reason as to why other sectors have been relatively less affected by the present day scenario.

The main factors influencing this stickiness are occupancy rate and Average Room Rate (ARR). Occupancy rate is a function of supply and demand. The present scenario is affected by both the demand and supply factors, with demand having the more potent influence. The two main demand drivers, the leisure and business travellers, have contributed to the reduction in occupancy rates. Overseas travel has been affected to a large extent due to the economic slowdown.

Corporates have found innovative ways to cut down on their expenses and there is a growing need for them to rationalise business travel. They have reduced their travel budgets, are staying at serviced apartments and guesthouses or even looking at options where they can avoid staying overnight. MNCs with significant exposure to the developed markets are taking the lead to drive travel associated business expenditures down as a part of their global strategy. Spending sentiments of consumers has been hit to a large extent owing mostly to fears of job loss and a resulting lack of confidence and low morale. The leisure consumers are hence looking to spend lesser on travel.

In addition to the demand slowing down, the supply is on the increase which would mean that the occupancy rates are set to reduce further at least for the next one or two years. All these factors contribute to the occupancy rate reducing significantly and this is a major reason contributing to the instability of the financial projections made by the various players. On the supply side, although there is an inherent demand for more supply in the long run, occupancy rates would see an improvement only with the revival of the economy.

Due to the hit on occupancy rate, hoteliers have been forced to cut down on the ARRs to attract both their business and leisure customers. The occupancy rate has also negatively affected the other closely linked revenue sources such as food and beverage, conferences and banquets.

Role of Funding Options

Traditionally, most developers have tended to plough back the surplus that they earn, into their business via investing in land banks. This makes them highly dependant on external sources for funding. The various equity funding options available in the market till now have been public or private equity which can be foreign (FDI) or domestic funding. In the present market scenario, there is a lot more uncertainty in cash flows associated with hotel projects than usual. This has led investors to be quite cautious when it comes to investing in or lending to hospitality projects.

With many of the real estate companies trading below book values, the public equity scenario is dismal. IPO market is almost non-existent. The last high profile real estate IPO which failed was the EMAAR MGF IPO in February 2008. Real Estate Index has fallen up to 80 per cent from its peak. Going ahead with secondary offerings or rights issues would likely meet with a negative investor response.

Private equity, while still being an option, has seen a slowdown. Investors are worried about the market bottoming out and there is a feeling that the correction in the hospitality sector is still not complete. PE players are avoiding common equity in SPVs but looking at structured investments with greater security and preferred returns. However, there are a number of funds which are actively looking to buy out or invest in distressed assets at enticing valuations.

Having said that, owing to the severe capital crunch, the market for new PE capital raising especially in real estate is difficult right now and is likely to remain so for the next two to three years. Where funds have already been raised, there have been cases of Limited Partners (LPs) not honouring their capital commitments.

Project loans for under construction projects are harder to come by with only the public sector banks lending. These loans are being disbursed primarily to promising projects with substantial asset cover guarantees. We are also witnessing cases of liquidity parched developers borrowing from HNIs at extremely high rates.

Bailing out Stranded Projects

A million dollar question on everyone's mind would be on how to bail oneself out of stranded projects.

Divesting a part of the stake in the project to gain capital may be one of the options. This may not be very easy in today's market. The project maybe valued at a much lower price than what is expected and may leave the seller with a raw deal from the transaction made. One could also think of repositioning the project. Instead of increasing the investment requirement for a project by planning a high end luxury hotel, one could look at serviced apartments and budget hotels at the moment to get through the times of credit crunch.

Another option would be to reduce the scale of the project. This can be done in one go or in phases. Phasing the project out in stages where part of the hotel could be operational in a relatively lesser time and with lesser investment than earlier planned would help ease the credit and liquidity crunch. There are quite a few operators who take a stake in the project as well. Accor is a good example of such an operator who have significant expansion plans in India. Tying up with the right investing operators would however not be as easy as it may look as these operators would choose only the best of the options available and they would have their own plans in place already.

Going back to the lender may be an option worth visiting, to see if they could restructure the existing loan. One could also go for refinancing or extending the loan. If the borrower has a good record, they could also look at finding a new lender as well, probably an HNI who would be willing to invest. However, if the only option left is to exit the project, the timing would need to be well thought out. If one waits too long for a good price, the price might just go lower. On the other hand one also needs to assess the urgency to exit the project as we would not want to end up in a situation where we would be forced to accept a price which would normally be unattractive.

Liberalisation of FDI Norms and its Impact on Expansion Plans

FDI has the promise to be a major factor in the economic development of the many developing nations of the world. With tourism being a major revenue earner for countries across the world, FDI norms liberalisation in this sector is a definite boost for the Indian economy. The government has been very liberal when it comes to FDI regulations in the hotel and tourism industry. According to the Government of India-Ministry of Commerce and Industry, 100 per cent FDI is permissible in the hotel and tourism sector on the automatic route subject to the automatic approval clauses. The additional restrictions, applicable to some sectors of real estate, such as area of development being at least 50,000 square metres, 50 per cent of the project to be completed before five years, no repatriation of funds before three years from date of minimum capitalisation released in 2005, are not applicable to the hotel and tourism industry.

The government has thus made a conscious effort knowing the fact that tourism can be a major source of revenue for the country which is still relatively untapped. Hence, the only effect that existing FDI norms can have on the industry is on the positive side. It is only a matter of time before investments in the hotel and tourism sector start flowing in freely once again. These investments would be more dependant on the inherent demand in the industry and the overall economic scenario. Once the credit crunch situation gets better, the inherent demand in the industry that one senses should help attract funds easily as compared to some of the other sectors.

Some say the worst is over and India will be getting back on its feet soon. However, the key is not just to wait and watch but to try and be one step ahead. Be ahead and decide on when to stop waiting. Only the best would survive and we would be lying if we said we weren't all eager to see who they really are.

The Hotel Organisation Framework

Both people and organizations need to establish a strategic framework for significant success. This framework consists of:

- a vision for your future,
- a mission that defines what you are doing,
- values that shape your actions,
- strategies that zero in on your key success approaches, and
- goals and action plans to guide your daily, weekly and monthly actions.

Your organization's success and your personal success depend on how well you define and live by each of these important concepts. In fact:

- Companies whose employees understand the mission and goals enjoy a 29 percent greater return than other firms (Watson Wyatt Work Study).
- U.S. workers want their work to make a difference, but 75% do not think their company's mission statement has become the way they do business.

Read more to find out how to develop a successful strategic framework for your organization and yourself.

Vision Statement

A vision is a statement about what your organization wants to become. It should resonate with all members of the organization and help them feel proud, excited, and part of something much bigger than themselves. A vision should stretch the organization's capabilities and image of itself. It gives shape and direction to the organization's future. Visions range in length from a couple of words to several pages. I recommend shorter vision statements because people will tend to remember their shorter organizational vision.

Personal Vision Statement

Your personal vision for your life can be as simple as a couple of words or as lengthy as 200 or more items you want to attain or accomplish. Mission or Purpose is a precise description of what an organization does. It should describe the business the organization is in. It is a definition of "why" the organization exists currently. Each member of an organization should be able to verbally express this mission. Additionally, each person needs a mission for his or her life. The alignment of your life mission with your organization's mission is one of the key factors in whether you are happy with your work and workplace. If they are incongruent, you are likely dissatisfied with your work choice.

Mission Statement Samples

> *"Our goal is simply stated. We want to be the best service organization in the world." (IBM)*
>
> *"FedEx is committed to our People-Service-Profit Philosophy. We will produce outstanding financial returns by providing totally reliable, competitively superior, global, air-ground transportation of high-priority goods and documents that require rapid, time-certain delivery."*

"To give ordinary folk the chance to buy the same thing as rich people."

"Our mission is to earn the loyalty of Saturn owners and grow our family by developing and marketing U.S.-manufactured vehicles that are world leaders in quality, cost, and customer enthusiasm through the integration of people, technology, and business systems." "In order to realize our Vision, our Mission must be to exceed the expectations of our customers, whom we define as guests, partners, and fellow employees.(mission) We will accomplish this by committing to our shared values and by achieving the highest levels of customer satisfaction, with extraordinary emphasis on the creation of value. (strategy) In this way we will ensure that our profit, quality and growth goals are met." (Westin Hotels and Resorts)

Values are traits or qualities that are considered worthwhile; they represent an individual's highest priorities and deeply held driving forces. (Values are also known as core values and as governing values; they all refer to the same sentiment.). Value statements are grounded in values and define how people want to behave with each other in the organization. They are statements about how the organization will value customers, suppliers, and the internal community. Value statements describe actions which are the living enactment of the fundamental values held by most individuals within the organization.

The values of each of the individuals in your workplace, along with their experience, upbringing, and so on, meld together to form your corporate culture. The values of your senior leaders are especially important in the development of your culture. These leaders have a lot of power in your organization to set the course and environment and they have selected the staff for your workplace. If you think about your own life, your values form the cornerstones for all you do and accomplish. They define where you spend your time, if you are truly living your values. Each of you makes choices in life according to your most important four – ten values. Why not take the time to identify what is most important to you and to your organization.

Why Identify and Establish Values?

Effective organizations identify and develop a clear, concise and shared meaning of values/beliefs, priorities, and direction so that everyone understands and can contribute. Once defined, values impact every aspect of your organization. You must support and nurture this impact or identifying values will have been a wasted exercise. People will feel fooled and misled unless they see the impact of the exercise within your organization. If you want the values you identify to have an impact, the following must occur.

- People demonstrate and model their values in action in their personal work behaviours, decision making, contribution, and interpersonal interaction.
- Organizational values help each person establish priorities in their daily work life.
- Values guide every decision that is made once the organization has cooperatively created the values and the value statements.
- Rewards and recognition within the organization are structured to recognize those people whose work embodies the values the organization embraced.
- Organizational goals are grounded in the identified values. Adoption of the values and the behaviours that result is recognized in regular performance feedback.
- People hire and promote individuals whose outlook and actions are congruent with the values.
- Only the active participation of all members of the organization will ensure a truly organization-wide, value-based, shared culture.

The following are examples of values: ambition, competency, individuality, equality, integrity, service, responsibility, accuracy, respect, dedication, diversity, improvement, enjoyment/fun, loyalty, credibility, honesty, innovativeness, teamwork, excellence, accountability, empowerment, quality, efficiency, dignity, collaboration, stewardship, empathy, accomplishment, courage, wisdom, independence, security, challenge, influence, learning, compassion, friendliness, discipline/order, generosity, persistence, optimism, dependability, flexibility. Although important aspects of your life and attention, these are not values: family, church, professionalism. If you define what you value about each of these, you are identifying the core value. As an example, the core value in family might be close relationships; in church, spirituality.

Want to see samples of values and value statements? These give you an idea of the depth and breadth in which organizations write their values. Search online for values and value statements and you'll find some that stretch to several pages, too. At Merck, "corporate conduct is inseparable from the conduct of individual employees in the performance of their work. Every Merck employee is responsible for adhering to business practices that are in accordance with the letter and spirit of the applicable laws and with ethical principles that reflect the highest standards of corporate and individual behavior...

"At Merck, we are committed to the highest standards of ethics and integrity. We are responsible to our customers, to Merck employees and their families, to the environments we inhabit, and to the societies we serve worldwide. In discharging our responsibilities, we do not take professional or ethical shortcuts. Our interactions with all segments of society must reflect the high standards we profess.".

Our Employees

- Our employees are the most valued assets of our company, essential participants with a shared responsibility in fulfilling our mission.
- We recognize that the quality, motivation and performance of our employees are the key factors in achieving our success.

"Accordingly, our Human Resources policies and practices are built on:

- Dedication to assisting every employee in reaching his or her full potential in both performance and reward.
- Commitment to diversity, equal opportunity and fair treatment.
- Promotion based on merit, and from within whenever possible.
- We want our organizational structure and culture to promote employee involvement, open communication, teamwork and cooperation."

Strategies are the broadly defined four or five key approaches the organization will use to accomplish its mission and drive toward the vision. Goals and action plans usually flow from each strategy. One example of a strategy is employee empowerment and teams. Another is to pursue a new worldwide market in Asia. Another is to streamline your current distribution system using lean management principles. A university Human Resources Development department established several broad strategies for growth. These included becoming the training and education resource of choice for all employees by offering one-stop access to any and all existing education and training resources.

Additionally, they determined key strategies for expanding their funding base and moving courses online for customer convenience. A Human Resources department devised strategies to develop a superior workforce. These included eliminating poor performers; hiring from several choices of excellent candidates, not just "settling" on a candidate;

developing succession planning; and increasing training and cross-training opportunities.

Sample Strategies

"The Human Resource Association of Greater Detroit's (HRAGD) efforts to advance its mission will include: The promotion of voluntary member interchange, observance of ethical and professional standards, the conduct of meetings and workshops on relevant human resources topics and issues, communication of our purpose and activities to the broader business community, cooperation with the Society for Human Resources Management (SHRM), as well as, other SHRM professional and student chapters and related Human Resources organizations and the community involvement of our membership.

The Association regularly publishes newsletters throughout the year which cover items such as monthly meeting highlights, future programs, Executive Board announcements, SHRM and legislative updates and general human resources news. In addition, a Membership Directory and member skills listing are published."

The San Antonio Express News developed these strategies.

- "Expand our customer base and enhance the franchise by pursuing multimedia opportunities.
- Deliver an award-winning level of journalistic excellence, building public interest, trust and pride.
- Provide vigorous community leadership and support.
- Instill an environment of internal and external excellence in customer service.
- Empower and recognize each employee's unique contribution.
- Achieve the highest standards of quality.
- Improve financial strength and profitability."

6

Restaurant Development

Traditionally, Indians were used to buying their sugar, wheat, pulses, rice etc. from their neighborhood baniya. The majority of food and food products were and still are retailed through neighborhood kirana (baniya) stores. A typical kirana store has a retail area of 200 sq. ft. and sells 500 to 800 stock keeping units (SKUs). The kirana stores focus on dry food products because the infrastructure for cold storage is lacking.

The majority of fresh produce is sold from the carts of travelling vendors. Such produce is deemed to be of low product quality, variety and hygiene. This concept is still popular in B-class and II Tier cities of India and giving employment to thousands of its inhabitants.

Initially the food retail format was seen in A-class cities like Mumbai, Delhi, Chennai which had co-operative stores like "Apna Bazaar" in Mumbai and "Kendriya Bhandar" in Delhi. Both were very successful and are operating many outlets in all strategic localities in the city. Escorts group in the late eighties diversified into non-auto sectors by getting into agri business or food business. It came out with first "Nanz" store at South Extension in Delhi in 1990.

The first visible sign of the change in food retailing was seen in mid-eighties. Around that time a few new food stores were set up in all metro cities in India. Calcutta was the only exception where it started a little later. At that time couple of leading food stores started operating such as "Morning Stores" and "Modern Stores" in Delhi, "Nilgiri" in Bangalore, and "Food Land" in Mumbai "Spencers Food Stores" in Chennai. Spencers were the first to tie up with a Singapore based large retail chain — "Dairyland" and had set up the food stores in Chennai. This was a technology tie up. In Mumbai, Garware group during the late eighties had set up a large food store, which is now reported to have been closed down. Until the late 1990s, food retailing has been concentrated in the south of the country. Southern India has been witnessing revolutionized activity in food retailing. It has thoroughly experienced the food retailing in various formats such as the supermarkets, hypermarkets and neighbourhood stores.

These include Food World, Subhiksha, Nilgiris, Margin Free, and Big Bazaar. The reason being that most entrepreneurs who started organised retail came from southern India and the cost of real estate in the southern region was less than other regions (particularly north and west). Since then, however, organised food retailing has emerged across the country, inspired by the presence of high potential markets in the north, west and east as well as the success of some non-food retailers and food services companies in these regions.

Food Retailing – The Buzz Word

Indian retail food industry has revolutionized shopping experience of Indian customers. Growing at the rate of 30%, the Indian food retail is going to be and no doubt is the major driving force for the retail industry. Food accounts for the largest share of consumer spending.

Food and food products account for about 50% of the value of final private consumption. This share is significantly higher compared to developed economies, where food and food products account for about 20% of consumer spending. Ireena Vittal, principal, McKinsey & Co in Food Forum 2008, said, "At US$ 175 billion today the food industry is likely to grow to US$ 400 billion by 2025.

The percentage of income spent in households will drive growth in the food market. Indian consumers are happy with store goods than branded goods and are very conservative on packaged goods. There are 10 million street vendors in India, of which 6 million only sell food. Currently, the retail food sector is US$ 70 billion and is expected to rise to US$ 150 billion by 2025. Food has the largest consumption in the Indian economy and will remain the single largest category." Modern state of the food retailing is not a demand led but the supply led one. Major spending on food and increasing usage of out of home food consumption represent a significant opportunity for food retailers and food service companies.

Speaking in Food Forum India 2008, on the government's role in the food retailing development, Dave said, "The retail stores need to empower its stakeholders and deliver what the consumer wants. The vision for 2020 should be appropriate extension network, implementation of appropriate practice at farmers' level and infrastructure in the country."

There are various factors paving the way to revolutionizing food retailing in India. Among them few are:

- Changing life styles and tastes
- Growing need for convenience
- Increasing disposable income
- Increasing numbers of working women
- Change in consumption patterns
- Higher aspirations among youth
- Impact of western lifestyle
- Plastic Revolution – Increased use of credit cards and debit cards.

Up-and-coming Food Retail Formats

With the changing food consumption patterns, consumers need for convenience, choice and value for money the setup of retail format is changing. The Indian consumers do visit about eight to ten outlets to purchase various food products, which make up the daily consumption basket. These outlets include neighbourhood kirana stores, bakeries, fruit and vegetable outlets, dairy booths and chakkies (small flour mills), which is very time-consuming and unproductive way of shopping for food. With changing lifestyle there is growing scarcity of time, and convenience in food shopping is emerging as an important driver of growth of one-stop retail formats that can offer consumer 'value for time' in addition to 'value for money'. These are giving an opportunity to various other retail formats.

Neighbourhood Stores

In India about 90% of food purchases are made within a distance of 1.5 km from the customer's home. This means that an organised retailer would need to have a 'neighbourhood store' close to customers in order to capture the share of wallet that is spent on food. These stores would cater to the consumer's daily and weekly needs. The outlets closest to a neighbourhood store in India are 'Safal' outlets operated by Mother Dairy in Delhi, Margin Free in Kerala and Subhiksha.

Supermarkets

This format caters to the consumers' need for choice and variety. These needs translate into 'more width' and 'more depth' in each category.

These stores cater to the consumers in a catchment area with a radius of 3 to 4 km and therefore need to be destination stores. A supermarket can cater to the consumers' weekly, monthly and occasional needs. Examples of supermarkets already in India are Food World, Trinetra and Nilgiri's.

Hypermarkets

Hypermarkets are essentially destination stores catering to the consumers' bulk shopping needs in both food and non-food categories. The key added values for the customer are 'choice' and 'value for money' because products are sold at a discounted price. The hypermarkets model of food retailing is new to India. Spencers (RPG), Big Bazaar (Pantaloons), Star India Bazaar.

Cash & Carry (C & C) Stores

These stores sell their products to their members only. The members are typically retailers and institutions. The key added value is a wide range of products under one roof, available at wholesale prices. Metro has started the first C & C store in India in Bangalore. The typical area of a C & C store is 70,000 to 100,000 sq. ft. and both food and non-food products are stocked.

Key Developments in Food Retail

The major development in food retail is consideration of Foreign Direct Investment (FDI) with a limitation that all companies would have to meet mandated export obligations. Food processing minister Subodh Kant Sahay told ET that "We are considering a proposal to allow FDI in food retail. It should be in such a way that it would boost our agriculture. Our farmers must also get benefits of economic liberalization". The government is also considering the opening up of the $330-billion retail market with adequate provisions to protect neighborhood stores.

In every retail format food trade is growing. More and more corporate houses such as HLL, ITC, Godrej and Reliance are already working into food retail. Huge increase is expected from the corporate players, which will help grow the entire food retail sector. Dabur's Amit Burman has also forayed into food retailing. According to Amit "Food and beverages retailing is a very attractive segment and with Lite Bite Concepts we are targeting Rs. 1,000 crore sales in a couple of years with around 200 outlets," Well-established players such as Subhiksha, Food Bazaar and Spencer's Daily are also tapping into backward linkages, while trying to match their expanding geographies with retail formats.

Also, most food retail players have been region-specific as far as geographical presence is concerned. Take the RPG Group's Food World, Nilgiris, Margin Free, Giant, Varkey's, all of which are more or less spread in the Southern region; Sabka Bazaar, Big Apple has a presence only in and around Delhi; names such as Haiko and Radhakrishna Foodland are Mumbai-centric; while Adani is Ahmedabad centric.

Retailers' Entrance in the Unbranded Food Space

Modern food formats like Food Bazaar and Spencer's have their eye on the unbranded part of the consumer's shopping basket. This constitutes as much as 60% of the total purchases and growing sharply, says AC Nielsen estimates. Retailers are offering a package of convenience and freshness, and have an edge over manufacturers that focus mainly on packaged conveniences. Food retailers are offering 'live kitchen' formats, which offer on-the-spot home-style gravies, dal, cooked rice and kneaded dough with options like grinding coffee fresh at store, idli batter, paneer, curd and cut vegetables.

Food for Retail Thought

Ratna Bhushan

First, some number crunching. According to a study on the food and grocery retail market by KSA Technopak, the country's overall retail sales now account for 44 per cent of its GDP. Food retail sales make up for close to 63 per cent of total retail sales. In absolute terms, food retail sales have grown from Rs. 3,81,000 crore in 1996, to Rs. 7,03,900 crore in 2001. And, just for the record, non-food retail sales have grown from Rs. 2,22,400 crore in 1996, to Rs. 4,19,000 crore in 2001.

Besides, the food and grocery sector now accounts for 14 per cent of total organised retail, after clothing and textiles (at 36 per cent) and watches and jewellery (at 17 per cent). Food and grocery retail offers the biggest opportunity for growth, provided levels of investment are high, says the KSA study. Now, a reality check. Modern, or organised retail, accounts for just about 1.6 per cent of the total retail sales in the country, estimated at Rs. 18,000 crore, says the KSA Technopak study.

The study further analyses that last year, for the first time in five years, retail shares of grocery dropped, even though in terms of absolute value, the shares remained stable. KSA Technopak attributes this to an international trend — even as total consumer expenditure rises, grocery shares slip at the cost of lifestyle-related expenses. A recently released CII-Jones Lang LaSalle report states that real estate has been the big deterrent to growth of the retail sector. The report highlights that areas that may require attention, consistency and radical change include area calculation, leasing costs and practices, deposit levels, operating costs and outgoings, property purchase practices, shopping mall building standards, and a legal framework.

Explains Arvind Singhal, Chairman, KSA Technopak, "Organised food and grocery retailing in India has a long, long way to go. The sector has not seen too many big entrants. The industry requires a lot more players. What it also requires is fundamental investments. That's not happening as yet." Agrees Raghu Pillai, President, Retail Business, RPG Enterprises, "There are not enough players. The business is not exactly cutting edge or sexy, the gestation periods are long, institutional funding is difficult, and there is none or little Government support. But I believe the industry will see large investments coming once the current ban on foreign direct investment is lifted. But that could be two-three years away."

Says R. Subramanian, Director of the Chennai-based discount retail chain, Subhiksha: "Food and grocery retailing is a tough business. Margins are low, and consumers are not dissatisfied with existing shops where they buy. For example, the next door grocery shopkeeper is smart and delivers good customer service, though not value."

Simone Tata's much-talked about food retailing venture under the Trent name, for example, is yet to take wing, even as there is talk of LifeStyle International planning a foray within this sector. As of now, while Chennai has some five organised food and grocery retail chains, other big cities such as Delhi, Bangalore, and Mumbai average only two-three such chains. Also, most food retail players have been region-specific as far as geographical presence is concerned.

Take the RPG Group's FoodWorld, Nilgiris, Margin Free, Giant, Varkey's and Subhiksha, all of which are more or less spread in the Southern region; Sabka Bazaar has a presence only in and around Delhi; names such as Haiko and Radhakrishna Foodland are Mumbai-centric; while Adani is Ahmedabad centric. Industry representatives say spreading presence across cities is a tough call. As Singhal points out, "Organised food and grocery retailing chains going national requires significant investments. Retailing within this sector is not just about the front-end, but involves complex supply chain and logistics issues as well."

Take FoodWorld, which came in first in the food and grocery retailing sector. The chain has no plans to venture beyond the Southern region just yet. "Our current plan is to focus on the Southern markets and achieve saturation. Maybe by 2005, we could look at the other regions, but there are no firm plans as yet," says Pillai. FoodWorld has a current sales figure of Rs. 350 crore. Subhiksha too is gung-ho about the future of the discount chain. Says Subramanian, "We deliver significant price value to the customer. We want to be the principal store of purchase for at least 40 per cent of all consumers living within 500-750 meters of the store, that is, within walking distance." Meanwhile, the RPG group plans to take its new formats such as Giant Hypermarkets national over the next three years. Grocery is a large component of this format, but not the only one.

Elaborating on the hurdles of going pan-Indian, Pillai observes: "Fundamentally, the way a basic grocery retailing model works is that the high setup costs in terms of setting up buying/distribution infrastructure is gradually amortised over a larger number of stores. The back-end costs without distribution centre costs, or what in retail jargon is called retail administration costs, should stabilise at around 2.5 per cent to 3 per cent of sales." Pillai says the obstacles of looking at a pan-India model for grocery are several. Given the federal nature of the country, the weak infrastructure and the major variances in eating habits in different parts of the country, one will have to replicate the retail administration costs for at least each region and therefore the gestation period of the project becomes huge.

"Of course, if one can get a model in place where the upfront store revenues scale very rapidly, then it is possible. Therefore, if one is to attempt a pan-Indian grocery foray, it will have to be in the hypermarket format with its attendant investment numbers and risk profile," he adds. Adds Arif Sheikh, President, Sabka Bazaar (owned and promoted by Home Stores India Ltd.): "While margins in the food and grocery business are only about 15 per cent, supply chain management costs are very steep. Therefore, it is difficult for food retail chains to go national."

Sabka Bazaar currently has 19 outlets in and around Delhi, and there are no immediate plans to spread wing. Sheikh presents another argument. According to him, there is so much potential to extract from individual regions, that players are in no tearing hurry to spread out. He cites a recent IMRB study, according to which in the six major metros, Delhi has the highest per capita consumption of food and grocery, among supermarkets. Chennai, the mecca of retailing, comes at fourth place. "This shows the high potential the sector presents. Chennai has some five supermarkets, and each of these are doing well for themselves. So there is enough scope to expand even in one single city." Sabka Bazaar is now generating sales of Rs. 11 crore from its 19 stores, says Sheikh. Pantaloon Retail (India) Ltd., which operates two types of retail formats, made its maiden foray in food and grocery retailing in the North late last month. Big Bazaar, Pantaloon group's discount store chain, has taken off to a roaring start in Delhi, says a company official. The Pantaloon Big Bazaar in Delhi is the sixth for the group, and the first in North India. According to a Pantaloon official, existing Big Bazaar stores in cities such as Hyderabad, Bangalore and Mumbai attract footfalls of 20,000 to 25,000 per day, more so during weekends.

While Big Bazaar is essentially a discount store retailing product categories ranging from food and grocery to apparel to footwear to home and interior products, food and grocery retailing forms a significant part of the chain's business. "Typically, while food and grocery retailing does well at the beginning of the month, the apparel sector sees maximum offtake during festivals," points out a Pantaloon Big Bazaar official. The Pantaloon group is now gearing up to open its next Big Bazaar in Nagpur within a few months time. Of course, this is the tip of the iceberg, and KSA Technopak's projections will well give a shot in the arm to the industry. Given that organised retail has been registering growth rates of approximately 40 per cent over the last three years, it is expected to grow to about Rs. 35,000 crore in 2005, and close to Rs. 70,000 crore in 2010.

And as an industry analyst elaborates, "Some years down the line, food and grocery stores will become dominating trade partners for the food industry, which, in turn, will be forced to offer special discounts and trade terms for them to get the shelf space in such stores. Also, once established, in-store label brands will become a real threat to the industry as manufacturers will have to compete with the store label brands which are generally very price-competitive." Replicating the success stories of names such as Sainsbury and Tesco may still be a distant dream for Indian food and grocery retailers, but at least the winds are blowing in the direction of growth.

Market Focus and Position

The industry's complexity has led to the evolution of very different organizational models. Many food and beverage companies are still organized along local or regional lines, with a presence in a limited number of categories, often those with a short shelf life. Other companies have taken a global, multicategory approach, remaining highly diversified in many different categories but with a small number of truly global brands. Only the industry's high-performance businesses have become successful category specialists, with a presence across most geographies but with a limited product portfolio, tightly focused on a handful of categories and power brands.

This strategic category domination is a key element of their market focus and position and also critical to the high-performance status of these companies. While their peers battle to build share and struggle for shelf space, high-performance businesses have successfully leveraged their top brands, targeting categories that have low private-label penetration and the potential to increase both the amount and frequency of purchase. High-performance businesses in this industry have consistently focused on being either No. 1 or No. 2 in a limited number of high-growth, high-margin categories or niches. Chewing gum giant Wrigley Co., for example, confines itself to the confectionery category. And although PepsiCo plays across numerous soft drink categories, its food presence is limited to a small global portfolio of snacks whose flavours and packaging are adjusted to accommodate local tastes around the world—a natural fit with its carbonates portfolio.

High-performance businesses achieve category domination with a selective approach to acquisitions, which concentrates on reducing portfolio complexity while increasing category domination, distribution power and geographic reach. Witness PepsiCo's acquisitions of Quaker Oats Co. and South Beach Beverages Co. (SoBe), with which the company sought to either gain entry into or reinforce its dominance in attractive, fast-growing categories. The Quaker Oats acquisition, which included Gatorade, was designed to bolster PepsiCo's competitive position vis-a-vis the Coca-Cola Co. in the energy drinks category, and SoBe reinforced PepsiCo's position in premium specialty beverages. Both brands are fast-growing, high-margin categories in line with the health trend—helping to counterbalance PepsiCo's traditional carbonates portfolio. More average performers, by contrast, still operate according to a global, multicategory model, which dramatically increases their exposure to business complexity and thus inhibits growth. One company has a presence across more than a dozen separate food and drink categories; another has an even more diverse product portfolio that includes a large number of local, often non-scalable and undifferentiated brands. The strategic category message, however, is clearly catching on.

French multinational Groupe Danone, for example, has been systematically shedding noncore businesses while refocusing its portfolio to concentrate on higher-growth regional opportunities and on health-conscious products like pro-biotic yogurt, where it now leads the market. Indeed, Danone is now enjoying its strongest revenue growth in a decade.

Distinctive Capabilities

Every high-performance business, in every industry, displays a unique set of connected business processes and resources that create value for its customers. Taken together, these processes and resources make up a company's distinct business formula, or its distinctive capability. Although these formulas can vary from company to company, there are three business characteristics that are common to the distinctive capabilities of all top performers in the food industry, which set them apart from their peers and are very difficult to replicate:

- Insight-driven marketing
- Customer and channel management
- Flexible and low-cost operations.

None of these characteristics would be as effective, of course, if they did not also rest on the exceptionally robust performance foundations that distinguish high-performance businesses—the sales and marketing, supply chain, finance, IT and HR functions that comprise a sound business infrastructure. Moreover, all three common characteristics work together to help make high performance possible.

Insight-driven marketing, for example, supports superior customer and channel management, and both depend on the flexible and low-cost operations that enable seamless execution. Only PepsiCo can lay claim to outperformance across all three characteristics.

Wrigley does well, but its high-performance status is partly due to being "category-advantaged"—the company is focused almost exclusively on the confectionery category, especially chewing gum, which is a high-margin product. Insight-driven marketing hinges on the ability to spot trends first, before the competition. High-performance businesses can do this because of their superior understanding of both market dynamics and consumer needs.

These companies relentlessly track key consumer trends in strategic geographies by means of exceptionally rigorous, sophisticated and fact-based business analytics that deliver relevant and insightful data. They then use the data to systematically manage the insights they have gained—not just to manage information. What's more, they make these insights accessible right across the organization to facilitate rapid and well-informed decision making. There is no direct correlation in this industry between the size of R&D investment and high performance. Instead, high-performance businesses distinguish themselves by rapidly capitalizing on consumer insight to deliver a continuous flow of new products to the market.

Incremental Innovation

High performers tend to have strong new-product pipelines to continuously refresh their portfolios. They also derive a large proportion of sales from products launched in the past three years. Innovations are often incremental rather than spectacular, science-driven or breakthrough in nature. But the continuous refreshment of a company's product portfolio is absolutely vital to the retention of consumer interest and the maintenance of retail shelf space. These refreshments include line extensions, repackaging and reformulations, as well as genuinely new products. Overall, incremental product innovation accounts for most of this mix and plays a critical role. Most of Wrigley's new products, for example, are line extensions or new flavours. However, by upgrading its R&D capabilities and restructuring its marketing team to focus on global brands and excellent local execution, the company has leveraged its unified commercial operations and centralized supply chain to consistently deliver innovation rates—measured as the percentage of sales from products launched in the past three years—above 15 percent every year since 2000.

High-performance businesses in this industry support their innovation capabilities by spending a higher proportion of sales than their peers—between 6 percent and 13 percent, compared with an industry average of 5.4 percent on a three-year average—on innovative marketing, revitalizing their brands through advertising and promotions. Take, for example, PepsiCo's repositioning of its portfolio on a better-for-you platform through the Smart Spot initiative. Smart Spot labelled products—more than 100 of the company's "healthier" products, including the Tropicana range of fruit juices—meet nutrition criteria based on recommendations from the Food and Drug Administration and the National Academy of Sciences. Although Smart Spot is currently confined to North America, it is earmarked for European rollout, and the company now devotes half of its media spending to the initiative.

To be sure, not all attempts to capitalize on the health and wellness trend have been successful. For one food giant, an effort to reformulate hundreds of products with nutrition in mind was compromised by the product portfolio itself, which included too many diverse categories.

Focus on Customers, Channels

Food and beverages companies must also contend with both the growing power of supermarkets and the private-label penetration this power reinforces. In addition, they face the challenge of a multichannel selling environment as the share of sales through alternative channels, including kiosks and vending machines, steadily increases. Indeed, customer and channel management is critically important. And with their laserlike focus on key customers and channels, high-performance businesses are well ahead of their competitors in this regard as well. Witness Kellogg Co.'s purchase of Keebler Foods Co., whose cookies and crackers are available in vending machines across the United States. The acquisition not only gave Kellogg critical mass in US snacks, it also allowed the company to distribute its own Pop-Tarts, Nutri-Grain bars and packaged cereals through many more channels, greatly extending its customer reach.

As with R&D expenditures, simply boosting investment in trade promotions does not guarantee better returns, so high-performance businesses go further. They not only employ integrated commercial planning to maximize the effectiveness of trade investments. They also use sophisticated analytics to evaluate the performance of past promotions, and include the results in the next round of promotional planning—all with an execution mindset worthy of a financial fund manager. Confronted with the complaints of frustrated shoppers who just could not find enough of its products on supermarket shelves, Campbell Soup Co. used its insights into how shoppers shop and store workers stock shelves to design a gravity-fed shelf system. The system, which shows store workers just which soups are running out and need replenishing, has been installed in outlets throughout the United States, Canada and Mexico. Since its introduction in 2004–05, the so-called iQ Shelf Maximizer has boosted sales by more than 8 percent in participating stores, and key outlets are performing significantly above the industry average in sales of condensed soups.

Performance Anatomy

Performance anatomy basically refers to a company's culture—which is, in turn, made up of its leadership values, strategic history and, most important, the winning mindsets that inform an organization's approach to executing its strategy.

In the food and beverages industry, a critical mindset is adaptability. High-performance businesses in this industry are just much better—not only than their competitors but also than their peers in related sectors, like alcoholic beverages or home and personal care, that enjoy greater leverage in their retail relationships—at working with and cooperating with their suppliers and customers.

Operating margins are lower than in related industries—a function of a relatively short product shelf life. So whether they like it or not, food and beverages companies are very dependent on external relationships and hence need to be tightly networked. High-performance businesses are especially good at third-party manufacturing, distribution and low-cost sourcing, and their relative dependence on their retail outlet customers also has led to close and highly successful working relationships. Some actually have integrated their supply chains with those of their customers so that information about consumption and demand can flow seamlessly between retailer and producer.

This industry's high-performance businesses have turned category focus, incremental innovation, targeted marketing and R&D investment, and ruthless cost control into a recipe that delivers long-term shareholder value. They have achieved this advantageous position by means of rigorous portfolio management and by developing highly flexible organizations with distinctive capabilities that enable them to seamlessly embrace and execute change. However, there are many challenges to the future value of the food industry. While consolidation continues, it is likely to be very gradual, as long as local taste and shelf-life issues limit economies of scale and most producers still juggle with the complexity of managing a diverse and often locally customized brand portfolio.

Accenture research suggests that the key to capturing future growth opportunities will remain a relentless focus on premium product categories—foods and drinks that satisfy at least two of the three big drivers of new demand (convenience, health and pleasure) and ideally all of them. Indeed, the high-performance businesses of the future will stand above their competitors because of their ability to exploit the big trends—for "fast and efficient nutrition," "guilt-free indulgence" and "quality convenience."

7

Beverage Industry

The food industry is on a roller coaster ride as Indians continue to have a feast. Fuelled by– large disposable incomes – the food sector is witnessing a remarkable change in consumption patterns, especially in terms of food.

Food retailing has come of age — from a period when food items were sold in small road side grocer shops & mandis, haats and bazzars by vendors to a stage when food products (processed and groceries) are retailed through supermarket stores where consumers can inspect, select and pick up the products they like in a comfortable ambience and still pay a fair price for the product and the merchandise and sometimes even pay less than the price they would have paid at the nearest food stores. Shopping for groceries is no longer a strenuous and uncomfortable affair. Instead, it is a pleasurable experience. From simple trading activity, food retailing is now heading to the status of an industry. Imagine yourself walking through the air conditioned lanes smelling fresh food and groceries, enjoying light music, experiencing five star ambiences and above all buying food products (vegetables, spices and beverages) without bargaining with the vendors. Food retail has surpassed the dominating apparel and accessories sector. "Contrary to the belief that fashion is the largest segment of organised retail in India, food & beverages is the major segment, worth Rs. 8,97,000 crore," said Arvind Singhal, Chairman, Technopak, at the Indian Retail Forum held in Mumbai. There is an old industry saying that " customer is king" Food retailers today will update that saying to "customers is the dictator" because of fierce competition, new technology and business practices the market power of customer is strong and growing stronger.

The Food Reta]il Tale

Traditionally, Indians were used to buying their sugar, wheat, pulses, rice etc. from their neighborhood baniya. The majority of food and food products were and still are retailed through neighborhood kirana (baniya) stores. A typical kirana store has a retail area of 200 sq. ft. and sells 500 to 800 stock keeping units (SKUs). The kirana stores focus on dry food products because the infrastructure for cold storage is lacking. The majority of fresh produce is sold from the carts of travelling vendors. Such produce is deemed to be of low product quality, variety and hygiene. This concept is still popular in B-class and II Tier cities of India and giving employment to thousands of its inhabitants. Initially the food retail format was seen in A-class cities like Mumbai, Delhi, Chennai which had co-operative stores like "Apna Bazaar" in Mumbai and "Kendriya Bhandar" in Delhi. Both were very successful and are operating many outlets in all strategic localities in the city.

Escorts group in the late eighties diversified into non-auto sectors by getting into agri business or food business. It came out with first "Nanz" store at South Extension in Delhi in 1990. The first visible sign of the change in food retailing was seen in mid-eighties. Around that time a few new food stores were set up in all metro cities in India. Calcutta was the only exception where it started a little later. At that time couple of leading food stores started operating such as "Morning Stores" and "Modern Stores" in Delhi, "Nilgiri" in Bangalore, and "Food Land" in Mumbai "Spencers Food Stores" in Chennai. Spencers were the first to tie up with a Singapore based large retail chain — "Dairyland" and had set up the food stores in Chennai. This was a technology tie up. In Mumbai, Garware group during the late eighties had set up a large food store, which is now reported to have been closed down. Until the late 1990s, food retailing has been concentrated in the south of the country. Southern India has been witnessing revolutionized activity in food retailing.

It has thoroughly experienced the food retailing in various formats such as the supermarkets, hypermarkets and neighbourhood stores. These include Food World, Subhiksha, Nilgiris, Margin Free, and Big Bazaar. The reason being that most entrepreneurs who started organised retail came from southern India and the cost of real estate in the southern region was less than other regions (particularly north and west). Since then, however, organised food retailing has emerged across the country, inspired by the presence of high potential markets in the north, west and east as well as the success of some non-food retailers and food services companies in these regions.

Neighbourhood Stores

In India about 90% of food purchases are made within a distance of 1.5 km from the customer's home. This means that an organised retailer would need to have a 'neighbourhood store' close to customers in order to capture the share of wallet that is spent on food. These stores would cater to the consumer's daily and weekly needs. The outlets closest to a neighbourhood store in India are 'Safal' outlets operated by Mother Dairy in Delhi, Margin Free in Kerala and Subhiksha.

Food Research Institutions in India

Produce Little Value

Food Science and Technology Education in India was initially masterminded by pure scientists in the field of chemistry, applied chemistry and biochemistry. The boderline between the basic science and technology and engineering was therefore not clearly demarcated at the initial stage. As a result, research projects that were undertaken in most of our premium food research institutions including Central Food Technological Research Institute (CFTRI) were designed on the line of basic science exploration in the areas of biochemistry, protein chemistry, nutrition and food processing. Those who have ventured into the processing and technology also focussed only on physiochemical changes of food during processing and process parameters optimization.

Those who have ventured a little ahead thus incorporated process conditions standardisations to improve product quality. Nothing therefore happened in terms of any major breakthrough in process technology in India. Our food research institutes including universities did very little in terms of technology upgradation and new product development which are of any commercial significance. Whatever little we have seen in new product development and product quality upgradation is the result of the efforts on the part of the industry largely triggered from the need as a survival strategy in the face of competition. Some of these research institutions also suffer from the syndrome of reinventing the wheel. Crores of rupees have been spent by young food researchers reproducing the knowledge which are either known and or explored elsewhere. This therefore has put the industry, in particular and the nation, in general into the back gear.

We have to painfully observe in various conferences and seminars that the research findings are presented with lot of gusto which are nothing more than the age old findings and established processes.

Another factor that has marked the failure of food research activities in India to create any dent in terms of value addition in the processing and technology is due to the fact that there was little or no collaborative efforts between industry and research institutions. The mutual mistrust and lack of confidence on the part of the industry leaders on the ability of the institutional research to deliver value has increased with the passage of time. As a result, researchers have ventured into their own chosen subjects while industries have decided to go it alone. Formation of an independent Ministry of Food Processing Industry which has now been reduced to the status of a department did not help change this scenario. The result is inevitable. While we can see a sea change in other industry categories in terms of product quality and value addition, in case of processed food industry changes are miniscule to say the least, and that too largely due to the efforts of the industry. On the top of it, some of our premium institutions are in reality in a state of decay in terms of quality of research and education.

The research activities that have been initiated earlier by the pioneers in food research and education have lost the inertia in the later years and thus died down. In this context we can remember the name of Prof. V. Subramaniam, first Director of CFTRI, Prof. A.N. Bose, first Director of Central Marine Product Research Institute in Cochin, Prof. A. Sreenivasan-First Director of Food Technology Dept. of BARC. Prof. Gopalan, first Director of Nutrition Research Institute (NII) at Hyderabad etc. CFTRI has seen some of the stalwarts in later years which include the names like Mr. C.P. Natarajan, Dr. H.A.B. Parpia, Dr. B.L. Amia and few others.

National Dairy Research Institute (NDRI) in my reckoning, do have a creditable record of quality research output and in that also contribution of Dr. K.K. Iya and most importantly that of Dr. N. Ganguly are noteworthy. In oil technology Dr. K.T. Acharya's and Prof. M.M. Chakraborti's contribution is also significant. In the areas of biotechnology and biochemical engineering Prof. T.K. Ghose's contribution is pioneering. He has, in fact, given the shape to biochemical engineering education and research in India and was associated with Jadavpur University, HBTI-Kanpur and IIT-Delhi. Defece Food Research Laboratory (DFRL) in Mysore also worked on projects of specific interest to our defence forces.

In the areas of research and education we now have a generation gap. After the retirement and or passing away of some of these above mentioned stalwarts most of these food research institutions have been reduced to insignificance.

If I describe some of those as "in a pathetic state of affairs" it will not be any exaggeration and in that list my old institution namely, Jadavpur University also features. The reasons of such state of affairs are many. One, – relatively inferior quality of people have come into the research and education, two, – the system has made them dull and non motivated, and most importantly, our stalwarts have not taken any pains to leave any legacy to continue. As a result, with their disappearance from the scene the things have drifted and ultimately came to a grinding halt. And that is a major failure. There are enthusiastic scientists like Prof. A. Sreenivasan who developed protein food by name 'Spert' – a product manufactured and marketed by Sandoz. Prof. Sreenivasan also developed the process for production of egg powder at Foods and Inns where he was a consultant.

Foods and Inns share still is quoted at Rs.60 today and the company is still doing the same thing that they used to do during Prof. A. Sreenivasan's time. When 'Spert' was launched during the late seventies I was discussing, one evening, with Prof. Sreenivasan at his Gautam Apartments flat in Bandra in Mumbai and asked him whether he really believed that there was a need of any protein food for those who can afford to buy 'Spert'. He confided in me and told me "Look Rajat if one takes full meals of only dal and rice one's proteins requirements is met and these are all humbug".

I responded by saying that "then the consumers for these so called protein foods are really taken for a ride." The marketers like us know that if there is no permanent value proposition, products do not have a long term prospect in the marketplace. Possibly, for this reason protein foods gradually disappeared from the market like fads. Of late, I see the decline of the sales of Complain in the hands of Heinz. Prof. Sreenivasan changed jobs in public sector research institutions like one changes or sometimes forced to change in private sector. He used to be a man of very strong conviction and a forceful character and as a result nobody liked him. But his contribution to the industry is significant. Prof. Bose was a strong disciplinarian and perfectionist. His contribution in food research and education in noteworthy. He used to come to the department in Jadavpur University exactly at ten in the morning and used to take a round of the laboratories and classrooms.

During his time a lot of research projects were there in the department which was in the global map with respect to food research and education. Today one cannot find a teacher in the department till twelve noon.

No one comes before that. Jadavpur University did pioneering work in rice process technology, marine products processing and protein technology etc. in earlier years. As it stands now the future development thrust for the processed food industry therefore largely has to be provided by the private sector industries itself. As the market is becoming increasingly competitive the innovations in terms of quality, cost, packaging and product variants and new products will be the name of the game. And private sectors will have to provide the support for their own survival. This is possible. For example, Pepsi Cola in USA has kept on their roll over a dozen very senior level scientists specialised in each area of their activities to support the company's competitive strategy.

This team of specialists are basically the technical backbone working for various ongoing and existing and future projects of Pepsi. In that team Dr. Shanti R. Bhowmik, a close friend of mine and a former director of CFTRI is there. Dr. Bhowmik spent 2-yr. time at CFTRI and having got fed up of the bureaucracy and the inner politics of the institution and poor level of research activities decided to return to USA again. This was narrated to me by Dr. Bhowmik. Of course, he has also praised some of the research scientists for their quality of work and dedication and in that list the name of present Director of CFTRI Dr. V. Prakash's name featured.

I wonder if India has to be the leader in this new millennium, technical competency has to be improved for our domestic industry so that we can have more Tata-Tetly kind of organisation being created in global scenario. And that can happen only with private sector initiatives. Let us not keep much hope on our institutional and Govt.. run organisation's research effort. That has not happened in the past and I don't see that is happening in future either. The reality is that past of food research in India was more glorious than what it is now.

Acquisition of Domestic Food Business by MNCs

Liberalisation has brought in through the entry of large multinational and transnational corporations, foreign investment in this sector. This resulted in competition, technological upgradation and market expansion. In the face of the competition, domestic Industries are gradually losing market share and thus selling their businesses to the new entrant MNCs well before the value of the brand and businesses drops further due to ongoing onslaught of multinational brands.

This is happening because MNCs have much greater resources to put behind their brand and business and also have long term vision and sustainability. Domestic industries are no comparison. The first attack came in soft beverages industry with Coke acquiring Parle brands and Pepsi acquiring Dukes and with the entry of Cadbury Schweepes in this sector entire soft drink industry is now in control of MNCs. MNCs such as Nestle, Brooke Bond and SmithKline & Beechern controlled earlier only hot beverages (both white and brown segments). But soft beverage sector was dominated by domestic industries. With Coke and Pepsi acquiring Indian businesses, total nonalcoholic beverage industry is now under control of MNCs.

Recently Sara Lee — a US multinational has acquired Nutrine — a large Indian bakery and confectionery business. Britannia is already under control of Danone group of France. Only large bakery and confectionery left to be acquired in private sector is Parle Products. And with the entries of confectionery giants like Perfetti, Wriggly and Agrilimen (a Spanish confectioner in joint venture with Dabur but in the process of acquiring Dabur's equity to have 100% control) confectionery and bakery sector, will also become the domain of MNCs. With Nestles' strong presence in Tomato Ketchup and Pickles and Hindustan Lever acquiring Kissan and Dipy brands from UB group through Brooke Bond route fruit and vegetable sector is also dominated by multinationals.

Heinz, the world's largest Tomato Ketchup manufacturer had acquired food business of Glaxo. Due to strategic restructuring of portfolio Glaxo decided to divest their dairy business with established brands like Complain, Glucon-D and Farex. Hindustan Lever, on the other hand, through a strategic alliance route, took control of Kwality Ice-cream as well as 100% Ice-cream brand of Jagatjit. Hindustan Lever with their own presence in dairy sectors, and with the introduction of Baskin Robbins and Walls has emerged as a dominant player in dairy segment, in general and Ice-cream segment, in particular. Hindustan Lever (HLL) also acquired Dollop Ice-cream brand from Cadburys'.

HLL, however, recently announced their intention to sell-off their Dairy unit in UP. Ice-cream industry, which is reserved for small-scale sector, has now been in the control of multinationals through a different route. The argument that ice-cream is actually a frozen dessert — a nomenclature that has been accepted by both food and law ministry of Govt. of India — paved the way for Hindustan Lever for this strategic acquisition.

The earlier successful domestic businesses such as Dalmia Dairy, Foremost Industry and Jagatjit Industry in dairy sector are all in deep trouble — and MNCs have taken a control of this sector as well. National Dairy Development Board (NDDB) with its strong brand Amul and with its deep root extended up to farmers level as a means of backward integration will of course, remains a significant force to reckon with. But nobody will deny that in branded dairy products Amul has to put up a constant fight against multinational brands.

Vadilal is also a significant player in ice-cream but their presence is limited in Western India and for how long they will remain has to be seen. Kraft Foods a unit of Phillips Morris is holding a licence to set up 100% owned entity and they are expected to come and set up their operation anytime.

In the convenience foods — 'Corn Products', a US multinational is fast making progress. This is an old company, which did not make any significant contribution in the Indian food business largely because of lack of interest from their principals. CPC-International is now fast making progress with their well known Rex and Brown & Poison and Knorr soup brands. Recently they announced the acquisition of DCW Chemicals — makers of Captain Cook brands, which ran into rough weather because of the objection taken by some miller in Haryana to whom allegedly DCW. has contractual obligations. Shortly, we will also have products in joint venture with Paoma Industries, the manufacturer of Rasna soft drink mixes and Campbell a world leader in canned foods. Godrej, on the other hand, has joined hands with Pilsburry a leading player in the convenience foods business to boost their business activities. Filsburry has already introduced instant Cake mix. In this category others including Gits brand are relatively smaller and regional players. Apparently, first change that we have witnessed is of acquisitions of domestic brands in frontiers of food business by MNCs and alongwith although at a much lower scale a few joint ventures.

Even the public sector undertaking, Modern Foods although making profit is up for sale in line with the Govt. policy of PSU disinvestment and ANZ Bank has been appointed to find a buyer for the same. The first lesson that we have learnt as the effect of liberalisation is acquisition of successful domestic food business by MNCs.

Global Competition

Ten years ago Indian processed food industries were crying about high taxation, lack of infrastructural support, nonavailability of quality raw material at competitive price, nonavailability of latest packaging machinery and packing material etc. as the major reasons for poor or sluggish growth of this sector. But the industry was still growing then, albeit not at the expected level. Competition was also there amongst domestic processors with their MNC counterparts. Because, large MNC food companies like Nestle, SmithKline Becheern, Britannia, Glaxo, Hindustan Lever etc. are there for ages.

But domestic industries were not worried about their presence. There was healthy competition. In some areas domestic industries were doing even better than some of their nearest competitors in multinationals. What went wrong then? Why domestic industries are now not able to fight multinational giants? This is because the rules of the game have changed. Post liberalisation, we have now entered into an era of survival of the fittest. Only couple of years ago we had only Amul Cheese. Britannia first successfully introduced Cheese from cow milk followed by the introduction of French cheese 'Le'-Bon" from Dabur-Le'-Bon joint venture.

Philips Morris — owner of Kraft Foods — is sitting waiting a formal licence to set up 100% owned company in India. They carried out lot of research for introduction of Kraft cheese in India. Their project now has been put in cold storage and they are still waiting and watching the market for processed food industry. Upto mid eighties Kissan was the number one brand in Tomato Ketchup and around that time the competition came from Maggie — a Nestle's brand. With Maggie launching several varieties of Tomato Ketchup there was a growth in the market. With Kissan and Maggie fighting neck to neck other smaller but established brands like Dipy's from Herbertsons, Volfruit from Voltas, Noga of Nagpur Orange Federation and SunSip of Wimco gradually disappeared from the market.

Delmonte now has joined hands with Paoma Industries, the manufacturers of Rasna Brands of soft drink concentrate and is expected to launch Tomato Ketchup shortly. The biggest global player in Tomato Ketchup Heinz is still waiting and watching. It was expected that they will launch Tomato Ketchup in Indian market soon. Some of the unknown local brands of course still existing only on price competition. The price competition has also kept some of the other categories of food products still alive. For example, the age old Corn Flakes from Mohan Meakin under the brand name Champion still sells almost the same quantity (reportedly 500 MT per annum) against the much better quality Kellogs brand which sells around 300 MT per year with all its variants.

Till today we have only Parle and Britannia as two major brands in biscuits. Kellog is entering that segment gradually. Cadbury and SmithKline Becheem have nominal presence with speciality biscuits. Shortly, we are going to see more cookies and speciality biscuits from Sara Lee, which has acquired Nutrine. In the snack foods category we have two successful Indian players namely Uncle Chips brand of Amrit Foods and Pepi of SM Dye Chem, others were local such as Fun Flip, Crax etc. Soon entered Pepsi with their Ruffles brand and soon extended to Indian snacks by introducing bhujjias which Bikanerwala makes for them to market. In confectionery we have over half a dozen global players struggling here for brand share and fighting against Indian players like National, Norton, Parle, Parrys etc. Amongst MNCs in this field leading are Perfetti, Wriggley, Agrilimen, Park Davis (with their chicklet brand).

Competition is also seen in organised food retail chains. Couple of years ago we had only Narula running such an organised retail food chain. Today we have everybody namely. McDonald, Kentucky's Fried Chicken, Dorninos, Pizza Hut of Pepsi's and many more. In some of these categories domestic brands are still a leader-for example, Uncle Chips, Frooty, Rasna etc. But how long they will be able to retain their leadership is a big question mark? If, potato price continues to remain at the present level possibly Pepsi's Raffle will still continue even after incurring losses but Uncle Chip will have to close its shutters.

As others are doing — for example Billy's Ltd. — an Indian company in technical assistance with Florigo of Netherlands had successfully introduced potato chips in Eastern India and was reportedly doing well. As potato price started shooting up the company could not afford to sell its brand at a competitive price and is now in the process of closing down. With highly fluctuating input price, domestic industries will be all the more vulnerable like the one as we have seen in case of Billy's. The second lesson that we have learnt is that in each category now we have global competition with more players expected to jump into the fray. Domestic processors will have to learn to survive competition. But consumers are the real beneficiaries, they have now a wide choice.

Technological Upgradation Leading to Superior Quality

Food processing industry in India has undergone a total metamorphosis over the last six to seven years, in terms of types, variety, quality and presentation which is a result of liberalisation leading to foreign direct investment in frontiers of processed food sectors. Multinational and transnational corporations made significant contribution. This was possible due to market significant technological upgradation in this sector. It is not that the latest state-of-the-art technologies in this sector were not known to us. On the contrary, we had the fullest capability and technical know-how. In seventies and eighties we used to talk about in seminars and conferences the new types of packaging, products and processes but industries never felt the necessity to upgrade or invest in new technology. Nor did they have the resources to support such programme. Reason was is the apprehension all around that there would be no market for such products. And we continued to produce products that are of traditional nature using age-old technologies. Besides, there would were licensing restrictions, reservation of many categories under small-scale sectors etc., resulting of into poor or negligible upgradation of the industry. Things have changed since then.

With the technological upgradation we now see an all round improvement in processed food products quality. The competition has forced the processors to improve and the upgrade the quality. Earlier we had limited categories, for example, jam, jellies, marmalades, squashes, cordials, ketchup and sauces in fruit and vegetable sector, ice cream, spray dried milk powder, condensed milk, butter and ghee in dairy sector, bread, biscuits and pancakes in bakery sector, hard boiled confectioneries, one brand and type of chewing gum and limited variety of chocolate in confectionery sector. Today we have not only better quality of these but also a lot of variants and product types and choices. There is also a significant improvement in packaging quality. In seventies we had only glass and cans as packaging materials. In eighties we had seen laminates and other plastic materials coming in.

Today we have the host of packaging types being used to market processed food products. Earlier we used to get fruit juices and ready-to-service (RTS) beverages only in glass bottles. Today we have tetra pack and also asceptic carton pack. Similarly, tomato paste earlier used to be sold in metal cans and the market for this was also very small. Today tomato paste is sold by Godrej Foods in asceptic consumer pack. In packaging of cheese and other dairy products considerable improvement in the product and packaging quality are evidenced. Cheese, as a product was not known to the Indian consumer in seventies and eighties. Only cheese that we had was cottage cheese.

Processed cheese was not there, not to speak of varieties of cheese as they are found and consumed in other countries. I remember during early eighties we had to develop a particular party near Delhi to supply Mozzrella cheese required for pizza to be sold through Mcdowells Fast Food chain which subsequently closed down.

Today although we don't have all varieties of cheese but we have seen a beginning. Britannia and La-bon cheese are definitely gaining ground. And we expect that when Kraft will enter this market there will be a revolution in processed cheese sector in India.

Kraft International has done considerable research on the possibility of producing world class Kraft cheese for Indian market and they came to the conclusion that the milk quality in India is not good enough to produce cheese of Kraft grade. Besides, Kraft cheese is produced from cow milk where as in India bulk of our milk is from buffalow. They even thought of importing the compressed casein block to Nepal under refrigerated condition and set up processing plant there for Indian market in order to take the custom duty advantage because quality is what they can not sacrifice. But that also was not found to be viable. I told Mr. Puno who is in charge of South East Asian region including Indian subcontinent that starting early is the key. I advised him to start the operation first and cow milk can be made available or can be organised.

But they had still the apprehensions. Britannia subsequently introduced cheese and their sole claim is "Cheese from cow milk" and has done very well if initial responses are any indication. And it is everybody's knowledge that Britannia is not manufacturing it themselves but it is being manufactured in a local plant near Pune under a subcontract manufacturing arrangement. Britannia is only marketing it. Although process technology support might come from their respective French collaborators namely BSN and LA-BON, but this only proves my contention that technology is known to us but we did not put it to application to tap new and emerging market. Competition is forcing the marketeers to look for better products and new products, which is a direct outcome of the liberalisation policy.

Even the traditional item like Indian snacks (bhujjia) and Bengali sweets manufacturers are also thinking to upgrade their manufacturing technology and product quality. Mr. Agarwal, Managing Director of Bikanerwala who supplies bhujjia to Pepsi Foods recently invited me to visit his plant at Lawrence Road in Delhi and said Pepsi's global chief also visited his plant and was highly impressed to see their process. When asked what exactly the improvement they have made in their age-old labour oriented process, Mr. Agarwal commented that the packaging of Bujjia is now fully mechanised.

Similarly sweets are also a serious trade worth Rs.16500 crore and in West Bengal alone the market is estimated to be Rs.1000 crores. The Sweet Traders Association in West Bengal recently held a seminar in Calcutta to devise ways of making the sweet making process more hygienic and to ensure optimum use of technology _ said Mr. Robin Pal, General Secretary of the Association. The implications of liberalisation has also reached these so-called traditional foods and the traders now are eyeing for the global market.

Under liberalisation regime consumer is the king. They are getting better value for money and they have now a wide choice to select from.

Proliferation and Extension of Food Brands

Food items are primarily processed to extend its shelf life and to preserve its nutritional value. The secondary purpose of processing of food is to deliver convenience, taste and appeal to the target consumers. Depending upon what consumer segments we are targeting the processing methods, type of food and its taste and packaging and total presentation varies widely. In a country like India where local taste preferences differ from region to region it poses a much bigger problem to produce food products which can have a much larger acceptance and hence a bigger market potential. But there are some food categories and types for which there is a universal acceptance and hitherto Indian processed food industry only were processing those generic category of foods for all India market. Even new entrants in the processed food industry were only adding brands in the traditional sectors. We have witnessed this phenomenon before liberalisation in different categories. And as a result, mortality rate of processed food brands were quite high. For example, when Amul came into the market with their Amul Butter-Polsons butter disappeared from the scene. And the successful brand went on extending it to other categories. Having tasted success, Amul brand has been extended across a range of items including cheese, cheese spread, shrikhand, chocolate and ice-cream.

Creativity in food industry was, to say the least, very low. There were of course small local companies who attempted to create products for catering to the local taste preferences but the market was so small that the products did not survive the test of time. For example Kissan launched "Bisebelle Bhath" a South Indian delicacy in Southern market in mid eighties only to withdraw a year later. We at Kissans did considerable work and developed instant rice but market research indicated that the market for instant rice would be insignificant and thus we had to drop the idea.

The same instant rice was used to formulate "Bisebelle bhath". Phillips Morris who got clearance recently for setting up 100% owned entities in India has announced their plans to introduce the instant rice under their global and popular brand "Minute Rice". And still there are others who tried to create universal appeal and introduced mass market product and have demonstrated big success stories. The example is Rasna from Pioma Industries. But how they did it is a different story and that will be covered in another article. Yet others have failed in such attempt. In mid eighties steel merchant of Mumbai Mr. Ravi Kiran Agarwal in a joint venture with Kwality Frozen Foods had set up Tasty Bite Eatables Ltd.-a company to get into frozen foods and North Indian and South Indian vegetarian and non-vegetarian ready-to-serve foods.

The concept was-warm and serve. A modern plant was set up near Pune. The products including Mutton curry etc. in retortable pouch were introduced but it did not click. A couple of years later they faced serious financial problems and subsequently the company was sold to Hindustan Lever-who tried hard to establish "Green Valley" frozen foods. It was also later on withdrawn. Welga Foods in Badaun near Bareilly similarly had to close down their frozen foods plant. Tarai Foods who were also contract manufacturers for Hindustan Lever is still struggling to exist. The only long term player in frozen foods particularly frozen vegetables is "Mafco" — a co-operative in Maharashtra. Food products that were in the high price range and were well ahead of their time did not succeed in India. And thus casualties in certain category were very high.

Before nineties the food industry in India was struggling to establish only the traditional food brands and there was very little or no effort to introduce new foods. In post liberalisation era we have host of new MNCs with superior marketing skill and bigger resource to their command have extended their brands to a wide variety of local foods and their variants including the areas which were protected niches of small local players. For example, Indian traditional snacks were only local brands even a couple of years ago. But there we have now even global brands. Kissan under UB-group used to sell and market only fruit and vegetable products. Today Kissan brand has been extended to even branded grocery items which were earlier the domain of small local players.

Pepsi's primary business is in soft drinks but in India they have gone into branding of traditional snack foods. Similarly Nestle-a swiss Food major-has introduced pickles in Indian market. In the traditional food items local companies should be able to add better value and hence can score higher in the market place. In seventies, 'Bisleri' was the only mineral water which had national presence and the sale was to the tune of approximately one hundred thousand cases valued at about Rs.60 lacs. Today mineral water market is said to be of Rs.200 crores and over hundred brands of mineral water are there.

Mr. Ramesh Chauhan of Parles thinks that mineral water market in next five years time will become Rs.2000 crores and based on that he has drawn up ambitious plan for his Bisleri mineral water. The competition in mineral water is so high that Mr. Ramesh Chauhan's own brother Mr. Prakash Chauhan who owns "Frooty" brand also introduced a mineral water under the brand name "Bailey". Of late we have multinationals entering the mineral water scene. "Evan" is recently launched which is a well known international brand.

Earlier we did not have any fruit juice in the market. Only canned juice and ready-to-serve beverages in bottles were available. Today we have number of brands in carton and tetrapack. Such as 'Onjus' of Enkay Texofood, 'Real juice' of Dabur, 'Jumpy' of Godrej etc. all packed in convenient asceptic cartons. We will be shortly getting more brands of fruit juice including 'Tropicana' from Seagram. The proliferation of brands are also seen in branded Grocery products. A few years ago we had 'Tata-salt' as the only refined iodised salt selling in the market and today we have 'Captain Cook' from DCW, 'Kissan Annapurna' from Kissan Products and Catch (with dispenser) from Hi-Tech Foods and more brands to come in. In some areas such as meat and poultry products branding, packaging, processing and distribution on a national scale has yet to be witnessed. But in many of the processed food categories, as we can see that the existing brand is either extended to a wide variety of foods such as Britannia to Cheese and Long Life Milk in tetrapack etc. or there are proliferation of brands. In this process, ultimate beneficiary is the consumer as they can expect to get the best value for their money. Competitive pressure will make that possible.

MNCs' Entering Traditional Foods Sectors

Mckensey did a study on the opportunity in India for food and agri business at the behest of Confederation of Indian Industries (CII). And as expected they projected a huge potential in food sectors and said that the real potential lies in traditional, local food and grocery items — but not so much in westernised processed food. Some of our big multinationals seem to have swallowed the Mckensey advise-pill and got into this sunrise sectors.

Historically, traditional food items were the domain of small local players. Grocery items earlier were sold loose and unbranded. Then some progressive traders started the cleaning, grading and primary packaging. And the next stage of development was branding of primary foods such as Atta (wheat flour), Rice etc. but those were mainly regional brands. Popular among these were "Rose" and "Shakti Bhog" brands in northern India. Whereas in traditional food items such as spice and pickles there were host of local brands with regional strongholds such as 'Cookme' spice powder in East, 'Bedekar' pickles in West, 'MDH-masala' in North etc., to name a few. And the food ingredients — nobody thought of. Only food ingredient that was there was tomato puree and paste in cans which in the recent times Godrej introduced in tetrapack. Edible oil in tin pack and later on in polyester jar and tetrapack were the first major step in branding grocery items. "Postman"— peanut oil from Ahmed Mills was one of the oldest popular brands.

Today we get variety of edible oils and NDDB and Marico are the leading players in this sector. Amongst MNCs we have "Mazola" corn oil from CPC and "Sundrop" from ITC Agro — a sunflower oil which subsequently has been acquired by CONAGRA-the fastest growing food company in America. With CPC and CONAGRA being involved in edible oil market this sector is going to be soon dominated by MNCs. The next major attempt to market a branded grocery item was done about a decade ago by Tatas by introducing the first refined iodised salt in poly bag by brand name "Tata Salt" and that was a success. The next big brand in this category is "Captain Cook" from DCW Chemicals who had plans in branded grocery items and thus the company introduced other items including wheat flour under the same brand name. But that was shortlived. During 1997 DCW Chemicals suffered a major setback and the company decided to divest this food business. The acquirer is Corn Products Co. (India) Ltd. — a wholly owned subsidiary of CPC-International a nine billion US dollar American multinational in food and grocery business.

The company has recently changed its name to Best Foods Ltd. CPC was a sleepy company operating in India for over fifty years and their performance was lacklustre. With their limited range of Rex and Brown and Polson brands of convenience foods, the parent company, although doing well globally did not have any commitment in India. In late seventies and early eighties when I was heading their project department many investment proposals were sent and notably among those were dextrose manufacturing project as CPC has a flavoured glucose brand in the portfolio and Knorr soup project. But project work used to be carried out by us endlessly but nothing got implemented. In post liberalisation era, this apparently sleepy company seems to have become active. The third brand of salt is "Kissan Annapurna" which is making a sustained effort to get market share. This brand which is now in Hindustan Lever's fold through Brook Bond acquistion who in turn acquired Kissan in early nineties have reportedly spent Rs.18 crores in advertising and got 14% market share in a Rs.200 crore branded salt category in a span of one year.

Tata Salt still holds 26 percent market share and Captain Cook's share is about 20 percent and balance forty percent is still with the smaller players. With the acquisition of "Captain Cook" in branded salt market MNCs are the dominant players controlling sixty percent of the market. The value addition in branded salt and pepper was really done successfully by a Delhi based local company Hi-Tech Foods belonging to Dharampal Satyapal of premium "Baba Zarda" (chewing tobacco) fame. Hi-Tech Food's `Catch' brand of salt and pepper in dispenser pack is a success story with upper middle class household and restaurant segments as the main customers. The sale of "Catch" is said to be around Rs.12 crores.

The first MNC to get into the branded spice business was Brook Bond who introduced the select premium priced spice range by name "Sona" in late eighties. The products were priced and packaged for higher income group. They struggled for couple of years to establish "Sona" brand but failed and was forced to withdraw in later years. Apparently we don't see any major MNC in branded spice but world leader in exotic spices "Macomac" seems to have plan to enter Indian market. The first MNC to introduce Indian pickles was Nestle with their Maggie brand. The products are still in the market. And as mentioned earlier, the first MNC to introduce traditional snacks (bujjias) is Pepsi under the umbrella of "Leher Namkins". It can be concluded that in traditional Indian foods MNCs cannot add much value through the involvement of their principals abroad. On the contrary, they will have to learn from the locals to derive advantage of their brand and resource muscle. Hindustan Lever is expected to enter branded grocery items though Kissan route in a big way. The company does significant export of branded rice particularly in Middle East market and therefore expected to introduce the branded rice shortly in domestic market as well.

Otherwise, in India so far branded packaged rice is limited to Basmati rice and there are many brands in this category and leading among them is "Kohinoor" — but all are from small manufacturers.

The grocery business is basically low margins and high volume business and thus it required multiple supply source to be strategically located to reduce the cost of freight and excellent distribution infrastructure and logistics management capability. Big houses like HLL, therefore are expected to do much better in this sector. In the food ingredients business MNCs have not yet traded. The only big player in this area is Dabur with their range of pastes such as onion, garlic, ginger and also mix of these for particular application. Current sales of these items which are sold under the umbrella brand "Hommade" is said to be Rs.5 crores and going by that standard it can be considered as a reasonable success. Very recently, "Cookme" curry paste has been launched in Calcutta. The market indicators point towards growth in the branded food ingredients business in coming years.

Pepsi is expected to get into this category and with their backward linkages with farmers whom they support with the high yielding variety of seeds for better crop yield, it stands to have an edge over others in this sector. One could have expected that Nestle would also jump into the fray in this sunrise food business — but their new Italian Managing Director Mr. Carlo Donati seems to have other priorities and they want to focus on major key brands. Price and quality are expected to be the major determinant in the success of grocery items and basic foods. Consumers in India would not be willing to pay much as the price of convenience. Big global brands to MNCs' in that context are therefore not much of significance.

Imported Foods in Indian Market

Not too long ago for buying imported foods we had to go to select markets-such as Modern Bazar. Vasant Vihar in Delhi or Fort in Mumbai. In other places one has to literally search for such choice food items. In those days importing foods were not permitted.

And we were told that these foreign made chocolates and soup mixes and cheese find their way to Modern Bazar through diplomatic routes in the sense that persons in diplomatic services bring with them these foodstuff and sell them to local stores. But the fact of the matter is that these food items are brought to India through what is called "Suitcase trade" in the concerned circle. It will not take time for readers to understand what the "suitcase trade" is?

It simply means to carry suitcase full of foodstuff by people frequently travelling overseas and selling and or delivering those to local traders and this happens in an organised manner. Those who can afford, have to pay a fancy price for those foreign foods. Although price was exhorbitant but the quality used to be distinctly better. Children love their Swiss chocolates, French Cheese and Italian pastas. General Foods (now known as Kraft Foods International)-subsidiary of Phillips Morris has a synthetic orange beverage by brand-name "Tang" found to their dismay that so much of Tang is selling in India and Nepal now that they started thinking what would be the loss of sales to their South East Asian subsidiaries from where it finds its way to Indian market, once they start manufacturing it locally.

In the last couple of years these imported foods are available almost in all leading shops in most of the shopping centres in the city. To my surprise while taking a stroll in Greater Kailash shopping centre, I found couple of those shops have stacked Champaign, sparkling wine and imported mineral water outside the shop alongside soft drinks and on getting curious when I peeped inside I found everything is available. You name it — it is there. I bought some MARS chocolate and came out. The way things are moving, some of these foreign companies in course of time will do only trading in foods.

There are local agents who now represent many foreign companies and regularly import foods in turn to supply to local retailers and stores. In big stores like Nanz, there are regular requirement being catered to by their local agents. In earlier years we used to see these phenomena in countries like say in Middle East. This trade in imported foods will be on the increase as the custom duty goes down. It will also fuel the growth of partial processing in India to take the advantage of price equation. For example, importing the product in bulk and carrying out re-packing operation here will be more economical than importing the finished product itself.

As we know that India has now signed the WTO (World Trade Organization) agreement, of course, being a signatory to this agreement is a lesser evil than not signing it at all. As per the terms of reference to this agreement, by year 2003, India has to put most of the items under Open General License (OGL) for import which means these items can be freely traded. We so far could announce around about hundred odd items under OGL and in that list shrimp, strawberry, rasberry and other fruits, have already featured.

With the recent announcement of the Commerce Ministry, we have now freed import of 894 items including consumer goods and agricultural products by putting them under Open General Licence (OGL). Another 414 items are removed from the "restricted" list allowing these to be imported against Special Import Licence (SIL) that can be procured in the market by importers at a small premium. Fruits like oranges and pomegranates, soft drink concentrates etc. are falling in SIL category whereas a range of marine food products, vegetables, assorted fruits and juices, spices, edible oils, jams, jellies etc. are brought under OGL. The peak rate of the basic import tariff is now 40 percent which is applicable to most consumer products. On some items such as milk products India's WTO commitment bind it to a zero duty. But in most other agricultural products the WTO restriction is substantially higher ranging from 150 percent in the case of processed foods to 300 percent for edible oils. It is interesting to note that India, as a part of its globalisation policy is reducing the general tariff structure much faster than the asking rate as per WTO.

The outcome of the same is that in India we now get "KIWI" — an Australian fruit from select outlets if we want to. Shrimp is also now imported into India. In a recent wealthy marwari marriage reception that I had attended, I found in the fruit counter all the fruits look different than what I am familiar about. For example, Guava and Apples were almost double the normal size that we get here. Plus there were unknown fruits. And I was told that all these fruits were imported from Bangkok. I was so tempted that I tried all varieties and filled my stomach with all these tasty exotic fruits only. And later on started thinking that what will happen to our fruits if these fruits are available at a competitive price in India. Can our farmers and fruit merchants become globally competitive in terms of price and quality.

We should see the writing on the wall and work in that direction. The Agricultural Products Export Development Authority (APEDA) should quickly assess the scenario and rise to the occasion to take appropriate action. All of us are seeing the ongoing battle European banana growers are fighting in the forum of WTO against Americans refusal to permit entry of European Banana in that country. If international fruit brands like "Chikita" and "Del Monte" start selling here, who is going to buy local fruits from our mandis and roadside vendors selling fruits on the top of hand-pulled trolleys?

Food Forum India: Redefining the Indian Food Business

The Food Forum India, the largest congregation of key, global and Indian, food retailers, manufacturers, organisations and minds in the food business will be held from May 6-7, 2008 at Renaissance, Mumbai. It will span the vast array of food business segments like food retail, food design, food processing, food logistics & support, food services, information & technology.

Conceptualised at the India Retail Forum (IRF), which saw the participation of leading brands, retailers and retail support organisations from across the globe, Food Forum India (FFI) was launched under the chairmanship of Subodh Kant Sahai, Union minister for food processing industries, with some 50 captains of the food world joining in to take up a series of support initiatives for the Indian food businesses.

The exhibition space covers all aspects of the food retail supply chain and has different exhibition zones such as Food Bites, Beverages, Food Support, Food Design, Food Space and Food Concepts.

F&G Retail Projections For 2010-11

- Reliance Fresh: To cover 70 cities, 784 urban towns and 6,000-odd rural mandis
- Future Group: 500 Spencer's Fresh, Daily, Super and Hyper
- Wadhawan Group: 1,500 Spinach/S-Mart/Sabka Bazaar outlets in 100 cities
- Subhiksha : 2,500 neighbourhood outlets across the nation
- Other major players firming up Pan-India plans include Bharti-Walmart, AV Birla Group (Trinethra/More), Heritage Foods (Fresh @, Hypercity, Dairy Farm, (Foodworld), Nilgiris, Radhakrishna Foodland, Influx, Landmark Group (Spar), Mother Dairy and Safal & region specific expansion by Jubilant Group (Jumbo Saver & Monday 2 Sunday), Hopcoms and Margin Free in South, Adanis and Arambagh Foodmart in East India among others. Most major retailers are expected to foray in to cash and carry model, to structure backend and take full advantage of large scale production, procurement, processing and also to put supply chain & logistics mechanisms in place.

Conferences: Several conferences will be held during the event.

Food Inspirations : The ability to do things differently has been one of the prerequisites to large scale success. Captains of successful food businesses will share their experiences and give insightful interpretations of the food industry.

Food Innovations : New ideas, products and concepts. Discussions on some of the most important innovations that have gained maximum popularity over the years. A look at possibilities for the near future.

Food For Thought : Presentations of leading global research and studies that are shaping the food industry today. Leading global food research and consulting firms and organisations will deliberate on key issues that guide the food business.

World Food Experience: The global market is today witnessing a mushrooming of numerous ideas and innovations that are radically altering the shape of businesses around the world. Focus will be on international ideas and insights, and include sunrise products from around the world and their implications for the Indian market.

Food Fight: Interaction between retailers and producers is of great importance to ensure the maintenance of an efficient chain that facilitates development of the industry as a whole. Food retailers and producers will debate on vital issues to determine the way ahead for the food industry in this session.

Investments In The Food Sector: Trade commissioners of key countries, governmental and regulatory bodies, international and domestic investors and corporates will debate upon investments in food processing, retailing, support and infrastructure.

Future of Food in India 2020: National and international vision leaders and key players of the industry will foresee the future of the business of food in India, and present some of the astounding possibilities of the future.

Awards: The Images Golden Spoon Awards (IGSA) to be announced at the event will honour enterprise, innovation and achievement in the business of food. Industry captains will celebrate excellence in the food business at a glamorous ceremony that will be the grand finale of Food Forum India. The IGSA awards will be benchmark of excellence, that all food businesses will aspire for, thus playing a vital role in the in the progress of the industry. Food and grocery accounts for 63 per cent share in the Rs. 1,330,000 crore (US$ 300 million) Indian retail market. Only one per cent of this segment was organised in 2007. Food, grocery and beverages constitute about 43 per cent of India's private final consumption expenditure, and yet only 11 per cent of organised retail market in 2006.

Opportunity in Food and Grocery

The Urban Middle Class continues to grow by 20-25 million annually. The population is young, better exposed to modern lifestyles, and has a preference for packaged food and beverages. This growing Indian Middle Class, especially the employed youth in the ITES, BPO and other Service sectors, have higher propensity to consume, fuelled by easy availability of credit due to popularization of plastic cards.

More than 1,000 Food and Grocery outlets operational across tier-I and tier-II cities and Retail space of over 3 million sq. ft. have come up for F&G supermarkets, department stores and hypermarkets. 25 major F&G Retailers emerged in less than a year and Retail sales in this segment grew by nearly 150 per cent over 2006.

Opportunity Logistics

Improved logistics, warehousing, state-of-the-art technology and availability of quality processed and packaged food are factors that will boost the growth of organised F&G retail in India. Indian corporates like ITC, Godrej, DCM Shriram have initiated the process of direct supply linkages with the farm. Global major Metro AG was the first to introduce up-to-date know-how logistics and supply chain management. Corporate major Reliance is investing heavily on this front. Wal-Mart too plans back-end operations with Bharti. Investments to the tune of US$ 23.5 billion in the food processing sector over the next three years is in the pipeline. This will undoubtedly create a huge demand for the food processing and packaging industry.. But keeping in view the vast farm sector and the surmounting demand for quality food products, there remains room for much more.

Opportunity in Food Processing

Nearly 80 per cent of agricultural produce in developed countries gets processed and packaged. It is just about 1.3 per cent in the case of India-a reason why less than one per cent of the F&G retail segment is organised. Even the existing organised F&G Retailers are finding it difficult to keep their stacks full & fresh. This is just the right time for global firms to invest in the food processing sector, especially so when the government seems eager to boost rural/farm incomes. Marine Food Parks and Agricultural Special Economic Zones are already being worked out to ensure that farmers are not displaced. The opportunity is huge.. and early movers will reap the maximum advantage.

Opportunity to Boost the Incomes of Indian Farmers

Organised F&G retail requires direct sourcing of bulk produce and this ensures a boon for farmers. Initiatives thus far, are proving the point as traditional mandis loose relevance, middlemen get eased out, and as a result there is substantial increase in the income of farmers. Adverse effects of fragmentation of land holdings can also be effectively countered. Initiative and Investment by Global companies can help make Cluster farming, Demand oriented farming and Raw material oriented farming the mainstay for Indian farmers.

India could well become the agri-business powerhouse in the export of fruits, vegetables, spices and food grains.

Opportunity for Food and Farm Supplies

More than 5,000 new outlets, 100 hypermarkets, 500 department stores and 2000 supermarkets are opening. Over 5,000 small and big existing outlets are to undergo a complete facelift. But the supplies are inadequate. Organised retail in India will need fresh and processed food and farm produce worth US$ 30 billion by the year 2010.

F&B (Servicing) Retail in India

Home-grown as well as international restaurant chains present in both high street locations and malls represent the organised food and beverages (F&B) services retail sector. This sector is in its growth phase and offers opportunities across a variety of retail formats. The Indian F&B services sector is estimated to be worth Rs. 70,000 crore in 2007, at current prices, out of which about Rs. 5,750 crore is accounted for by the organised sector. This is roughly 8.2 percent of the market being organised as compared to just 6.9 per cent of the market being organised in the previous year. This F&B services sector has increased its share from 4.7 per cent of the total of Rs. 1,200,000 crore retail market in 2006 to about 5.26 per cent of the Rs. 1,330,000 crore retail market in 2007, as per preliminary estimates by Images F&R research.

Report – India's Food Processing Industry

The Food Processing Industry sector in India is one of the largest in terms of production, consumption, export and growth prospects. The government has accorded it a high priority, with a number of fiscal reliefs and incentives, to encourage commercialisation and value addition to agricultural produce; for minimising pre/post harvest wastage, generating employment and export growth.

Important sub sectors in food processing industries are:-Fruit & Vegetable Processing, Fish-processing, Milk Processing, Meat & Poultry Processing, Packaged/Convenience Foods, Alcoholic beverages & Soft drinks and Grain Processing etc. As a result of several Policy Initiatives undertaken since liberalisation in August 1991, the industry has witnessed fast growth in most of the segments. As per a recent study on the food processing sector, the turnover of the total food market is approximately Rs.250,000 crores (US $ 69.4 billion) out of which value-added food products comprise Rs.80,000 crores (US $ 22.2 billion). Since liberalisation in Aug 91 and up-till Feb 2000 proposals for projects of over Rs.53,800 crores (US.13.4 billion) have been proposed in various segments of the food and agro-processing industry. Besides this, Govt. has also approved proposals for joint ventures, foreign collaboration, industrial licenses and 100%export oriented units envisaging an investment of Rs.19,100 crores (US $ 4.80 billion) during the same period. Out of this, foreign investment is over Rs. 9100 crores (US $ 18.2 billion). Processed food exports were at over Rs.13,500 crores (US $ 3.2 billion) in 1998-99. Out of these exports, rice accounted for 46%, whereas marine products accounted for over 34%. Primary food processing is a major industry with lakhs of rice-mills/hullers, flour mills, pulse mills and oil-seed mills. There are several thousands of bakeries, traditional food units and fruit/veg./ spice processing units in unorganised sector. In the organised sector, there are over 820 flour mills, 418 fish processing units, 5198 fruit/ veg processing units, 171 meat processing units.

India is the world's second largest producer of fruits & vegetables, but hardly 2% of the produce is processed. India is the land of spices producing all varieties worth over Rs. 3500 crores (US $ 900million) amounting to 25-30% of world production, which is processed for value-addition and export. It grows 22 million tonnes of oilseeds covering most of the varieties. Other important plantation products include tea, coffee, cocoa and cashew. It has large marine product and processing potential with varied fish resources along the 8041 km. long coastline, 28000 km. of rivers and millions of hectares of reservoirs & brackish water. India's livestock population is largest in the world with 50% of world's buffaloes and 20% of cattles, but only about 1% of total meat production is converted to value added products. India is the largest milk producer in the world and about 15% of the total milk production is processed through the organised sector. Size of the semi-processed and ready to eat packaged food industry is over Rs. 4000 crores (US $ 1 billion) and is growing at over 20%.

With India's food industry witnessing explosive growth in line with the country's on-going economic development, there has been a marked move towards trying to get more out of the country's immense agricultural industry. Despite being the world's leading producer of cattle, milk, tea and pulses and the second largest producer of fruit, vegetables, rice, wheat and sugarcane worldwide, India accounts for just 1.5% of global processed food trade. The government estimates that the cost of boosting this figure to just 3% would be US$25bn, with India's primary focused agricultural and food supply chain having to dramatically reconsider standard industry practices in order to boost secondary output. Fortunately, the government is not alone in attempting to fund this seismic shift. A vast population, steady urbanisation and GDP growth that is forecast at 7.9% annually to 2012, have helped ensure that multinational investment interest in the market is massive. More encouraging than this is that multinationals alone are not being left to drive development; local corporations are also playing a huge role in the process. Mos notable has been the involvement of Indian companies in the food and beverage industry, whose primary business interest was formerly elsewhere.

Over the past 12 months this has seen fast-moving consumer goods manufacturer Hindustan Lever – 52%-owned by Dutch giant Unilever – attempt to grow its food division, via the heavy marketing of popular brands, such as Knorr and Lipton, and reduce its dependence on its health and personal care products. Perhaps even more significantly than this, burgeoning food sales have seen cigarette industry number one and two – ITC and Godfrey – launch new food products in a bid to establish themselves as key players within this industry. Looking at the industry more broadly, almost all of India's leading conglomerates – Tata, Reliance, RPG, Aditya Birla etc. – are now participating in the industry to some degree, many having chosen the explosive grocery retail as a starting point. Likewise, former food category specialists, such as Amul Dairy, are now looking to become industry generalists in a bid to broaden their growth prospects (Amul has recently announced its interest in further non-dairy snack food launches).

Investment from all of these companies, as they battle to boost sales and build market share, should help to lift India's contribution to global processed food trade in the long term. In the short-to-medium term, the impact will be on internal processed food sales. Included in this report for the first time this quarter are our forecasts for the country's processed food industry. To 2012, we expect processed food output to increase by 44.2% to US$90.1bn, while packaged food sales in the country climb by 67.5% to US$21.7bn. On a per capita basis, it is forecast that a per capita packaged food spending increase of 56.5% to US$18.06 in 2012.

Food Processing – A New Era in India's Economy

The agriculture sector has come a long way since independence. With the advent of green revolution, India has transformed itself from a country of shortages to a land of surpluses. With the rapid growth of the economy, a shift is also being seen in the consumption pattern, from cereals to more varied and nutritious diet of fruit and vegetables, milk, fish, meat and poultry products.

This has resulted in the development of a sunrise industry namely the Food Processing Industries. The food processing sector in the country with its vast potential has emerged as one of the major driver of economic growth. It is encouraging to note that while the country's GDP growth rate had increase from 3.5 per cent in 2002-03 to 9 percent in 2006-07, the food processing sector has grown from 7 per cent to 13.1 per cent during the same period. India is a country of over 1.10 billion consumers, there is a large untapped domestic market of 1,000 million consumers in the food processing sector and 200 million more consumers are expected to shift to processed food by 2010. It is the second largest producer of fruits and vegetables in the world.

There is a huge wastage of perishable food items in the country due to lack of proper food processing facilities and the level of processing is only about 2.2 per cent. However, India has tremendous potential to unleash large scale process based farm activities to exploit the emerging globalbusiness opportunities.

Incredible Opportunities

India's homogeneous market size endowed with growing incomes and changing life styles has created incredible market opportunities for food producers, machinery makers, food technology and service providers. Food processing industries has great export and employment potential. The policies are investor-friendly and more importantly technological and human resources are available aplenty in the country. The competitive edge enjoyed in terms of raw material and labour offers lucrative opportunities. However poor perception of quality and the indifferent image of Indian products is preventing Indian food products to penetrate global markets in a big way.

While developing countries like Thailand have exploited the global markets in a big was by fine-tuning quality management aspects of their food processing industry, India are yet to make a headway on this front. Production of high quality processed foods meeting international quality standards & regulations may very well open new frontiers for Indian food products. This will not only create a dynamic and competitive domestic food processing industry but will also enable India to become a major player in the global food market. An attitudinal change towards quality is essential.

Several thousand crore worth of farm produce is lost every year due to inefficient postharvest practices for storage and processing. On one hand is the growing demand for food products, which are difficult to meet due to limited resources and on the other, there exist abnormally high wastage in farm sector due to inefficient technology in storage, processing and handling. It is, therefore, imperative to introduce state of the art technology in the food-processing sector to minimize post-harvest losses. It also calls for a concerted attention to a few selected food products where India has or can develop a competitive edge over other countries.

FDI

The sector has been attracting substantial FDI also and is among the top ten sectors getting FDI equity. FDI up to 100 per cent equity is permitted under the automatic route in food and infrastructure like food parks and cold chains. There are many areas for investment in this sector which include mega food parks, agri-infrastructure, supply chain aggregation, logistics and cold chain infrastructure, fruit and vegetable products, animal products, meat and dairy, fisheries and seafood cereals, consumer foods/ready to eat foods, wine and beer, machinery/packaging.

Productivity and Progress

It is essential to understand the dynamic relationship that exists between productivity and progress. The basic fact is that until both the farmers as well as the processors are convinced of benefits that accruc through productivity, the productivity campaigns will remain ineffective. So the main challenge is to introduce the concepts of productivity and make it work under a variety of constraints for the sustainable growth of the industry. In the process of globalization, the Indian food processing industry will be facing increased competition, particularly in domestic markets in addition to the uncertainties prevailing in the international markets.

It is in this context that emphasis must be given to improve productivity and quality. Undoubtedly, better performing firms will have a competitive edge over others. In order to maintain the tempo of productivity and quality, the National Productivity Awards have thus assumed much greater significance.

Ministry of Food Processing Industries on its part, is leaving no stone unturned to achieve the multiple objectives of stepping up the growth, higher farmer income, reduction in wastage, providing nutritious and safe food and enhancing employment opportunities. It has initiated measures to deal with the major constraints being faced by the industry such as affordability and cost of processed foods, linking of farmers and processors, supply chain and post harvest technology, infrastructure, finance, food safety, hygiene and taxes. With the active support and cooperation of all the stakeholders the ministry is confident of providing the necessary momentum for the rapid growth of the food processing sector and usher in a new era in the Indian economy.

Vision 2015

Given the strengths and opportunities of food processing sector, a Vision 2015 has been developed by the Ministry of Food Processing Industries, together with an appropriate strategy and implementable action plan so as to enhance farmer income, generate employment opportunities, provide choice to consumers at affordable price and contribute to overall national growth by increasing: the level of processing of perishables from 6% to 20%, value addition from 20% to 35% and share in global food trade from 1.5% to 3%. The vision 2015 of the Government for the food processing sector aims at enhancing and stabilizing the income level of the farmers by assuring wider and better choice by enhancing dynamism, competitiveness, by ensuring safety and quality of food by introducing a transparent and scientific system of standards. To achieve these aims a transparent and industry friendly regulatory regime is proposed to be established. Making the sector attractive for both domestic and foreign investors. Achieving integration of the food processing infrastructure from farm to market. Having a transparent and industry friendly regulatory regime. Putting in place a transparent system of standards based on science. To achieve the stated Vision, Ministry of Food Processing Industries, has prepared Action Plan for energizing the food processing sector during 11th Plan.

Main Initiatives

Cold Chain: To address the situation and with a view to create a modern cold chain for preservation and value addition of perishables, during the 11th Plan, the Ministry is launching a revamped comprehensive Cold Chain Infrastructure Scheme for creating integrated cold chain infrastructure at different levels – farm level primary processing centre-cum-cold chain, collection/aggregation centres and Strategic Distribution Centres (SDC). The SDCs will have integrated infrastructure facilities like material handling equipment, refrigeration, IQF/Blast freezing facility, Frozen/CA/MA Storage, Modern Packaging Facilities, ancillary equipment like X-ray, weigh bridge etc. The SDCs will be linked to retail supermarkets.

Mega Food Park : A new scheme of Mega Food Parks in the country is proposed which is envisaged to be a well defined agri/ horticultural processing zone containing state of the art processing facilities with support infrastructure and well established supply chain. The proposed scheme aims to provide a mechanism to bring together farmers, processors and retailers and link agricultural production to the market so as to ensure maximization of value addition, minimize wastages and improve farmers' income. The Mega Food Park is designed ultimately to link the farmers with the retail markets with minimizing of the intermediaries. These food parks will function as sourcing hubs for the retail outlets. Abattoirs: Hygienic and scientific slaughtering as well as optimum utilization of byproducts are issues of grave concern of the Indian Meat Industry.

It results in tremendous waste, contamination and avoidable cruelty to animals. Ministry is launching a comprehensive scheme for modernization of existing abattoirs/establishment of modern abattoirs at 100 locations across the country on a PPP mode. Capacity Building: Ministry of Food Processing Industries has also taken up quality assurance, R & D, HACCP, Human Resource Development and Establishment of laboratories to support the Food Safety and Standards Act. Ministry of Food Processing Industries have taken many steps to give impetus to this sector which include virtual delicensing of the sector, inclusion in the priority sector for lending, allowing 100% FDI except in alcoholic beverages and retail, several duty and tax reliefs, financial assistance for infrastructure building, setting up of food processing units etc. In case of export-oriented units, foreign investment is permitted even in case of items reserved for small scale sector. In addition, the export oriented units are given a number of incentives and concessions under the Export-Import Policy, such as, duty free import of capital goods, raw materials and intermediates, export income being exempt from Corporate Tax etc. FDI inflow in food processing is becoming stronger.

Recipe for Success

The global packaged food and nonalcoholic beverages industry, with more than 30 distinct product categories, is complex and highly fragmented—and worth about $2 trillion,or the rough equivalent of the GDP of the United Kingdom. The top 20 players account for less than one-quarter of the market, which is characterized by vast differences in local taste preferences, shelf-life considerations and food technologies.

All of these factors have combined to inhibit consolidation. However, deal activity has picked up in recent years as more companies have sought focus by trying to unravel diverse and undifferentiated portfolios. Yet even with increased consolidation, most companies are struggling to sustain margins. Rates of growth and profitability vary significantly across the 30 product categories. Sales growth of bottled water far outstrips that of carbonates, for example. And sales of ready-made meals are almost double those of pasta. Such differences reflect rapidly evolving patterns of consumer demand—a reflection, in turn, of profound changes in demographics and lifestyle. More women in the workforce and increased urbanization have fuelled worldwide demand for convenience foods. At the same time, the rates of obesity and food-related diseases like diabetes have skyrocketed, powering a parallel desire for "healthy" food as well as a similarly health-related boom in organic foods, especially in developed countries.

Meanwhile, as consumers in many countries become wealthier, more informed and thus more confident, they have developed an interest in eating for pleasure and have cultivated a taste for exotic, ethnic foods. There are, to be sure, significant differences globally in these trends. Interest in healthy nutrition rises in line with disposable income, while the growth in convenience consumption is a function of both rising incomes and the increased sophistication of local retail networks. Emerging markets offer sizable growth opportunities, if only because of their relatively low per capita consumption rates. The bulk of future growth, however, will come from North America, Western Europe and the Asia Pacific region, where the impact of the three new drivers of the demand—convenience, health and pleasure—is the strongest. High-performance businesses know this, and they have positioned themselves to take full advantage. Accenture defines a high-performance business as one that consistently outperforms its peers through economic and industry cycles as well as changes in leadership. Our extensive cross-industry research has identified three building blocks that underpin high performance in any industry—market focus and position; distinctive capabilities; and performance anatomy—and that all high-performance businesses have mastered. Here is what these building blocks look like in the food and nonalcoholic beverages industry.

Sidebar

About the Research

The peer group set for the study comprised 13 global, publicly traded companies that all boast worldwide sales of more than $5 billion annually. In addition, they all derive at least 75 percent of their sales from food and beverages, and 30 percent of these sales are outside their home region. All provide branded packaged products (rather than food or beverage ingredients). Four companies emerged from our analysis as high-performance businesses. All distinguish themselves on measures of revenue growth, profitability, return on capital and working capital management. They also deliver superior economic profit, which has allowed them to produce consistently superior returns for their shareholders—more than double the industry average over the past five years.

More important, their returns on invested capital consistently outstrip those of their competitors, thanks to both higher margins and a higher percentage of sales per invested capital in each of the past three years. Indeed, high-performance businesses have grown nearly twice as fast as the industry average by focusing on high-growth categories and by implementing selective acquisitions to round out their portfolios and extend channel and geographic reach. However, only two of the four companies have consistently delivered superior returns to shareholders over both long and short time frames, as well as superior revenue growth and profitability and high future value expectations.

Case Study 1

PepsiCo: A discerning eye for acquisitions: Just 10 years ago, it looked as if PepsiCo had lost the so-called cola wars. Its profits lagged those of archrival Coca-Cola by almost 50 percent, and its market capitalization had slumped to less than half that of the Atlanta-based beverage giant. Since 1996, PepsiCo has turned challenge into opportunity, reshaping its portfolio with an approach to acquisitions that has given the company strategic category domination—the essential element to succeeding at market focus and position, one of the three building blocks of high-performance business, in this industry. So much for history. The key to PepsiCo's success is the selective nature of its M&A strategy. With the purchase of The Quaker Oats Co., South Beach Beverage Co. (SoBe) and Seagram Co.'s Tropicana Products division, the company has made strategic acquisitions in the water, sports drink and juice categories—all fast growing, thanks to the "healthy eating" trend that is one of the factors transforming the industry.

PepsiCo also has expanded (again selectively) into the packaged foods sector—more specifically, into snack foods, where its Frito-Lay division now enjoys a 60 percent share of the US market.

By acquiring top regional brands in attractive markets, PepsiCo is also huge—and growing—overseas. In February 2005, it took full control of a joint venture it had established with General Mills (said to be the largest of its kind in Europe) that makes and sells snack foods from Madrid to Moscow. Other recent acquisitions include Sara Lee Corp.'s nuts business in Belgium, the Netherlands and France, and a leading Polish snack foods company.

Case Study 2

Wrigley: Chewing up the competition: The Wm. Wrigley Jr. Co. has come a long way since 1892, when its founder first marketed a primitive form of chewing gum made from spruce gum and paraffin in Chicago. Today, the $4 billion company sells its popular brands in more than 180 countries. Indeed, with more than 60 percent of sales outside North America, Wrigley reigns supreme as the world's No. 1 maker of chewing and bubble gum.

These are hardly Wrigley's only products. Times have changed for a company that marketed just three chewing gums—Spearmint, Doublemint and Juicy Fruit—for more than 75 years. The growing popularity of sugar-free gum brands that promise to freshen breath, whiten teeth or fight tooth decay have made the gum market a target for candy companies like Wrigley's fast-growing rival, UK-based Cadbury Schweppes, which snapped up Pfizer's Adams confectionery unit, including the Dentyne and Bubblicious brands, in 2003.

Wrigley knows that insight-driven marketing—one of the important elements that distinguish high-performance businesses in this industry —is the key to sustaining its supremacy. So the company has been busily boosting product development.

Its innovation efforts often take the form of beefing up old favourites—pellet forms of Big Red and Juicy Fruit, for example. Wrigley invests heavily in its innovation capability and processes.

It spent $50 million to build a Global Innovation Centre—and it is reaping the rewards. Since 2001, the contribution from new products has averaged 15 percent to 20 percent of Wrigley's global sales—a significant increase over the single-digit figures of the 1990s.

Wrigley also has been on the selective acquisition trail—another key characteristic of high-performance businesses in this industry.

Historically, Wrigley focused exclusively on the gum subcategory and relied on organic means to grow the business. However, with increasing consolidation in the confectionery category and growing competitive pressures in the core gum market, Wrigley has responded with a string of acquisitions. In 2001, Wrigley bought Velamints and since then has been steadily adding to its range of non-gum mints, with products like Extra sugar-free mints.

In 2002, its $12.5 billion bid for the Hershey Company floundered when the sale was called off. In 2004, however, the purchase of the Spanish Joyco gum and confectionery business strengthened Wrigley's position in such key confectionery segments as bubble gum, candies and lollipops, and also boosted its presence in Europe and key emerging markets, including China and India.

In 2005, Wrigley resolutely entered the US sugar confectionery market with the acquisition of Kraft Foods' LifeSavers, Creme Savers and Altoids brands. Finally, in January 2007, the purchase of an 80 percent stake in Russian premium chocolatier A. Korkunov gave Wrigley an important foothold in a booming consumer marketplace.

8

Food Planning and Management

The food industry, be it the processing industry or the catering industry, is one of the largest and most needed industry in the world today fulfilling one of our three basic needs, i.e., food. Its growth rate is phenomenal, growing by leaps and bounds to provide three square meals to our rapidly increasing population and keeping pace with the ever-changing demands of the population.

The developments in the food industry can be traced back to surplus food which needed to be preserved for a rainy day. Food preservation is not a new phenomenon. Our forefathers understood the basic principles underlying food preservation and practised them using natural ingredients and the forces of nature like sunlight and ultraviolet rays till newer and more scientific methods were developed. Improvement in equipment and machinery has made it possible to increase the capacity of food processing plants greatly. The shelf life of perishable foods has increased dramatically with the invention of the refrigerator and the use of dry ice.

With the advent of the wheel, surplus food was transported several hundred miles. As early as in 1850, milk was transported by special milk trains and tank trucks over a distance of several hundred miles with negligible loss in quality. Food which was perishable was moved thousands of miles before it was processed, stored, and consumed. Over the past few decades, the food industry has witnessed a significant change. The market has witnessed such a flood of food commodities, superior in quality and available all year round. Ice cream filled cones and nuts in ice cream retaining their crunch, fresh milk stored on the shelf for months, and crisp croutons in a ready to serve cream soup are a few marvels of food science and technology.

With these advances in science and technology, the consumer has an unlimited choice of meals to choose from all year round. The aesthetic value of food is important. To be able to offer the consumer quality cuisine, basic knowledge of food science and its applications is necessary. Every food handler should know the composition, structure, and behaviour of food and the changes that take place during cooking, holding, and storage as well as what happens to food once it is consumed, i.e., its digestion, absorption, and metabolism in the human body. The study of food is today accepted as a separate discipline called food science.

Definition: Food science is a systematic study of the nature of food materials and the scientific principles underlying their modification, preservation, and spoilage. To understand food science, the basic concepts of physics, chemistry, mathematics, and biology and their applications, i.e., biochemistry, microbiology, and food technology, are necessary to prepare, package, store, and serve wholesome, high quality products. All foods are chemical compounds which undergo various chemical reactions at all stages from production to consumption. These reactions are based on the laws of chemistry. Many processes used while preparing food involve physical changes apart from chemical changes.

Matter exists in three states-solid, liquid, gas. In general, as the temperature is increased, a pure substance will change from solid to liquid and then to a gas, without change in chemical composition. However, many organic compounds will decompose, undergoing various chemical reactions, rather than a change of state when temperature is raised. Many foods are complex mixtures of chemical substances. In processed foods, additives are added to improve colour, texture, flavour, etc., and these additives are also chemical compounds. It undergoes further chemical changes during storage, cooking, processing as well as in the human body during digestion of food by action of chemical substances. Physical aspects of food such as the various food systems are of colloidal dimensions. Food is subjected to various physical conditions during preparation and storage which affect its quality such as temperature and pressure changes.

Food chemistry is the science that deals with the composition, structure, and properties of food, and with chemical changes that take place in food. It forms a major part of food science and is closely related to food microbiology. The chemical composition of food dictates which microorganisms can grow on it and the changes which take place in the food because of their growth.

The changes may be planned and desirable or may result because of contamination, causing disease, i.e., causing food poisoning and food infection or just spoiling the food rendering it unfit for consumption. Microorganisms have basic growth requirements, namely, food, moisture, temperature, time, osmotic pressure, pH, and the presence or absence of oxygen. Food chemistry and food microbiology are intimately related to food processing because the processes to which food needs to be subjected to improve its taste, texture, flavour, and aroma depend on its composition and ingredients. The time and temperature for food processing depend not only on the chemical composition of food but on its microbial load and the type of packaging to be used. The growing public demand for meals away from home has made the problem of serving safe wholesome food more critical and challenging. This makes it imperative for food handlers to understand and implement the basic principles of the food science to enable them to prepare and serve high quality products over extended lunch hours.

The Need for Convenience Foods

Rapid urbanization and changes in social and cultural practices have modified the food habits of the community. Industrial development in Indian cities has compelled labour from villages to migrate to cities in search of employment. It is estimated that within the next ten years, half the world's population will be living and working in urban areas. Increase in buying power and long hours spent away from home commuting to work places, make convenience foods a necessity in every home. The ever-increasing market for convenience foods, be it tinned, canned, chilled, frozen, or preserved, presents a whole array of complex operations in food processing. This weaning away from the traditional fare of yesteryears provides a tremendous and urgent challenge to the food industry: serving safe, attractive, and nutritious food that is wholesome and bacteriologically safe and conforms with quality standards.

The urban workforce does not have the time or inclination to follow the traditional recipes and would rather pick up packed, clean, and reasonably priced meals rather than return home from work and do domestic chores. Most food consumed in developed countries is in the form of *convenience foods*. Convenience foods are foods that require little labour and time to prepare. A pack-et of frozen green peas is a convenience food since it requires no shelling. A pack-et of whole wheat flour is also a convenience food as it has already been milled. A packet of instant idli mix is more of a convenience food, and 'ready to eat' or 'heat and eat' foods like chicken keema matar or canned palak paneer are most convenient since they need no further cooking.

Many different types of convenience foods are available in the market today. The speed and efficiency of cooking and service increases dramatically with the use of convenience foods, giving the caterer, homemaker, or working professional more time to devote to other activities. The convenience food revolution is possible because of a wide variety of chemicals which are added to food not only to preserve it but to enhance its overall quality. These numerous chemicals, tested and permitted by law to be added to food are called *food additives*. Today, convenience foods are being specially packed for caterers and are avail-able in large catering packs. Manufacturers of specialized food supplies pack food so that it fits into standard catering equipment, e.g., catering packs that fit into vending machines. The caterer can choose between smaller packs and larger packs that are economical.

Convenience foods need to be handled with care because one source of infection can contaminate thousands of prepacked items. Take-away meals should not be kept for a long time, hygiene should be practised in processing plants, and time and temperature control should be observed during storage. Leftover contents in large catering packs should not be stored in the open. Convenience foods help by saving considerable time and effort. However, the cost of convenience foods compared to home-prepared foods should be considered before purchase. Some foods may not be costlier while others may work out to be expensive. For people who have to rush home from work and prepare a meal, such foods purchased on the way home or stacked in the deep freezer are not only time-saving but also convenient.

Convenience foods vary widely in their palatability, nutrient content, and cost. The consumer can choose from a bewildering display of snacks, soups, sauces, fruit chunks and juices, desserts, meat, and vegetable preparations and gravies in the ready to eat and ready to cook form. They need to be warmed up in a microwave before they are served. Canned foods, commercially prepared chappatis, snacks both sweet and savoury, main course, vegetable preparations, soups, gravies, sauces, breakfast cereals, bakery items, deep frozen foods, dry ready mixes, etc., are not only time saving but convenient to cook and store. Thus, food science covers all aspects of food, from the properties of food materials and influences of all factors affecting food, beginning from growing the food to harvesting or slaughter, i.e., all stages from the farm to the table, from raw food till it is consumed like processing, nutritive value, shelf life, novel sources of food, fabricated food and food analogs, conservation and reuse of resources to make more food. A study of food science and nutrition will be of benefit to all food professionals.

The food industry is a fast-growing industry that applies the principles of food science and technology to offer the consumer a wide array of fresh and processed foods to meet their nutritional needs, wants, and budget. These foods are available under different brand names, all year round in delectable flavours and assorted preparations. The aesthetic value of food is an important criterion in its acceptability. Every food handler should be aware of the composition, structure, and behaviour of food and what happens to it during processing and after consumption. The systematic study of food is called food science.

All foods are chemical compounds and under-go physical as well as chemical changes. The various food systems are of colloidal dimensions and various physical conditions such as temperature and pressure affect its quality. Food science is intimately related to food chemistry, food microbiology, and food processing. To understand this, the basic concepts of physics, chemistry, mathematics, and biology are necessary. The growing demand for meals away from home has made the problem of serving safe and wholesome food critical and challenging. With rapid urbanization and changes in food habits and lifestyles, and increase in the number of couples who have little time has caused a shift in focus from farm-grown fresh foods to partially or totally processed convenience foods. These foods require little labour and time to prepare and are useful to both caterers and homemakers. The shelf life and acceptability of these foods are enhanced by the use of permitted additives. The consumer can choose from a wide range of 'ready-to-cook' and 'ready-to-eat' foods.

Interactions in Food Technology, Agriculture, and Nutrition

The last 30 years have witnessed spectacular increases in food-grain production in India, from 51 million tonnes to more than 130 million tonnes. A sizeable buffer stock has also been built up to face the likely shortages arising out of uncertain production levels (DES 1975).

***Table** : Food-grain Production*

Food grains	*1950/51*	*1966/67*	*1978/79*
Cereals	42.41	65.88	119.20
Pulses	8.41	8.34	12.16
Total	50.82	74.22	131.36

Source: DES 1975.

Various national projections indicate that food-grain production must be doubled to meet the needs of an estimated population of more than 950 million by the turn of this century. Since food grains constitute the principal source of calories, proteins, and other nutrients , careful efforts are necessary not only to conserve them against qualitative and quantitative losses but also to upgrade their nutritional and acceptability features. Thus, a systems approach has become crucial for integrating the production, conservation, and nutrition of food grains to get maximum benefits from national efforts.

Table: *Daily Per Capita Food Consumption and Recommended Levels*

		Recommended level (g)	
Food materials	***Consumption (g)***	***ICMR***[a]	***Task Force on***
Cereals	434	412	376
Pulses	34	60	64
Green leafy vegetables	21	125	116
Other vegetables	71	50	61
Roots and tubers	-	87	69
Fruits	10	30	40
Milk	69	100	189
Fats/oils	12	40	39
Meat and fish (and egg)	14	30	23
Eggs	-	30	15
Sugar/jaggery	19	35	38

a. Indian Council of Medical Research

Source: Gopalan et al 1971, Gopalan and Narasinga Rao 1971; NCST 1972.

Breeding of new food-grain varieties has been directed to increasing per hectare yields and resistance against field-borne microorganisms and insect pests. Advances in food technology and nutrition have, however, given some insight into the desirable features that need to be considered in breeding programmes. This paper attempts to highlight some salient features of the processing, storage, and nutritive value of food grains produced in India so as to understand the interphase linkages between production and post-harvest conservation.

Technological Considerations in Evolving Strategies for Varietal Development of Food Grains

About 70 per cent of food grains produced in India are retained for farm-level consumption and the rest moves along a chain of agencies before it reaches the consumption points. Post-harvest conservation by modern procedures is therefore a crucial need to prevent the dissipation of national efforts to raise food production levels. The incidence of bunt in wheat, chalky grains in rice, and Gibberella infection in maize, and the impairment of processing qualities as a result of pre-harvest infection have engaged the attention of scientists in recent years. The expertise in food conservation built up during the last 30 years has found increasing application, but basic information to evolve varieties with desirable storage, processing, and nutritional or organoleptic qualities is important in meeting future needs. Variable production levels in different years emphasize the need for varieties that give maximum yields during processing and suffer minimum losses during post-harvest handling and storage.

Processing

Food grains harvested from standing crops are dried and processed before cooking and consumption. Milling is used to obtain rice from paddy, dhals from pulses, and flours from wheat and millets. The wastages inherent in some traditional practices have been minimized through improved processing technology and equipment design. The physico-chemical features of food grains need attention in varietal development programmes.

Rice

About 50 per cent of all cereal production consists of rice, represented by numerous varieties exhibiting diverse per hectare yields and physico-chemical features. Research and developmental efforts have focused on the best utilization of paddy varieties grown in the country through:

a. minimizing qualitative and quantitative losses during harvest and post-harvest handling and drying stages;
b. improving the milling yields of rice by appropriate drying and milling procedures, and the development of milling equipment;
c. adapting processing procedures to improve nutrition and acceptability;
d. utilizing by-products; and
e. product development for diverse needs.

The investigations at the Central Food Technological Research Institute (CFTRI) have conclusively shown that inherent grain structure and harvest/post-harvest drying practices directly influence the milling behaviour of paddy.

Paddy is currently harvested at 16 to 18 per cent moisture level because of difficulties in getting labour, drying space, and other amenities during harvest periods. Harvesting at this stage results in shattering and sun-checking of grains ultimately reflected in heavy breakages and reduced milling yields. Harvesting at higher grain moisture levels of say 20 to 24 per cent (indicated by the presence of 1 per cent milky grains), and a controlled drying procedure with an intermediate conditioning stage, is suitable for farm level use, and also reduces milling breakages. Breeding of crack-resistant varieties, the second approach, overcomes frequent process alterations and equipment designs. Crack-resistant and low-shattering selections from pushpa, vani and madhu varieties have been identified, tested and released by the CFTRI for mini-test trials through the University of Agricultural Sciences, Bangalore, Further, a chalky variant of Alur sanna (a rice variety), which seems to cook into discrete, fluffy grains even without ageing, has also been identified by the CFTRI for further trials.

The influence of physico-chemical characteristics on the storage, packing, and processing of rice has been examined as an aid in post-harvest conservation. For example, grains with low length: breadth ratio exhibit higher bulk density (and lower porosity), indicating that a given volume of round grains has a greater weight than slender grains. Similarly, the friction coefficient of grains increases with moisture level, contributing to handling and packing problems. Brown rice and highly milled rices, characterized by low friction coefficients, pack well, while intermediate milled rice, particularly from parboiled paddy, packs badly because of high friction and low bulk density (DES 1975). Yellow discoloration of rice preharvest has also been a problem in some parts of the country. Varieties of rice with a high amylose content cook into dry and flaky products, while those with a low content into pasty products. The gelatinization temperature (GT) of starch has proved to be an important quality criterion and low-GT rices are preferred for puffed products (Bhattacharya 1979). Data such as these are extremely useful in developing varieties capable of yielding cooked products that suit the diverse food habits of Indian populations.

Breeding of varieties with a higher bran oil content, and weak or no bran-lipase activity, is also indicated in relation to the edible oil requirements of the country. Breeding for low husk content would lead to higher yields of edible material, but the storage qualities of such varieties would need scrutiny.

Coarse Grains

Coarse grains consisting of jowar, maize, bajra, and other millets account for about 25 per cent of total cereal production.

Table: Some New Hybrids and Varieties of Millets Evolved or Recommended in Recent Years

Crop	*Hybrids and new varieties*
Jowar	CSH-1, CSH-4, CSH-5. CSH-6, CSH-7R, CSH-8R (all hybrids).CSV-3 (370), CSV-4 (CS 3541), CSV-2 (303), CSV-5 (168), CSV-6 (604) (kharif varieties).SPY-86, FR varieties (few) (rabi).
Maize	Deccan, Ganga Safed-2, Hi-Starch, Him-123, Ganga-5, Deccan-101 (all hybrids), Amber, Jawahar, Kisan, Vikram, Sona, Vijay (all composites), Shakthi, Rattan, Protima (nutritionally superior Opaque-2 composites).
Bajra	BJ-104, BK-560, NHB-5, PHB-10 and 14, CJ-104, CK-560 (stable hybrids resistant to downy mildew), VZM-composite (resistant to mildew).

Sources: Ganga Prasada Rao 1976; Joginder Singh 1976; Murthy 1976.

They are dryland crops capable of withstanding variable climatic conditions. Recent years have witnessed the evolution and commercial cultivation of hybrids, new varieties, and composites characterized by good yields, disease resistance, and adaptability to different cropping systems.

Coarse grains yield cooked products of harder texture than rice and wheat because of a fibrous bran layer that is relatively resistant to water permeability during the cooking process, and also of hard and horny subaleurone layers.

Milling procedures and equipment (Desikachar 1976) have been evolved that remove 10 to 15 per cent of grain layers as bran to obtain grains and flours without serious impairment of nutritional qualities. Large-sized and damaged starch granules present in the grains of certain varieties of maize, jowar, and bajra are conductive to higher water uptake by flours and soft cooked products.

Wheat

Over 90 per cent of the wheat produced in the country is ground in chakkis to obtain flour of about 95 per cent extraction, used for making various unleavened breads such as chapati and poor). Only about 2 million tonnes pass through roller flour mills to yield maida and white flour used in bakery products. New varieties in various stages of development and cultivation are systematically screened for characteristics needed for the manufacture of bread and biscuits (Shankar and Amla 1979). Comprehensive data have become available from the Indian Agricultural Research Institute (IARI), the CFTRI, and the Food Grains Research Centre at Hapur. A programme has been undertaken at the CFTRI to gain an insight into the protein characteristics of wheat and their relationship to the quality of chapati, the most important means of utilizing wheat in this country.

Some attempts have also been made to define chapati quality by sensory methods and to correlate the data with instrumental methods of analysis (CFTRI 1977-1981). Translation of these criteria into physico-chemical characteristics could help in evolving varieties specially suited for chapati.

Pulses

Pulses are the principal means of raising the protein quality of Indian cereal-based dietaries. Pulse production has not exceeded 12.5 million tonnes, although consumption requirements for 1980181 can be estimated at 15 million tonnes (at 60 9 per capita per day for a 684 million population). To minimize the wastages in traditional milling practices and hence nutrient losses, improved procedures and milling equipment have been evolved for commercial use. This technology has been used by industry for the milling of pigeon-pea almost throughout the year, independent of the climatic conditions, which play an important role in traditional practices (Kurien 1979). Milling conditions are also being optimized for mung bean, chick-pea, urd bean, cow-pea, kidney bean, horse gram, winged bean, and peas by suitable adaptation or modification of the technology developed for pigeon-pea at the CFTRI. Wide variations in physical properties and chemical composition of each of these pulses and their varieties are to be expected in different regions and cropping systems. These properties would influence the milling behaviour of pulses, necessitating expensive changes in technologies and equipment. Intra-and inter-varietal differences in physico-chemical properties should be exploited to upgrade the milling quality of the grain, without sacrifice of yield and duration.

Storage

Food grains in the hot and humid countries of Asia suffer qualitative and quantitative losses from insects, microorganisms and rodents during post-harvest handling and storage. Impairment of organoleptic and nutritional qualities and health hazards arising from insect and fungal metabolises, are well-known effects of inadequate grain protection measures and undesirable storage conditions. Food grains handled by government agencies benefit from improved storage practices, but not those remaining in farm storage.

To eliminate or minimize such losses, pesticidal chemicals and their formulations are used widely for prophylaxis or destruction of insect pests both pre- and post-harvest. Pesticide residues are monitored and regulated under Indian food laws to ensure safety to consumers. Increasing hazards from the pesticide residues on food grains accumulating in the human system either by direct consumption or through animal-based foods, have led to an intensification of research on non-toxic insecticides, biological methods of control, and breeding of varieties resistant to pre-harvest infestation.

A mass of experimental data on the varietal resistance of different food grains to storage pests has been put out from various parts of the world. More often than not, the susceptibility or resistance of high-yielding varieties to storage pests is tested just before release for commercial cultivation. Attention to pest resistance is important at all stages of the breeding programme. Maintaining desirable genetic characteristics on a national scale of cultivation is difficult and expensive.

Sixty-seven varieties of rice have been tested for field infestation by Angoumois paddy moth (Sitotroga cerealella) and graded for susceptibility (Kittur and Patel 1972). Genetic resistance of certain rice varieties to this storage pest has also been reported from the United States (Cogburn 1977). Information on susceptibility or resistance of wheats grown in India to storage pests such as the rice weevil (Sitophilus oryzae), or khapra beetle (Trogoderma granarium), Rhizopertha dominica, and Tribolium castaneum have also been generated to help in breeding and cultivation.

In maize, Angoumois paddy moth is found to damage varieties with a high amylose content (Fergason et al. 1970). Reports from Africa indicate that local varieties are more resistant to insect infestation than improved varieties and hybrids, because of hard kernels and complete coverage of cobs by sheaths (Adams 1977; Dobie 1977). Resistance and susceptibility of India maize varieties to Trogoderma granarium and Rhizopertha dominica have also been tested. Six genotypes (M-25-1, CSH-1, CSH-2, CSH3, CSH-4, and CSH-5) of Indian jowar have also been tested and the degrees of resistance to storage pests ascertained (Krishnamurthy et al. 1976). Varietal resistance of pulses to storage pests has also been indicated in India. Trials on chick-pea have shown that grains of indigenous varieties G-24 and G-30 are more tolerant than new varieties to the pulse beetle (Callosobruchus chinensis) because of a wrinkled surface and tough coat (Gupta and Mishra 1970). Continuous efforts are necessary to develop and maintain pest-resistant germplasm of different food grains so as to economize on the costs of storage and infestation control.

Breeding for Improved Nutritional Quality

Breeding for nutritional quality has mainly been directed to improving the protein content, which may or may not be reflected in increased levels of specific essential amino acids. The dwarf wheats cultivated in India contain 12.5 - 16 per cent protein and 2.21 - 2.9 9 of lysine per 100 9 protein (Deosthale et al. 1969). The protein content of improved sorghum varies from 7 to 10 per cent, and that of lysine from 0.9 to 2.6 9 per 100 9 protein. Lysine is the amino acid that limits the nutritional quality of sorghum protein; however, there is overwhelming evidence to show that excess of dietary leucine (another essential amino acid) results in a conditioned nicotinic acid deficiency. More recént studies have shown that the leucine/isoleucine ratio may be as important as the leucine level in causing pellagra. Deficiency of lysine is also relevant in bajra and ragi as in other cereals (Srikantia 1976). Tannin present in the testa of sorghum grains at about 1 per cent level is known to reduce protein digestibility and availability by binding some of its fractions. Most Indian varieties contain less than 0.1 per cent tannin and it may not be of much significance. However, recently the National Institute of Nutrition indicated that the big-availability of iron from a variety of jowar that contained 136 mg/100 9 of tannin was lower than in one containing 20 mg/100 g of tannin.

Of the common cereals, the big-availability of iron from jowar is least and iron deficiency anaemia is common among poorer sections of the population. A low tannin content in jowar is therefore a desirable breeding feature (Srikantia 1976).

Very little attention seems to have been given to the carbohydrates of food grains be they cereals, millets, or pulses, although animal experiments indicate that flatulence can occur by feeding food grains containing stachyose (CFTRI Annual Report 1980/87), and that protein quality can be affected by the level of digestibility of dietary starches. For example, feeding the field bean and some of its carbohydrate fractions to rats affected the absorption of calcium and nitrogen. Detailed carbohydrate profiles of food-grain varieties appear relevant in breeding programmes in terms of nutrition, processing and culinary practice (Srikantia 1979).

The impact of scientific advances in raising food-grain production levels and building buffer stocks could in future years be diluted by agro-climatic uncertainties and population growth. Accordingly, efforts have been intensified to develop sturdy varieties capable of withstanding adverse conditions, resisting infestation, and giving high per hectare yields. Research and development in post-harvest conservation of food grains have begun to provide a fund of information on physico-chemical characteristics that influence milling yields, cooking behaviour, and sensory qualities. Inherent crack-resistant feature of paddy for better milling yields and low breakage of rice, the influence of carbohydrate make-up and starch characteristics on cooking qualities and digestibility of rice and millets, imbalances in amino acid profiles causing nutritional deficiencies like pellagra, and hard texture coupled with a wrinkled surface in grain as a deterrent against pest infestation, are some specifics that merit consideration in breeding programmes.

Commendable advances in breeding, post-harvest conservation and nutrition have been made, but only through isolated efforts. Technologies and equipment have also been developed to process varieties under commercial cultivation, but may not cope with the diversities in physico-chemical characteristics of different food-grain varieties. Constant interaction among breeders, post-harvest technologists, nutritionists, and extension specialists is necessary to integrate the developments in various disciplines and evolve a systems approach that will result in raised production levels and optimal utilization without sacrifice of nutritional or sensory qualities.

While the evolution of varieties characterized by high productivity and disease resistance will continue to have a high place in breeding programmes, genetic translation of such desirable attributes as milling yield, cooking quality, acceptability, nutritive value, and post-harvest infestation is a challenge to the scientific community. Coordination between the areas of agriculture, food technology, and nutrition needs to be reflected in practice (and not just as policy) in the evolution of food-grain varieties possessing the best possible attributes of production, utilization, and nutrition. Such interaction has a very crucial role to play in the food system.

Generating Multidisciplinary Action: The Importance of Interface Activity between Agriculture, Food Science, and Nutrition

The spectre of hunger, poverty, and malnutrition continues to stare at mankind. It represents a multidisciplinary challenge of no small magnitude and therefore requires a multidisciplinary approach to find a solution. Science and technology have been able to make meaningful contributions to socioeconomic development only when they have acted in an interdisciplinary manner to solve the problems.

The United Nations University has therefore recognized the value of such an approach and has given special attention to organizing activities that would involve teams of scientists (both social and natural), technologists, policy-makers and planners (including development economists) and the implementers of programmes to collectively look into the major problems of mankind and find solutions for them through co-operative efforts.

The United Nations University is doing this in the hope that the concerned disciplines will stimulate each other consciously and create a comprehensive and dynamic system capable of multidisciplinary action that could increase the pace of progress towards establishment of a more equitable and just social order in this world. This effort could convert the vicious circles in which we are caught at present into dynamic development cycles. What can agriculture, food science, and nutrition contribute towards this effort? And how can all three fields interact with each other and with other areas in order to benefit society? These questions need to be critically examined.

It is with this objective in mind that the UN University has supported the organization of interface workshops. It is hoped that the present workshop on the interfaces between agriculture nutrition, and food science will provide an opportunity for better understanding of the whole system in greater depth and in relation to actual problems, so that more meaningful multidisciplinary solutions can be sought through cooperation between the scientific communities concerned in other fields. The world population, which at present stands at about 4,300 million, is expected to reach a figure of well over 6,000 million by the year 2000 (FAO 1979). Agricultural production has barely kept pace even with the present need. The requirement of food, even to meet minimum need, will be nearly twice the present production level by the turn of the century and the challenges for the next century would become much greater.

Food losses continue to be high and take away from mankind a substantial amount of what is produced with a great deal of inputs and human effort. The consequent qualitative deterioration of food, resulting from infestation by rodents, insects, and microorganisms, adds to the problem of malnutrition. Prevention of these losses would increase and improve food supplies without additional demand on land, and raise nutritional standards. The UN University looks to this workshop to provide multidisciplinary leadership, and for its recommendations that may be useful in moving forward more rapidly towards solving this global problem, which is among the greatest challenges facing mankind in the twenty-first century scientifically, socially, and politically. In this, the efforts of the organs, organizations and bodies of the United Nations system will have an important role to play, but the real efforts needed will have to come from the countries themselves where the problem really exists.

The Role of Science and Technology

The phenomenal rate at which science and technology continue to develop is clear from even one single indicator: 3,000 words of scientific literature are published every minute. Yet their impact on developing countries has been far from satisfactory. Only a few developing countries have benefited. These are the countries that have recognized the nature and magnitude of their problems, and have built capabilities in the form of human resources and institutions able to use the available knowledge, generate new knowledge, and further bring about its interaction with society to produce technologies that can be absorbed into the social system.

It must, however, be noted that the interaction that has taken place between science and society in advanced countries cannot always be the same as that required in the developing countries because of the fact that conditions are vastly different. There is a need in the developing countries to bring about more meaningful and deliberate interaction between science and society if technologies are to be generated that would be really useful to them. Trained human resources that can bring about the interaction must be created, that is, people who understand not only the disciplines of science and technology, but also the interfaces involved in ensuring a multidisciplinary effort.

Only then will the results produced be such as to bring real benefit to the countries by triggering self-reliant and long-lasting processes of progress. The developing countries, which represent nearly 70 per cent of human-kind, account for barely 5 per cent of the world expenditure on research and development in science and technology.

If they have to achieve the desired results, every effort must be made to build their capabilities and optimize their impact through creation of multidisciplinary networks of cooperating institutes. The UN University is giving special attention to the need for this type of development in its Medium Term Perspective for 1982/87 (UNU 1981). The present poverty and socioeconomic stagnation has resulted in creating a condition where 65 per cent* of the world population live on about 15 per cent of the world income (Parpia 1979). The economy of these countries is primarily based on agriculture; therefore, it is through agriculture and related fields of economic activity that resources have to be generated that would contribute to overcoming poverty and bringing nutritious food within the reach of the common man. To talk of nutrition in isolation from raising income levels and increasing food supplies would be like telling the poor that if they do not have bread they should eat cake.

The Approach for Developing Countries

When one considers the available potential, there is a great deal of hope for improving the situation. It is unfortunate that such negative aspects as the limitation of resources, population growth, and environment have received greater publicity than the positive aspects. To exploit fully the resources available. There is an urgent need for both the political will and the provision of financial resources to build scientific capabilities.

The Post-harvest Phases

Despite the emphasis on raising agricultural production, shortages of food continue, showing that such efforts must in future follow a different course. Some of these represent intelligent estimates and indicate the need for much more data to be collected. These losses are not only quantitative but qualitative in nature. Within four weeks of insect infestation, the protein efficiency ratio (PER) of wheat and legumes can come down substantially, while the food itself becomes unacceptable through development of undesirable metabolites.

Policy Planning and Management of an Integrated Agriculture and Nutrition Technology Network

Missing Link

Agriculture, nutrition, and food science have seldom been discussed together. Somehow, discussions on overall planning and policies for agriculture have remained isolated from food science and nutrition. However, taking the overall need as a working base, nutritional inputs and requirements are projected so as to work out per capita availability and consumption. Agricultural production will continue to remain short in relation to overall nutritional requirements.

Advances in food science and technology have been made, and various appropriate technologies applied. It is disheartening to observe that despite the existence of a very large fund of knowledge for bringing about technological changes, overall adoption of new technologies that involve agricultural produce has been slow, even when acceptance of the new technology is considered to be in national interests.

Policies and Planning

Is integrated management of agriculture policies and planning feasible in India? Agriculture is a state subject. No amount of policy planning at the central level can be effectively implemented uniformly on an all-India basis. This means, therefore, that policies will have to be broad-based and that implementation will occur according to the specific needs of the area, or, for that matter, the crop system. Coordination and integration at an all-India level have been attempted through well-devised interactions between policy-makers and the implementing agencies. Repeatedly over the years policymakers have recognized that planning should be at the base level, and, therefore, policies should be evolved at national level. Under the circumstances how do we go about planning an all-India crop pattern? For certain categories of production, such as those that are of a perennial nature, some planning is possible since one can estimate the areas under such plantations.

But when it comes to general agricultural crops, the pattern of production would vary depending on many factors, primarily decision-making on the part of the individual farmer. Planning in agriculture therefore must establish linkages with the farmer, and some means will have to be found to involve him in the adoption of the plan: otherwise no worthwhile policy can be evolved. It will thus be necessary to know how the farmer will react to various policies in deciding his own plan. We will also have to determine what his options are, as well as his reactions to any new ideas, and how far he is convinced of the significance of things considered beneficial. So far no attempt has really been made to have the primary producer comprehend any cost-benefit ratios, or to know how he would benefit by adopting a policy strategy evolved at district, state, or central level.

In the present socioeconomic and political system, it would indeed be important to establish full rapport with the primary producer. This can be achieved to a large extent by interacting first with selected farm leaders, and have these leaders transmit to the farmers the overall need for policies and planning in the total national context. Through such means, there could be widespread adoption of agricultural policies and planning. However, it is recognized that even with the diverse nature of a subcontinent like India, considerable success has been achieved in improving the overall agricultural situation. The Green Revolution, with its significant adoption of high-yielding varieties all over India, has many lessons for us. Perhaps the techniques employed in extension need much wider appreciation and adoption. Although there may be shortcomings, agricultural development has in itself been epoch-making.

Inputs

With the high population growth rate in India, there would have to be continuous effort to improve food production. Agricultural production can be considerably increased in India because circumstances are favourable. It has been shown that a very high rate of crop productivity can be achieved, and from the achievement of the research stations one can visualize how much potential there still is to improve overall production. The lab-to-land programme can provide many examples of feasible adoption of high productivity. The basic need for any human being is food, and in the Indian context, even shelter and clothes are less important. If we decide as a policy to have adequate food for everyone, an all-out attempt must be made to attain the needed production through agriculture by way of a plan that would match agricultural production with nutritional needs.

This is feasible, but it does seem that our policy perhaps lacks this recognition of a need for a national nutritional uplift. Some of the policies adopted are discouraging, and do not seem to help the attainment of a higher rate of productivity. Inputs like seed, irrigation, fertilizer, and pesticides are the basic requirements for attaining a high rate of production. Take for example the use and cost of fertilizer. Since fertilizer is essential to productivity, in the initial stages all encouragement was given to the use of fertilizer. However with the recent considerable escalation in cost, the overall demand for fertilizer has decreased, and this has substantially (10 per cent) lowered agricultural production.

Is this in the national interest? would it not have been better to continue to encourage the use of fertilizer and help the farmer achieve higher rates of production? Similarly, for other inputs like pesticides, power, and fuel for irrigation, the policy should be to minimize their costs. It is a tragedy that whenever there is a shortage of power, the first restriction in most states falls on the rural feeders; this restricts use of irrigation, at a time when it is most required. Certain advanced countries, and even developing countries, have helped achieve higher rates of productivity in agriculture by assuring a supply of inputs at very low cost. Even in India, if we were to produce much more of any foodstuff, it could be an export earner. Considering the overall potential of agricultural development, prospects for India becoming a net exporter of agricultural produce rather than having to depend on imports are very good. The rate of productivity in agriculture can also be further increased by giving special incentives to those who attain a higher-than-average rate of productivity. Such incentives would attract many farmers, and might give the direction needed to attain specific production aims of any commodity. Many forms of incentive have been designed for industrial development and for export, but in the area of agriculture such forms are very few. In reality there is a negative approach to higher agricultural production, since urbanites and policy-makers continue to scoff at any successes made in agriculture.

Agricultural Prices Commission

The Agricultural Prices Commission (APC) is an important agency that can be effectively used as a mechanism of planning and of attaining some integration in agriculture. This role has not so far been fully visualized for the APC. It deals only with working out price support for selected agricultural commodities. To be used as an instrument in policy implementation, APC must broaden its mandate, since it is the prices of agricultural commodities that largely determine the decisions of the farmer. So far the APC has perhaps not given consideration to the nutritional aspect of agricultural commodities. No weightage seems to have been given directly to nutritional need in fixing prices, though in recognition of the overall shortfall in such agricultural commodities as oilseeds or pulses, higher incentive prices have been given. In recommending an overall "food basket" of balanced nutrition for the country, it may not be feasible to advise APC to encourage higher prices for any products that would improve the overall nutritional needs of the nation. As a matter of policy, however, a recommendation should be made that a nutritionist may be included as a member of the APC, with the intention of influencing pricing policies from the point of view of nutrition.

Integration of Policies

There is a serious lack of integration in the formulation of policies by various ministries. It would appear that often the exigency of the situation is overrated and the perspective plan is sacrificed. To give an example, the policy decision that has been made in regard to sugar price, levy excise duty, and export, in spite of integration at the highest level, suffers from lack of perspective, and has not taken into consideration the high potential for sugar production nor its effect on producers and consumers.

Similarly, the decision to import 1.5 million tons of wheat as an expedient reaction to a particular situation may have a long-term effect on the production of wheat, in which India has attained an international record of productivity would it not be possible to evolve a long-term policy, by which the farmer would be assured of prices that are reasonable, which is linked with any escalation (such linkages are in operation for all dearness allowances) and which is guaranteed for a period of five years? This would enable the farmer to work out a plan of rotation according to his own feasibility. Another example is the price of milk. Most urban areas in India now have public sector dairies. Milk prices of these dairies are artificially kept low, resulting in substantial losses to the exchequer and, of course, in no significant improvement in the purchase price of milk. There is therefore a lack of any incentive for a higher production of milk, and this would naturally reduce the overall availability of milk and milk products. Not only is the pricing policy affecting milk production, it is also affecting the nutrition of people.

Credit

Credit again is an instrument that can really help attain higher agricultural production, but this instrument has not been properly used. General availability of credit is based on the cost of specific crops. However, only a few banks have linked a higher rate of productivity to higher credit. Such linkages between credit and productivity would enable the farmer to use effectively more inputs and improved technology. Apart from short-term credit for the crop, there is also a real need to organize better credit linkages for land development, irrigation and such post-harvest facilities as storage, handling, and marketing. This has not been recognized. Agricultural production would be diluted through large wastages for lack of post-harvest handling facilities. Damage to perishable commodities would be especially higher without proper post-harvest facilities at the farm level and all through the marketing chain.

The processing and marketing of various agricultural commodities deserve better terms of credit. With many of them, the producers' interest can be protected only if commodities are properly preprocessed, packaged, and marketed. However, credit is sometimes restricted and is now given at a lower rate of interest only towards production.

But if full benefit of greater production is to be acquired, extension of credit to the later steps of handling, packaging, and transport would not only protect many food commodities from deterioration, not only in terms of quantity but of product quality and nutrition. Much could be done in preventing if easier terms of credit were made available for these purposes. Not only must credit be provided, but incentives may have to be designed to improve the overall handling of all commodities.

Marketing

Planners often consider agricultural production as a base for all policies. This is highly erroneous. A country that is predominently rural, with an obvious lack of rural development, suffers when the infrastructure needed for proper marketing of agricultural commodities is missing. Post-harvest handling, processing, and marketing of agricultural commodities influence individual nutrition. In other words, it is not sufficient to evaluate the availability of nutritional foodstuffs by considering just the overall production of agricultural commodities. It is necessary to understand how the marketing of food has been organized and how the needs of each consumer have been met. A study of the public distribution system through ration shops, of the Food Corporation of India and of other agencies that are handling such programmes as Food-for-Work, shows how ineffective are the means to properly protect food and service the consumer. Not only are the costs high, but the deterioration of food in terms of quality and nutrient content is very evident. Surely there is a need for much better understanding of how post-harvest technology could be the means for improving substantially the quality of food.

It may also be relevant to ask whether it is necessary to continue a policy of rationing, recognizing that there is an overall significant reduction in the quality and nutrition of food. Why would it not be possible to replace the entire programme by one of Food-for-Work, which has relevance to the use of manpower and the employment of food as a resource? Extension of the Food-for-Work programme could also generate employment in the private and public sectors, or enhance a self-employed status. This programme could perhaps adopt nutritional criteria as a means for improving the nutritional status of the lower strata of the community. Market yards and mandis could also be used in monitoring and evaluating standards and the quality of agricultural commodities. This would also help in improving handling, storage and processing of the trade commodities. Agro-industries are on the threshold of an expansion programme. However, it is unfortunate that most agriculture commodities needed by these industries are not produced in accordance with the requirements of industry since there is hardly any link between industry and agriculture. An isolated exception is sugar, where productivity has been very effectively linked with the quality of sugar-cane. Establishing linkages between agriculture and agro-industry would help to improve the status of food technology and most likely nutrition. Vertical integration through use of an agricultural commodity would contribute substantially to overall economic progress.

Integrated Use of Agricultural Commodities

An important area affecting both nutrition and food technology lies in the utilization of agricultural produce to full potential. In developed countries, producers receive maximum benefit out of such total utilization of agricultural produce. This is achieved through vertical integration, utilizing each and every by-product of agriculture. Food science and technology could significantly contribute to this end of improving the status of agricultural commodities in terms of higher utilization. Moreover, many of these commodities could contribute greatly to nutrition. It is not necessary that all processes produce items for human use; there are many innovative technologies that could use agricultural commodities as cattlefeed, fertilizer, and fuel. Some studies have been made to prepare balance sheets of all inputs into agriculture and its outputs. Through such studies, one can perhaps evaluate, if not the cost-benefit at least the nutrition-benefit ratio for important agricultural commodities. If this were done, we could perhaps achieve a proper interphase of agriculture, nutrition, and food science.

9

Food and Labour Cost Control

If you are running a restaurant or food service business, you understand that the most important costs under your control are food (including beverages) and labour costs — together, known in the industry as prime costs. Being able to compare these costs — in a percentage format — against typical scenarios of other restaurant businesses is helpful in the management of your business. Costs Vary Widely By Type of Restaurant. Both food and labour costs vary with the type of food service operation. As a rule, luxury restaurants will have higher food and labour cost percentages than casual dining or fast-food restaurants. The product sales mix, quality of food and service, pricing and hours of operation will impact your food and labour cost percentages. Furthermore, state minimum wage differentials and differences in tip credit allowances (towards minimum wage) affect the labour cost percentage. The extent of beverages sales — as part of the food mix — has a considerable impact on total food cost percentages.

How Food and Labour Costs are Calculated

Food and labour costs are calculated as a percentage of the total volume of sales. If a restaurant does $20,000 per week and the total cost of food and beverages is $7,000 for that week, then the food cost is considered 35 percent. If, at the same restaurant, labour (including payroll taxes and benefits) equal $5,000 for the week, then the labour cost is 25 percent. Total prime costs are 60 percent in this example.

What Are the Ranges?

Certain fast food restaurants can achieve labour cost as low as 25 percent, while table service restaurants are more likely to see labour in the 30 percent to 35 percent range. Food costs (including beverages) for the restaurant industry run typically from the 25 percent to 38 percent range, depending upon the style of restaurant and the mix of sales.

Look at Prime Costs to Determine Success

In order to make money in the restaurant business, prime costs should generally be in the 60 percent to 65 percent range. How that breaks down between food and labour is less important than achieving a prime cost maximum that produces a satisfactory profit. So if one of the prime costs is in the higher range, the other prime cost must be in the lower range to achieve profitability. Remember it is the combination of food and labour that creates the bottom line.

About Labour Costs

The majority of labour costs stem from paying employee wages and salaries. To obtain a more accurate picture of the restaurant's labour costs, divide the front-of-the-house labour with the back-of-the-house. Front-of-the-house labour includes wait staff, floor managers, hosts, bussers and bartenders. Back-of-the-house includes kitchen staff and dishwashers. As a small-business owner, also include the portion of all employee benefits that you pay, such as group health insurance, in your labour costs.

Labour Cost Percentages

Varying industry standards put labour costs between 30 to 35 percent of the restaurant's total sales. The standard for manager salaries should be around 10 percent of total labour costs, leaving 20 to 25 percent of labour costs for hourly employees. Labour costs tend to fluctuate depending on your restaurant's busy and slow seasons, so it's a good idea to average your weekly labour costs to obtain your monthly labour costs. You can then use your monthly labour cost averages to obtain your annual average labour costs.

Overstaffing

If you find your labour costs are higher than the industry standards because of overstaffing, examine your staff schedule and cut your staff down to a "skeleton crew" whenever possible. This applies to both front and back-of-the-house staff. If you have a kitchen manager or executive chef who schedules back-of-the-house staff, discuss your labour cost concerns and goals with her so she can schedule her staff accordingly.

Employee Productivity

Low employee productivity is also a factor in higher labour costs. To increase employee productivity and decrease the restaurant's labour costs, consider cross-training your front-of-the-house staff. For example, train some of your wait staff behind the bar. This way, on slow nights you won't have to staff a bartender because the server can take care of your guests' drink orders. For back-of-the-house employees, consider training them on additional food stations. Doing so will enable one person to work multiple stations on slow nights.

Controlling costs isn't so much about reducing them as it is about maximizing the value for your guests. Restaurateurs tend to look at theft, over portioning and shrinkage in terms of what it does to us as owners and managers. If we are to take a customer-centric approach to the problem, we begin with the question "What is the end result of these actions on my guests?" Theft is an easy example. An employee that steals from you causes your Cost of Goods sold to increase which must be compensated for by raising prices. Raising prices in turn decreases the value of the customer's experience. The long term effect of this is that the customer count decreases which leads to lower sales.

A customer-centric look at over-portioning may at first look like a benefit to customers, but nothing is truly free, so if they aren't paying for it in the French fries on their plate, they'll pay for it with a beer price that could be priced 25 cents lower. While this may seem insignificant, the next point isn't so benign. Over-portioning is rarely consistent. This means that the customer that is delighted with the huge portion of French fries will be disappointed with a normal portion on their next visit. Major players in the fast food industry have shown how to handle this problem head on. McDonald's has changed their portions and packaging over the years to make it physically impossible to over-portion their fries. This means that your fry box always seems to be spilling over with fries. It shows how seriously they take consistency in their business and gives us a glimpse at how they have become the world's number one operator. Shrinkage or spoilage is the third issue that not only hits our bottom line but also our customers. Inefficient purchasing creates crisis situations (we need to get rid of this lettuce) and inferior product for your guests. Not ordering enough on the other hand creates shortages and also results in unhappy guest experiences.

Seven Strategies

So we've seen that these things hurt our guests as well as ourselves. What can we do to fix them?

Menu Development: Do you have a Products Standards Manual? If you do, do the portions listed reflect what's actually going on day-to-day. We've seen situations where the portion size listed in the manual was 40% less than what was actually going onto plates. Correcting this meant actually changing the size in the manual and adjusting pricing and purchasing decisions accordingly.

Portion Training: When a new team member comes on board, are they shown how to estimate portions? Do they check those estimates against a scale or other measure?

Prep Guides: How do you decide how much raw product to prep into your restaurant made sauces and other items? Key decisions like this should be thought out with all of the appropriate information at hand.

Purchasing: Reduce the number of vendors you deal with - How many suppliers do you work closely with? Have you spelled out expectations on produce, meats and other perishables? Do you go back and forth between suppliers, focusing on price rather than quality? Instead, try focusing on one main supplier and establish strict expectations with them for quality. Nearly all suppliers treat customers like that better than the "shoppers". By concentrating your volume, you'll gain leverage with the supplier as well.

Systemize Ordering: How do you decide how much product to order? Here's a hint, if you're sitting at a desk to do your order, it's probably wrong. Great operators walk through the restaurant's coolers, freezers, and dry storage while deciding how much to order. In addition, they refer to the previous few weeks of usage to root out any trends or opportunities in their purchasing. As well, they see the condition of what's in stock and act accordingly.

Systemize Receiving: Do you have a process for receiving? There are four basic steps to receiving the order

- Check for completeness and accuracy
- Check for quality of product, especially produce and meats
- Contact your representative for any credits
- Date all products received.

Inventory Controls

Appropriate inventory controls are critical to closing the loop on controlling your costs. While they can be simple, the solution should be robust enough to alert you to trouble spots in your kitchen and on your menu. Always keep in mind that your Cost of Goods Sold Percentage only tells you about a part of your business. It won't tell you if your customers are unhappy with portion sizes or if your service levels are suffering. It's up to you as an excellent operator to balance all of the areas of your business.

Labour Cost

Operating a restaurant involves many expenses. Essentially, you incur labour costs when you have employees working for you. Labour is an operational expense in just about any restaurant, predominantly including hourly wages for staff members.

Labour Cost Awareness

Labour costs are typically understood as a percentage of sales. To figure your labour cost, use this equation:

$$Payroll \div Total\ Sales = Labor\ Cost\ Percentage$$

OR

$$\$7{,}000\overline{)\$1{,}400}\quad 20\%$$

Many restaurants hope to run a labour percentage below approximately 20 percent. When the costs begin to climb, anxiety levels rise as well. Still, simply paying your employees less will not solve labour cost issues. The keys to controlling labour costs are improving workplace productivity and scheduling your employees wisely.

Control Your Labour Costs with Improved Worker Productivity

Increasing productivity improves your overall operation by building employee skills and confidence. Take time to provide your staff with sufficient training and communication.

Cross-Train Your Staff

Cross-training is beneficial to both the employee and the business, since the worker will have a wider range of skills and be able to help in multiple areas of the restaurant. This allows the manager to schedule fewer workers while still being able to achieve the same production and service standards. Some suggestions for cross-training include:

- Train your prep cook to handle the grill
- Train your hostesses to work as back-up servers
- Train bussers to help run food to customers.

Conduct Frequent Staff Audits and Reviews

Another great way to help improve productivity is to perform regular audits. Take the time to watch and assess your employees' performances. If you find that a large portion of your employees' work days includes inordinately long breaks or downtime, it might be wise to revise your schedule. Conducting face-to-face reviews with each member of the staff will help communicate your thoughts and concerns.

Control Labour Cost With Precise Scheduling

Make sure you have constructed a budget to help keep track of your annual sales and expenses like labour. Through your budget, allow a percentage of your sales to cover labour expenses. Then, create a staffing schedule to reflect your budgeted allowance for labour expenses. The following tips elaborate these guidelines:

Break down your annual budget: Break down your annual budget into monthly budgets to help divide the money into weekly sections. This will give you a weekly budget, from which you can determine labour costs and make an appropriate staffing schedule.

Design a new weekly schedule for all employees: Relying on a fixed schedule week after week fails to acknowledge shifts in projected sales, changes in the weather or other factors that can affect your business. Adjust the number of staff scheduled each week to keep compliant with weekly budget constraints.

Monitor clock in/clock out times: After every shift, make sure that all employees have punched in and punched out exactly according to the schedule. Managers can usually use tools within the Point of Sale (POS) system to monitor and alter this information when necessary.

Discuss all schedule change requests in advance: Switching shifts can create problems when people start to work overtime, working more hours than the budget allows and potentially breaking a law, if the workers are youths. Be sure a manager is constantly aware of any proposed changes in the schedule.

Avoid Over-Staffing

It is often tempting to schedule more people than necessary in order to ensure that the business runs without any kinks. The reality is, however, that there will always be a few kinks in the restaurant business. Scheduling too many employees will increase your labour costs and reduce your overall profit, hurting your business overall. If you find that you have over-scheduled, you can send staff members home early. Train your people to work quickly, accurately and efficiently while also treating guests with respect and care. This allows you to operate at a high standard while still hitting your target labour percentage. Whether opening a restaurant for the first time, or simply hiring due to employee turnover, be prepared to keep constant tabs on your staffing needs.

In the restaurant industry, a manager often needs to hire for the same position more than once. Learn to determine which positions you need to successfully run the business in order to find and keep the best staff members.

Know Your Staffing Needs

If you are opening a restaurant for the first time, you will need to determine your staffing needs with as much accuracy as possible. Even if you have run your business for a while and need to hire again, consider the following first:

- The type of restaurant you run (i.e.: fine dining, casual dining, fast food etc.)
- The type of food service you offer (i.e.: deli-style, buffet-style, fine-dining, etc.)
- The type of food on your menu—this determines what you need to cook and which kitchen stations you require
- The number of tables or seats available in your restaurant—this determines the number of servers you will need.

After you operate the restaurant for a while, you will begin to see the shifts and trends in daily and weekly business, and you will get a feel for which people—and how many people—you need for each part of the day.

Determine the Critical Positions for Your Operation

Know your concept before determining what position you will need to fill. For instance, a fine dining restaurant needs a chef and a sous chef, to start.

However, a fast-food drive-thru will need a drive-thru order taker and fry-cooks. Additionally, consider the positions that will have direct contact with customers or guests. Hiring respectful, friendly and engaging people will help define the face of your operation and deliver the memorable customer experience you want.

Determine How Many Employees to Hire

Before hiring, be sure to consider the number of employees you should bring on. It helps to start out with a few more employees than necessary in case some staff members do not work out. At the same time, be sure your annual budget can accommodate the number of people you are looking to hire. Essentially, consider the following guidelines:

Assess the number of tables, seats or service stations: The number of tables you expect to serve will help determine the number of servers you need on staff.

Consider the layout of the kitchen and different kitchen stations: The layout of your kitchen and the cooking stations affect the number of line cooks or kitchen staff you require.

Consider your busiest times first: Make sure your busiest times, typically lunch and dinner, are adequately staffed. For instance, you might need to staff more people from 11am-1pm than you would in early morning hours,

Stay within the means of your budget: Your budget will not only determine how much you can afford to pay your employees, but how many employees you can have working at a time to keep your labour cost down.

Use a Sales and Guest Projection Chart.

A staff chart is helpful when determining how many employees to schedule. The chart below shows the number of guests anticipated each hour, as well as the projected sales the restaurant achieve each hour. This information determines the number of staff members needed per hour as well. You can organize your chart by number of expected tables if you do not know the expected hourly guest number. Be sure to consider your restaurant type, service style and layout when designing your chart, and keep operating efficiency and customer service as your priorities.

JOB POSITION	*# of Customer Per Hour*					
(# of each required)	*10*	*25*	*50*	*75*	*100*	*150*
Front of House						
Server	1	2	4	5	7	10
Busser	0	1	1	2	2	3
Bartender	1	1	1	1	2	2
Hostess	0	0	1	1	2	2
Back of House						
Line Cook	1	2	3	3	4	6
Dishwasher	1	1	1	1	1	2
Expeditor	0	0	0	1	1	1

Manage Your Labour Cost

When you begin to hire, or bring on more people, labour cost is a concern. Complete a comprehensive staffing schedule for all the staff you anticipate needing in your establishment. Cover all of your busy times and think about staffing according to the Sales and Guest

Projection Chart. For instance, you decide that you will need about four servers scheduled during the lunch hour. After you determine the average hourly wage for each position, you can simply multiply the average hourly wage by the hours required on your schedule. This is your labour cost. Compare this number with your operating budget, and make sure the labour cost does not displace profits. This will help you control your labour expenses.

Find the right people

Once you have considered your budget, the positions your restaurant needs, and how many people to hire, the real search begins. With a plan in place, you can focus on finding the right people for your operation and watch your operation become more successful before your eyes.

Controlling Food Costs

Controlling food costs starts with inventory organization and control. Over and over we have found that reducing inventory levels and organizing food storage areas will significantly reduce food costs. It is a simple axiom: When you have excess and disorganization you have waste.

The Best Guess Inventory/Order System

This system works best when your chef/kitchen manager has been able convince you that ordering is a complex procedure that you the manager/owner should not get involved in. Only someone with his/ her many years of experience can understand the obscure secrets of food purchasing.

The system works like this:

- In the middle of the lunch hour rush a waitress runs out of crackers. (Side station stocking problem?)
- She rushes to the store room but does not see the crackers because two cases are hidden under other things. (Poor organization problem?)
- She then rushes to the chef, who is busy on the line, and tells him you are out of crackers.
- The chef was to busy to leave the line and check the storeroom.
- That afternoon whatever salesperson walks in first will get an order for crackers. (Forget price, we need them now!) And because we ran out the chef doubles the order to four cases.

- Now we have six cases of crackers that will sit in the storeroom for who knows how long. (Your money is sitting on a shelf earning nothing)
- Murphy's Law says it is only a matter of time until someone stacks a couple of cases on #10 cans on top of the crackers.
- Chances are good that before you can use up all those crackers, you will have one or more cases of cracker bits and crumbs.

There you are: Inadequate side station stocking and poor food storage organization caused a panic in the middle of the lunch rush resulting in a panic purchase of excess inventory, without checking prices, which resulted in overstocking and spoilage. The really scary part is that this is standard operating procedure for many restaurants.

Helpful Hint

In many instances we have eliminated 20% to 50% of the shelves and storage areas to encourage the kitchen to keep their inventory lean and mean. In some cases of extreme overstocking this alone has resulted in reducing food costs by more than 10%. A rule of thumb we have found to work well is: Order to bring your inventory up to a two order period par level. That is: If you order an item daily, such as produce, order enough to have a two day supply including the inventory you have on hand. If you order dry stores weekly, subtract the inventory you have on hand from what you expect to use over the next two weeks and order the difference. With this simple concept you should never run out of product, and never have more than a two order period inventory on hand. Check out the inventory/order system chapter for details.

Food Storage

While state Health Departments have gotten tougher in this area, many restaurants still loose product to freezer burn, contamination and spoilage because of improper storage procedures. Even worse are those restaurants who loose customers because they serve less than fresh meals.

Want to know what improper storage is costing you?

- On the sly, after all your employees have left, take an inventory of everything in your freezer and walk-in that is not properly wrapped, covered or date marked.
- In the next day or two take a second inventory to see how many of these items are still not properly stored. Check for rotation to see if the oldest items are used first.

- Now cost out the items that are still improperly stored. Multiply this by 365 days. Bet that number gets your attention.
- Give your kitchen crew a break by assuming that half of those items will be used up before they spoil. Chances are that even half of your annual spoilage cost will get you thinking what you could do with all that extra money.

Portion Control

Advance preparation can have a critical impact on food costs. Just as you would not stop to drain the swamp when the alligators are nipping at your butt, your cooks will not worry about portion control when deluged with orders during a rush. Advance preparation and portioning not only saves food cost dollars, it also results in a more efficient kitchen, with a more consistent product and faster service to your customers.

Helpful Hint: A quick check of the previous weeks menu score provides a good guide as to how much to prep for a given day and meal period.

Purveyor Shopping

Regularly scheduled requests for bids/quotes from both your current suppliers and new suppliers can loop some more off your food costs. This is an area where you can delegate, up to a point.

- Have one or more of your employees make the calls, using the specifications from your inventory/order form. If a new supplier offers a good price, ask for samples.
- Do not let the employee change your specified supplier on the inventory/order form without your approval.
- Review the price offered and check the quality of the sample before changing purveyors. If you have any doubts, check their service and the consistency of their quality with other restaurants in your area.
- Have a receiving procedure that checks price, quality and quantity at your door. One way is to post your inventory/order form on a clipboard at the back door. The person receiving the delivery certifies that price and quantity of the delivery matches the inventory/order form as well as checking for quality. Exceptions can be noted on the back of the form, and signed by the delivery driver, with management follow-up.
- A double check is to have your bookkeeper check invoiced prices and quantities against quoted prices and amount ordered quantities on the inventory/order form

The Lowly Dishwasher

Being the lowest in the pecking order in a restaurant, the dishwasher's potential for profit maximizing is often overlooked. More than anyone else he/she can tell you what is coming back from your dining room. How much of your food costs are going into the trash because of excessive portions or just because customers do not like an entree, vegetable or condiment? Changing a garnish, eliminating a vegetable or reducing a portion may allow you to reduce the menu price, making you more price competitive with the same profit.

The Back Door

The back door is where a good portion your profits can go, if you let it.

- The most obvious step is to keep your back door locked. This will require you to install a door bell outside for deliveries. In addition local fire codes may require an emergency exit bar on the door. Be sure it includes an alarm that must be deactivated by management or designated kitchen personnel before the door can be opened.
- Keep the area outside your back door clean and tidy. As much as is practical you want to eliminate places where stolen food product can be hidden until the thief gets off shift.
- Check your garbage. It is a common trick to wrap a couple steaks up and hide them in the out going garbage. You may also realize considerable saving in lost linen and silverware costs by checking the garbage.
- If you are designing a new kitchen, locate your freezers and walk-ins, where you keep high cost items like meat and seafood, as far from the back door as possible. Make it harder to sneak things out.

How To Make It All Workable

Just like everything else in your restaurant, you are the key to making food cost control work. We favour the two person spot check and prosecute method.

The Two person check:

- Designate whoever has authority to open the back door to check all garbage before the dishwasher carries it out. If the inspector does his/her job theft will be reduced by requiring two person collusion.

The spot check:

- This is where management insures the inspector is doing his/her job. This is also where management gets their hands dirty and spot checks the garbage at unexpected times. This clearly establishes you are committed to controlling back door theft. It also validates that you do not ask your employees to do anything you will not do.

The prosecution:

- You may choose not to go through the hassle of calling the police and actually prosecuting a thief. What you can do is:
- If your cook/garbage inspector catches a dishwasher taking food out with the garbage, establish that the dishwasher is actually the thief and fire him/her. After a severe reprimand the first time, the same dishwasher caught taking food out again is reasonable proof of his/her guilt in our minds.
- If you wait outside and find stolen food in the garbage after your cook has inspected the garbage, fire the cook.
- It is very possible the cook who allows stolen food to go out the door is negligent rather than a thief. No one likes to root through garbage. By firing this cook you will insure that the next cook/inspector will really check the garbage.
- Help your cook/inspector. Provide heavy vinyl or rubber gloves and apron for use while inspecting the garbage.

A Couple Tricks To Reduce Breakage And Spoilage

- The very first step in breakfast preparation should be to set a supply of eggs out to temper, even before the grill is turned on. Egg yokes are less likely to break if the egg is cracked at room temperature.
- If you use frozen portion cut steaks, layer the steaks in a shallow hotel pan then cover them with clean cooking oil. With this simple procedure:
- The steak's cooler shelf life will be doubled. And, you will have better tasting steaks because the oil prevents the steaks flavourful juices from draining off.
- When broiled the oil seals in the steaks flavour, without leaving any after taste.
- With a longer shelf life you can keep more steaks defrosted, eliminating the need to defrost in a microwave, or attempt to broil a frozen steak if you sell more than expected.

10

Food Tourism in Different Countries

Food in Africa

Africa is the second largest continent in the world. There are 54 countries on the continent, and each one has something special to offer. Africa is known for its beautiful diamond and gold mines, the Nile River, and the ancient Egyptian culture that resides in the desert. Some visit Africa to see history, while others visit Africa in order to have an adventure.

Traditional Cuisine

The food in Africa became the cuisine it is today thanks to the availability of the local fruits, vegetables, meat and grains. Green vegetables are the main source of vitamins and are included in most meals in Africa. The greens are often picked when they are very young. They are washed and cut up and are boiled with other vegetables and spices. While there are some common ingredients in the many different countries, each one has their own specific style and types of foods.

East Africa

East Africa is the home of the people who raise cattle. In early days, sheep, goats, and cattle were seen as forms of currency and were often not eaten. Instead, the animal might be given to the father of a bride or the widow of a warrior. Foods that are commonly eaten in East Africa include corn, rice, curries, lentils, pickles, and other exotic flavours. When meat is cooked, it is often roasted or cooked into a nourishing stew.

North Africa

North African cuisine is rich with spices that came from the Arabs. Things like nutmeg, ginger, cloves, and saffron are found in a number of the dishes that are made in North Africa. Couscous was brought to the inhabitants of North Africa thanks to the Berbers, and quickly became a main staple of daily living.

West Africa

West African cuisine is known to be heavy and filled with starchy ingredients. There is also a lot of fat included in the dishes that come from West Africa. Some of the common ingredients in the countries in West Africa include cinnamon, potatoes, yams, cassava, plantains, citrus fruits, and pineapples. Many of the dishes are either roasted, boiled or fried, and the root vegetables are often mashed. Fish is served frequently in West Africa. Some of it is dried, other times it is cooked fresh in olive oil.

Southern Africa

Southern African cuisine has been changed by the number of immigrants that have migrated to the countries. Curries and chutneys are eaten frequently, as are kebobs and fish stews. Seafood is used heavily and wild game is eaten often as well. European beers are available to drink, as are more fruit beverages made from the local citrus population.

Central Africa

The cuisine in Central Africa is filled with starchy foods, grilled meat and tons of different sauces. Chicken is a popular meat, so is crocodile, antelope, warthog and monkey. It is said that the most traditional type of African cuisine can be found in Central Africa, as not many people migrated there until only recently.

Food in Argentina

Argentine is located in the southern tip of South America. There are a number of popular cities in the country, including Buenos Aires. Buenos Aires is the capital of Argentina and has been made popular by a number of things, among them the musical Evita, which portrayed the life of Eva Peron, the wife of the president. San Juan is known for it's wine and it's beautiful scenery, and La Plata is also a popular tourist destination.

Traditional Cuisine

The cuisine in Argentina is compared to Spanish and other European cuisines. Argentina is a country that is rich in beef, meaning that red meat is common in the culture. Wheat is also a major export, meaning that white bread and other wheat-based foods are also used frequently in the culture.

Proteins

Proteins are very popular in the Argentine culture, so protein is served at almost every meal. Grilled meat, such as steak and ribs, is a staple. Pork sausage and blood sausage, or chorizo or morcilla, are also very popular and are often eaten for breakfast or lunch. Meat is breaded and fried and eaten as a snack, and sometimes are eaten with a side dish of mashed potatoes. Empanadas are another popular snack in the culture and can be found at a number of food carts in the larger cities. Sandwiches are often served for lunch. Argentina sandwiches are generally a white bread that has no crust and is filled with cured meat, lettuce and cheese. Sometimes the sandwiches are bought at a local store and are eaten for dinner.

Special Occasions

Mate is a traditional drink that is created from dried leaves and twigs of the yerba mate plant. These leaves and twigs are placed in the bottom of a special cup, which is also called a mate, and the dish is sweetened with sugar. Hot water is poured into the drink and it is sipped through a metal or cane straw, which is called a bombilla. This drink is often shared at a party or special occasion, being passed around until the drink is gone.

On Christmas it is a tradition to serve a pork that has been oven-roasted, while on Easter, eggs are always served and meat is avoided. Empanadas de vigilia, or empanadas that are created with tuna and cod, are often served at this time of year.

Italian Influence

Italian food is seen frequently in Argentina cuisine. Pizza in Argentina looks very like a calzone, both of which are Italian foods. The faina is a thin bread that is made using chickpea flower and is often served with a sweet wine. Pasta is eaten very often in Argentina. Fettuccine, gnocchi and ravioli are three of the most popular pasta dishes served and eaten in Argentina.

Food in Austria

Austria is a land-locked country that is located in Central Europe. It is surrounded by culture in the forms of Switzerland, Germany and the Czech Republic. Austria was dealt a blow when World War II occurred, but it has since come back and is becoming a hot tourist destination. It has an old-world charm and beautiful scenery. Many tourists find themselves visiting it in order to go hiking. The Austrian Alps have a number of different trails and shelters which allows even the most novice of hikers to enjoy themselves.

Traditional Cuisine

The cuisine of Austria is considered to be one of the most transcultural cuisines in Europe. Most of the world knows Austria for it's delicious pastries and sweets, but there are many different types of foods that are created in the country.

Traditional Dishes

One traditional Austrian dish is wiener schnitzel. Wiener schnitzel is piece of veal that has been coated in breadcrumbs and fried. It has become a popular dish all over the world. Some people confuse the dish with a type of sausage, due to the name. Powidl is another well-known dish. It is created using plum. The plums used for this stew are generally picked as late in the season as possible, so as to add sweetness to the dish. It is cooked for a few hours and is stored in the winter in traditional crockery. Gulasch is an extremely popular dish that is served in Austria. It is often spelled goulash and came, originally, from Hungary. It is just as popular in Austria. The dish is created using beef, onions, paprika and some red peppers. The meat is cut up and browned. Onions, garlic and peppers are added to the mixture in order to brown, and then water is put into the pan. Potatoes are sometimes added to the dish in order to thicken the stew a bit. Goulash is often served with dumplings or wish mashed potatoes.

Sweets

A number of popular sweets have come out of Vienna, including vanillakipferl. Vanillekipferl are small biscuits that are flavoured with vanilla and are often served at Christmas times. Guests in the country may also find them in Viennese coffee shops. Sachertorte is an extremely rich chocolate cake. It was created in 1932 and consists of two layers of chocolate dough with apricot jam in the middle. The cake has dark chocolate icing covering the top and sides and is served with a dollop of whipped cream.

Apfelstrudel is another sweet treat served in Austria. It is a pastry jacket that is filled with sugar, cinnamon, raising, bread crumbs and apples. Some recipes call for rum in order to add more flavour to the pastry.

The pastry is sealed and is baked until it is brown. The dough part of the pastry should be extremely thin and crispy when it comes out of the oven. Powdered sugar is sprinkled on top of it and sometimes vanilla ice cream is put along side of it.

Food in Brazil

Brazil is the largest, and most-visited, country in South America. Rio de Janeiro is one of the more popular cities in the country. It is a city on the coast of the country, loaded with beaches and hospitable people. Brasilia is the capital and contains beautiful buildings and cathedrals. Sao Paulo is another popular city. It is the richest city in Brazil and is also considered to be the most trendy city in the entire country.

Traditional Cuisine

The cuisine in Brazil is different in every region. Each region has made the best of the resources available to the people, creating dishes that compliment the people as well as the landscape.

The South & Southeast

Food in the south generally consists of sun-dried meats or flame grilled meats and fresh vegetables. Potatoes are not generally used in the culture, but may be found in the form of potato chips at local stores. Food in the southeast is known for it's distinctive cooking styles. There are a number of local cheeses that are popular in that section of the country. Rice and beans is a popular dish. Black beans are usually used in this dish. Many of the dishes are of German and Italian influence. The state dish is Moqueca Capixaba. This is a stew that is made with fish, garlic, tomatoes, cilantro and onions. Soy and olive oil are used in the meal and it is cooked in a clay pot.

North & Northeast

The north has a number of rain forests which means that the diet generally consists of root vegetables and fish. Sometimes strange meats, such as alligator meat, are used in some dishes, such as Picadinho de Jacare. In the northeast, fertile plains and lots of rain equal abundant vegetation. Cattle ranches thrive in this area which means that beef is abundant and is cooked with regularly. Seafood is also used, as are a number of tropical fruits, such as mango, passionfruit, and pineapple.

Traditional Dishes

Strangely enough, pizza is extremely popular in Brazil. It is made in a wood-fire with a thin crust, a slight amount of sauce and a mild white cheese. There are some toppings, which may seem strange to some travellers, such as guava jam, banana, chicken and chocolate. Many Brazilians put ketchup on pizza, and gourmet pizza, such as pizza that may include shrimp and cheese. Definitely strange foods for people that are not used to it. Hot dogs in Brazil are served with a number of different condiments, such as peas, olives, mashed potatoes, quail eggs and potato sticks. These hot dogs area available in street carts in the larger cities, and may be found in restaurants in some of the smaller cities. Pinhao is a type of pine nut that is eaten as a snack. They are found from a tree that grows in southern Brazil. The nuts are prepared by being boiled, and are stored until the winter months.

Food in Belgium

Belgium lies in Western Europe. Brussels, the capital of the city, is generally the first tourist attraction for most visitors to the country. Most people who live in the country feel that Brussels is not a good representation of the entire culture, but it does have some beautiful architecture and interesting historical buildings. Bruges was the world's biggest city and has been entirely preserved. It is considered to be the biggest historic centre in Europe and has been called one of the most beautiful cities in the world. There are a number of medieval gardens and historical things to see and enjoy.

Traditional Cuisine

Belgium is known as a country where the food is delicious and comes in massive quantities. The dishes are often described as simple, but are made with taste in mind, not presentation. One typical dish is moules frites, which is simply fried mussels and chips. A popular side-dish is stoemp, which is made using mashed potatoes, bacon, cream and root vegetables. This side-dish is often served alongside sausage. Waterzooi is a traditional Belgian stew. The dish is created using fish, carrots, potatoes, leeks, an egg yolk, cream, butter and fish or vegetable stock. The vegetables are fried with peppercorns and then stock is added and brought to a boil. Fish is thrown in and the dish is allowed to simmer. The fish is ten removed and cut. Egg yolk is then put into the stock along with cream and heated until almost boiling. The cut-up fish is added and the dish is ready.

Vlaamse stoofkarbonaden is another popular stew. It is very similar to a Beef Bourguinon, which is made using beef that has been stewed in red wine and cooked with garlic, carrots, onions and other vegetables. Vlaamse stoofkarbonaden is almost exactly the same recipe, but instead of red wine, beer is used to cook the beef in.

Chocolates

Belgium is known around the world for its delicious chocolates. One popular chocolatier is Neuhaus. This chocolate store was begun in Brussels in 1857. It has stores in over fifty countries and supplies chocolate to even more. The chocolate out of Belgium is known to be creamy, rich, and utterly delicious.

Beer

Another popular export from Belgium is beer. Belgian beer comes in many different shapes and colours, from a lager to a lambic or Flemish red beer. There are thousands of cafes in Belgium that offer Belgium beer, and there are thousands of places in the world where you can get beer that has been brewed in Belgium. Many beer connoisseurs believe that Belgian beer should be served at "cellar" temperature in an appropriate glass. Every type of beer in Belgium has it's own specific glass. These glasses are often created by the brewery and are said to enhance the flavour of the beer.

Food in Cayman Islands

The Cayman Islands are a group of islands located in the Caribbean Sea. They are a favourite destination of tourists as well as divers. There are a number of beautiful beaches in the Cayman Islands. Grand Cayman is the largest island and tends to be where the tourists head, but there is much to be found on Little Cayman and Cayman Brac as well. Seven Mile Beach is a popular tourist destination. It is located on Grand Cayman. There are a number of resorts directly off of Seven Mile Beach that tourists can be pampered at.

Traditional Cuisine

The Cayman Islands were founded by people coming from Jamaica and Great Britan. These people learned how to farm and fish on the island and eventually raised chickens and pigs. As time passed, the people learned how to catch turtle, lobster and conch, as well as how to cook with them. Most Cayman dishes are still simple meals, often using a meat, a bread or starchy vegetable, coconut milk, and a few simple seasonings. Most traditional dishes take a long time to cook, and are extremely labour intensive. Conch stew and turtle stew are two favourite dishes and are made using ingredients that can be found in and around the home.

Eating Out

There are a number of different places to eat out on the Cayman Islands. One popular restaurant is Sea Harvest Restaurant. This restaurant resides on the Grand Cayman island. It has a beautiful view of the Caribbean Sea and has a full lunch and dinner service. Many tourists enjoy sitting under umbrellas as they have their meals. Another restaurant that is popular is the Bamboo restaurant, which resides at the Hyatt Regency Grand Cayman Resort. This restaurant is considered by many to be the best sushi bar on the island. There are a number of different types of dishes available, including Asian dishes and traditional cuisine.

For Mediterranean cuisine, tourists should head to Café Mediterraneo. Café Mediterraneo offers traditional, light Mediterranean cuisine, such as pasta, seafood and chicken served in delicate sauces. An extensive wine list is available and the restaurant is conveniently located off of Seven Mile Beach. Hemingways is another restaurant that is located off of Seven Mile Beach. It is a fine dining restaurant and the owners advise that would-be diners reserve a seat in advance, as the restaurant is extremely popular, both with locals and with tourists.

Food in Canada

Canada is the largest country in North America and the second largest country in the world. It is considered to be one of the wealthiest countries in the world and is known for the beautiful landscapes and the culture. Montreal is one city that visitors flock to. It is the largest city in the Quebec province and is home to the largest population of French-speaking people in North America. The country is known for it's trendy culture and it's nightlife. Toronto is another popular destination, as is Calgary, which was known for the 1988 Winter Olympics. Quebec City is considered to be the oldest city in North America.

Traditional Cuisine

Cuisine in Canada varies depending on which province the tourist is visiting. Most cuisine is related to French, American or British foods. In the northern territories, wild game is popular, while in the Quebec province, one can hear the echoes of the French past in the cooking.

Traditional Dishes

There are a number of traditional dishes that can be found around Canada. One popular dish Canada is poutine. Poutine is created by putting large steak fries into a deep dish and adding beef gravy and cheese curds. The curds melt into the gravy and it creates a delicious blend of simple flavours. Haddock and chips is another popular dish that can be found in most restaurants and food stands in the country.

Fiddlehead ferns are cooked in a number of different dishes, and are often served as a side dish. These vegetables can only be picked for a short time, and must be cooked thoroughly in order to avoid the Fiddlehead breaking down and causing vitamin B deficiencies. Montreal smoked meat is identified as the food of Montreal. There are a number of extremely well-known smoke houses, including Jarry Smoked Meat, Chenoy's and the Main Deli, where visitors can get some smoked meat or a smoked meat sandwich. It is possible to find smoked meat in other parts of the country, but most connoisseurs of smoked meat believe that the only true smoked meat can be found in Montreal. It is so popular that some deliver the meat by mail-order. A traditional smoked meat sandwich will often be served simply, with mustard, a side of chips and coleslaw and a pickle.

Meats

Some other popular meats served in Canada include wild game such as Venison, Partridge, Bear, Moose and Caribou. Often these meats are marinated and cooked a certain way in order to take the gamey taste out of the meat. Side-dishes may be fairly strong. Surprisingly, fruit tends to go well with these gamey meats, taking the strong taste down to a tolerable level. Sea food is also very popular in Canada. Salmon is cooked in most established restaurants, and many journey to Canada simply to go Salmon fishing. Lobster is another bit of seafood that is served frequently in Canada, as is Atlantic Cod.

Food in Cambodia

Cambodia is a country that is located in Southeastern Asia. It shares a border with Vietnam and Thailand. Visitors to Cambodia are immersed in a very different culture than most are used to. There are a number of things to see, such as the Angkor Archaeological Park, which holds the ruins of the Khmer civilization, and Phnom Penh, which is the capital.

Traditional Cuisine

The cuisine in Cambodia is known as Khmer Cuisine. This food ranges from simple fare to fanciful dishes that were created for royalty, and is a cuisine that must be tried by anyone that loves food. One mainstay of Khmer Cuisine is prahok. Prahok is a fish paste that is created when fish are cleaned and ground together. It is then left to sit in the sun for at least 24 hours, salted, and sealed in a jar that s full of salt. It takes at least twenty days for the Prahok to be considered rip, but most let their Prahok ferment for up to three years.

Prahok gives a distinctive flavour to any dish that it is used in. When it comes to spices, most people who live there use a variety of basil, heartleaf, chives, coriander and perilla in their dishes. Chili was brought to Cambodia in the sixteenth century and is now used in a number of dishes. Other popular spices include star anise, tumeric, Kaffir lime leaves and ginger.

Vegetables and Fruits

The country does have a number of unusual fruits to offer the casual tourist. Some of these include bitter melon, yardlong bean, winter melon and luffa. These are often added to stews and soups. Squash is used often in dishes, as is baby corn, broccoli, snow peas and bok choy. These are often mixed up, fried, and made into a stir fry dish. Fruits are extremely popular in Cambodia as well. The durian is one popular fruit, as are the mangosteen and the sapodilla. Other more traditional fruits, such as mango, banana and papaya can be found in the country and bought for very little. Many inhabitants of the country believe fruit to be a dessert.

Traditional Dishes

Amok trey is one traditional and simple dish that is served in Cambodia. It is a fish that has been cooked in a coconut milk along with curry, wrapped in banana leaves, and steamed. Bai cha is also served at restaurants and is a fried rice that is made using garlic, soy sauce and Chinese sausage. A meal may be started with Bok l'hong, which is a salad that is made using papaya, string beans, cherry tomatoes and roasted peanuts. Sometimes fish sauce and crabs are included in the salad. Loc Lac is a stir fry dish that is made using beef, red onions, cucumbers, tomatoes and lettuce. Lime juice is served alongside of it so that consumers can dip their food into the juice. Cha knyey is another popular stir-fry dish, made with a spicy chicken, jalapenos, peppers and beef curry. This dish is extremely spicy, and some visitors find that they can not handle the heat of the dish.

Food in China

China is a large country that lies in Eastern Asia. Size-wise it is equivalent to the United States, but it has the largest population in the world. There are a number of cities that intrigue travellers, including Beijing, which is the capital city, and Guangzhou, which is one of the richest cities in China. Nanjing used to be known as Nanking and was the capital of China for a time. Now, however, it holds a number of monuments and relics to interest in the historian.

Shanghai is the most famous city in China, known for it's shopping opportunities and riverside scenery.

Traditional Cuisine

Chinese cuisine is considered to be one of the most diverse types of cuisine in the world. Chinese chefs are able to take cuisine from the many different parts of the country in order to create their dishes. Most Chinese dishes, however, have either a carbohydrate, such as rice or noodles, along with vegetables, fish or another form of meat. Chopsticks are used to eat most foods, and ceramic flat-bottomed spoons are used to enjoy soups and other liquids. Because chopsticks are used, most dishes are made of bite-sized pieces that are easy to grasp with the wooden sticks. In a traditional Chinese meal, each diner is given a bowl of rice while other dishes are laid on the table. The diner is then able to chose from the accompanying dishes, taking a bite of one thing, and then of another. The rice is the only dish that remains in front of the diner the entire time.

Traditional Dishes

There are a number of dishes that are common throughout the entire country. One of these dishes is guotie. Guotie is a dumpling that is filled with meat or vegetable. These are often called potstickers in North America. The traditional Guotie is filled with pork, scallions, cabbage and ginger and is first fried and then steamed. Pickled vegetables are also extremely common to find for lunch or dinner. They are often put on top of the white rice and eaten with it.

Some dishes are known world-round as belonging to the Chinese cuisine. One such dish is Peking Duck. Peking Duck is created using a specific variety of duck, known as the Peking duck. The duck is slaughtered and air is pumped through the neck cavity in order to pull the skin away from the fat. It is then hung and glazed with maltose syrup. After it stands for 24 hours, the duck is roasted. Traditionally the duck should be roasted in a hung or closed oven made of brick. When being served Peking Duck in a restaurant, diners should look for the chef to carve the duck in front of them. The skin is usually first dipped in a garlic and sugar sauce while the meat is carved and served with steamed pancakes, plum sauce and scallions. Cucumber and carrot are often the vegetables of choice to accompany the duck. Traditionally the duck should be placed in the pancake and eaten by hand. The remains of the duck, such as the fat and bones, are often taken home by customers in order to be made into a soup.

Food in Croatia

Croatia is located in Southern Europe. It is surrounded by the countries of Slovenia, Serbia and Hungary. It is often visited by people wanting to get a taste of the past. Split is an ancient city that has a number of Roman ruins in it, and Zagreb, the capital of the nation, also has a number of ruins in it. Omis is a coastal town that boasts of beautiful beaches, as does Ruskamen. The Kornati National Park is frequented by hikers and explorers, as is the Kornati National Park.

Traditional Cuisine

Croatian cuisine is divided into a number of different regions. Each region has a different taste that it is known for. For instance, the Slovonian region is known for it's meat and game dishes, while Istria has light dishes that are of Italian descent. Dalmatia uses Mediterranean influences to create light, tasty dishes, and Middle Croatia is popular for heavy dishes and home-made cheese.

Traditional Dishes

Soup is often served as the first course in some restaurants of Croatia. Manestra is one popular soup. It is created using corn as a base and may include meat. Often, if it has meat in it, it is turned into a stew and is used as a main course. Vegeta is a product that is sold commercially. It is used to season broth. Some add vegetables to it and make a warm winter soup, while others make a light summery soup out of it. Meat is often cooked and served simply. Veal, Turkey and Lamb are three of the popular proteins. Sometimes these meats are served with dumplings, other times they are cooked and served in a wine sauce. Janjetina is a lamb dish that is made when the lamb is roasted and is served with Mediterranean herbs, while Purgerica is a Christmas turkey that is stuffed with apples, bacon and chestnuts before it is roasted. Side dishes often include a lot of vegetables. Sataras is a side dish that is made using bell peppers and other vegetables. These vegetables are chopped up an are roasted and served alongside a meat dish. Mlinci is made using thin, dried bread that is doused with boiled water and salt.

Wine

Wine is very important in Croatia. It is served with most meals and is becoming a profitable industry for the country. When the Romans ruled Croatia, wine was created and refined. Once the Ottoman Turks came into possession of the country, their anti-alcohol laws prohibited wine from being made. Now that wine is becoming vastly popular in most of the countries in the world again, Croatia is building a thriving wine industry. The warm weather and mild winters are ideal for grape production.

Food in Costa Rica

Costa Rica is a beautiful tropical country located in Central America. It borders both Panama and Nicaragua and has the Caribbean Sea on one side and the Pacific Ocean on the other. Costa Rica is Spanish for "rich coast". There are a number of different places that tourists will enjoy, including the capital of San Josë, the Manuel Antonio National Park, and Tamarindo, a famous beach town on the North Pacific coast.

Traditional Cuisine

Costa Rican cuisine uses a lot of fruit and vegetables in the dishes. One staple that is used frequently in Costa Rica is gallo pinto. Gallo pinto is a rice and beans mixture. It is created differently in different parts of the country, but always has a speckled appearance. This food is often eaten three times a day: once with breakfast, once with lunch and again with supper.

Traditional Dishes

Casado is a traditional lunch dish. It is made using rice, fried plantain, beans and salad. Sometimes chicken or pork is served alongside of it. It is sometimes served during dinner, but is more often found on the menu for lunch. Fried zucchini, ayote and chayote are main ingredients in a number of popular dishes. Potato, onion and pepper are also found frequently.

Plantains

Plantains are also fried frequently and served as a dessert or in a meal. Plantains are a member of the banana family. Plantains are more firm than bananas are and are not quite as sweet. They are used mainly for cooking, not for eating raw. Only the plantains that are extremely ripe taste good when they are raw. When they are green, they taste like a potato does, and when they are yellow then are much softer and a bit sweeter.

Beverages

Coffee is served in most homes for breakfast. Costa Rican coffee is very strong and a visitor may need to cut it with cream or sugar. Another traditional drink for breakfast is agua dulce, or sweet water. This is made when sugar cane is boiled down and is solidified into a mold. Some of the solid form is scraped off into boiling water to create a sweet drink, known as agua dulce. Another sweet drink are refrescos. These are fruits that have been liquefied and diluted with either milk or water. They come in a variety of different flavours, including melon, strawberry, mango and passion fruit. When it comes to liquor, residents of Costa Rica drink guaro. Guaro is created from sugar cane and is very similar to rum. It is generally mixed with juice or soda before it is imbibed. There are a number of different types of guaro available to purchase. There is also a number of different beers to purchase in Costa Rica, including Heineken and Pilsen.

Food in Cuba

Cuba is a beautiful island located in the Caribbean. It is located between the North Atlantic Ocean and the Caribbean Sea. Many people visit Cuba for the beautiful beaches and the amazing nightlife. Havana is the capital of the country, and is known as the place where everything is available. Baracoa is a beach-side town that is many people own property on, and Santa Clara is the home of the Che Guevara mausoleum. Cuba is certainly the place to go for those who want fun and frolicking in the sun.

Traditional Cuisine

Cuban cuisine is considered to be a fusion cuisine. It is a mixture of flavours from Africa, Spain and, of course, the Caribbean. African cuisine infiltrated the island when African slaves were used on the sugar cane plantations in the country, and Spanish cuisine came into the picture due to the fact that most of the tobacco plantations were worked by poor Spanish peasants.

Traditional Dishes

One Cuban dish that has made it's way to the mainland is a Cuban sandwich. A Cuban sandwich is created when a long piece of Cuban bread is piled with roast pork, Serrano ham, Swiss cheese, pickles and yellow mustard. It is pressed and cut in half. This dish has become extremely popular in a number of countries, but especially in the United States. Most of the southern states offer a Cuban sandwich on their menu, made the same way as it is made in Cuba. Some add tomatoes and lettuce into the sandwich. This is considered by many to be unacceptable.

There are other popular sandwiches served in Cuba. One is a medianoche sandwich. This sandwich is made almost exactly the same way as a Cuban sandwich is, but it is made with an egg loaf instead of Cuban bread. A pan con lechon is another pressed sandwich. This one is made with roast pork, Cuban bread, onions, and mojito. A variation on the pan con lechon is the pan con bistec, which uses flank steak instead of pork. The Elena Ruth is a well-known sandwich, created using roast turkey, cream cheese, and fruit marmalade. The frita is often considered to be the Cuban version of an American hamburger. It is made with ground beef, onions, and paprika, and is served on a small hamburger bun. It is also topped with mojito sauce and is served with French fries.

Desserts

Desserts are extremely popular in Cuba, mainly because the majority of the trade going out of the country is sugar based. Desserts in Cuba range from being very simple, such as sugar and fruit being added together, to very difficult, such as the dulce de guayaba. Dulce de guayaba is made using Guava paste, which is created by mixing together gelatine, sugar, and guava.

A churro is a Spanish dessert that has become a favourite in Cuba. It is a sweet fried pastry that is often covered in powdered sugar. Marmalade is used in a number of desserts, either as a filling or a topping, and the local Plantain fruit is used frequently as well, sometimes fried and sometimes soaked in a rum mixture.

Food in France

France is located in Western Europe and is an extremely popular tourist destination. Paris, the French Riviera, the Castles of Loire Valley, and Mont Saint Michel are just some of the things that attract people to visit the beautiful country. Paris is known as the birthplace of fashion and cuisine. In fact, many times a chef's education is deemed incomplete until he has traveled to France to study.

Traditional Cuisine

The food in France is considered by most to be the most refined and glorious food in the world. It was not until the 20th century, however, that the food was refined to the delicious and beautiful cuisine it is now. Before that, most chefs used seasonings with a heavy hand and drowned their meats in one sauce or another. There are, however, some delicious dishes that were created in France during that time and have stood the test of time. Some of them have been refined by modern chefs, but many of them are still eaten on a daily basis by inhabitants of the country.

Traditional Dishes

There are a number of traditional dishes that are both served in restaurants and eaten by locals. One classic and simple dish is Biftek frites, which is basically a steak cooked and served with fries. Poulet frites is chicken that is served with fries. There are some dishes that are extremely gourmet, and are created the best by the masters of French cuisine. One such dish is coq au vin. Coq au vin is served around the world and is known as French cooking at it's finest. It is created by using a chicken, preferably an old hen, brandy or wine, salt pork, garlic and button mushrooms. The chicken is cut into strips and is par-boiled and sautéed. Carrots, onions and celery is added to the mixture, as is garlic. Wine is then poured into the pot, often along with stock, until the liquid fully covers the solid ingredients. After it has cooked, the sauce is strained so as to remove the vegetables, and mushrooms are added and served along with the chicken.

Desserts

Many know France for the delicious and decadent desserts and pastries that have come out of the country. Chocolate mousse is a favourite, and is a light, fluffy form of chocolate pudding. One popular, and well-known, dish is Crème Brûlëe. Crème Brûlëe is created when pastry chefs create a rich custard that they top with a sweet, hard caramel. Sugar is then put on top of the dish and is burned on, often by using a blow torch.

Wine

Wine is an important part of French culture and cuisine. It is served during a meal in every gourmet restaurant, and many have sommelier's on staff in order to properly match the wine up with the meal. Wine from France is shipped around the world, and many vineyards have won national awards multiple times for their delicious wines.

Food in Germany

Germany is a country that has received a bad reputation to most of the world due to World War II. The country, however, is beautiful to visit. It holds a number of amazing pieces of architecture, as well as important museums and wonderful shopping. Beautiful churches are located in the city, as are world-class theaters. Frankfurt and Munich are the two most visited cities in the country, but Germany is so much more than just those two cities. That that visit outside of the main cities find that amazing country sides, friendly folks, and delicious food.

Traditional Cuisine

Most German cuisine uses a good amount of pork, chicken and beef. It is estimated that a Germany citizen eats over 60 pounds of meat a year. Game meats, such as boar and rabbit, are available to purchase in many grocery stores, and are often found on menus in prestigious restaurants.

When it comes to breakfast, most German people find themselves eating toast with jam, eggs and very strong coffee. Sometimes deli meats or cheese are served on top of bread, or toast, in the morning. Some meat spreads, such as Leberwurst, which is the German word for liver sausage, are marketed to be used on toast in the morning. Muesli, a cereal that has become popular around the world, is another favoured morning dish. Supper tends to be very similar to breakfast in that it's a light meal. The heaviest meal of the day tends to be lunch, which is eaten around the noon hour. Families sometimes get together and eat Brunch, which is a meal that is midway between breakfast and lunch. These is the way that celebrations are often celebrated, and most families enjoy having an excuse to spend time together.

Beverages

Beer is extremely well-known and liked in Germany. There are a number of different kinds of beer that are served in the country, including lager beer, black beer, and mixed bear. Some mix lager and cola, such as Diesel and Colabier, while others mix lager and lemonade, such as Radler or Alsterwasser. Wine is imbibed in the country, and is found in most fine-dining restaurants. Coffee in Germany is stronger than most Westerners are used to, but is not quite as strong as espresso. Tea is popular in some of the country, but not all.

Bread

Bread is served frequently in German cuisine. One may find toast on their plate in the morning and a sandwich at supper time. The German culture has over 6,000 different types of bread, from white to black to everything in between. There are over 1,000 types of rolls and pastries, and over 17,000 bakeries in the country. Rye-wheat bread is the bread that is the most consumed, followed by toast bread and whole grain. It is common to find a sweet roll wrapped around a Bratwurst and served by a roadside vendor, especially in the larger cities.

Food in Indonesia

Indonesia is an archipelago, or a country that is split between a number of islands, that lies in both the Indian and Pacific Ocean. It is a beautiful country to visit, with dozens of amazing beaches and beautiful volcanoes to visit. Each island has a big of a different feel, but all of them welcome tourists with open arms. Adventurers will love the islands for their beauty and wilds, and those looking for a relaxing vacation can find it in Indonesia as well.

Traditional Cuisine

Indonesian cuisine is extremely diverse, which makes sense because of the wide majority of different islands that makes up the country. Indonesia has always been involved in trade, which means that the culture has always been one to use ingredients that are not native to the islands. Visitors to the country need to know that most meals are eaten with the fork held in the left hand, and the spoon held in the right hand. Like many Asian countries, rice is a staple and is included in most meals. Most often rice is eaten plain with a protein and vegetable dish on the side. Sometimes it is steamed in coconut leaves, in a process that is called ketupat, or is made with rice wine.

Traditional Dishes

There are a number of traditional dishes that are very popular on many islands in Indonesia. One dish that is found on a number of menus is Nasi goreng. Nasi goreng is a fried rice that is made with a number of different ingredients. Sometimes fried crackers and chips are added to the fried rice, while other times leftovers from the evening before are added and the dish is eaten for breakfast. When the cook replaces rice with noodles, it is called mee goring, and is often eaten for lunch or dinner.

Rendang is a dish that is both refreshing and filling. It is used by the tribal people as a ceremonial dish and is often served only during festivities. It is created when beef is cooked with coconut milk and other spices over several hours. The liquid disappears and the meat begins to fry. After the meat is fried, the dish can be either served or saved, under refrigeration, for a few months. It is often served with a rice cake.

Sayur asem is also a popular dish that is offered at the beginning of a meal. It is a soup dish that has a number of vegetables, such as long beans, peanuts, bilimbi and corn. The dish becomes very sour and is considered to be extremely refreshing at the beginning of a meal. Another soup dish that is served at the beginning of a meal is called soto. This dish has a chicken broth, chicken or pork, and vegetables in it. It is similar to a Western-style chicken soup, but can be created with beef instead of chicken.

Food in India

India is a very diverse country, and is considered by some to be the largest democracy in the world. There are miles of deserts, beautiful cities, and spiritual centres that are visited by thousands on a daily basis. Tropical forests are available to adventure through, and amazing shopping beckons all tourists. Many find themselves journeying to one of the many temples that are scattered throughout the country, even if they are not spiritual, simply to view the amazing architecture. The Taj Mahal is one temple that people flock to, for its beauty and amazing story.

Traditional Cuisine

Food is considered to be a vital piece of the culture. Families make time during the day to sit down and enjoy a meal together, generally three courses or more, and food is abundant in the many festivities that the citizens go to. A large number of people in the culture are vegetarians, meaning that those vegetarians that visit the country have a number of options when it comes to eating. Spices, such as ginger and cumin, are widely used in traditional dishes. In most parts of the world, the word "curry" is used for specific spices, but in India, curry is used to describe gravy. Lentils and dairy products are used heavily in the cuisine, and flat breads are also found served along side a number of dishes.

When it comes to protein, goat and lamb are the favoured meats. Kebobs are sometimes served and can be found in street stalls for a quick meal. A lot of times, proteins are fried in oil and served with rice, noodles or vegetables. Chicken is also used in cooking. Meat gravies are popular and are served whenever proteins are served by themselves.

Traditional Dishes

Sambar is a dish that is generally served for breakfast. It is a chowder that is created when toovar, a type of pea, is cooked with tamarind. Spices and flour are put into the broth in order to thicken it, and often other vegetables are added. In the morning, sambar is most often served with vadai, which is created when mashed potatoes are seasoned with spices and are fried. Vadai look very similar to a Western doughnut, but is much spicier. Vadai can also be served in a bun for fast food.

Chicken tikka masala is a dish that has become very pouplar in other parts of the world. It is created when chicken chunks are marinated in yogurt and are cooked in an outdoor, or tandoor, oven. Coconut cream and tomato are often used to create a sauce, and chicken is then put into the sauce. It is generally served over fried rice and a flat bread accompanies it so that the diner can be sure to get all of the sauce off of their plate.

Tea is very popular in India. Darjeeling is one popular tea, and Assam is another. However, most meals do not come with wine or tea. The beverage is served either after, or in between, meals.

Food in Iceland

Iceland is a country located in Northern Europe. Over eleven percent of the country is covered with glaciers, but the country is not as cold as many believe it is. Most visitors tend to head to Reykjavik, which is the capital of the country, as well as the largest city. There are many more things to see in the country, beyond the borders of Reykjavik, such as coastal towns, glacial river rafting, and the largest puffin colony in Europe.

Traditional Cuisine

Most Icelandic dishes have either fish or lamb as the protein. Fresh produce is often eaten as well, and dairy has a place in the heart of Icelandic cuisine. Unlike some countries, Iceland is extremely clean. This means that the majority of the restaurants and markets are extremely clean, and the food that comes out if it is pristine.

The fish that is caught around the island include haddock, halibut, herring and shrimp. This means that fresh fish can be found at all times of the year. Many recipes smoke the fish, or grill it, giving it a smoky, delicious flavour. Lamb is also smoked frequently in the country, and one or the other is included in just about every dish. Sheep are not raised in small quarters, but are allowed to range around on the mountains. This makes the meat lean and delicious. The Icelandic government does not allow hormones to be used in the country, so all of the meat, including the chicken and turkey, is very tasty and is hormone-free.

The hormone-free policy also means that the dairy products in Iceland are completely pure. Dairy is extremely important in most

Icelandic dishes, and it has been estimated that one citizen of the country eats at least 100 gallons of dairy in a year, either through milk, cheeses, or other dairy products. There are over eighty different types of cheeses made in the country, and a number of them have won international awards. As for other produce, hearty vegetables such as potatoes and cabbages are grown outside, but the majority of other fruits and vegetables are grown in heated greenhouses.

Hakari

One delicacy in Icelandic culture is hakari. Hakari is the word for shark, and this specific dish has become a popular one for tourists to try. It is created when a shark is captured and cut up. The meat is then buried in a chamber and is kept there anywhere from two to six months. It is allowed to decompose naturally. After it reaches a specific state of decomposition, it is unburied and is eaten. Many tourists eat it with brennivin, which is a very strong alcoholic beverage. Some that have tried it say that it tastes like a strong cheese, while others swallow without truly tasting it. It is one Icelandic delicacy that has to be tried to be believed.

Food in Hungary

Hungary is a land locked country that is located in Central Europe. The country holds a number of attractions for visitors, including the capital of Budapest and other smaller cities, such as Nyiregyhaza and Szeged. Nyiregyhaza has a beautiful water resort and a museum village that shows what Hungary was like hundreds of years ago, and Szeged is known as the sunniest city in the entire country. Hungary boasts beautiful scenery and architecture, including castles and baroque architecture.

Traditional Cuisine

Hungarian food is known to be spicy and warm. Spices such as black pepper and paprika are used in a number of dishes, and garlic and onions are also two favoured spices. There are a number of different types of soups and pancakes, generally stuffed, that are served frequently in the country. Lunch is considered to be the largest meal of the day, and generally begins with a soup followed by a meat dish. Dessert, or fruit, comes after. Dinner is a lighter meal, and may have dishes that are similar to breakfast dishes.

Traditional Dishes

Goulash is a dish that is known around the world and originates from Hungary. In Hungary, goulash is a soup that is made when meat is cut up and browned, with seasonings such as pepper, salt and paprika. Water is then added to the meat, along with garlic, onions and peppers. Potatoes are often added as well, in order to thicken the soup a bit. When it is cooked, it is then served with mashed potatoes or polenta. Halaszle is another popular soup dish in Hungary. It is made with fish, onion, chili peppers, and spices. The tails and heads of the fish are also added into the soup, creating a very fishy flavour to it. Bread is served with the soup, especially when it is extremely hot, so that the consumer can sop the juice up with the bread.

Stuffed pancakes are also very popular and are eaten either for breakfast, dinner or dessert. One type of stuffed pancake is called Palatschinken. This is a thick pancake and can be filled with fruit, nuts, chocolate sauce, or a combination of them all. Sometimes confectioner's sugar is put over the pancake, along with chocolate sauce. When filled with cheese, meat or vegetable, the dish becomes suitable for diner or as part of lunch. Galuska is a Hungarian dish that is created when potatoes are grated and mixed with egg and flour in order to form a batter. The batter is then filled with cabbage, onions and batter, and is boiled. Kolbasz is one of the types of meats that is served on its own, and is served in stews. It is a smoked sausage that is created out of pork shoulder, salt and garlic. It is smoked cold and is hung to dry. Egg casserole is one dish that is dependant on Kolbasz.

Food in Jamaica

Jamaica is a beautiful Caribbean island that is located directly south of Cuba. It has become one of the number one tourist destinations due to the beautiful beaches, warm weather and wonderful hospitality. Guests on the island can enjoy swimming, rafting, shopping, and a number of other things.

Traditional Cuisine

The cuisine in Jamaica is filled with spices and light meals. Pork and chicken are the two proteins that are eaten the most. Fish is sometimes served, but chicken is the main protein included in most dishes. Jamaican's drink more tea than any other island in the Caribbean, mostly due to the fact that the British tried to civilize the Island inhabitants. The habit caught on, and now tea is included in a meal at least once per day for most Jamaicans.

Jamaican Jerk

Jerk is a sauce that is used in a lot of different Jamaican dishes. It is used to marinate chicken, pork, or fish, and the meat is then often barbecued. Jerk sauce is made using allspice, bonnet peppers, cloves, scallions, thyme, cinnamon, garlic and nutmeg. The mixture of ingredients gives the meat a spicy, yet sweet, taste that is appealing to a wide variety of people. Jerk is often prepared in large amounts to be served to a crowd. Jamaican Jerk Chicken is served in a number of places throughout the world, and is often a very popular dish on the menu.

Traditional Dishes

There are many times that tourists will see the words "Jamaican patty" and will not understand what the phrase means. A Jamaican patty is a pastry that is filled with spices and other fillings, such as chicken or shrimp. It is sometimes referred to as a turnover. Curried goat is another dish that is served frequently, as is ackee and saltfish. Ackee and saltfish is the national dish of Jamaica. It is created by sautéing a salted cod with onions, peppers and other herbs. Bacon is often served over the dish, along with tomato slices. Tourists should definitely head to one of the sugar cane fields. There, they simply need to pick a piece, pull it apart a bit and suck on them. The taste is sweet and will give you enough energy to get your through many hours of walking or sight seeing. Other fruits and vegetables grow plentiful on the island. Grapes, however, do not, and are fairly expensive to purchase.

Food in Italy

The beautiful country of Italy is a favourite among businessmen and tourists alike. The country boasts many beautiful pieces of architecture as well as a romantic atmosphere for any vacationing couple. Art is plentiful in the country, and luxury abounds in some of the larger cities. Some consider Italy to be the home of fashion, and many beautiful shops can be found in Florence and other large cities. The mountains are exquisite, as are the scenic lakes and old castles.

Traditional Cuisine

Italian cuisine is known around the world for its refined taste and beautiful presentation. Surprisingly enough, some of the main ingredients for most of the favoured Italian dishes, such as potatoes and tomatoes, were not originally grown in Italy. The foods were not grown in Italy until after the Americas were discovered. Finally, in the 18th century, the popularity of these ingredients grew, and they were suddenly planted and used in a number of dishes. In one of the finer restaurants, diners will be expected to sit through at least three to four courses. In fact, many of the citizens of the country serve at least three courses during their main meal as a way of spending time with friends and family. Holidays bring out the best in Italians, and often meals can last hours or the better part of a day! When dining out in a fine restaurant, visitors should expect to be offered an antipasti, which is an appetizer, the primo, or first course, which is usually pasta or a soup, and a secondo, or second course, which is fish or some type of meat. A contomo is the word used for a side dish, which may be a salad or some sort of a vegetable that has been cooked. Cheese and fruits, or formaggio, is often served for dessert, but occasionally dolce, or desserts such as cookies or cakes, are served.

Coffee is very important in Italian culture and is served at the end of every meal. Most Italians drink espresso, which is a concentrated coffee. It is served in a very small cup because it is so concentrated. Another form of coffee served is cappuccino, which is generally imbibed in the morning and is often topped with steamed milk. Caffe latte is an coffee drink that is created when espresso and steamed milk are put, in equal parts, into a coffee cup. Because the espresso is not quite as concentrated, it is served in a normal cup, instead of a demitasse.

Wine

Italian wines are vital to a traditional Italian meal. There are three regions in Italy that create wine, and these are Piedmont, Tuscany, and Veneto. Most restaurants will have wine that was produced in one of these regions, and all of the wine is superb. Some restaurants have sommelier's. The entire purpose of a sommelier is to match your meal with a wine that will bring out the taste more fully. Wine is also fast becoming important in other cultures in the world as well.

Food in Israel

Israel is a small Middle Eastern country that lies along the coast of the Mediterranean Sea. It is also bordered by Egypt, and is considered to be the Holy Land. It is a very economically developed country that is urbanized, and is very safe for travelers to visit. There are a number of historical cities that are interesting to visit, such as Akko, Nazareth and, of course, Jerusalem. Jerusalem has become the spiritual and political capital of Israel, and is sacred to three different religions.

Traditional Cuisine

Israeli cuisine is based mainly on traditional Jewish foods. There is, however, a large debate about foods that are considered to be from Israel, as the country is known for being a refuge for immigrants.

Many believe that the high number of immigrants means that the majority of the food that comes out if Israel is not true Israeli food, but is, instead, a mixture of foods from a number of different cultures.

Traditional Dishes

Aside from the debate, there are some foods that are thought to be from Israel, and others that are extremely popular in the highly-populated country. The pita, for one, is a very popular bread that is known around the world. It is said to be the national bread of Israel, and is popular for a number of reasons. It is extremely soft, for starters, and is an interesting and different way to eat meat with bread. The pocket in the pita makes it very easy to eat the sandwich without spilling things out of it. The pita is used in a number of different ways in Israeli cooking. One way is to put falafel balls, along with some vegetables and condiments, into the bread and to eat it that way. Chicken soup is an extremely popular dish around the world that is said to have come from Israel. This dish started with the Jewish culture. Back in ancient times, many Jewish families were poor. Chickens were very inexpensive to raise, and became the main protein of the culture. In trying to stretch the chicken as far as it could go, innovative cooks learned how to make the best of the bird by boiling it and adding some of the vegetables from their garden. Today, chicken soup is considered to be a restorative meal. There is a delicious blending of nutrients that seems to help the body recover faster from illness, and the steam from drinking chicken soup tends to help clear the sinuses and helps to relieve symptoms.

Chamin is a dish that is most often served on the Shabbat morning. It is a dish that is created by stuffing vegetables, such as red peppers or eggplant, with rice and beef. The vegetables and other ingredients, like chicken or another kosher meat, are left to cook overnight in a slow cooker. The meal is eaten in the morning and is most often served with coffee.

Food in Ireland

Ireland is a beautiful country, filled with rolling hills and beautiful green meadows. Visitors to Ireland can find everything, from excellent pubs and shopping to medieval towns and amazing museums. The country has held onto history, but has accepted the future, and is the perfect blend of the old world and the new world.

Traditional Cuisine

Those visiting Ireland should be aware that most restaurants and pubs use only fresh local ingredients, and that meat or dairy are included in a majority of the dishes created. Most of the meals are fairly heavy and tend to suit the damp climate to a t. There are excellent fish restaurants available to eat at, and Irish beer is not to be missed.

The Potato

The potato is famous for being the cash crop of Ireland. Almost a million people died when, in 1849, the potatoes were subjected to blight and were unable to be harvested. Since then, potatoes are used frequently, but are not depended on as the sole source of food. Some of the traditional stews that kept the poor alive during the famine are considered by some locals to be "famine food", and are eaten without much joy.

Traditional Dishes

There are a number of hearty traditional dishes that are still popular in Ireland. One such dish is called colcannon. Colcannon is a dish created by mixing mashed potatoes, salt, pepper, butter and kale together. This dish was found regularly on plates during the famine, and is still eaten today. Champ is a similar dish, and is made by mixing mashed potatoes with scallions that have been diced up.

Irish stew is famous for coming from the beautiful country. Irish stew is made by using lamb or mutton. Sometimes the trimmings would be used to create the stock, and would then be thrown away after a thick stock was created. Vegetables, such as turnips, carrots or parsnips, were added along with the meat that was edible. This hearty stew now appears all over Europe and is a very popular dish on a cold winter's evening.

Beer

When it comes to drinking in Ireland, tourists are always encouraged to try a Guinness. Guinness bear is brewed in Dublin and is now shipped around the world. It has a rich flavour and a creamy head, making it an appealing beer even to those who are not that fond of beer. Amazingly enough, it has been discovered the Guinness is actually beneficial to dink. This is because there are antioxidants that help to prevent cholesterol from being deposited onto the walls of the heart.

Eating Out

When it comes to eating out, tourists have to basic options. They can choose to eat at a traditional food at a pub, or they can choose to eat the newer haute cuisine at one of the many gourmet restaurants available in the larger cities. Both types of restaurants have excellent meals associated with them, and many visitors find that they stop at both types of restaurants on their trip.

Food in Mexico

Mexico is an extremely popular tourist destination for a number of reasons. The country has everything a visitor would want: beautiful beaches, amazing shopping, exciting historical monuments, and delicious food. In fact, it is one of the top ten tourist destinations in the entire world! Those visiting Mexico may find themselves confused by the traditional cuisine. Much of Mexican cuisine has been brought to the United States and has been changed to suit the different palates there.

Traditional Cuisine

Real Mexican food does not come out of a fast food restaurant. Real Mexican food is extremely colourful and very spicy. Spanish explorers brought their dishes over from the homeland, and mixed their dishes with traditional Aztec meals, creating an eclectic, spicy, colourful mixture. The food in Mexico varies depending on the area that tourists are visiting. For instance, southern Mexico is most known for chicken dishes, while northern Mexican dishes rely more on beef for protein.

Traditional Dishes

One appetizer that most tourists will find on their menu is Spanish rice. This is created using white rice and mixing it with garlic, onions, tomatoes and other spices. It is an excellent start to any meal. Pambazo is another popular appetizer. It's created by dipping bread into a pepper sauce. The dish is very spicy, but is the perfect start to most traditional Mexican meals. There are a number of meals that are popular for the main course. One popular meal is the burrito. A Mexican burrito is a simple, but delicious meal, created by filling a flour tortilla with beans, rice or meat. It is often eaten for lunch by the locals, and can be spiced up and served gourmet style in some of the more expensive restaurants. Chimichanga's are burritos that have been deep-fried. This creates a crispy outside, and a soft inside.

Carne asada is Spanish for grilled meat. This meat is served in a number of dishes, including burritos, fajitas and the ever-famous tacos. Very rarely is carne asada served alone. Sometimes, however, the term carne asada stands for a large barbecue, where friends and family are invited. A large portion of grilled meat is served in the middle of the table, with a number of different side dishes served to compliment the meat.

Liquid Refreshment

Chocolate is known more for being a drink than for being a dessert in Mexico. It is often served for breakfast in the place of coffee. Tequila is the drink that is most recognised as being from Mexico. It was created by the Aztecs in the 16th century, when they let the agave plant ferment. Spanish conquistadors brought Brandy with them to the new world, but once they ran out of that, they began making their own tequila. Now certain parts of Mexico have become known as "party centres" due to the constantly flowing tequila. Those specific cities are great for bringing tourists in, but are also cities that tend to have problem with crime and people abusing the alcohol.

Food in Malta

The small country of Malta lies in the Mediterranean Sea directly south of Sicily. It is a beautiful island country that boasts of amazing beaches and a proud history. There are stone temples that lie in the country, as well as a number of caves and rock formations that have to be seen to be believed. The country has been inhabited since the Neolithic era, meaning that the architecture in the country is both old, and astounding.

Traditional Cuisine

Maltese cuisine is an extremely eclectic mix of Mediterranean dishes. Many non-natives made their home on the island, bringing the dishes of their home country along with them. The majority of those that moved to Malta were from Italy, so the Maltese diet is heavy with Italian influence, but is still very distinct.

Traditional Dishes

Soup is served often in the warm country. There are a number of traditional soups that can be found on menus, such as Soppa ta' l-armla, or widow's soup. Rumour has it that the dish was named such because neighbours would descend upon newly created widows, giving them produce from their gardens. The widow would then put everything into a pot, creating a thick, vegetable soup. When the soup is almost done cooking, raw eggs are cracked and left to coagulate on the top. When they are firm, the soup is done. Kusksu is another hearty soup served often on the island. This soup is created using pasta beads with tomato paste, chicken stock, onions and garlic.

For a comfort dish, look to Mqarrun il-Forn, or baked macaroni. This is a macaroni that is created using a Bolognese sauce, egg, peas and bacon. Ross il-Forn, or baked rice, is extremely similar, except is created using curry as well as macaroni noodles. Meat is served frequently on the island, but some if it look strange to Western eyes. Fenkata is a very popular dish. It is created by frying rabbit meat, and then simmering it in red wine for a few hours. A thick sauce is often served over the meat. Stallion meat is another strange meat that tourists may shy away from trying. It is used frequently in meals, and is sometimes fried with a white wine sauce. Maltese sausage is created using pork, sea salt, and a number of different spices. It is cooked in a variety of ways, and is sometimes eaten raw. Dolphin fish is a meat that is found frequently on menus in the country. It is not a dolphin, but is, rather, a small fish that is found in abundance around the island. It is often coked by being fried, or put into a pastry of some sort.

Gbejniet are small cheeses that are created using sheep's milk. These cheeses are served often during lunch or supper, possibly because they can stay fresh a very long time without needing to be kept cold. They come in fresh, peppered, or sun dried, and are found in barrels of water in the store. They have a sharp taste, and a creamy texture.

Food in Malaysia

Malaysia is located in South-East Asia. It is a developing country that has mixed the best of the old ways, with new technology. There are a number of things to see and do in Malaysia, including visiting the many national parks and jungles, and the amazing beaches. There are a number of tropical islands that belong to Malaysia, and are the perfect places to go for a relaxing, or romantic, get away! The capital city of Kuala Lumpur has a number of exciting things to see, and has cuisine available to purchase from every corner of the world!

Traditional Cuisine

Rice is one of the main staple foods in Malaysia. The rice generally comes from Thailand, and has a delicate flavour to it. The short grain rice from Japan is sometimes eaten, but it is more common to find long grain rice in the dishes than any other. Noodles are also found in a number of traditional dishes. When it comes to meat, chicken tends to be the protein of choice. There are a number of farms that raise chickens, but some are allowed to roam free and are captured and cooked.

This dish is called kampong chicken, and is considered to be a very nutritional dish, because the chickens that roam free have less body fat on them. Other types of proteins that are consumed are fish and other seafood, such as prawns or shrimp.

Traditional Dishes

Keropok lekor is a traditional snack that is eaten in Malaysia. Keropok lekor are a dish that is created by frying flour crackers and flavouring them with fish or prawns. These are sometimes home made, but are often created in a factory and are purchased in a bag. Ikan baker stands for "burned fish", and is the term Malaysians use for seafood that they grill, often with a banana leaf. Squid and stingray are also sometimes grilled and sold at roadside stands.

Nasi Lemak is considered to be the national dish of Malaysia, although it has never been officially labelled as such. It is created by soaking rice in a coconut cream. The rice is then steamed, and herbs and screwpine leaves are sometimes put into the pot to flavour the rice more. Cucumber slices, anchovies and peanuts are often served with it, along with pickled vegetables, spicy sauces and a hard boiled egg. This hearty meal is considered to be a breakfast dish and is sold in almost all the roadside stands. There are some dishes that are reserved for special occasions. One such dish is the ketupat. This is a dumpling that is created when rice is wrapped in a woven palm leaf pouch. The pouch is then boiled, and the rice becomes compressed inside of the palm leaf, making it turn into a rice dumpling. Curry is often eaten with ketupat. Sometimes, the palm leaves are formed into a shape, such as a crab or a turtle, in order to celebrate specific dates in Malaysian history.

Food in Lithuania

Lithuania is a small country that is located in eastern Europe. It is a country full of history and intrigue, and is often visited by those wishing to explore the past. The large cities are full of old castles and museums that show the many struggles that the Lithuanian's had to go through in order to retain their independence.

Traditional Cuisine

When it comes to food, Lithuanian's eat hearty. Meat, vegetables and potato is generally served for the evening meal, and pork tends to be the protein of choice. Vegetarians will have a difficult time finding dishes with no meat on them, and vegans will find that it is almost impossible to find a dish that has no meat and no cream sauce. Barley, mushrooms and other greens are also eaten frequently, as they grow well in the climate. Bread is also eaten during most meals, especially rye bread. Dark rye bread is served with butter or cheese, and may be flavoured with onions.

Traditional Dishes

Soups are often served at the beginning of a meal, or for lunch. Cabbage soup is one traditional favourite, and is made with carrots, onions or ham. Cucumber soup is a meal that tourists may find in some restaurants. It is created when cucumbers are blended and served, often with carrots. Sauerkraut soup is created when cabbage is fermented. The fermentation process gives it a very sour taste, and it is always served with bread. Vistos sultinys is the Lithuanian name for chicken soup, and is very popular in the country. When it comes to main dishes, look for fairly heavy meals and plates filled with potato and meat. Desra is a type of sausage that is created in Lithuania. It is often served smoked. Blood is occasionally added, but it is not considered to be a blood sausage. Cepelinai is a delicious meal that is found in the majority of restaurants in the country. It is a dumpling that is created using grated potatoes and ground meat. It is often served with bacon and sour cream sauce on the side.

Kotletai are patties that are made of minced meat and other veggies. They are served with a meat sauce and potatoes. Saslykai is another popular meat dish in Lithuania. It is when pork cubes are skewered and grilled. Sometimes they are marinated to obtain a specific flavour before they are grilled.

Beverages and Desserts

Lithuanian desserts are often a cake that has fresh fruit baked into it. They are rarely covered with frosting or icing. Tortes are also popular, but are mainly saved for special occasions. Ledai, or ice cream, is especially popular in Lithuania, and is served just about everywhere. Beer is the beverage of choice. It used to be that beer was taboo, but after the country won its independence, it has become very popular. Many Lithuanian beer makers have won awards for their beers world wide. It has become a must for tourists to try locally produced Lithuanian beer.

Food in Japan

Japan is a beautiful island country that is visited by millions of tourists and business people every year. The majority of people visit the Tokyo area, but some venture outside of the large city in order to see some of the beautiful regional areas. Japan is a country that has everything available for its guests. When visiting Japan, tourists can choose to eat cuisine that is from other cultures, or to enjoy some of the more traditional dishes that are available to consume.

Traditional Cuisine

In Japan, rice and noodles are considered to be staples. Most dishes have at least one of these ingredients in them, and dishes that do not are served with rice or noodles as a side dish. Fish is also a staple, as the entire island is surrounded by healthy fishing grounds. A traditional meal could include some Japanese rice, soup, and pickled vegetables. In Japan, most people do not eat at a table and chairs. Instead, they sit on small pillows that surround a low table.

Chopsticks are often used to eat food, and low, shallow spoons are used for soup. These spoons have become popular in gourmet cooking, and are often used to serve a small serving of food. Lunch in Japan is a simple meal. It is called donburi and is a bowl that is filled with rice and topped with either meat or an egg. There are a number of different names for these bowls, including oyakodon, which is donburi that is topped with an egg and chicken, and unadon, which is donburi that has eel and vegetables on top. In larger cities there are delivery people that bring the dishes hot from home to the place of business. This means that the workers get hot, fresh meals on a daily basis.

Sushi

Sushi is a meal that has found popularity all over the world. It is created by combining vinegared rice with ingredients such as uncooked fish and vegetables. There are a number of different types of sushi. The most popular is nori, which is sushi that is rolled inside a sheet of seaweed. It is often served with wasabi and is meant to be eaten in one large bite.

Traditional Dishes

Gyoza is one dish that is very popular in Japan, as well as elsewhere in the world. It is a dumpling that is filled with meat or vegetable and is steamed. A soy sauce is generally served with it to allow for dipping. Okonomiyaki are another popular food in Japan. The word means "as you like" and is a cross between a pizza and a pancake! The dough is made by mixing flour, water, eggs and cabbage together. After that has been mixed together, other ingredients can be added. Some popular ingredients are shrimp, mushrooms, beef, chicken, or dried seaweed. The batter is then poured onto a hot plate and is cooked as a pancake would be. Restaurants cook these fresh and create the mixtures specifically for each customer. Some popular toppings are soy sauce and mayonnaise.

Food in Netherlands

The people of the Netherlands are known as the Dutch. It is a beautiful land full of historical landmarks and plenty of things for tourists to do. There are dozens of museums in every area, and no visit to the Netherlands would be complete without purchasing a pair of their famous wooden shoes. Traditional Dutch food is very basic, but the larger cities have an abundance of food, from a variety of cultures, to choose from.

Traditional Cuisine

Traditional Dutch cuisine is fashioned by the agriculture around it. In the early 20th century Netherlands, girls were sent to a school where they were trained to be domestic servants and were taught to cook simple, inexpensive meals. This trend became popular, and the food that was readily available became the food that was cooked. Vegetables, for instance, are a staple in the culture, and are used in almost every rural dish.

Dinner Meals

A traditional dinner meal in the Netherlands consists of a meat with gravy, a vegetable, and a potato. Sometimes this mix is put together in the form of a stew. One traditional meal is called Hutspot. This meal is created by mashing together potatoes, onions and carrots. Often a piece of meat is served either next to, or on top of the mixture. Hutspot is eaten with a chop of beef shoulder every October third, when the Dutch celebrate Leidens Ontzet. This is a holiday celebrating the time when, in 1574, the Spanish soldiers invading the country were flooded out a huge storm. Pea soup is another staple in Dutch cuisine, as is boerenkoolstamppot. Boerenkoolstamppot is when potatoes are mixed with kale and served with rookworst, a type of sausage. Gravy is also served over the mixture. Zuurkoolstamppot is another similar meal, but uses sauerkraut mixed in with the potatoes to give the meal an extra "zing". Dessert is generally a sweet product, such as yogurt or pudding.

Fast Food

When it comes to fast food in the Netherlands, visitors need to be prepared. A typical order at a fast food stand would include French fries with mayonnaise, ketchup or a heated peanut butter sauce, and a fried meat, such as a croquette or a frikandel. A Frikandel is similar to a traditional hot dog but is much more spicy and is served cut open with a peanut butter sauce on it. Mayonnaise to the Dutch is different than the traditional French mayonnaise. It is much sweeter and is more firm than most are used to. It does contain less fat, but is considered to be just as unhealthy as the French mayonnaise is. Delicious meals, that are not fast food, can be found in the larger cities, such as Amsterdam. Dutch gourmet cuisine is full of traditional ingredients that are used in different ways. Visitors to the cities can also find restaurants that specialize in cuisine from around the world.

Food in Morocco

The small country of Morocco lies bordered by the Mediterranean Sea and the Sahara dessert. It is a beautiful dessert country that is visited for a number of different reasons. Some people head to the beautiful beaches, such as those in Agadir and Rabat, while others head to cities like Fez or Marrakech to see the history of the "old world". All tourists visiting Morocco agree, however, that the cuisine can't be beat.

Morrocc Cuisine

Because Morocco is a country that borders the ocean, it has long been a place where other cultures come to trade. This means that Moroccans were able to take a little bit of every cuisine that they liked and mesh them together. This is what Moroccan cuisine is known for! Chefs in Morocco can take the best of their locally grown fruits and vegetables, as well as the number of spices that are either imported, or grown, in the country, and create amazing meals.

Lunch

The midday meal, or lunch as other parts of the world call it, is generally the most extensive meal during the day for Moroccan's. Hot and cold salads are often served, as well as lamb or chicken and other meats and vegetables. Bread is a staple and is eaten at almost every meal. Another thing to note is that Moroccans do not generally use utensils. Instead, they use their fingers or their bread to get the food from the plate to their mouth.

Traditional Dishes

Couscous is one dish which is extremely popular in Morocco and is believed to have originated there. Couscous is made using small wheat granules that are coated in wheat flower. The granules are then steamed, using either water or chicken broth, and served with vegetables and meats. And when it comes to meats, lamb is the preferred meat in Morocco. Unfortunate it is fairly expensive to purchase, and beef has begun replacing it in many traditional Moroccan dishes. Another popular Moroccan dish is Pastilla. Pastilla is a dish that is created using a bird called a squab, or rock pigeon. The pigeon is fried in oil, and then the oil is cooled and mixed with beaten eggs. The meat is then layered onto dough and is sprinkled with powdered sugar before being served.

Beverages

Morocco is an extremely dry place, and guests to the country may be looking for drinks on every corner. Strangely enough, the most popular drink in Morocco is a warm drink! Green tea, spiced with mint, is consumed at least once a day, and is considered to be an extremely important ritual. The tea is often poured from the tea pot very high up in the air, so that bubbles can form in the tea before it is drank.

Fast Food

Guests to the country will find fast food available in any of the larger squares in the city. Dairy shops, which offer breakfast and other types of dairy products, are available, as are shops which serve sandwich's, often called bocadillo's.

Food in Mongolia

Mongolia is located directly between China and Russia. Its landlocked position has made the residents of the country dependant on the food they create, and the nomadic lifestyle is still the way the majority of people survive. Inside of the larger cities, tourists can find a vast array of different foods available. Outside of the cities, they are subject to eating traditional Mongolian cuisine.

Traditional Cuisine

The average population in Mongolia shows that approximately 4 people live in every square mile. This means that the countrymen have learned how to survive on the animals and plants that they could grow for themselves. Meat is used in most dishes, as is dairy. A lot of animal fat is used in a number of the dishes, and is considered to be healthy for the Mongolians, as they need extra fat in their body to be able to survive the extremely harsh weather.

Most Mongolians are extremely hospitable people. Anyone that is invited into a yurt, or home, is considered to be a guest, and all guests are treated with honour. Every guest will be given some food, and it is good etiquette to at least take a small taste of the dish. Refusing to do so is a snub to the home's owner. If the guest does not care for the dish, they should pass it back to the host only after they have tried it. Mutton is the most frequently cooked meat in the rural areas of Mongolia. The meat is often cooked on it's own, with no other sauces or ingredients. There are some other traditional ways that the meat is cooked, however. One way is to fill dough with mutton and then seal it off. The dough is then boiled in water, or mutton fat, and served with rice or noodles. These dumplings are a classic dish that is surprisingly tasty. On a special occasion, mutton can be cooked using stones that have been taken straight out of the fire. The meat is put into a sealed can, or the stomach of an animal, and is put onto the stones to cook. This process takes a fairly long time, but creates extremely moist and tasty mutton meat.

Eating Out

When in the large cities, guests will be able to choose their cuisine. A number of popular types of restaurants have found their way to Mongolia, including Italian and Spanish. Those visiting Mongolia, however, should definitely strive to try traditional Mongolian fare. They may find it to be a bit heavy, but the heaviness is a nice comfort to have on a very cold winter's evening.

Food in Nepal

Nepal is the country located directly in between China and India. It is a mountainous country, having eight of the highest peaks in the world within its borders. There are a number of things for tourists to do within the country. The shopping is always good, as is visiting the many museums. Nepal, however, is one of the best places to go for outdoor people. Many visit the country in order to raft or take part in a jungle safari. And, of course, some visit the country to climb the peaks of the highest mountains in the world, including Mt Everest and Mt Kathmandu.

Nepal Cuisine

Nepal is very different from most countries when it comes to food. There is a huge amount of cultural diversity, which means that there have been a number of different cuisines that have emerged. Really, there is no one set type of cuisine that is considered to be from Nepal. Instead, there are a number of different types of cuisines. This is excellent for the tourist, as it means they will get to experience a number of different types of food instead of having to stick with just one. There are a few dishes that are linked straight to Nepalese cuisine. One dish is lentil soup. This is a vegetarian dish that is made with lentils and other vegetables, such as carrots, potatoes and onion. Everything is then pureed together and it is served hot. This dish might be followed by bhat, or boiled rice, and tarkari. Tarkari is a vegetable curry which is extremely spicy and very delicious. The entire meal may be served with beer, as it is created in a number of different towns in the country. Westerners need to beware: Nepalese beer is often not served cold.

Nepali citizens do eat meat, but not as often as they eat vegetables. Curried meat is available to purchase, but most people save it for special occasions, as it is extremely expensive. Guests in the country are likely to be surprised that cows are not eaten in the country. Instead, water buffalo are the main meat of the country. Tourists may see the word "buff" on a menu. "Buff" is short for water buffalo. The taste is remarkably similar, but the water buffalo is a bit more gamey tasting. Another favoured dish is Gurr. Gurr is created by grinding up raw potatoes and mixing potent spices in with it. The mixture is then fried and made to look like a pancake. Cheese is almost always served with Grr. Visitors to the country might be hesitant to try lassi. Traditional lassi is created by mixing curds with water. Sometimes rosewater or other flavourings, such as mango or strawberry, are put into the drink. This is a drink that should be imbibed when the weather is warm, and tastes much better than it sounds.

Food in North America

North America is an extremely diverse culture. Some call it a melding pot, because many people immigrated to the continent from other cultures. Many French immigrants settled in Canada, but while the French influence is still there, it has been diluted over centuries of other cultures finding their home in the beautiful wilderness as well. The Mexican people have a more tightly-knit culture, as their ancestors passed down the "old ways" successfully to the younger generation. The United States is extremely diverse, with older traditions staying in the east and newer traditions popping up in the west.

Canada

Canadian cuisine began with the French but has since morphed to include some of other cultures, including those of Great Britain and the United States. Those living in the province of Quebec still tend to cook French food. Their dishes are hearty fare that has simple flavours, all of which meld together well. In the wilds of the North, game is much more popular and is eaten on a regular basis. One can get caribou, moose or venison without much trouble. Smoked meat is delicious in Canada, especially in the city of Montreal. Salmon is on the menu frequently, especially when visiting either coast of the country.

Mexico

Traditional Mexican food has been handed down through generations of family members. It was created by using the available resources, which means that many of the dishes are very spicy. This is because spices were always plentiful in Mexico. Spanish rice is familiar to most. It is a dish created by blending garlic, tomatoes, onions and a few other spices in with white rice. The result is a spicy rice that goes perfect as an appetizer. Chicken is popular in the southern area of Mexico, while beef is the main protein in the northern area. Both areas make a version of burritos. This meal is a filing one that uses thin tortilla's as a base. Some put rice in the tortilla, others put meat, and still some use leftover beans as a way to be economical. Burritos had their start as a way to eat food cheaply and easily, but have now become extremely popular in many parts of the world.

The United States

When people immigrated to the United States hundreds of years ago, they settled on the east coast. This may be why most of the food in the east coast is more reminiscent of the past than the food in the west coast is. In the east, the food tends to be very filling and warm. This may be because of the difficult and long winter months. Stews are extremely popular, as are other dishes that can be combined in one pot, such as casseroles. Beef and chicken are the two most popular proteins. In the northeast, citrus has to be shipped in from the south or the west, as there is not a long enough growing season for it to thrive. Those in the west coast live on a much lighter fare. People moving to the west from the east met people from other cultures and integrated their food into the recipes they currently had. This made a new type of food called fusion, which is when foods from two different cultures are meshed together. Fruit is popular in the west because it grows so well in the bright sunshine.

Food in Okinawa, Japan

Okinawa is a prefecture, or island, that is located in Japan. It is considered to be the largest island in population as well as in size. There are a number of islands that make up the Okinawa Prefecture. Some are famous for their beaches while others are known for their beautiful jungle atmosphere. The climate of Okinawa is hot, making it the perfect place to visit for those looking towards a tropical vacation.

Traditional Cuisine

Okinawan cuisine is extremely different from the cuisine normally served in Japan. Okinawa has a different climate and vegetation, which means that it is nothing like the food available on the mainland. Most people in Okinawa exist on whole grains and vegetables. Meat is served, but not extremely often. Of the meat that is served, Spam, Soki (a type of pork spare rib) and other pork meat are the favourites. Both white rice and brown rice are served, as well as noodles, but that is truly the only similarity between Japanese and Okinawan dishes.

Traditional Dishes

One traditional dish is chanpurû. Chanpurû is a stir fry dish that is made in a number of different ways. Each way is slightly different, but each way has vegetables, tofu and a type of meat or fish in it. Sometimes pork belly is used as the meat, other times tuna is. One favourite is Gôyâ chanpurû. This is made with a bitter melon (known as the gôyâ melon), as well as other vegetables, tofu, Spam and bacon. Other chanpurû is made with pasta and eggs. Okinawa soba is a dish that is so popular in Okinawa, it was named after the country. It is a noodle soup that is made using thick wheat noodles. The noodles are then topped with either scallion, pork belly, pork ribs, pickled ginger or a fish cake. Often diners add Korean pepper to the dish in order to spice it up. Okinawa soba can be found in almost any restaurant on the island. Another popular dish is taco rice. Taco rice is begun with a base of rice. Lettuce is then laid on top of the rice and taco meat is piled on top of that. Cucumber, cheese and tomato are crumbled over the mixture to complete it. Sometimes the dish is served in a tortilla roll. This meal is served frequently for lunch and is found in many school cafeterias.

Drinks

Awamori is an alcoholic beverage that is made only in Okinawa. It is created by distilling rice. This drink is exported to Japan, although the exported brands are not as strong as those that stay inside the country. It is also sometimes called island sake.

Food in United States

The United States of America is one of the most powerful nations in the entire world. It is the third largest territory and has a history of different races and cultures living in it. There is something for everyone in the United States, from a number of different music venues to attend, to sporting events, to historical avenues. The cuisine in the United States is as varied as the culture is.

Origins of American Cuisine

American food differs depending on which area of the country a tourist is in. Those visiting the south will likely find a breakfast of grits and sausage gravy and biscuits, while those visiting the north will often order pancakes with real maple syrup. A breakfast in California is often very light, with fruits and toast as the main dish. Each area has it's own needs and tastes, and it's very obvious to those that visit the areas what the needs and tastes are.

The Northeast

Foods in the northeast tend to be heavy and filling. A lot of the traditional dishes are warm dishes, such as stews and soups. This is because people had to have full, warm bellies in order to work in the heavy winter snows. Citrus has to be shipped in from warmer states, and the only vegetables and fruits that can grow are those that grow during the three month summer season. Beef tends to be eaten frequently, along with chicken, as it can be raised locally.

The South

Food in the south is always warm, like the hospitality. Grits are a favourite in the south. Grits are a porridge that is made from corn that has been coarsely ground. Some say that it is an acquired taste, while others love it from the first second they eat it. Coca-cola is the typical soft drink in the south, and most southerners will tell you that they're drinking a "coke", no matter what soft drink they have in their hand.

Fast Food

The United States is full of fast food restaurants. Every large city will have at least one, if not a dozen, fast food restaurants. McDonald's is most globally known, and serves hamburgers and fries, as does Burger King, Wendy's and In and Out Burger. Other fast food restaurants include those that serve pizza, like Pizza Hut and Little Ceasars, and those that serve fried chicken, like Kentucky Fried Chicken.

Beverages

Wine has become extremely popular at restaurants in the United States, and almost every high-class restaurant will have an extensive selection to choose from. Beer is served in every bar, and in a wide majority of restaurants. Some beer is specific to the location, such as Sam Adam's beer, which is created in the Northeast.

Food in Trinidad and Tobago

Trinidad and Tobago is a country that is made up of two Caribbean Islands that reside off of the coast of Venezuela. Trinidad and Tobago are two popular vacation destinations, due to the Caribbean atmosphere and the beautiful views. When it comes to food, Indian roots means that a lot of the dishes are extremely spicy, so tourists that do not like spicy food need to be sure to let their waiter know that they want the food toned down a bit.

Traditional Cuisine

Curry chicken is a meal that is often served for lunch and supper in Trinidad and Tobago. It is a simple meal, which includes chicken that is spiced with saffron and curry powder. A curry flavoured sauce is served over the chicken. The dish was brought to the islands by indentured servants that arrived from India, where it was a popular "poor man's" dish. Roti is often served with the dish. Roti is a flat bread that is rolled out and pan fried. Callaloo is another dish that tourists are likely to find on the menu at a nice restaurant. It is a side dish that is created with dasheen leaves and water spinach. Coconut milk or other ingredients such as lobster or Chile peppers can be added to spice up the meal. The dish is served in a stew or soup consistency. Breakfasts in Trinidad and Tobago are generally light. They tend to include a lot of fruit, such as bananas, oranges and pineapples. Some other dishes served for breakfast include bread and cheese, fried potato, and black pudding.

Bake and Shark is a well-known dish. It is served on the coast, often near Maracas Bay. The dish is created with pieces of shark that are deep fried and served in a fried bread. Sauces are served with the dish. Barbecued chicken is also found on many Trinidad and Tobago menu's. The dish can be found in fine restaurants and in roadside stands. It is cooked with spices from the island, and may taste different than most people are used to, but many tourists find it absolutely delicious.

Eating Out

There are a number of different restaurants that one can eat at while in Trinidad and Tobago. One restaurant is called La Terrazza. La Terrazza is owned by a husband and wife duo. The husband, Chef Stefano, is in charge of the kitchen, while wife Kisha takes care of the diners. The food is wholly Italian, and is considered by some to be the best in the Caribbean. Emerald is another well-known Trinidad and Tobago restaurant. Emerald caters to those who want to taste traditional Caribbean dishes, including shrimp and fish fillets. Desserts include chocolate cake and a delicious coconut ice cream.

11

The Menus Planning

Get an insight into the Indian vegetarian recipes and dishes. Vegetarian cooking of India is easy and simple. Vegetables are an integral part of our food and we consume them in a number of ways. For pure vegetarians India is a heaven. India can boast for its innumerable varieties of tasty and nutritious vegetarian dishes. Indians like their vegetable curries real hot 'n' spicy and so add a number of spices to make them really exotic. These are also prepared using different methods of cooking like baking, boiling, frying etc. We offer a number of tempting Indian vegetarain recipes of dishes like Navratan Korma, Shahi Paneer etc. to the connoisseurs of taste.

Vegetable Recipes

- Bhindi Bhaji
- Hara Chana Masala
- Sindhi Kadhi
- Stuffed Tomato
- Makhani Arbi Masala
- Stuffed Bhindi
- Rajma Rasmisa.
- Ghiye Ke Kofte
- Malai Kofta
- Navratan Korma
- Vegetable Curry
- Pindi Chana
- Stuffed Capsicum

Aloo Recipes

- Aloo Dahi Wale
- Aloo Ghobi
- Aloo Rassewale
- Baigan Aloo
- Aloo Palak
- Stuffed Aloo.
- Aloo Dum
- Aloo Ki Sabji
- Aloo Took
- Dum Aloo
- Methi Aloo

Paneer Recipes

- Chilli Paneer
- Matar Paneer
- Paneer Bhurji
- Paneer Kofta
- Paneer Makhani
- Shahi Paneer
- Paneer Tikka
- Paneer Parantha
- Paneer Makhana Curry.
- Kadhai Paneer
- Palak Paneer
- Paneer Sandwich
- Paneer Korma
- Paneer Pasanda
- Paneer Pakora
- Microwave Paneer Matar
- Paneer Coconut Gravy

Baigan Recipes

- Baigan Bharta
- Baigan Kalongee
- Stuffed Baigan.
- egetable Recipes.

Bhindi Bhaji Recipe

Ingredients

1 pound okra

2 medium onions, chopped

1/4 tsp garlic paste or powder

1/4 tsp coriander paste or powder

1/8 tsp cumin

3 large tomatoes

2 tsp oil

1/2 cup chopped cilantro.

How to make Bhindi Dopiaza :

- Cut the tip and the very bottom from the okra just to clean it, but do not slice.
- Heat oil in a pan over medium heat. Add onion and cook for 3 minutes.
- Add all ingredients except okra, tomato and cilantro. Cook for 3 minutes. Add okra, then cook for 6 to 8 minutes. Garnish with tomato and cilantro.
- Serve the bhindi bhaji with rice, naan or pita bread.

Lauki Ke Kofte Recipe

Ingredients

For the kofte:

4 cups (500 gms) Ghiya or Lauki (bottlegourd), peeled and grated

1/2 tsp Ginger paste

1/2 tsp Sendha namak (rock salt)

1/2 tsp Kali mirch, pissi (black pepper powder)

2 tbsp Singhare ka atta (waterchestnut flour)

Oil for deep-frying

For the Gravy

2 tbsp Ghee (clarified butter)

1 tsp Jeera (cumin seeds)

1 tsp Ginger, finely chopped

1/4cup (50 gms) Dahi (yogurt), beaten smooth

1/4 cup Khus-khus (poppy seeds) soaked in milk for 1/2 hour

1 1/2 tsp Dhania (coriander) powder

1 1/2 tsp Sendha namak (rock salt)

1/4 tsp Chilli powder.

Hara dhania (green coriander), chopped for garnishing.

How to make Lauki ke Kofte:

- Squeeze water out of the ghiya; mix in salt, ginger and black pepper. Suite over high flame, to dry up excess liquid and leave to cool.
- Add singhare ka atta, mix well and shape into walnut sized balls.
- Deep-fry koftas to a golden brown over high flame and keep aside.
- Heat ghee; add jeera followed by ginger and suite to a light brown.
- Grind the khus-khus into a paste. Add dhania powder, salt and chilli powder and suite till oil separates.
- Add 2-3 cups water and bring to a boil, then simmer for about 10 minutes. Add koftas and dahi, simmer for another 2 minutes, and serve hot. Garnish the lauki ke kofte with hara dhania.

Navratan Korma Recipe

Ingredients for Navrattan Korma

3 cups - Boiled vegetables (9 varieties-potatoes, carrots, green peas, french beans, cauliflower, capsicum, cabbage, bottle gourd, cluster beans).

150gms - Grated paneer

3 - Tomatoes

2 - Grated onions

1 1/2 tsp -Ginger paste

1 1/2 tsp - Garlic paste

Salt To Taste

1 tsp - Turmeric Powder

1 1/2 tsp - Red chilli powder

1 tsp - Coriander powder

2 tsp - Garam Masala Powder

2 tbsp - Cream

6 tbsp - Vegetable oil

1 tbsp - Ghee

1 cup - Milk / water

1/4 cup - Dry fruits (cashew nuts, raisins)

Coriander leaves for decoration.

How to make navrattan korma :

- Boil tomatoes till tender. Allow them to cool. Then peel off the tomato skin to make puree. Readymade tomato puree can also be used.
- Take 1 tbsp ghee and slightly fry the dry fruits for about 1 min on medium heat.
- Heat oil in a pan. Fry onions and ginger-garlic paste till golden brown.
- Add salt, turmeric powder, red chilli powder, coriander powder, garam masala and fry for 2-3 minutes.
- Next add tomato puree and dry fruits. Stir well and cook the mixture for 4 minutes. Ensure that the mixture doesn't stick to bottom of pan.
- Add milk (use water alternatively). Bring it to boil. Reduce the heat and cook until the gravy becomes thick.
- Add paneer to the gravy and stir well.
- Finally add all the vegetables to the above gravy and cook for 5-7 minutes.
- Serve the navratan korma hot. Put cream and chopped coriander leaves on the navaratna korma decorate.

Stuffed Tomato Recipe

Ingredients

5-6 medium size Tomatoes / Tamatar

100-150gms Paneer grated or mashed

1 Onion finely chopped

Finely chopped Coriander leaves

2 Green chili (finely chopped)

Salt, Red chili powder to taste.

Gram Masala to taste

1/2 tsp turmeric powder

1 tbsp grated cheese

1 tbsp oil.

How to make Bharwan Tamatar:

- Wash the tomatoes and set dry.
- Cut the top of tomato (tamatar) like a cap. Gently scoop out the centers. Keep aside the scooped portion and chop the cut tops.
- Heat oil in a kadhai add chopped onions and green chilies till tender.
- Now add the pulp and chopped tomato and fry for a minute and all dry masalas and fry for a minute more.
- Add paneer ,mix well and cock for a minute.
- Fill tomatoes with the mixture.
- Top with grated cheese and chopped coriander.
- Place tomatoes in a cooker container. put little butter and pressure cook for one whistle. (or you can also bake it in a hot oven at 200 degree c for 20 minutes.
- Serve the stuffed paneer tomato hot.

Indian Vegetable Curry Recipe

Ingredients

1/2 medium-sized (100g/4oz) aubergine (eggplant) cut into 2cm x 1cm/¾in x 1/2 in sticks

2 small carrots (100g/4oz), peeled and cut into 2cm x 1cm/¾in x 1/2 in sticks

100g/4oz/1 cup peas

100g/4oz/1 cup French beans, cut into 2.5cm/1in pieces

1 medium-sized potato (100g/4oz), peeled and cut into 2cm x 1cm/ ¾in x 1/2 in sticks

50g/2oz/ 1/2 cup freshly grated coconut

4 fresh hot green chillies

2 tbsp white poppy seeds

1 1/4 tsp salt

3 medium-sized tomatoes, roughly chopped

1 tbsp natural plain yogurt

1 tsp garam masala

2 tbsp chopped, fresh green coriander.

How to make Vegetarian Curry:

- Place the aubergine (eggplant), carrots, peas, French beans and potato in a medium-sized saucepan. Add 250ml/8fl oz/1 cup water. Bring to the boil. Cover, turn the heat to medium and cook for 4 minutes or until the vegeatbles are just tender.
- Meanwhile put the coconut, chillies, poppy seeds and salt in the container of an electric blender. Add 150ml/5fl oz water and grind to a fine paste. Set aside.
- When the vegetables are cooked, add the spice paste and another 150ml/5fl oz water. Stir and simmer gently for 5 minutes. Now add the tomatoes, the yogurt and the garam masala. Stir gently to mix well. Bring to the boil and simmer gently for 2-3 minutes. Turn into a serving dish and garnish the vegetable curry with the fresh coriander.

Makhani Arbi Masala Recipe

Ingredients

Arbi (medium size) - 250 gms

Besan (gram flour) - 2 tblsp

Oil (tel) (tel) - 3 tblsp

Ajwain - 1/2 tsp

Onion (pyaj) (chopped)- one

Green chilli (slit) (deseeded and chopped)- one

Red chilli (lal mirch) powder - 1/2 tblsp

Chopped coriander - 1 tblsp

Salt (namak) - 1/2 tsp or to taste

Lemon juice - 1/2 tblsp

Garam masala - 1/4 tsp.

Makhani Gray

Tomatoes (tamatar) (chopped roughly) - 250 gms

Ginger (adrak) paste - 1/2 tsp

Garlic (lasan) paste - 1/2 tsp

Green chilli - one

Red chilli (lal mirch) powder - 1/2 tsp

Laung (cloves)- 2

Choti elaichi (green cardamom)- one

Salt to taste

Butter - 2 tblsp

Honey- 1 tsp

Kasoori methi - 1 tblsp.

How to make Makhani Arvi Masala :

- Pressure cook the whole arbi with three cups of water to give one whistle.
- Keep on low flame for 2-3 minutes.
- Remove from fire. Cool and drain.
- To prepare makhani gray, put tomatoes in a bandi, add one cup of water, ginger and garlic paste, green chilli, red chilli powder, laung and chot elaichi.
- Boil. Cover and cook on low heat till it is reduced to a saucy consistency.
- Remove from fire.
- Blend in a mixer.
- Strain into a clean pan.
- Add butter. Stir in honey.
- Add salt to taste.
- Keep on fire.
- Boil. Simmer on low flame for 1-2 minutes.
- Add kasoori methi and remove from fire.
- Keep the makhani gray aside.

- Peel and flatten each piece or arbi.
- Sprinkle some salt and red chilli powder on it.
- Sprinkle dry besan.
- Overturn the pieces and sprinkle salt, red chilli and besan on the other side too.
- mix, so as to coat lightly.
- Heat oil on a large tawa, add half the arbi and suite over medium heat till golden.
- Shift the fried arbi from the centre to the sides (periphery) of the tawa.
- Add the rest of the arbi, fry and shift to the sides.
- In the same oil, add ajwain, when it turns golden, add chopped onions, grated ginger and green chilli and suite for three minutes.
- Add 1/2 tsp salt.
- Return the arbi to the centre, add red chillies and half of the coriander.
- Fry for a minute.
- Add the prepared makhani gray and fry until the arbi is coated with the gravy.
- Adjust seasoning.
- Sprinkle lemon juice, garam masala and the remaining coriander.
- Stir and serve immediately.

Pindi Chana Recipe

Ingredients

1 cup chickpeas (kabuli chana)

1 tea bag or 1 tbsp black tea leaves tied in a cheesecloth

21/2-inch ginger, 3/4th of it shredded finely for garnish

2-3 tbsp oil

2 onions chopped

2 tsp garlic, finely crushed

2 green chilies, sliced

3 medium sized tomatoes, chopped

2 tsp ground coriander

1 1/2 tsp ground cumin

1/2 tsp turmeric powder

1/2 - 1tsp red chili powder or as per taste

Salt To Taste

1/2 tsp garam masala

finely chopped coriander leaves.

How to make Pindi Chole:

- Soak Chole in water overnight or for about 6 hr.
- Cook the chole with salt and enough water in the cooker for about 20 minutes or till fully done.
- Drain, reserving 1 cup of cooking liquid.
- Finely chop the remaining ginger. Heat oil and suite onions till golden, then add garlic and chopped ginger and green chilies. Suite for 5 minutes.
- Add tomatoes, coriander, cumin, turmeric and chili powder and suite over low heat until the oil separates.
- Add chole, the reserved cooking liquid, salt and half of the coriander leaves. Simmer, uncovered until the liquid has been absorbed.
- Add a pinch of garam masala and serve pindi chana sprinkled with the remaining garam masala, coriander leaves and shredded ginger.

Stuffed Bhindi Recipe

Ingredients for Stuffed Bhindi

1 pound Okra (Bhindi), washed and dried

3 tbsp - oil

1 tsp cumin seeds (jeera)

1 medium sized onion, chopped

2 green chilies, seeded and chopped

3/4-inch ginger, finely chopped

A pinch of Asafetida powder

1 tomato chopped

Stuffing

3 tsp coriander powder

2 tsp turmeric powder

2 tsp ground fennel (saunf)

2 tsp dried mango powder (amchur)

1/2tsp chili powder or to taste

Salt To Taste.

Preparation of Stuffed Okra:

- Cut the stalk of each okra and make lengthwise slit.
- Combine stuffing ingredients and mix well. Stuff each okra with the mixture.
- Suite cumin with the little oil until it starts to crackle.
- Add onions, green chilies and ginger. Suite till onion turns transparent, then put in asafetida and cook for a few seconds.
- Add tomato and cook until it turns pulpy.
- Add the okra and cook for 5 minutes until tender and well coated with the sauce (masala).
- Serve stuffed bhindi hot with chapati, paratha or rice.

Stuffed Capsicum Recipe

Ingredients

5-6 Capsicum (simlamirch)

2 boiled potatoes

2 tbsp boiled green peas

1 Onion finely chopped

1/4th tsp turmeric powder

Red chili powder to taste

1/4th tsp Garam masala

1/4th tsp Dry mango powder (amchur)

Salt To Taste ;

Oil/ghee for frying

Preparation:

- Wash the capsicum and boil them whole till they are tender (not too much), drain water and keep aside to cool.
- Mash the boiled potatoes.
- Now in a pan heat 2-tbsp oil/ghee and add chopped onion and fry till it turns golden brown.
- Now add all spices, mashed potatoes and peas and fry for few moments.

- With a sharp knife cut the stem of the capsicum and take out seeds from the top gently and add the stuffing in it.
- Now take oil/ghee in a kadhai and fry the stuffed capsicums on all sides.
- Garnish the bharawan capsicum with grated paneer, chopped coriander leaves and thinly sliced rings of tomato. Serve hot.

Rajma Rasmisa Recipe

Ingredients

Rajma (kidney beans)- 200 gms

Cumin seeds - 1/2 tsp

Onions (pyaj) (medium-sized and chopped) - 3 nos.

Fresh tomato (tamatar) puree - 1 cup

Ginger (adrak) paste - 1 tblsp

Green chillies (chopped)- 3-4 nos.

Cumin seeds powder (jeera powder) - 1 tsp

Coriander powder (dhania powder) - 1/2 tsp

Red chilli (lal mirch) powder -1 tsp

Salt (namak) - to taste

Oil (tel) - 2 tblsp

Curd (dahi) - 1/4 cup

Green coriander leaves (dhania patta) (chopped)- 2 tblsp.

How to make Rajma Rasmisa :

- Pick, wash and soak the rajma overnight.
- Boil the soaked rajma till well cooked.
- Heat oil, add cumin seeds.
- When it crackles, add chopped onions.
- Saute it till light golden brown in colour.
- Add ginger paste and garlic paste and suite it.
- Add the tomato puree and suite it.
- Now add the green chillies, cumin seeds powder, coriander powder, red chilli powder, curd and salt.
- Cook the masala for 5-6 minutes.
- Add the rajma, mix it well and add half a cup of water.
- Cook it for another 15- 20 minutes.
- Garnish with green coriander leaves.

Aloo Dahi Wale Recipe

Ingredients

500gm aloo (potatoes) boiled and peeled

1 tbsp ginger-finely sliced

a pinch asafoetida

1 tsp cumin seeds

1/2 tsp garam masala

2 tsp coriander powder

2 tsp salt

1/2 tsp chilli powder

1/2 tsp turmeric powder

1/2 cup yogurt (curd)

3-4 green chillies

2 tbsp clarified butter

1 tbsp coriander leaves-chopped.

Preparation:

- Break the aloo (potatoes), by holding each in the palm of your hand and closing the fist. Keep these unevenly broken potatoes aside until further use.
- Heat the ghee, add cumin and asafoetida. When the cumin splutters, add ginger and suite till slightly fried.
- Lower the flame, add yogurt 1 tbsp at a time, stirring vigorously until all of it is well blended.
- Add garam masala, coriander, salt, turmeric and chilli powder. Stir a few times until well mixed, add potatoes and green chillies, turn around over high heat, until they look slightly fried.
- Add about 2 cups water, bring the mixture to a boil, and then simmer uncovered for about 15 minutes.
- Serve aloo dahi wale hot, garnished with coriander leaves.

Recipe For Aloo Gobi

Ingredients for aloo gobi masala :

450gms Potatoes

450gms Gobi (Cauliflower florets)

2 tbsp Oil

1 tsp Cumin seeds

1 no. Chopped green chillies

1 tsp Coriander paste

1 tsp Cumin paste

1/4 tsp Chilli powder

1/2 tsp Turmeric paste

1 tsp Chopped coriander leaves

Salt To Taste.

How to make Aloo Ghobi :

- Par boil the potatoes in a large saucepan of boiling water for 10 minutes. Drain well and set aside.
- Heat the oil in a large frying pan and fry the cumin seeds for about 2 minutes, until they begin to splutter. Add the green chilli and fry for a further 1 minute.
- Add the cauliflower florets and fry, stirring, for 5 minutes. Add the potatoes, the ground spices and salt and cook for 7-10 minutes, until the vegetable are tender.
- Garnish the aloo gobi with coriander and serve with tomato and onion salad and pickle.

Aloo Badiyan Rasedaar Recipe

Ingredients

500 gm aloo (potatoes) - peeled, boiled

5-6 badiyan

2 tbsp oil

1 tsp cumin seeds

1 tbsp salt

1/2 tsp turmeric powder

1/4 cup yogurt-beaten smooth

2 1/2 cups water

1 tbsp coriander leaves.

How to make Aloo Badiyan Rasedaar :

- Break the potatoes, by holding them in your palm and closing your fists.

- Heat oil and add the badis in very briefly-just put them in, quickly turn them over and remove from oil, keep aside. They should barely get darkened.
- In the same oil, add cumin, when it splutters, add the potatoes and fry over high flame but just slightly. Add salt, turmeric and badis.
- Stir-fry till mixed well. Add enough water to cover the potatoes and badis, bring to a boil and simmer, till the badis get soft, but hold their shape.
- Add the yogurt and mix well and serve the aloo badi curry immediately garnished with coriander leaves.

Aloo Took Recipe

Ingredients

500 gm aloo (potatoes) -peeled and cut into rounds

Oil for deep frying

1 tsp salt

1 1/2 tsp red chillies-coarsely pounded

1/4 tsp black pepper

1 tsp dried mango powder.

How to make Aloo Tuk:

- Heat oil in a kadahi to a point when a piece of potato put in, comes up at once. Put in the potato rounds, lower flame to medium and fry to a creamish colour, with the edges a little darker.
- Remove from kadahi, drain excess oil. Put aside to cool a little.
- Once cool, flatten by pressing between palms.
- Just before serving, reheat oil and re-fry aloo (potatoes) to a golden brown, over high flame to make them crisp on the outside and fully cooked inside.
- Drain excess oil on absorbent paper. Mix in salt, red and black pepper, dried mango powder and coriander and serve hot aloo took.

Aloo Baigan Recipe

Ingredients

1/2" piece of ginger root

2 Minced green chilies

1/4 cup Shredded unsweetened coconut

1/2 tsp Garam masala

4 tbsp Ghee

1 tsp Black mustard seeds

1/2 tbsp Whole cumin seeds

1/8 tsp Asafetida

6 md Potatoes, boiled & cubed

1 tsp Turmeric

1 tbsp Coriander

1 sm Eggplant in 1" cubes

1 tsp Salt

3 tbsp Fresh coriander, chopped

1 tbsp Lemon juice.

Preparation of Aloo Baingan:

- Combine ginger, green chilies & coconut in blender with 1/3 cup of water till smooth. Add garam masala & pulse for a few seconds. Set aside.
- Heat ghee. Whe hot, add mustard & cumin seeds & fry for a few seconds. Stir in the asafetida & almost immediately put in the potatoes. Stir fry for 5 minutes Then pour in the mixture from the blender. Add the turmeric, coriander, eggplant, salt & half the fresh coriander. Mix very gently so as not to break the vegetables.
- Reduce heat & fry very gently until the liquid has evaporated. In the aloo baigan mix lemon juice & remaining coriander greens & serve.

Dum Aloo Recipe

Ingredients for Dhum Aloo

900gms Aloo (Potatoes)

33/4th cups water

Salt To Taste

Ghee or oil for deep-frying

1 cup ghee

1 large Onion (finely chopped)

4 tbsp tomato puree

140 ml curd

4 tbsp hot water

1 green pepper (seeds removed and sliced)

1tsp garam masala powder.

Spices

4 cloves

4 bay leaves

6 black peppercorns

4 green cardamoms

1 brown cardamom

1piece cinnamon stick.

Paste

1 large onion (chopped)

12 flakes garlic

2 tbsp ginger

6black peppercorns

1 tsp poppy seeds

1 tbsp coriander seeds

1 tsp cumin seeds

2 dry red chilies

1 tsp turmeric powder

A pinch of ground mace

A pinch of ground nutmeg.

How to make Kashmiri Dum Aloo:

- Scrape the aloo (potatoes), prick all over with a fork and soak in the water with little salt for 2 hours.
- Dry the potatoes on a cloth and heat the ghee or oil.
- Deep fry the potatoes until golden brown. Drain and set aside.
- Heat the measured ghee in a flameproof pan and fry onions with all the spices until golden.
- Grind the paste ingredients to a fairly smooth paste and stir into the onions.
- Cook for 10 minutes. Stir in the tomato puree, curd and salt.

- Add the aloo (potatoes) and hot water and stir over a low heat for 5 minutes.
- Sprinkle the dum aloo with pepper and garam masala and cook for few minutes.

Kadhai Paneer Recipe

Ingredients

250 gms Cottage Cheese (Paneer)

3 Capsicum (Shimla Mirch)

4 Onion (Pyaj)

4 Tomato (Tamatar)

1 " long piece Ginger (Adrak)

1 tsp Red Chili Powder (Lal Mirchi)

2 Bay Leaf (Tej Patta)

4 Cloves (Lavang)

1 piece Cinnamon (Tuj/Dalchini)

Little Orange Colour

4 tblsp Clarified Butter (Ghee).

How to make Kadhai Paneer:

- Cut cottage cheese, capsicum in long pieces.
- Grind onion, tomato, ginger, salt, red chili powder and orange colour.
- Mince cloves and cinnamom.
- Heat clarified butter in a pan.
- Add bay leaf, cloves, cinnamon.
- Then add onion, tomato, ginger paste.
- Continue cooking it on medium flame till ghee/oil begins to separate.
- Add paneer and capsicum pieces.
- Cook on low flame.
- When the capsicum are done put off the flame.
- Take off the fire and serve hot.
- Serve with nan or paranthas.

Mattar Paneer Recipe

Ingredients

450gms /1lb shelled Mutter (green peas)

250gms / 1/2lb Paneer How to make paneer

2 medium onions (chopped)

6 cloves garlic (crushed)

1 tbsp grated ginger

2 green chilies (chopped)

250gms / 1/2 lb tomatoes (peeled and sliced)

Salt To Taste;

1cup curd / plain yogurt

1 tsp turmeric powder

1 tbsp coriander seeds

4 bay leaves

2 cups water

1/2 cup ghee / vegetable oil

To Garnish:

Garam masala powder

Chopped coriander leaves.

12

Restaurant Food Safety Management

A little more than a decade after global warming, gradually disappearing rain forests and endangered species ruled our collective conscience, new concerns have started to dominate our concerns: pesticides, mad cow disease, *e-coli* genetically modified foods, fungicides, growth hormones and food safety.

In this first decade of the 21st century, food safety is the environmental issue (75 percent of North Americans claim to be concerned about the wholesomeness of the food they consume). Even a larger percentage is concerned about processed food, yet a huge proportion of the population buys processed and prepared food due to time constraints. These days, people are time poor but cash rich. Considering the fact that in the recent past more ground beef had to be recalled than anytime before 1990 shows how vulnerable we all are.

It used to be that food manufacturers wanting to export to Canada had to pass stringent health inspections carried out by specially trained officials before they were allowed to ship a unit of their product, but this policy has been relaxed. Also every slaughterhouse had to have an inspector (provincial or federal) but this policy has been relaxed in most cases.

These days the North American consumer has more opportunity to sample food from different part of the world. You can now buy haricot beans from Kenya, Kiwi from New Zealand, Israel, Chile, or Italy, pineapple from Thailand, herbs from Costa Rica, avocados from the Caribbean, avocado oil from New Zealand, papayas from Brazil, okra from India and mangoes from Central, America oysters from France, swordfish from Chile, cod from Norway and even dried fish from Maldives. Some of these foods may be contaminated due to illegal means of irrigation with untreated sewage.

Restaurants are just one link in the food-supply chain; their role against food borne illness is crucial. In Canada approximately 10,000 cases of food borne diseases are reported annually, of which 30 percent result in death. The Atlanta based Centre of Disease Control (CDC) estimates that about 70 percent of all food borne illness outbreaks occur in foodservice operation compared to 20 percent traced to homes. Food processors account for three percent but this figure is increasing.

It is obvious that the restaurant industry particularly the fast food industry must train all food handlers more vigorously, hire healthy individuals and take every possible precaution to serve wholesome foods. This will cost but it better to be safe than sorry. I can recall a few ago the Jack-in-the-Box tragedy that cost millions and even more in lost business and reputation. All equipment and literature are readily available at affordable cost. Managers just need to implement a well thought out education seminar, then maintain standards.

Ingesting food that has been contaminated by bacteria, viruses, parasites or chemicals causes food borne illness. Food-safety hazards can be introduced into food service operations in a number of ways, such as food, equipment, supplies and customers. The hazards may be biological (bacteria, viruses, parasites and fungi); chemical (cleaning supplies, pesticides, and food additives); or physical (dirt, broken glass and crockery that accidentally get into food). Diseases can also be spread by cross-contamination, which is the transfer of harmful substances or microorganisms to food by a variety of means. Utensils, washcloths, and human hands can contaminate ready-to-eat foods. Contamination can also occur via food-to-food, such as when thawing meats drip on ready-to-eat foods.

Major Food Borne Illnesses Include

Salmonella: A large group of bacteria, salmonella can make people sick with a disease called salmonellosis. These bacteria are found in the natural environment, animal feed and animal intestines. Salmonellosis symptoms may include diarrhoea, abdominal cramps, vomiting and fever. These symptoms usually appear six to 48 hours after exposure and can persist for several days. Foods that are most likely to carry salmonella bacteria include raw and undercooked meats (especially poultry), raw milk, eggs and sprouts. Fruits and vegetables can become contaminated with salmonella bacteria if they have been exposed to contaminated soil, or have come in contact with a contaminated product or surface (such as a countertop or hands during food preparation).

Prevention: avoid cross-contamination, refrigerate food, thoroughly cook all meat to proper internal temperatures, rapidly cool cooked meats, practise good personal hygiene and proper hand washing.

Shigella: A pathogen found in the intestinal tract of humans, shigella is rarely found in other animals. Its presence in foods is a sign of human contamination and lack of hygiene by food handlers. Another means of transmission is ingesting of contaminated water, such as water supplies contaminated by untreated sewage. Consumption of shigella-contaminated food or contact with infected people may lead to shigellosis. Symptoms include diarrhoea, abdominal pain, fever, vomiting and dehydration. The most common foods to carry shigella are salads (potato, shrimp, tuna, chicken, macaroni, fruits, and lettuce). Chopped turkey, rice balls, beans, puddings, strawberries, spinach raw oysters, luncheon meats and milk may also carry shigella.

Prevention: Avoid cross-contamination; avoid fecal contamination from food service employees by practicing good personal hygiene and proper hand washing; use sanitary food and water sources.

E.Coli 0157:H7: This is found in the intestines of cattle, poultry and other animals. When an animal is butchered, the bacteria can be transferred to the meat's outer surface. E.Coli 0157:H7 infection can be spread by hand-to-hand contact with an infected person or even from surfaces he/she may have touched. A small number of people who become infected with E.Coli 0157:H7 do not get sick at all; some experience flu-like symptoms; others experience severe, even life-threatening symptoms. Symptoms include diarrhoea, severe abdominal pain, vomiting and low-grade fever. It may cause an unusual type of kidney failure and blood disorder called haemolytic uremic syndrome (HUS).

Although HUS is commonly called "hamburger disease", un-pasteurized milk untreated water, vegetables and un-pasteurized apple juice/cider contaminated with E.Coli 0157:H7 have made people ill. Ground beef may be easily contaminated by E.Coli0157:H7, due in part to its preparation. The grinding process spreads bacteria, generally found on the surface, throughout the meat.

Prevention: Thoroughly cook ground beef to at least 70 C (158 F) for 15 seconds; avoid cross-contamination; avoid fecal contamination from food service employees by practising good personal hygiene and proper hand washing

Attitude Towards Coffee Drinking by Coffee Consumers and Non-Consumers in India

In promoting -a product it is important that consumers' attitude towards the product is fully evaluated. Attitude is an individuals enduring perceptual, knowledge based, evaluative and action oriented process with respect to an object or phenomenon.

The three components of attitudes are a) belief component (cognitive) or a person's awareness or knowledge about a product b) feeling component (affective) or a respondent's liking and preference for a product and c) behavior component is the readiness to respond behaviorally or what one has done or doing.

In the marketing context, the knowledge component provides information for decisions regarding the consumers' awareness or knowledge about product features, ad campaigns, pricing, product availability etc. while the belief component provides information for decisions regarding determining buyers' positive or negative feelings, preferences of organizations marketing programme as well as those of competitors.

The behaviour component is the respondents' intention to buy and actual purchase behavior. The aim of this paper is to present some of the key findings of attitude of Indian consumers towards coffee drinking. In order to understand the consumer perceptions and attitudes towards coffee and in the context of other beverages and also to understand the attitude towards coffee with respect to quality, variety, price and additives especially chicory; positive and negative associations related to consumption as well as drivers and barriers to coffee consumption etc., a consumer attitude survey was commissioned during 2006.

The study was conducted in urban locations across the country and in rural areas in the southern part of the country. The results were analysed by zones (South, North, East and West India), type of consumer (regular drinker who drinks 1-2 times or more of coffee everyday including yesterday), occasional drinker who drinks coffee once in the last 6 months, but not yesterday) and non-drinker who had not drunk coffee at all in the last 12 months), Socio-Economic Classifi-cation (SEC) (SEC A, B, C, D with SEC A representing the highest economic strata and SEC D being the lowest strata) as well as different age groups. The salient results of the attitude survey is presented below.

Spontaneous Recall

Spontaneous recall measures whether a respondent recalls a beverage spontaneously without any aid. Both coffee and tea enjoy high spontaneous recall rate of 81 % and 95% respectively- both in urban and rural areas. These are followed by plain milk and carbonated soft drinks. It may be emphasized here that even in the non traditional markets of non-south, coffee has fairly higher recall of over 70%.

Top of Mind Category Recall

Top of Mind (ToM) beverage is a subset of the beverages, which are spontaneously recalled first without any aid. Tea has the highest ToM recall across both urban and rural markets. While 66% of the respondents recall tea, only 22% named coffee as the first beverage. ToM recall of coffee is higher in traditional coffee strong holds such as Tamil Nadu and Karnataka. Across the country ToM recall for coffee is higher among SEC A, B & C than SEC D.

Consumption

In Karnataka and Tamil Nadu, the percentage of those who drink coffee more than 2 times a day is higher than in other regions. Rural Karnataka has comparatively higher percentage of persons drinking coffee more than 2 times everyday than to urban areas. There is 33% of this group in rural areas while there is only 28% who drink coffee as frequently in urban areas.

Top Beverages Consumed by Coffee Drinkers

Even among regular coffee drinkers, tea is entrenched as a regularly consumed beverage. In rural Tamilnadu, tea is far more a regular beverage even among regular coffee drinkers than in urban Tamilnadu. These findings indicate the opportunities that exist to increase the depth of coffee consumption among regular coffee drinkers by recognizing competitive strengths of tea.

Consideration Set of Beverages

To determine the choice set, respondents were asked to name the first choice beverage, the second choice beverage, beverages that will be considered for drinking and beverages that will never be considered for drinking. Among regular coffee drinkers, though coffee is the first choice among 67% of overall respondents, about 31 % of regular coffee drinkers mention tea as their first choice.

This is especially true in coffee markets of Kerala, AP and the non-south regions. Among occasional drinkers, coffee is a first choice beverage only among a small majority. This indicates the scope to increase coffee drinking even among regular coffee drinkers in most markets.

The observations of the urban market hold good even for the rural markets. Especially in rural AP and Kerala, tea is a first choice beverage among a larger proportion of regular coffee drinkers. In rural Tamil Nadu, tea is far more entrenched as a regularly consumed beverage among regular coffee drinkers.

Among the occasional drinkers of rural market, not only consideration to drink coffee but also trial of coffee is found to be quite high. However, future consideration of coffee is low among non-drinkers of coffee especially in Tamil Nadu, Karnataka and AP. This suggests that there are strong barriers against coffee drinking among non-drinkers in these traditional coffee strongholds. As such non-drinkers either urban or rural, may be the most difficult to convert.

Attitudes Towards Beverages

To understand attitude drivers to beverages, the statement "Overall Best Beverage" was treated as the independent variable and a battery of 23 statements were treated as dependent variables. The respondents were asked to rate each of the statements using a 5-point scale in which 1 is Strongly Disagree and 5 is Strongly Agree. The various statements were grouped thematically into three groups - family beverage, health and status connotations. Overall, the best beverage description is explained by dimensions of whether it can be consumed at home by most family members, whether it is healthy and if it is modern (keeping up with times).

The results of regression analysis brought out that in Tamil Nadu, coffee has moderate association on 'Family beverage'. However, it is strongly associated with special occasions and hence has high status connotation. In Karnataka, coffee has very strong association with 'Family beverage'. It also has special/high status perceptions. In AP, perception of tea is very close to coffee on key dimensions. Tea comes across mainly as an evening cup. In Kerala, tea has higher positive associations on key dimensions of family, health and status. In the North, East and West, coffee is largely a social or out-of-home drink. coffee is associated with high status, modernity, ideal for cold weather suggesting it is a special and occasional drink.

Perceived Occasions :In Home and out-of-Home

Among the regular coffee drinkers of North and West, coffee is an evening drink more than a morning drink. Where tea is the 'first cup' choice among regular coffee drinkers in urban Kerala, presence of tea is high in rural Karnataka among regular coffee drinkers. Tea constitutes the evening cup among regular coffee drinkers in urban AP, Kerala and West. Coffee has the highest association in the out-of- home environment especially, at a restaurant/hotel and at special events/functions.

Beverage Evaluation Criteria

Respondents were asked to rate the beverages on evaluation criteria using a 5-point agreement scale. The largest difference in rating between coffee and tea is in Karnataka and rural AP. In rural Karnataka, product scores for coffee are lower than in urban Karnataka. There is more usage of instant coffee in rural Karnataka than in urban Karnataka. In rural Kerala, coffee scores higher on aroma than tea, possibly due to higher penetration of local filter ('katang') coffee

Barriers and Drivers of Coffee Consumption

Among the regular drinkers (especially those who drink one cup a day), health is found to be a major barrier to more frequent consumption. Among occasional coffee drinkers and non-drinkers, the key barriers are: L Habit 2. Non-consumption by other family members, and 3. Price. Taste is an additional barrier among non-drinkers in North, East and West and Tamil Nadu.

Coffee, like any other drink is 'habit' forming. Family drinking is a key for early adoption. Most regular and occasional drinkers started drinking coffee while they were less than IO years old. They first drank at home and were introduced to the beverage by a family member. The exception is the North, where most started out-of-home and were introduced to coffee by a friend. This is an important driver for future consumption growth and addressing the youth in the promotion programmes will help in formation early coffee drinking habits.

Place of Consumption of Coffee: In-Home vs out-of-Home

Coffee drinking at home is prevalent even among occasional drinkers indicating no entry barrier. In the West, rural Tamil Nadu, Karnataka and AP, there are occasional drinkers who drink exclusively outside the home. Data suggests that price is a barrier to regular consumption with family. In the North, proportion of people who drink coffee outside the home exclusively is the highest.

The consumption occasions outside home coupled with the highest frequency of consumption in those places tell us where coffee is consumed most outside home. There appears to be low penetration but high consumption of coffee in offices and colleges - this finding represents a possible opportunity area to promote the category in these locations.

Intuitive and Easy-to-use

Table Service's intuitive touchscreens put the user in control with the touch of a finger, making operations and customising the system a snap, allowing you to decrease training time and increase employee productivity. With Aloha, it's easier than ever to enter orders, manage guest checks, run Promotions and process payments.

Powerful Management Functionality

Whether you have weekly promotions or daily menu changes, Aloha's built-in Event Scheduler lets you program events that are automatically activated at a specified time. Special messages can be entered to appear on screen, keeping your employees informed. Aloha's comprehensive reporting package allows you to keep track of real-time sales results and other data.

With extensive front-of-house reporting features like real-time sales statistics, product mix reports, employee check-in stats and server sales, you're able to spend more time with the customer and still keep up with the latest profit margins and performance measures.

Virtual Order Processing

With Aloha Table Service, communication flows sooothly and seamlessly from your wait staff to the kitchen staff. Voids, order changes and adds can now be handled effortlessly through the Aloha system eliminating unnecessary trips to and from the kitchen. And with Aloha's menu item availability feature, you're able to count down selected items or specials as they're ordered so servers never order out-of-stock items - which ensures your customers will continue to receive only the best possible service.

The Table Service Advantage

Aloha Table Service offers advanced point-of-sale functionality, intuitive Window-based touch screens, open architecture, built-in redundancy, extensive front-of-house reporting and much more to meet the exact needs of your business. The peerless pas system provides you with the tools to effectively and efficiently manage your operations. No matter how you configure it, the end result is always a smooth-running, seamlessly integrated system.

Benefits

- Order processing ease
- Powerful management functions
- Unparalleled menu management capacity
- Built-in security system
- Modular, flexible design that allows the system to meet current and future needs
- Detailed report and audit tracking
- Automated scheduled menu and promotion events
- Fast and easy to train.

Life in the restaurant industry is extremely fast-paced, and with every new day comes new challenges. Though you may not be able to predict everything that will go wrong on any given day, with Aloha Table Service you can be prepared to face it head on. Aloha Table Service is the key to reliability and performance for your hospitality POS needs.

Unmatched performance, functionality and features :

- Intuitive touch-screen interfaces
- Built-in redundancy
- User-customisable screens and screen flow
- Menu management
- Comprehensive reporting package
- Microsoft Windows-based

- Several graphical user interfaces
- Performance measurements for servers
- Open architecture
- Off-the-shelf, non-proprietary hardware
- Enterprise capabilities
- Extensive kitchen chit printing options
- Simple cheque or item splitting and combining functionality Aloha Table Service.

Table Reservations

Say goodbye to inefficient and messy manual reservation books, grease pens and dirty rags. Reserv IT software accepts reservations from any workstation in your restaurant, across multiple restaurants, even through your company's website.

As you book reservations, this Windows based software actively tracks your guests' history and preferences, so your entire staff can make them feel at home and offer truly personalized service. This information can also be mined to support targeted marketing efforts based on customer habits, birthdays, anniversaries, special request and more.

With its easy-to-read screen and point-and-click functionality, Reserv IT software reduces errors, centralizes reservations for multiple locations, and lets you process more reservations with fewer people staffing the phones. It's just one of many ways In Touch is changing the industry, providing a wide range of products to increase your revenue, enhance the guest experience, and improve your bottom line.

Table Availability Notification

Visual prompts immediately let host staff know when tables become available, even in large restaurants, multi-level facilities, or enclosed rooms. Faster seating reduces congestion, creates more inviting atmosphere, and increases table turn around. Ability to see the status of the restaurant without walking the floor. Automatic server paging speeds up service, prevents walkouts, makes guests happier, and earns more return visits.

Automated Waiting List

Maximize utilization of tables with the systems automatic suggestions. The Acc Quote feature provides precise wait times, reducing customer dissatisfaction and walkouts. Simplified process reduces staff frustration and turnover. PC-based system eliminates paper passing and appearance of confusion.

Balanced Server Rotation

Server rotation system tracks the number of times a server is seated last seated. Eliminate double and triple seating of servers. Sense of fairness keeps staff happier and reduces turnover.

Improved Decision Making

Ability to monitor restaurant status at a glance. Aids day-to-day management. Historical data provides performance benchmarks and reveals new opportunities. Many of the worlds best and busiest restaurants have discovered that the old Book, no longer meets their needs. With Reserv IT for reservations you now have the tools to allow you to control your operations better.

In Touch Table Management

In Touch Reserv IT touch screen software takes the guesswork out of table management, preventing walkouts and getting customers seated in record time. A customized, colour-coded display of your floor plan shows table status at a glance provides accurate wait times dynamically updated throughout the day based on seating trends and table turns prompts your host staff when space becomes available, and automatically rotates servers to fairly distribute the workload. It's also exceptionally easy to use, reducing training costs and preserving best practices in an industry marked by chronically high turnover. It's just one of many ways In Touch is changing the industry, providing a wide range of products to increase your revenue, enhance the guest experience, and improve your bottom line.

Guest Recognition

Instant view histories, notes, preferences, current reservations. Reduce time spent constantly taking down names and phone numbers. Help new employees to offer personalized service immediately.

Multiple Points/Multiple Locations

Avoid making guests wait while someone looks for the reservation book. Save time and prevent errors. The Quick View feature provides the ability to view table availability for all restaurants in the system. Provide a central number for all locations.

Reservation List Management

Provide guests with options of different reservations at multiple locations. Add guests to a computerized wait list and eliminate mistakes.

Enhanced automatic table selection method designed to increase seat usage efficiency when selecting tables for a reservation. Automatically releases selected tables when the party size is decreased, and selects additional tables when party size is increased.

Customer Relationship Marketing

Base promotions on specific histories, preferences, holidays, special requests, etc. Increase number and frequency of future visits. Save money by focusing your marketing efforts. The Reserv IT floor plan shows the current status of all your guests. Seating allocation is a simple point and click operation and you are able to look at individual sections or the total tables in the outlet. Interfacing to your system provides immediate feedback to your hostess.

Restaurant Promotion: Wine Tasting

The Basics of Hosting a Wine Tasting

Specialty dinners, such as dinner theater, fundraisers or a wine tasting are great way to get extra business through the door in slow times. They work well for both large and small groups and are ideal for those slow weekends in between the busy seasons. Wine tastings are especially popular, because people love good wine and good food, especially when they come together.

What is a Wine Tasting?

A wine tasting is just that. Guests enjoy sampling various wines, usually from a particular region and converse with a sommelier (a wine expert) about the wine- how it is made, the difference between the various wines and how to select a wine for home. A sommelier can explain the subtle differences between each wine, and answer questions guests might have about the wines.

Along with wine, a specialty menu is served, which is designed to compliment the wine. You can serve an informal buffet of appetizers and finger food or a full sit down dinner. For example, if the evenings theme is wine from Italy, you could serve authentic Italian dishes, such as fresh tomato bruschetta and tiramisu.

Why Should I Host a Wine Tasting?

A great non-seasonal promotion. In Maine (my neck of the woods), March is the month of Restaurant Doldrums. Too late for skiers, to early for summer people.

We host a wine tastings to lure people out in the bitter winter weather, with the promise of good food and drink. A wine tasting is a also a chance to showcase new foods and bring in new customers.

How do I Plan a Wine Tasting

First check with your local liquor laws to see if there are any specific rules around a wine tasting. Unless your state has some odd law about serving wine (and some states do) a wine tasting is usually covered by your regular liquor license. Next, you will need to reserve a sommelier. A sommelier is just a fancy name for someone who knows a lot about wine.

The wine sales rep for your restaurant should be able to put you in contact with a sommelier, or act as the sommelier himself. If the salesperson does it, it is usually a free service because you are purchasing wine from them. You then need to settle on a wine list and menu, make up promotional flyers and advertisements and print tickets.

But Won't all my Customers get Drunk?

Not if you host your wine tasting properly. While there are always a few people who will throw back goblet after goblet of wine, like its going out style, most people who attend a wine tasting have a genuine interest in experiencing new wines and learning about the wine process. However, a wine tasting doesn't mean your staff should ignore their TIPS training. Anyone who is exhibiting any signs of drunkenness should not be served any more alcohol. Also remember that you are not serving a full glass of each wine on the menu. You are giving customers a *taste* (hence the name) each wine. The amount of wine served should equal 3 regular glasses of wine, or half a bottle of wine.

Restaurant Promotions

Restaurant promotions, whether daily, weekly, or monthly are great ways to show customer appreciation and bring in some extra business at the same time. Promotions can range for a nightly happy hour to an annual customer appreciation day, with drink and dinner specials.

Happy Hour

Many restaurants with a bar or lounge area offer happy hour specials during the week. Happy hours are geared toward working people, to entice them to stop in for a drink after a long day at work. Along with reduced drink specials, many restaurants offer inexpensive or free appetizers such as chicken wings, taco bars, or chips and salsa.

Live Music

Offering live music on a certain night of the week is a great way to bring in extra business. Music can range from local bands playing in the bar or pub to a live jazz or piano player in the dining room. The music should fit your restaurant theme and cater to your core customer demographic. If you have a quiet, upscale restaurant with a majority of customers in their 40s, 50s or older, a loud rock band is probably not going to go over well. However, if you have a restaurant and pub in a college town, that same band might bring in loads of local students.

Open Mike Night

If you want to offer some sort of entertainment, but don't want to pay for it, offer a "open Mike" (short for microphone) night. Locals are invited to sing, play musical instruments, tell jokes, or read poetry. You may be surprised at how many people show up for these local nights. Along with aspiring entertainers, many of their friends and family will come out to support them, and have a drink and an appetizer or dinner. Slower mid-week nights, like Tuesday or Wednesday are ideal for an open mike night.

Two-for-One Specials

Twofer, as we call it at our restaurant, offers customers two entrees for the price of one. To keep food cost under control, offer a special two-for-one menu, with a limited selection of entrees. Or rotate the menu, offering different dishes each week. Because two-for-one specials are geared toward the budget-minded customer, avoid offer pricey items, such as lobster or large cuts of beef. Simple menu items, such as chicken pie, baked haddock, and stuffed pork chops all have low food cost, and are popular dishes with diners.

Contests

Everyone loves a contest and the chance of winning a free gift. Contests are better suited for restaurants with a pub or bar, but there is no rule that you can't have one in your diner, bistro or cafe. Contests can range from naming a new dessert dish to winning the weekly football pool.

Prizes can be something as simple (and inexpensive) as a gift certificate for a free meal to cold hard cash. Free t-shirts, if you carry them, mugs or other restaurant related retail items also make great promotional gifts.

Sport Night Specials

Running special promotions during various sporting seasons is another way to get customers into your restaurant. Again, this is more ideal for a bar or pub. Monday Night Football, a Superbowl Party, or the World Series all offer untapped sales potential. Offer special drink and dinner discounts for those events.

Lockkeeper's Restaurant

Bottom Line

Lovely, wood-paneled Lockkeeper's is a special restaurant, with excellent service, delicious and creative cuisine, and a warm and inviting atmosphere.

Pros

- Excellent service and warm inviting atmosphere
- Innovative and tasty food (including the best lobster in Cleveland)
- Extensive wine list, including many offerings by the glass
- Four-diamond AAA rating
- Patio overlooking the Cuyahoga River.

Guide Review - Lockkeeper's Restaurant

Lockkeeper's Restaurant is an elegant fine dining restaurant, located along the Cuyahoga River in Valley View, Ohio, just south of downtown. The spacious, wood-paneled eatery specializes in fine, American-inspired cuisine and changes its menu each season in order to take advantage of the freshest ingredients.

Lockkeeper's has been honored with many awards, including AAA's prestigious four diamond designation and *Wine Spectator Magazine's* 2004 Award of Excellence. Lockkeeper's features a scenic, wrap-around patio, open between Memorial Day and Labour

Day, as well as the elegant *Sommelier Room*, a private upstairs dining room.

Rome Restaurant

The Bottom Line

You can eat cheap in Rome, but can you find a good, sit-down restaurant meal that doesn't set you back many Euros? Yes you can, especially if you venture out of the main tourist areas. We discovered *Antica Osteria da Giovanni* while walking between Vatican City and Trastevere.

The menu and prices looked almost too good to be true, especially for a restaurant mentioned in *Gambero Rosso*, an Italian wine and food magazine. We tried *Antica Osteria da Giovanni* for lunch and we were very pleased.

Pros;

- Well-prepared, reasonably priced food based on the Marche region
- Off the beaten tourist track.

Cons;

- Menu is limited
- You'll have to go out of your way to get there.

Description;

- Antica Osteria da Giovanni serves simple, well-prepared food at bargain basement prices.
- Antica Osteria da Giovanni has been in business for over 50 years and mentioned in Gambero Rosso.
- Antica Osteria da Giovanni.

Antica Osteria da Giovanni's menu of the day has only some of the items on the menu posted in the window, based on what's fresh in the market. Although it's not a huge selection, you'll find sufficient pastas, rice, and soup for the first course and several meat and fish choices for your second course.

I started with rice and endive for about 2 euro. Now, for 2 euro I wasn't expecting much but I was surprised at both the wonderful taste and the large portion. James had a perfectly al dente tagliarini topped with a traditionally small amount of intensely-flavoured ragu—

satisfying, especially considering the 3 euro price. But he was much more impressed with his second course, fresh anchovies topped with a vibrant *piziolla* sauce. My grilled fresh fish (the most expensive item on the menu at 11 euro) was perfectly prepared.

We often order the house wine; it's usually quite drinkable and costs less than a bottle from the list. In this case the house wine was bottle of good DOC wine from Lazio and a half liter cost us only 2 euros, a price hard to find even in a store. A bottle of mineral water added on 1 euro, a salad was 1.55, and bread and cover was.75 each. Our total bill was 26.80 euro, including tax and service. Here you won't find an English menu or gourmet food, and you'll probably be the only tourists in the restaurant, but you'll enjoy a simple well-prepared meal at bargain basement prices in a restaurant that's been serving Romans for over 50 years.

Bibliography

Auty, R.M. : *Patterns of Development: Resources, Policy and Economic Growth,* London, 1995.

Balch C.N.C, P. : *Prescription for Nutritional Healing,* New York, U.S.A: Avery Publishing Group, 1997.

Bhutani, R.C.: *Fruit and Vegetable Preservation,* Biotech Books, Delhi, 2003.

Britton, S. and Clarke, W.C.: *Ambiguous Alternative Tourism in Small Developing Countries,* Suva: University of the South Pacific, 1987.

Carlsen, J.; S Charters, Edith Cowan University: *Global Wine Tourism*, Cabi Publishing, NY, 2006.

Charles, G.: *International Dictionary of Food & Cooking,* Chicago, Fitzroy Dearborn, 1998.

Clark, Mona: *Interpersonal Skills for Hospitality Managers,* London, Chapman Hill, 1995.

Cliff, S. and Grabowski, P.: *Tourism and Health: Risk, Research and Responses,* Pinter, London, 2000.

Copeland, R. A., *Enzymes: A Practical Introduction to Structure,Mechanism, and Data Analysis*, New York, 1999.

Cornish-Bowden, A.: *Fundamentals of Enzyme Kinetics*, Portland Press, London, 1995.

Davies, R.: Tourism and Food Safety. *Tourist Health: A New Branch of Public Health,* Cabi Publishing, *NY,* 1988.

Dayal Shambhu: *Ethical Foundation of Hotel and Hospitality Managemen*, Akansha, Delhi, 2006.

Dhaka , J.M.: *Economics of Agricultural Production and Farm Management,* Aavishkar Pub, Delhi, 2009.

Donald, M.: *Customer Service in the Hospitality and Tourism Industry,* Englewood Cliffs, Prentice Hall, 1994.

Eckel, Peter J.: *College & University Foodservice Management Standards,* Westport, AVI Pub. Company, 1985.

Fersht, A. : *Enzyme Structure and Mechanism*, W. H. Freeman, New York, 1977.

Fletcher, J.: *Tourism Principles and Practices,* London: Pitman, 1998.

Fromm, H.: *Initial Rate Enzyme Kinetics*, Springer-Verlag, New York, 1975.

Gautam Arvind : *A Concise Course on Hotel and Hospitality Management*, Axis Pub, Delhi, 2010.

Gunjan Goel: *Applied Dairy and Food Microbiology,* Agrotech, 2005.

Gutfreund, H.: *Enzymes: Physical Principles*, Wiley-Interscience, London, 1972.

Hacker, J.B. : *Nutritional Limits to Animal Production from Pasture,* Farnham Royal: CAB, 1981.

Harrison, Ruth: *Animal Machines: The New Factory Farming Industry.* London: Vincent Stuart, Ltd., 1964.

Hays, Judi Radice: *Restaurant & Food Graphics,* Glen Cove, PBC International, 1994.

Hennessy, S., Greenwood, J.: *The Role of Tourism in Local Economies: A Pilot Study of Looe, Cornwall,* University of Exeter, 1986.

John Prince: *Dairy Farming: Being the Theory, Practice, and Methods of Dairying*, New York, 1888.

Johnston, J. R. : *Molecular Genetics of Yeast, a Practical Approach.* IRL Press, Oxford 1994.

Judi Radice: *Restaurant & Food Graphics,* Glen Cove, PBC International, 1994.

Khurana A.D.: *Handbook of Catering, Hospitality and Tourism,* Mohit Pub, Delhi, 2008.

Kochhar B.K.: *Principles of Hospitality and Tourism Management*, Cyber Tech, Delhi, 2011.

Kumar Saurabh Dixit: *Promises and Perils in Hospitality and Tourism Management*, Aman Pub, Delhi, 2006.

Lata Bhattacharya: *Biochemistry of Nutrition*, Discovery, Delhi, 2010.

Madhukar Manoj: *Hospitality Industries in Next Millennium*, Rajat, Delhi, 2001.

McCollum EV.: *A History of Nutrition*, Boston: Houghton Mifflin; 1957.

Michael, C. Hall, Brock Cambourne, Liz Sharples, Niki Macionis: *Wine Tourism Around the World: Development, Management and Markets*, Elsevier, 2000.

Mydral, G.: *Economic Theory and Underdeveloped Regions*, London: Methuen, 1957.

Nancy N.: *Choosing a Career in Hotels, Motels, and Resorts*, New York, Rosen Pub. Group, 1997.

Narang, R.K.: *Fruit and Vegetable Preservation Techniques*, APH Pub, Delhi, 2010.

Norman G.: *Hotel, Restaurant, and Travel Law: A Preventive Approach*, Albany, Delmar Publishers, 1993.

Paul B. : *Food Biotechnology in Ethical Perspective*, Aspen, CO: Aspen Publishers, 1997.

Pearce, P.L., Moscardo, G.: *Tourism Community Relationships*, Oxford: Pergamon, 1996.

Peter J.: *College & University Foodservice Management Standards*, Westport, AVI Pub. Company, 1985.

Piszkiewicz, D. : *Kinetics of Chemical and Enzyme-Catalyzed Reactions*, Oxford University Press, New York, 1977.

Purich, D. L. : *Enzyme Kinetics and Mechanism Part D, Developments in Enzyme Dynamics, Methods in Enzymology*, Academic Press, San Diego, CA, 1995.

Ratti Manish: *Hospitality Management : Theories and Practices*, Rajat Pub, Delhi, 2007.

Rhykerd Charles L. : *The Cycles of Plant and Animal Nutrition*, Scientific American Books, San Francisco 1976.

Rosemary E.: *Managing Employee Relations in the Hotel and Catering Industry*, London, Cassell, 1995.

Segel, I. H. : *Enzyme Kinetics: Behavior and Analysis of Rapid Equilibrium and Steady-State Enzyme Systems*, John Wiley and Sons, New York, 1975.

Sharma Hemant: *HRM in Hospitality Industry*, ABD, Delhi, 2006.

Sharma Sunil: *Planning and Development of Tourism and Hospitality*, Rajat Pub, Delhi, 2007.

Shepherd, D. : *Homeopathy for the First Aider*, Sussex, England: Health Science Press, 1953.

Simmons, D.: *Community Adaptation to Tourism: Comparisons between Rotorua and Kaikoura*, New Zealand. Tourism Management, 2002.

Singh Gagandeep: *Global Aviation and Hospitality Management*, Book Enclave, Delhi, 2008.

Thomas Bernauer : *Genes, Trade and Regulation : The Seeds of Conflict in Food Biotechnology*, Universities Press, 2005.

Thomas, F.: *Introduction to Management in the Hospitality Industry*, New York, Wiley, 1995.

Tramontano, A., : *Antibodies as enzymes*, Trends in Biochemical Sciences,1987.

Tripathi, Pramila: *Botanical Pesticides in the Management of Post-harvest Fruit Diseases*, Daya, Delhi, 2005.

Waller, Keith: *Improving Food and Beverage Performance*, Oxford, Butterworth-Heinemann, 1996.

Wickens, E.: *Tourism and Health: Risk, Research and Responses, Pinter, London,* 1997.

William H.: *The Chef's Guide to Practical Restaurant Cookery*, New York, Van Nostrand Reinhold, 1988.

Index

❑❑❑